The Complete Idiot's Guide to Word 2000

tear here

The Word 2000 Screen

Email is integrated into the Word screen.

Adaptive menus and toolbars change to meet your needs.

The Standard and Formatting toolbars merged into one.

Click here to see remaining buttons.

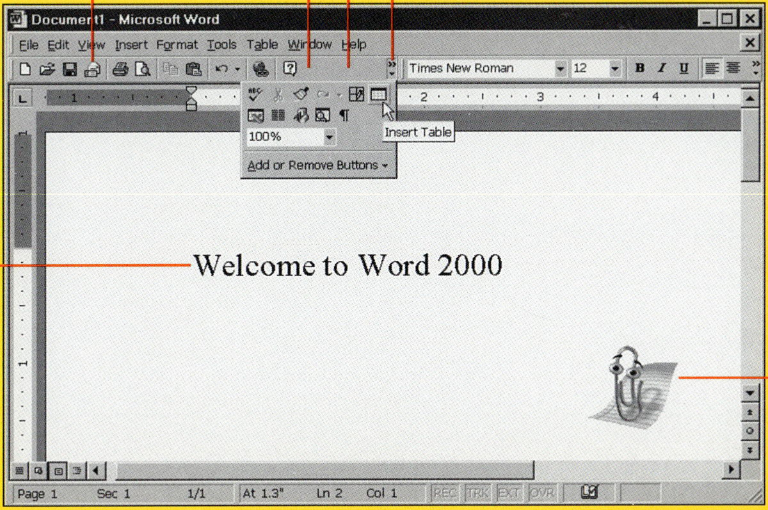

The new Click & Type lets you start typing anywhere.

Choose one of the new annoying helpers.

Word 2000 holds a few new surprises

Copy and Paste on Steroids

Each can hold different copies; click to paste them.

Miscellaneous Good Stuff

Productivity tools available inside Word 2000

Convert entire folders of existing documents at once.

Mailing labels are in here (Letters & Faxes).

Brochure and phonebook are in here (Publications).

Lots of web page designs (Web Pages).

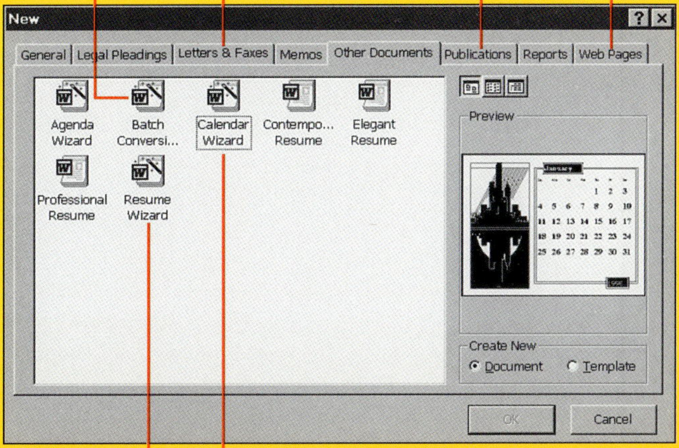

Great résumé templates.

The Calendar maker.

QUE®

Handy Quick Keys

Task	Keyboard Shortcut
Save my document	Ctrl+S
Print it	Ctrl+P
Oops! Undo that!	Ctrl+Z
Switch between open documents	Ctrl+F6
Famous "Go To" window	F5 or Ctrl+G
Cut	Ctrl+X
Copy	Ctrl+C
Paste	Ctrl+V

Jumping Around With Quick Keys

To Jump To:	Keyboard Shortcut
Beginning of document	Ctrl+Home
End of document	Ctrl+End
Top of screen	Ctrl+PageUp
Bottom of screen	Ctrl+PageDown
Next Paragraph	Ctrl+Down
Previous Paragraph	Ctrl+Up
Beginning of Column	Alt+PageUp
End of Column	Alt+PageDown
Go to previous place	Shift+F5 or Alt+Ctrl+Z

Miscellaneous Quick Keys

Check Thesaurus	Shift+F7
Print Envelopes	Alt+T+E
Open	Ctrl+O
Repeat	F4
Close Word	Alt+F4
Bold	Ctrl+B
Italic	Ctrl+I
Underline	Ctrl+U
Cancel	Esc
Go Back	Shift+F5

THE COMPLETE IDIOT'S GUIDE® TO

Microsoft® Word 2000

by Daniel T. Bobola

Que®

A Division of Macmillan Computer Publishing
201 W. 103rd Street, Indianapolis, IN 46290

The Complete Idiot's Guide to Microsoft Word 2000

International Standard Book Number: 0-7897-1860-X

Library of Congress Catalog Card Number: 98-86979

00 99 8 7 6 5 4 3 2 1

Interpretation of the printing code: The rightmost number of the first series of numbers is the year of the book's printing; the rightmost number of the second series of numbers is the number of the book's printing. For example, a printing code of 99-1 shows that the first printing of the book occurred in 1999.

Printed in the United States of America

Although we cannot provide general technical support, we're happy to help you resolve problems you encounter related to our books, disks, or other products. If you need such assistance, please contact Macmillan Tech Support at 317-581-3833 or via email at support@mcp.com.

To order other Que or Macmillan Computer Publishing books or products, please call our Customer Service department at 800-428-5331 or visit our online bookstore at http://www.mcp.com.

Executive Editor
Angie Wethington

Acquisitions Editor
Stephanie McComb

Development Editor
Todd Unruh

Managing Editor
Tom Hayes

Technical Editor
Bill Bruns

Project Editor
Karen S. Shields

Copy Editor
Victoria Elzey

Cover Designers
Dan Armstrong
Barbara Kordesh

Designer
Barbara Kordesh

Illustrator
Judd Winick

Production Team
Wil Cruz
Carl Pierce
Elise Walter

Indexer
Larry Sweazy

Contents at a Glance

Contents

Dedication

To Melissa

Introduction

You're certainly not an idiot, but if Word 2000 makes you feel like one, then you need a book that can help. You don't need a book that assumes you are, or want to become, a Word *geek*. You also don't need anyone telling you that Word is one of the most sophisticated and complex word processors in the world, because you've probably already learned that the hard way. You are a busy person working hard in a busy world, and you just want to get your document written, printed, and available for future use.

Word 2000 is the latest version of the world's most popular word processing program. You'll find plenty of new features that will ensure its popularity far into the future, such as adaptive menus and toolbars, creative themes, Web page templates, easier graphics, superb integration with the Office 2000 product suite, and an artificial intelligence help system to show you how to use it all. And, to prepare you for work on the Internet, Word 2000 comes with a complete set of advanced Web Tools for creating pages on your own Web site.

Why Do You Need This Book?

With so many computer books on the market, why do you need this one? Because it focuses on getting your work done. This book is different because it won't assume that you know anything at all about how to use Word 2000. If you need some assistance coming up to speed with Windows in general, a Windows Primer has been included in the back of this book. If you want more information on Windows, you might pick up *The Complete Idiot's Guide to Microsoft® Windows 95/98*, or *The Complete Idiot's Guide to Microsoft® Windows NT/2000*.

This book doesn't assume you have the time or the interest to learn everything there is to know about Word 2000. The most common tasks are broken down into easy reading chapters that you can finish in a short period of time. Simply open the book when you have a question or a problem, find the answer, and solve your problem, and then get on with your life.

How Do You Use This Book?

For starters, this isn't a novel you can take to the beach and read from cover to cover. I suppose you could, but people would talk. Rather, it's a book to guide you through tough times while you're at work or home. When you need a quick answer, use the Table of Contents or the Index to find the right section. Each section of the book is self-contained with exactly what you need to know to solve your problem or to answer your question.

You can follow along with any example in the book. If you are supposed to press a particular key on your keyboard, that key will appear in **color**, as in:

> **Press Enter to continue**.

And buttons or tabs you work with in dialog boxes are bold fonts:

> Click **OK** when you're finished in the **Save As** box.

Sometimes you will be asked to press two keys at the same time. This is called a key combination. Key combinations appear in this book with a plus sign between them. The plus means you should hold down the first key while you press the second key listed. Here's an example:

> Press **Alt+F** to open the **File** menu.

In this case, you should hold the **Alt** key down and then press the letter **F**, and something will happen on your screen. Then you can let both keys back up; the order doesn't matter. The **Alt** key is popular; it's used with practically all the letters on the keyboard to do one thing or another. These key combinations are explained throughout the book chapters and also on the tear-out card inside the front cover.

Also included throughout this book are special boxed notes that will help you learn more of the basics, and some of the advanced stuff, too:

Techno Talk

These contain more of the advanced material that you can safely ignore if you don't have the time or the interest.

Check This Out

These boxes contain helpful hints, definitions, and shortcuts for clarifying some subjects and getting your work done even faster.

New Word 2000 Features

Experienced users of Word will benefit from discovering these completely new features in Word 2000.

Note

Here's where you'll find interesting tidbits of information that might be useful for you to know.

Part 1

Creating Your Masterpiece

Your computer is a busy machine. It handles the latest games, surfs the Web, and scans photos of the boss so you can distort them later. But once in a while you need to do some real work. Computers can do that, right?

Sure they can! So let's buckle down and prepare to be productive! Write some reports, generate memos, and print your heart out, because you've got Word 2000 and this book. Together we can make the basics of creating documents less of a chore so you can get back to the finer things in life. Whatever they may be.

Chapter 1

The Top 10 Features of Word 2000

Word 2000 is probably the greatest word processor ever created, but you may need a friend to show you where all the good stuff is hiding. When you don't have time to search the rest of this book, you can check this chapter for the major improvements to Word 2000 that will help you create a better document.

Quicker Installation

Only the basics are installed with Word 2000, improving the speed of the installation and lowering the initial amount of disk space required. That makes it less intimidating if you are a beginner. Oh, but don't worry, all the new (and old) features are still available and at your fingertips. Just click on the feature menu item or toolbar button and Word 2000 swings into action. If the feature isn't yet installed, Word automatically installs it for you and makes sure it's always available from now on (of course, you may want to keep that CD handy).

Click and Type

Want to start typing in the center of a new page? Go ahead! Word 2000 now lets you ignore the tabs or formatting. Instead, just double-click where you want to start typing and type!

Personalized Menus and Toolbars

No, not customized, actually *personalized,* and just for you! And you don't have to lift a finger! Word 2000 observes the features you use most, then automatically changes the order or location of that feature to make it faster and easier to reach the next time you need it.

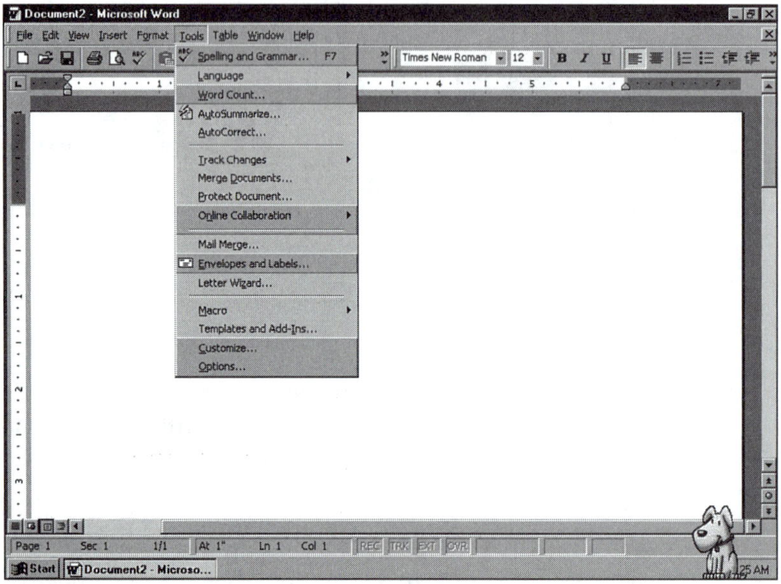

Figure 1.1: Word remembers the commands you use most.

Simplify Document Design Using Themes

Save time making your Word 2000 web pages look more attractive by using the new Themes feature. It's a lot easier than using the old styles or earlier web tools, and you'll avoid any chance of bad combinations of colors or design. Just click any of the new themes (described in Chapter 22) and all the custom-coordinated bells and whistles will find themselves in your document.

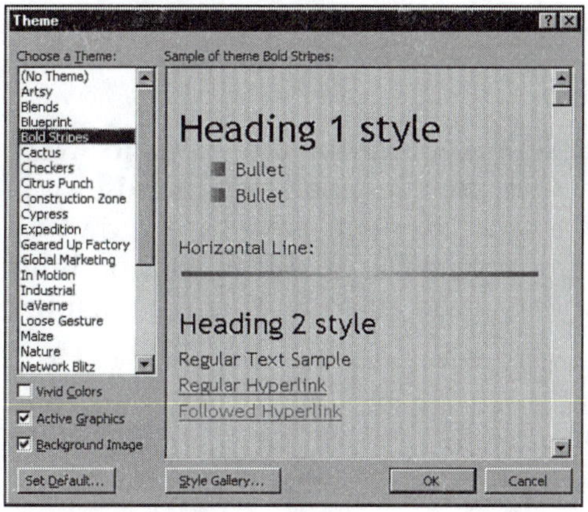

Figure 1.2: Themes help you design web pages.

Easier to Use Multiple Documents

Tired of all the clicking required to move yourself between several open documents? Now you are just one click away, because each Word 2000 document shows up as a task on your taskbar.

Easier to Maintain in both Word and Web Format

Before Word 2000, you had to decide on one format or the other, then generally stick with it. Trying to go back and forth usually meant losing some formatting or contents. Word 2000 now keeps all information with the document, so you can go from Word to HTML/XML and back to Word and still have your stuff appear the same.

Tables Inside of Tables

It might not be high on your list, but the ability to stick one complete table inside another (it's called nesting) is a big deal for some. Chapter 14, "Importing a Fine Piece of Text," gives you all the scoop on creating tables in your documents.

Improved Help Now Demonstrates Features

Reading help screens is boring. Watching an actual demonstration is cool. Word 2000 adds many of these in the improved Help program. Next time you need help with a feature, look for an "Explain How," then sit back and watch how an expert might do it. Chapter 4, "Basic Editing and Text Formatting," describes more ways to get help in Word 2000.

Group Editing with Newsgroup-style Web Comments

No need for yellow-stickies on your printed documents. Now you can share comments live, online, with your collaborating friends using the group editing features of Word 2000. Insert comments anywhere and you can start a running dialog just like a newsgroup on the web. And there's no limit to the number or location of these comments. Read all about them in Chapter 17, "Using More Word 2000 Tools."

And once you begin collaborating on a document, you'll want to know when changes are made and by whom. How about an email? Word 2000 can track these documents and automatically send an email to notify you of any changes.

Figure 1.3: Make comments and track changes online.

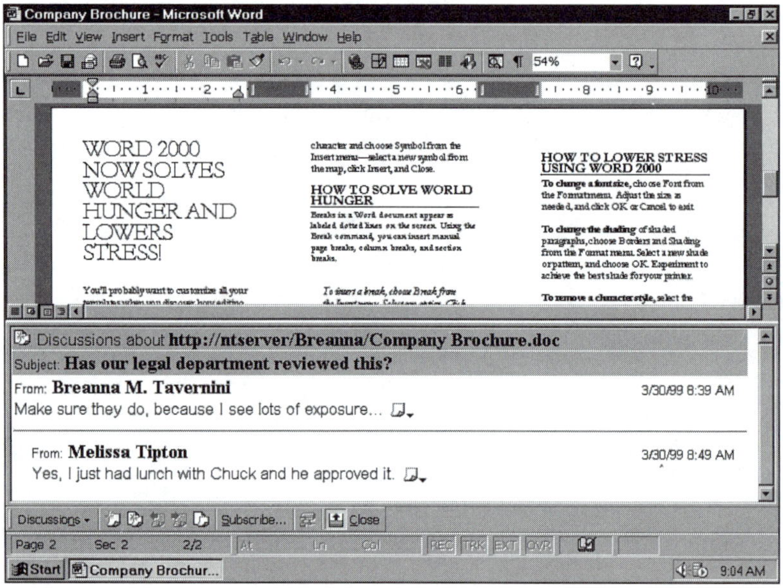

The Clipboard Holds a Dozen

The new Office Clipboard can hold up to 12 selections, and it keeps them handy and visible for you. You'll see the Clipboard toolbar appear the instant you make a second selection of anything. Save time gathering all of your selections first, and then zip around your document depositing them wherever needed. Chapter 5, "Proofing Tools (Spelling, Grammar, and the Thesaurus)," shows you how.

Figure 1.4: The new Office Clipboard holds more text.

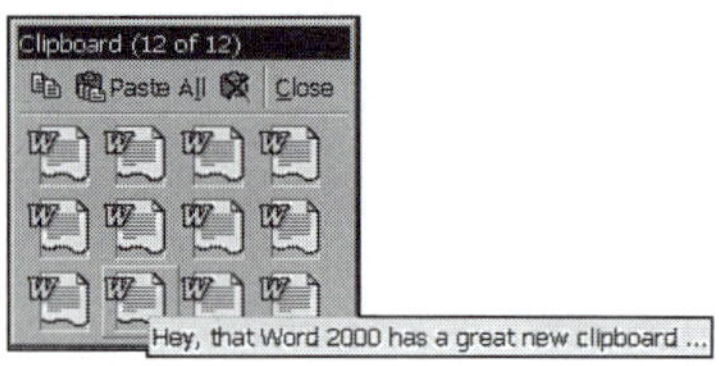

Chapter 2

Word 2000 Basics

In This Chapter

- Starting Word
- Word 2000 toolbars and menus
- Typing and printing a simple letter in Word
- Changing your mind and editing text
- Sampling a wizard to create an attractive memo

Chomping at the bit? This chapter provides a quick review of the basics you'll need in order to navigate your way through the new world of Word 2000. Open the gates, and let's begin!

Starting Word 2000

You can start Word 2000 in either Windows 95/98 or Windows NT/2000 by clicking on the **Start** button, selecting **Programs**, and clicking the **Microsoft Word** menu command. The following figure shows which menus to open.

Figure 2.1: Starting Word 2000 in Windows 95/98/NT/2000.

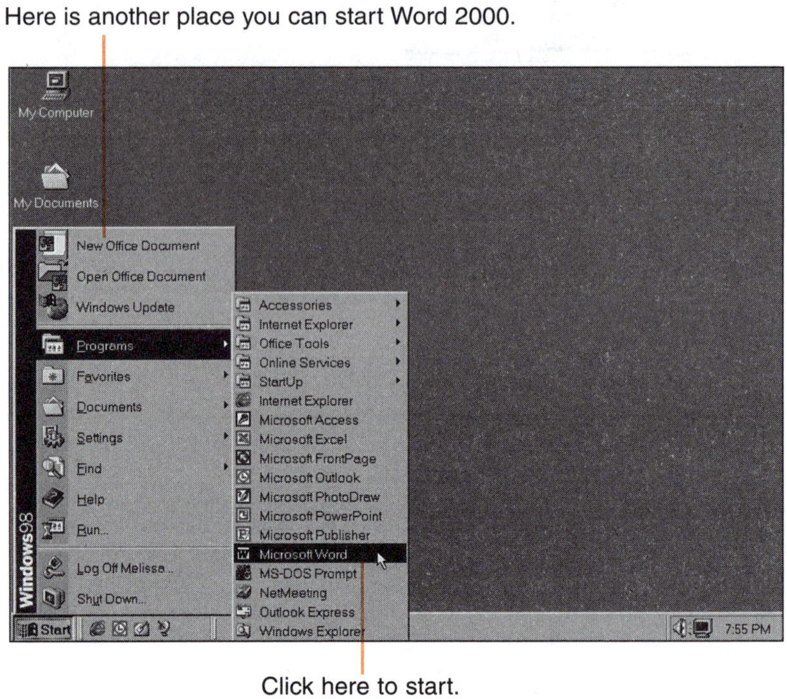

The following figure shows what the majority of users see when they open Word 2000. Nothing has been created yet. The largest part of the display screen is white with nothing in it. This represents a blank sheet of paper ready for you to type on. You will be using the computer keyboard to type words onto this simulated sheet of paper. That's easy enough to understand. But what are all these gadgets on the screen?

More Buttons!

Can't find a button you remember from earlier versions of that toolbar? Click the **More** buttons to find them. You'll find a **More** button on each toolbar; it's the last button on the right.

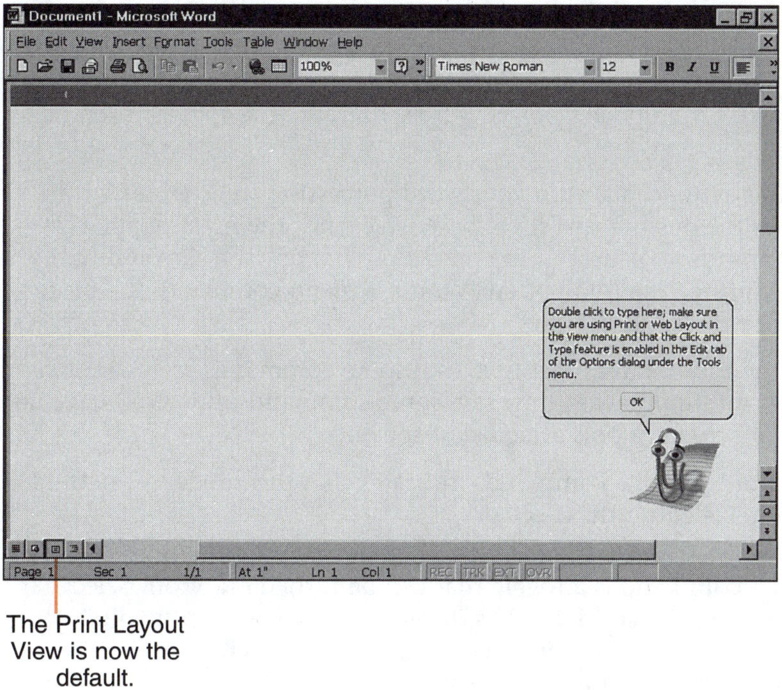

Figure 2.2: Welcome to Word 2000.

Welcome to Word 2000

Think of this chapter as your visual index for finding help about the Word screen. It is a top-down description explaining what you'll see and how to use it.

Title Bar

The title bar is always visible at the top of your screen, as long as the monitor is turned on. Hey, this Title bar is important! Word 2000 places the name of the document you're currently working on in this title bar. It's a quick way to identify your current document. Beyond that, the title bar also contains the three title bar buttons (Minimize, Maximize/Restore, and Exit) that control your Word 2000 window.

Menu Bar

Take a look at the row of words near the top of your screen. See the words File, Edit, View, and so on? These words make up the *menu* bar. It's called the menu bar because it holds a bunch of menus—and menus organize the features of Word. So, when you need something from Word, like printing or adding a footnote, just look for it in these menus. A click of the mouse opens a menu, and then click the feature or command you desire.

So what's new on the menu in Word 2000? I suggest you try the new adaptive and personalized features—they're easy to experience. When a menu first opens, you'll see a few items. But hold that menu open for more than a few seconds, and you see more items—the ones that aren't as popular. This is Word's attempt at keeping life simple for you.

It gets better. The menus actually adapt to your word processing style. Finding the footnote feature may be tedious the first time, because it's not the most popular menu option. But if it warms your heart and you choose it a few times, you'll find it appearing faster in the future. The more often you use a menu command, the more likely it will be near the top of this list.

If you look closely at the View menu, you'll see that some commands are plain, like Header and Footer, and do simply what they say. Some commands, however, have an icon in front of them or other symbols attached at the end:

- The gray box in front of some commands indicates that this mode (or method of doing something) is currently selected.
- The check mark is a standard way of indicating that an option is "on." For example, the Ruler command is a toggle that can be turned on or off. Select such a command when the check mark is displayed, and you turn it "off." When the Ruler command is on, the ruler appears on your screen below the formatting toolbar. When it's off, the ruler is hidden.
- An ellipsis (...) at the end of a command brings up dialog boxes enabling you to choose from many options and settings.

Figure 2.3: The View menu is displayed.

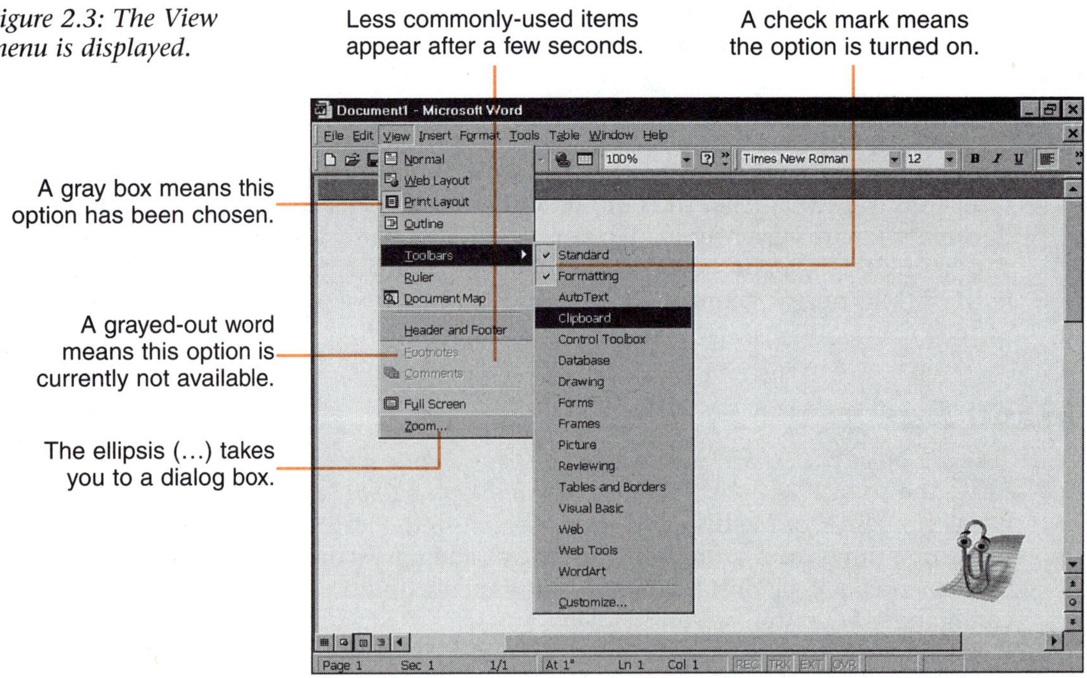

The Adaptable Toolbar

Just under the menu bar is a neat row of icons called the Toolbar. Depending on your needs, you can view one or more toolbars at once. If you're an old hand with Word, you'll notice this first toolbar is actually a combination of the most widely used buttons from the *Standard* and *Formatting* toolbars. Not only can you be looking at more than one toolbar, but they can share the same row of icons. You can see the buttons that don't fit by clicking the More Buttons icon.

With Word 2000, you can easily change the order of buttons you see or even add new ones. This also applies to all toolbars. Chapter 20, "Customizing Word 2000," gives you the scoop on customizing your toolbars. But for now, we'll stick to describing the "original" toolbars.

The Standard Toolbar

The standard toolbar contains icons (or little pictures) of the tasks the average user is most likely to use. That's the average user according to Microsoft, of course.

Table 2.1 The Standard Toolbar Buttons

Icon	Button	Description
	New	Creates a new, blank document based on the normal (the most common) template.
	Open	Find and open an existing document.
	Save	Saves current document.
	Print	Prints the current document.
	Print Preview	View the current document as it will appear when printed.
	Spelling and Grammar	Start the proofing tools at the current insertion point. Grammar checking is now included here.
	Cut	Remove the currently selected text or objects.
	Copy	Take a copy of currently selected text or objects to be pasted elsewhere.
	Paste	Insert the previously selected text or object that was cut or copied.
	Format Painter	Click to copy the formatting from one paragraph to another.
	Undo	Please forget what I just did and put it back the way it was.
	Redo	After an Undo, you might want to Redo the same thing.

continues

Table 2.1 CONTINUED

Icon	Button	Description
	Insert Hyperlink	Converts selected text to a hyperlink.
	Tables and Borders	Displays the toolbar that helps you create and edit tables and table borders.
	Insert Table	Click to display and choose a grid size that creates a table in your document.
	Insert Excel Worksheet	It does exactly that! It inserts a new spreadsheet.
	Columns	Displays and creates custom text columns in your document.
	Drawing	Displays the powerful new Drawing toolbar.
	Document Map	New in Word 2000, a view for a quick browsing of large documents.
	Show/Hide	Toggles the display of non-printing characters, such as spaces, tabs, and paragraph symbols.
	Zoom Control	Displays a menu of different screen enlargements, to better view your document.
	Microsoft Word Help	Starts the animated help creatures described in Chapter 3, "Help! Using Word 2000 Awesome Help."

The Formatting Toolbar

Here are the buttons you will probably use to spiff-up the appearance of your words in your document. These buttons help you select fonts, font sizes, make text bold or italic, and perhaps center your words in the middle of the page. Chapter 4, "Basic Editing and Text Formatting," describes using these buttons in more detail.

The Ruler

This ruler is not your average ruler. If you hold a six-inch ruler up to your screen, you may discover that the two rulers don't match in size, and you may have the urge to return your copy of Word 2000 as defective. Resist that urge. Word is fine, and so is the ruler. The Word 2000 ruler is used to set and display tabs and to indent paragraphs. The ruler is also accurate in size, but the measurement you see is for the future printed page, not the page you see on your screen. What you see is usually larger, and that's helpful for your eyes. You can learn more about setting tabs by using the ruler in Chapter 9, "Enhancing Your Paragraphs and Pages with Formatting Options." If you don't care to see this ruler (most beginners don't need the extra distraction), you can get rid of it by clicking the **View** menu and removing the check from the **Ruler** command.

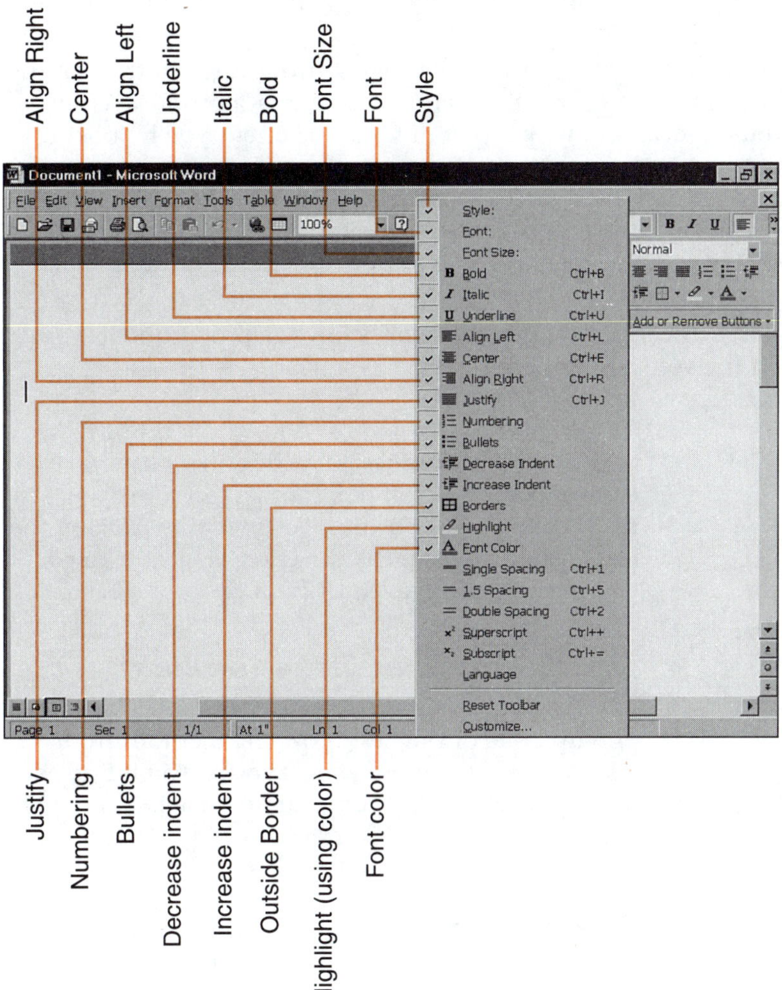

Figure 2.4: The Formatting toolbar buttons.

The Scrollbars

The horizontal and vertical scrollbars are used to travel throughout your document. The most helpful of the two available is called the vertical scrollbar, but you can recognize it as the thing on the right. The vertical scrollbar in Word represents the length of the document. The top arrow represents the top of the document, and the bottom arrow represents the bottom of the document. The area in between the two arrows represents all of the pages, but the most important part of the scrollbar is that small square. That square represents the current spot you are viewing on the screen. As you move up or down the screen (or page), the square moves, too, showing you where you are in the document.

- To scroll your document up one line of text, click the Up scroll arrow at the top of the scrollbar.
- To scroll down one line of text, click the Down scroll arrow at the bottom of the scrollbar. Riding up and down the vertical scrollbar is the proportional scrollbar marker. It gives you an idea as to which part of your document you're looking at (if the marker is near the top of the scrollbar, you are near the top of your document). If it's thin, you have a large document. If it's fatter, you have a smaller document (thus named proportional). Drag the scroll marker up or down to move quickly through the pages of your document. Click the marker to see the current page number.
- To scroll one page at a time, click either above or below the proportional scrollbar marker in the vertical scrollbar.

Another scroll option if your mouse has a wheel

Purchased a mouse lately? The newer models come with a wheel between the buttons. You can use this wheel to scroll through a document two ways: hold the mouse still and spin the wheel to scroll, or press the wheel (it will click) and drag the mouse to scroll smoothly.

Near the bottom of your screen, you'll find the horizontal positioning bar, with arrow buttons on each end and a scroll box (or marker) somewhere in between. You can position your view by clicking the bar or the arrows in the direction you want to go; this moves the page left or right on your screen.

What's That Thing in the Scrollbar?

The **Select Browse Object** is used to display a pop-up table of the best browsing methods from which you can choose your favorite. You'll find the icon on your vertical scrollbar and details on how to use it in Chapter 8, "Can't Find It? Look Here!"

Status Bar

More interesting information about your document is stored in the *status bar* at the bottom of your screen. Most helpful is probably the page number. If you have nothing else to do, you can click in different parts of the screen and watch the numbers in the status bar change. These changing numbers are the coordinates of your whereabouts, or text cursor position, on the page. Isn't it useful to know you are 5.8 inches from the top of your printed page, at line 28 and column 13? Microsoft thinks so.

Don't Like What You See? Change Your View!

You can quickly change your view at any time by clicking one of the four View buttons near the bottom left of your screen, in the horizontal scrollbar. These represent your choice of view, whether it's **Normal**, **Web Layout**, **Print Layout**, or **Outline** view. You can also open the **View** menu and click to choose the view you prefer.

This is for the default **Normal** view. You won't be bothered by headers, footers, page numbers, and so on; you'll see only the plain text document. It's the fastest of the view choices.

Word 2000 introduces a new view called **Web Layout**, designed to make text easier to read onscreen, instead of showing you exactly how it will look when printed. Try it, and notice sentences wrap to stay within the borders of your screen, and smaller text is enlarged. It's ideal for working with Web documents. It provides the look and feel of an active Web page for faster creation and editing.

In **Print Layout** view, you actually see the representation of a sheet of paper on your screen. That's helpful when you are trying to balance text and graphics on the screen and also to see what might be stored in your margins (such as page numbers or footnotes).

Outline view provides an easier way to manage larger documents, just as an outline helps organize your thoughts. The left column of your screen displays the outline format of the current document, but you need to be applying styles consistently for it to be helpful.

Creating a Quick and Simple Document

Think of your Word 2000 screen as a sheet of paper. And imagine your keyboard as your old typewriter (youngsters can ignore that remark). Now just start typing. Everyone can hunt-and-peck out a document, so don't worry if your typing skills aren't the greatest. That's the good thing about Word 2000—most of the minor errors that slow down a professional touch-typist are automatically corrected! Most misspellings, grammatical errors, and forgotten capitalization or punctuation can all be corrected for you. You simply concentrate on getting your thoughts down onto paper (or should I say the screen?). Just start typing.

Enter Text into a Word 2000 Document

Start a new document and your cursor (starting point) is placed automatically so you're ready to start entering text. If you don't like that spot, just double-click anywhere on the page and Word enables you to start typing at that precise spot. It's called Click & Type, and this new feature of Word 2000 gives you complete control over the organization of your document, without resorting to manual tab adjustments.

Click & Type Anywhere!

Forget about the details. With Word 2000, you can now just double-click anywhere on a new page and begin typing.

As you type, your words appear on the screen. Keep typing, and do not press **Enter** when you reach the edge of the screen. Just keep typing. Word 2000 will automatically move your words to the next line as needed. This is called *word wrap*, and it's the most basic feature of any word processor. When you get to the end of a complete paragraph, you press **Enter**. Here are some more hints on entering text in a Word document:

- **Press Enter only when you reach the end of a paragraph or to insert a blank line**. If you want to divide an existing paragraph into two, move the cursor to the dividing point (between sentences) and press **Enter**. To put two paragraphs back together, move to the first letter of the second paragraph and press **Backspace**.
- **Use the spacebar to insert a single space between words or sentences**. Do not use the spacebar to indent or center text on a page. Yes, lots of people like to do it, but it's a bad habit because different fonts assign different sizes to the space. If you mix fonts, things won't line up or center properly.
- **Press Tab (not the spacebar) to indent the first line of a paragraph**. Spaces are not just blank holes on the page; they are real characters. Depending on the fonts you choose for your text, your paragraphs can look uneven if you use the spacebar to align them. Using the Tab key enables Word 2000 to line things up for you.
- **A dotted line marks the end of a page**. Just ignore the dotted line when you see it. It's there to tell Word for Windows where one page ends and another begins. If you add text above a dotted line, the excess text flows to the top of the next page automatically. You can also force the end of a page (before it's full) by pressing **Ctrl+Enter**. When you do this, the dots multiply (get more dense) to show that this is a *forced page break*.

No Mistakes?

If you're a careful typist, you won't have to look through the rest of this book to find out how to back up and change things (Chapter 4), how to ensure things are spelled correctly and are grammatically correct (Chapter 5), or how to skip backwards to locate and replace something (Chapter 8).

Word Wrap Rap

With word wrapping, words are automatically advanced to the next line of a paragraph when they "bump" into the right margin. Likewise, you can insert words into the middle of a paragraph, and the rest of the paragraph is adjusted downward automatically. If you change the margins, paragraphs adjust automatically.

Quicker Alternatives to Snazzy Documents

Want to create a professional-looking report for your boss without straining your cranium? Let a wizard show you how.

A wizard is like ordering up some fancy custom stationery whenever you want it. You pick the kind of document you want (like a fax or a memo) and then tell it what you want (general appearance, size, and so on), and the wizard will instantly prepare your Word 2000 screen to look exactly as you requested. You just fill in the missing words in order to save yourself from wasting time on the trivial aspects of a document.

Word 2000 Document Wizards

To find these wizards, you have to start a new document, but unfortunately you can't simply click the **New** button on your toolbar. You must open your **File** menu and click the **New** command (certainly looks like the same icon, doesn't it?). Oh well, it's just one of those quirks of Word. You'll see something similar to this:

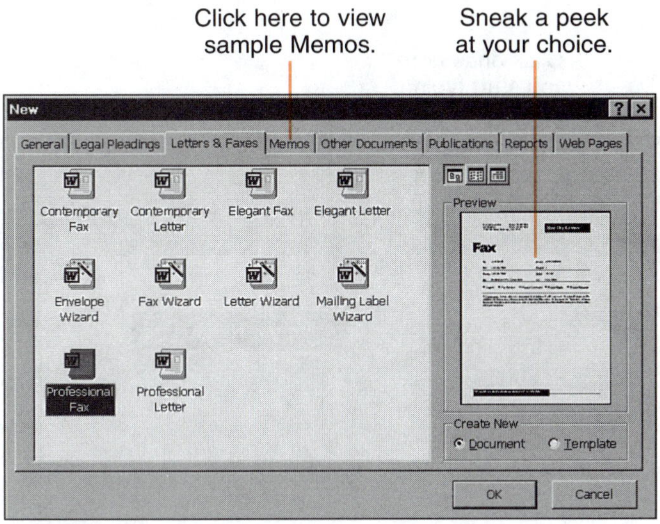

Figure 2.5: Prepared document styles organized in categories.

Just above the central display you'll see tab headings, such as Letters & Faxes, Memos, General, and others. Click the **Memos** tab.

Memo Me This, Mr. Wizard

Double-click the **Memo Wizard** to get it started. The wizard comes to life and begins asking you questions about how you want your memo to appear. You can participate in this banter as much or as little as you feel necessary. You can even skip through the whole thing by doing nothing more than pressing the **Next** button. Press the **Next** button six times and you've completed all of the questions. Press the **Finish** button at the checkered flag.

Just like magic, nice big letters and lines are painted on the page. The parts of the memo are easy to figure out. Someone already stuck the date in for you. They even put your name in the **From:** line! All you have to do is tell the computer who this memo is intended for.

Look at what's written next to the **To:** line. Inside the brackets you will find the suggestion to **Click here and type names**. Try it. Move the mouse arrow until it rests on any word between the brackets. Click the left mouse button once. The sentence changes in appearance, turning light gray in color, anticipating activity from you. Now type your boss's name—or your dog's name if you're just practicing. They may even be the same, for all I know. The typed name appears and replaces the brackets and sentence. You're ready to move on.

Similarly, you can click the optional **CC:** area and type a name for the carbon copy, or click the **RE:** area and type something regarding what this memo's about. Don't need or want them? You can also click them and press **Delete** to remove them.

Figure 2.6: A spiffy memo in a jiffy.

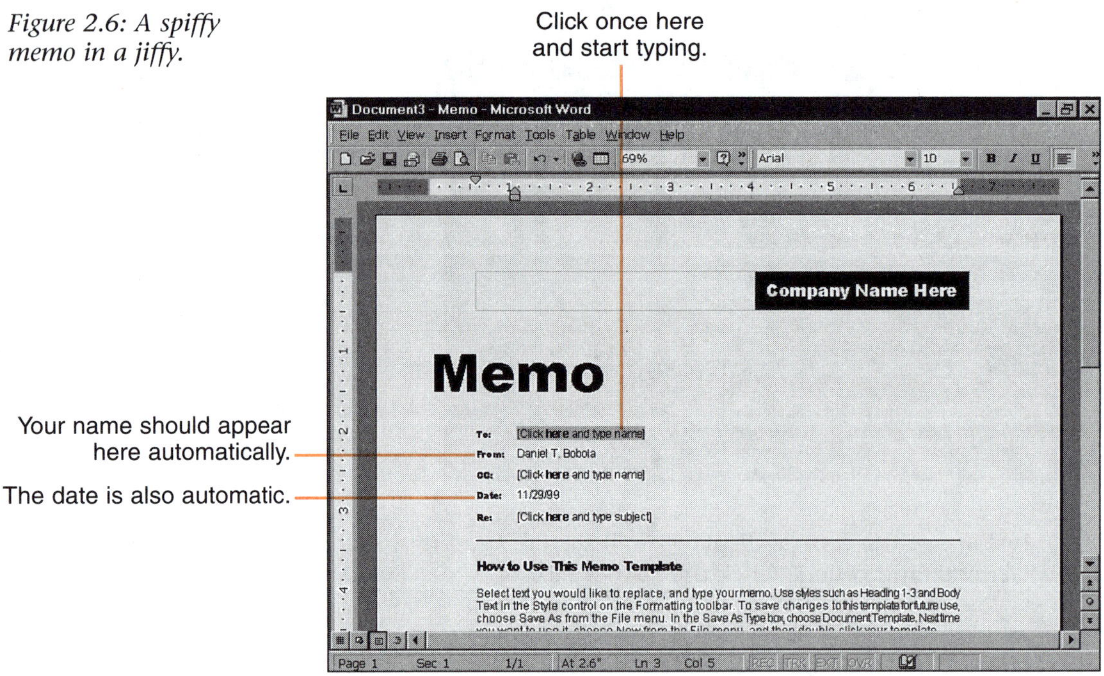

Now move the mouse arrow down to the part that says **Click here and type your memo** text. This is the main body of the memo. Go ahead and type the memo to your boss. When you finish, you'll have a document that's good enough to print.

Oops! Editing Basics

Correcting typing mistakes in Word 2000 is easy. Simply press the **Backspace** key to back up and erase text to the left of the insertion point, or press the **Delete** key to erase text to the right of the insertion point.

How do you correct a mistake found in the middle of a paragraph? You simply have to move the insertion point (that skinny blinking cursor) by clicking on the spot where you want it to go. Now you can use the **Delete** key or the **Backspace** key to remove the unwanted text.

You can quickly get rid of entire words by double-clicking them and pressing the **Delete** key.

Save That First Document

Before trying anything as daring and daunting as printing your new document, the golden rule is to *always save your work first*. Saving a document is simply making sure that everything you now see on your screen is recorded inside your computer, so it's there the next time you want it, which may be weeks, years, or never.

Click the **Save** button on your toolbar. Word 2000 understands that you want to save your new document, but it needs some information from you. Basically, what do you want to call the thing? Since you'll probably have loads of documents soon, you need to name each one so you will recognize it the next time you need it.

Messing Up While Cleaning Up?

If you happen to delete something by mistake and you want to undo the deletion (get the text back), simply press the **Undo** button on the Standard toolbar. In fact, you can keep clicking **Undo** to undo any number of your last actions, in reverse order.

Notice that Word 2000 has already suggested a name for your document. This name is actually the first few words of your document, and more than half the time this might be good enough. You can either type in a new name now, or leave it as it is. Word 2000 automatically saves all your documents to the My Document folder, which is pretty handy. To complete the saving process, click the **Save** button as shown.

Figure 2.7: Saved by the button.

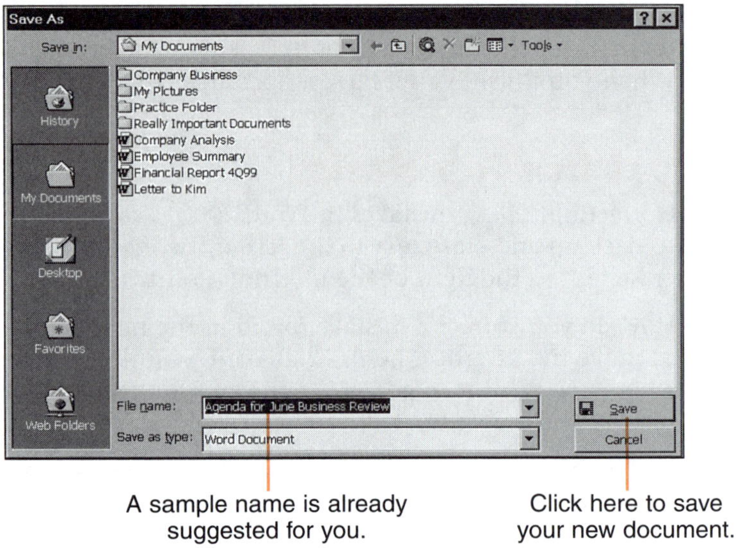

To learn more about saving things in Word 2000, including some helpful options available to you (like changing the folder where you save your documents and automatic timed backups—in case you forget), turn to Chapter 6, "If It's Worth Saving, Save it!"

And Printing That First Document

If it's good enough for you, it's good enough to waste paper on. Click the **Print** button on the toolbar. That's it. Seriously, that's it! If you want another copy, press the button again. If you've been blessed with good fortune, your computer is connected to a printer, your report is already finished, and you are happy. You may also want to experience some of the control you can have over your printer. Open the **File** menu and click **Print**, and you'll find the box enabling you to change such items as printer settings, paper bin source, number of copies, and so on.

If, on the other hand, nothing happened, you are probably feeling rage, anger, and hatred. That's common when dealing with computers. Call your spouse or significant other and tell them you'll be a few minutes late. Then turn to Chapter 7, "Previewing and Printing a Document," to learn more about printing.

Closing Down and Going Home

When you think you've had enough, give your computer a few more seconds of your time. Don't just turn the power off, or you may have an unfortunate surprise (like corrupted documents) waiting the next time you start up.

To properly close your documents, open the **File** menu and click **Close** to close the current document. If any changes have been made to the document since you last saved it, Word gives you the chance to save it before closing. Continue closing all other documents you may have currently open. To close Word, open the **File** menu and click **Exit**, or click the **Exit** button in the title bar. Finally, to close Windows 95/98/NT/2000, click the **Start** button on the Task bar, click **Shutdown**, and click the **Yes** button. Your computer will turn off automatically or display a message saying it's safe to power off your computer.

The Least You Need to Know

You don't have to know much about Word 2000 to get some productive work out of it.

- How do I start Word 2000?

  Click the **Start** button, point to **Programs**, and click **Word 2000**.

- How do I get around in Word 2000?

  Click the toolbar buttons, open the menus, slide the scrollbars, watch the status bars, and don't be afraid of experimenting!

- Can you make it easier to get me started?

  Try using one of the built-in wizards, such as the Memo Wizard. It takes care of the formatting and placement; you just type your message.

- Will my document be here tomorrow?

  Only if you save it. Be sure to click the **Save** button and give your document a name and a home.

- Is it hard to print?

  Not if you have a printer! Click the **Print** button and your document will be printed with the default settings. If that's not good enough for you, try peeking at Chapter 7.

Chapter 3

Help! Using Word 2000 Awesome Help

In This Chapter

- Getting good help fast
- Putting your Office Assistant to work
- Making your Assistant behave
- Using the Help Contents, Answer Wizard, and Index

Good help is hard to find, but relax—you've found this chapter. This chapter is dedicated to helping you help yourself with Word 2000. Word is an incredibly sophisticated program, so it's no wonder that we sometimes slow down when using a new feature or remembering an old one. Word provides help for absolutely every function and feature within Word, mostly through gadgets called Office Assistants. They're worth the click to get them started. You may find yourself looking for help just for the fun of watching the program go get it.

The Office Assistant

Microsoft expands the use of these critters in Word 2000. At first, it may seem silly to have a dopey dog or bouncing ball sitting in the corner of your screen. But these *Office Assistants*, as they are called, grow on you. Each one tries to guess what you need help with based on the previous actions you've performed. Or, you can ask your Assistant directly for help whenever you want, just by clicking it. You'll have the option to search for specific help on something or type in a question, and the Assistant will provide relevant Help topics.

Different Assistants are available and each has a slightly different personality; some are more animated and have lots of sound effects (like the dorky robot called *F1*), and some are more quiet and reserved (would Einstein have used the "genius"?). No matter which Assistant you choose, they all have the same purpose, which is to help you solve your word processing problems and learn to use Word 2000 quickly and painlessly.

Why Should I Try an Assistant?

Assistants provide the convenience of one-stop shopping. It's one place to look for all the help that exists. It's got enough intelligence to stay out of your way and yet give you a subtle hint when it can guide you to a better way of doing something. And help appears at the appropriate time. For instance, you won't be bothered with help in placing a table across multiple pages until your table starts growing across multiple pages.

Also, the Assistants can warn you before you do something dumb. Try to close Word before saving all your files and you may hear a dog yapping on your screen, trying its hardest to protect your document. It's the right amount of silliness to awaken you before making a big mistake.

Figure 3.1: The Office Assistant can provide the help you need.

Choosing Your Own Assistant

The Assistant starts automatically when you start Word. If you accidentally close your Assistant, click the **Office Assistant** button on your toolbar (or press **F1**). You'll always see the same assistant until you decide to change it.

To change your Assistant, click anywhere on the Assistant and click the **Options** command. You'll see the box that includes the **Gallery** where you can sample each of them. If one doesn't work out for you, throw it back and try another (even more are available from the Microsoft Web site). Click the **OK** button to set the current Assistant to be your latest buddy.

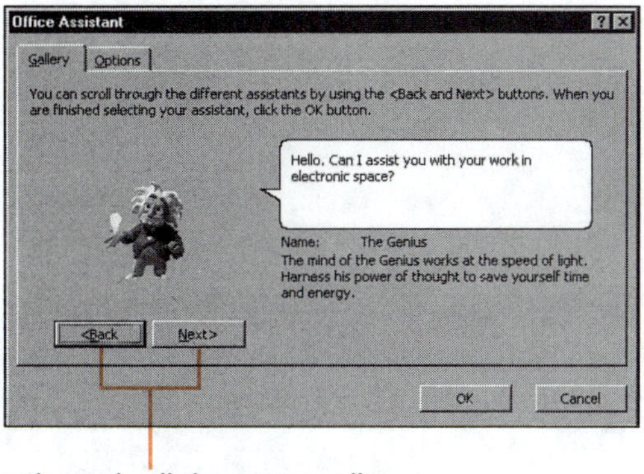

Figure 3.2: You can pick your friends and you can pick your Assistant.

Don't Forget the Tip

You may find it amusing to have your Assistant on the screen all the time. If you don't make many mistakes, the Assistant won't have much need to help you. In fact, your once-animated Assistant may appear to be bored stiff. But that doesn't mean it's asleep! It keeps watching, and if it has a relevant idea for your current activity, a small light bulb icon will appear in the upper-right corner of the Assistant window. To see the idea, click the light bulb.

These tips automatically suggest ways to use Word 2000 more quickly and efficiently, as when you're trying to create a big table or trying to change margins or tabs. The tips are also a great way to get a lot of information about what's going on with some of the new features in Word 2000.

If you don't want to wait for the light bulb to appear, you can see the tips by right-clicking your Assistant. In the menu that appears, click the **Tips** option. If more than one tip is currently available, you'll be able to browse through them by clicking the **Back** and **Next** buttons.

Asking Your Assistant for Help

The Assistant can't always read your mind, so if you want to ask it a question, go right ahead. Just click it! A balloon of information appears on your screen. The top half lists help topics related to your current activity, and the bottom half has navigation buttons taking you to the other help functions, such as Tips screen and Search. In the middle you see a box where you can type your personal request.

Have some fun. You can ask for information using common everyday language, and you'll get the help you need—also in plain English. For example, type **How do I create a Web page?** In response, your Assistant provides a list of possible answers (all about creating a Web page), and you can choose any or all of them to get more help. Be as creative or bold as you dare with the questions you type—it's a great stress-reliever—it may even help answer your questions.

Your answers are delivered to you on the right side of your screen, now called **Microsoft Word Help**. If there isn't an exact answer, you can click any of the next-best-guess alternatives to get full details of each topic.

Figure 3.3: Ask your Assistant for help.

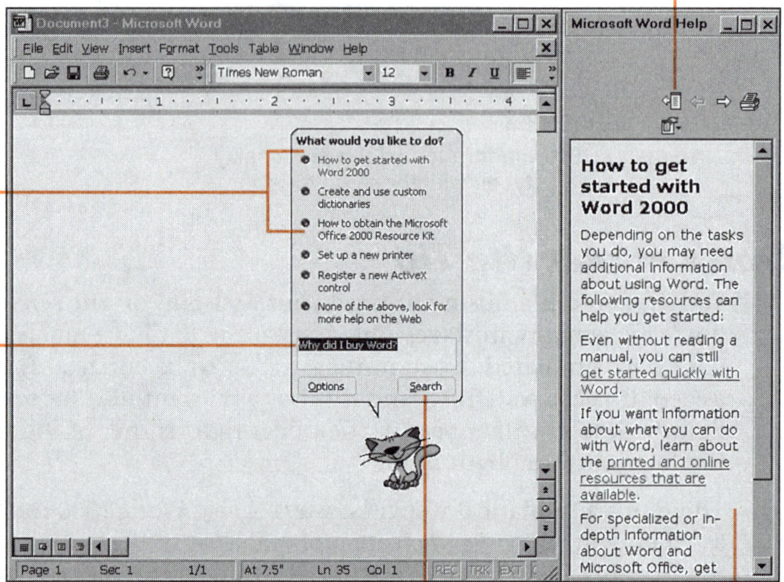

Customizing Your Assistant

You don't like something about your Assistant? You prefer not to hear the sound effects? You want to be bothered only with tips of the highest priority? Then customize your Assistant!

Word 2000 provides a customization menu to tweak how much or how little your friend helps. To open this menu, click anywhere on your Assistant and click the **Options** command. Here you'll find lots of good choices. Among the better ones:

- **Guess Help Topics** This option keeps the Help engine running in the background to anticipate the help you'll need based on your actions.
- **Keyboard Shortcuts** You can have the keyboard equivalent of all help tasks for those whose fingers are quicker on the keyboard than with the mouse.
- **Only Show High Priority Tips** This shows only the tips that relate to time-saving features.

- **Show the Tip of the Day at Startup** This is a painless way to slowly and steadily ingest all the features and tips of Word 2000.

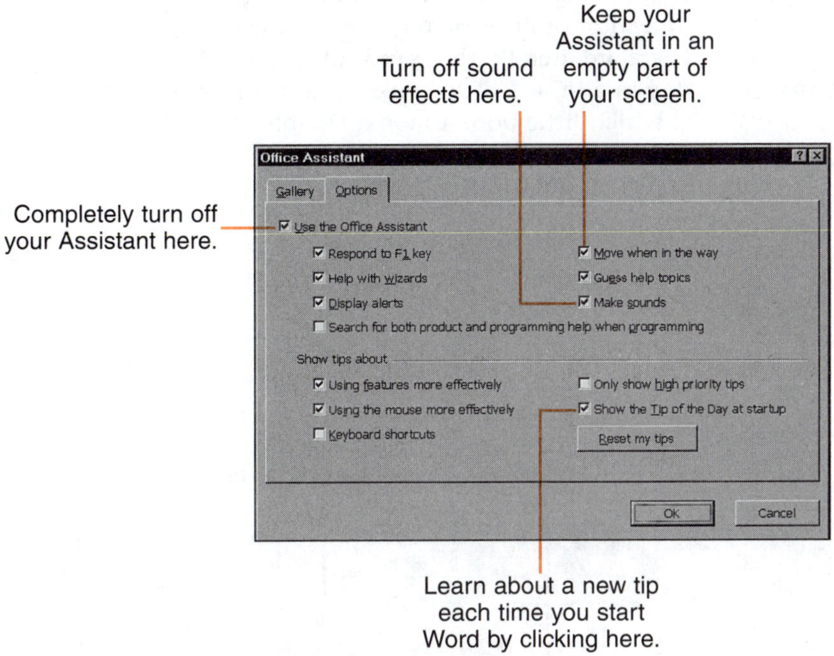

Figure 3.4: Make your Assistant behave by customizing it.

The Help Menu: A Library is Stuffed Inside

So where are all the paper manuals that used to come with Word? The information is still in there, but it's not written on paper anymore. All the Word 2000 manuals, and there are actually dozens of them, are included inside the Word program. The help is loaded into your computer during installation and is ready when you beckon it. The easiest way to browse these help books directly is to click the **Show** button on the **Microsoft Word Help** screen. The screen will expand and show you the full **Help** dialog box options. Now you'll see a dialog box where you can browse books, look up something in an index, or search for specific combinations of words.

What Happened to the Help Key?

In Microsoft Word 2000, the **F1** key now brings up the Office Assistant by default. If you prefer to have the **F1** key open the **Help Topics** (the look-it-up-yourself method), you must change your Assistant Options. Click your Assistant and choose **Options**. Remove the check from the **Respond to F1 key** option, then press the **OK** button. It's back.

Shut the darned thing off already!

Hate your Assistant? Word 2000 improves your ability to shut it off and keep it off. It's now the first option on the Options screen.

The Little Help Books

With the Help screen open, click the **Contents** tab to bring it to the front. You'll be treated to a collection of little Help books arranged by category. There are literally thousands of pages of help available in all these little books. You just have to decide in which little book to look. Double-click a book and you'll see it open and display specific answers to related questions.

Figure 3.5: Reading the online help books.

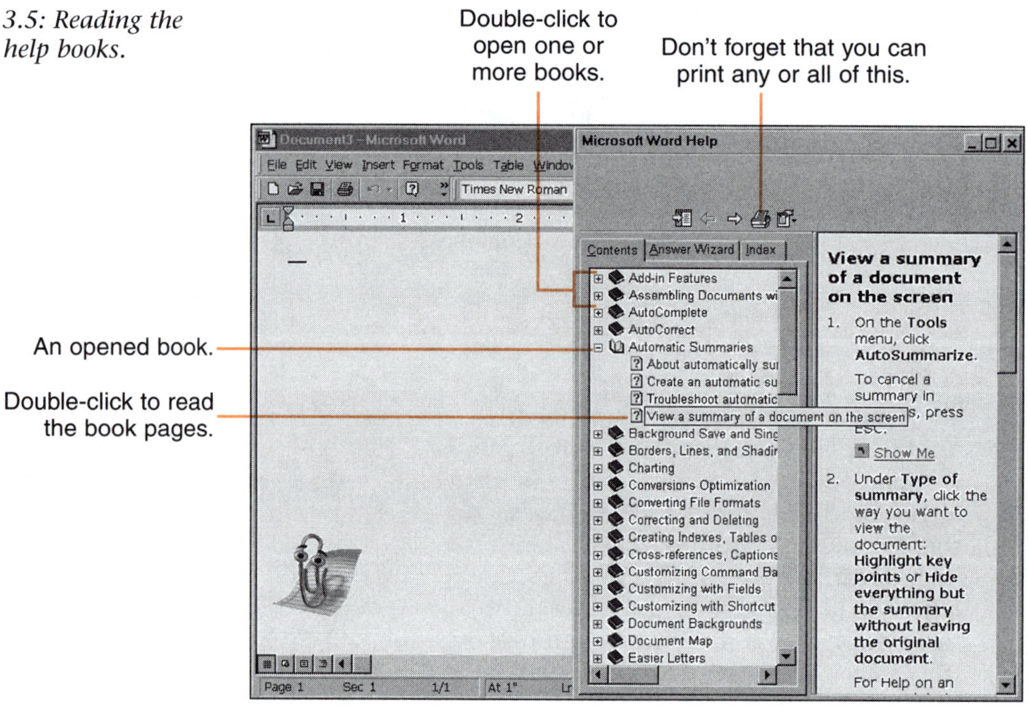

The Answer Wizard is Back

The second tab in the **Word Help** dialog box is the **Answer Wizard**, revived from an earlier version of Word. Use it just like the Assistant, typing in your question and clicking Search. You'll get the same answers as the Assistant, and you may prefer the larger writing area.

Prefer the books over the Assistant?

You can also go directly to these help books every time by turning off the Assistant. Click the Assistant, click **Options**, and choose **Turn Off Office Assistant**.

Browsing the Help Index

With the **Help Topics** open, click the **Index** tab to bring it to the front. In the Number 1 box, type the first few letters of the word you want help with, and the text box below it fills with the closest matches. Then you can click or use the arrow keys to browse around in the list until you find what you're looking for. Double-click to view the contents. You can click **Print** to get your answer in writing.

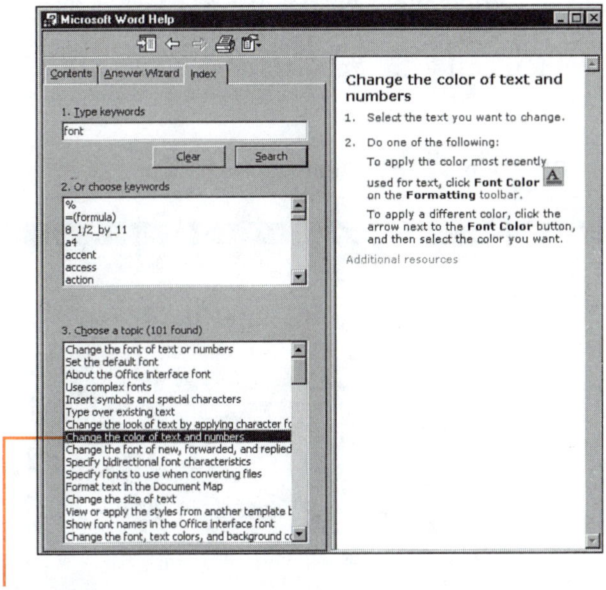

Figure 3.6: Finally someone understands me.

Print It!

You can also print any of these helpful screens by clicking the **Options** menu in the Help screen and choosing the **Print** command.

Click the "What's This?" Command to Point and Learn

You can use the **What's This?** command on the **Help** menu to learn just about anything on your Word 2000 screens. You can discover what a button on a toolbar really does, what format codes are applied to any text in your document, or learn more details about an option before you choose it.

For example, let's say you don't have a clue as to the purpose of the button sitting next to Paste on the Formatting toolbar. Open the **Help** menu, click **What's This?**, and then click that unknown button. This help feature won't activate that button, but instead provides a descriptive dialog box telling you this is the *Format Painter* button, and it's used to copy formatting. It even tells you how and when you might want to use this button.

As another example, what if you want the details on some interesting formatting that captures your eye inside a document you've just received? Click the same **What's This?** button and then click directly on the formatting you want to explore. You'll be rewarded with detailed formatting information of every aspect from font to paragraph and page details.

Figure 3.7: Discover formatting information with this pointer.

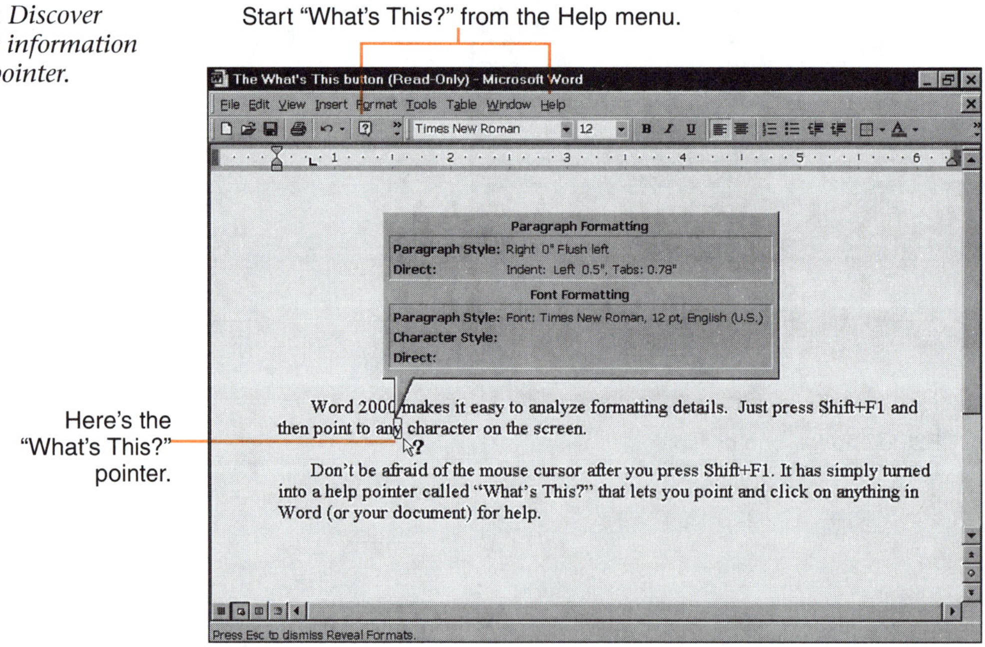

If you change your mind and want to get rid of the **What's This?** pointer and return your normal mouse arrow, click anything just to unload it, or you can press the **Esc** key. This action returns you safe and sound to normal operation.

Help from the Web

The fourth item on the Help menu is called **Office on the Web**. It provides a direct link to Microsoft's Web site, containing the very latest information and tips. When you choose one of these options, Word 2000 will start your Internet Web browser and point it to the right place.

WordPerfect Users Can Join the Bandwagon

If you happen to know WordPerfect but are new to Word, try the **WordPerfect Help** command. It's a great way to put your previous knowledge to productive use. You'll find a great cross-reference guide of the commands you're familiar with and demos of how this task is accomplished in Word. If you are a WordPerfect user who really hates Word but must use it, you can always use the combination keys you remember from WordPerfect, and they function correctly in Word! How the heck did that happen?

Show Me the Videotape

If you are lucky, you will run into a useful new feature called **Show Me** that actually performs or demonstrates a feature on your current document. These are easy to identify in your searches for help because they include the **Show Me** icon. There are hundreds scattered throughout Word, and most are smart enough to save your document automatically before trying anything too serious. Sit back and watch the action!

Oops! I think I Broke It!

Troubleshooting is easier in Word 2000. Just enter the word **Troubleshoot** in your Assistant (or in the Answer Wizard or Index portions of the Help Topics), and you'll find dozens of step-by-step procedures to guide you through the problem.

Figure 3.8: Show Me demonstrates features in Word 2000.

Detect and Repair

Word 2000 includes a new feature on the Help menu called **Detect and Repair**. Use it when you think Word is acting too weird to continue. This feature tells Word to try and cure itself by inspecting and reinstalling components like fonts, templates, and other noncritical files. You won't cause any additional harm by running it.

The Least You Need to Know

Getting help in Word 2000 does not require a call to 911. It's much easier to use the built-in Help features described in this chapter.

- What if I need help fast?

  If you're using Word 2000, just ask your Assistant (if you can't find it, press the **F1** key). You'll get the complete online help program.

- Can I just point to something on my screen and get specific help about it?

  Sure. Just press **Shift+F1** (or click the **What's This?** command on the **Help** menu) to get a help pointer, and move it anywhere on the screen to click the exact detail that may be troubling you.

- What's this bouncing paper clip doing on my screen?

  That's the new Word 2000 Office Assistant, and the paper clip is one of eight personalities programmed to help you. They sense when you need help and offer suggestions. They provide room to type questions and search for answers.

- Do I have any control over this Assistant?

  Yes, you can change the urgency levels for specific events, alter the sound effects, and even shut him up for good. Just click your Assistant and choose the **Options** command to locate the settings.

- Can you help me troubleshoot my problem?

  You said the magic word. Use the word troubleshoot during your Help sessions, in combination with another word describing your problem (such as troubleshoot printing), and you'll receive specific tips on getting you out of that bind.

Chapter 4

Basic Editing and Text Formatting

In This Chapter

- Different ways to select text
- New options in Cut, Copy, and Paste
- Choosing Bold, Italic, and Underline
- Changing fonts and font size
- Copying a good format

So now you've got words on the page, and they basically say what you want to say, but there's no pizzazz?! You want more. You've seen it in magazines, posters, and those impersonal form letters in the mail. Wild formatting, huge lettering, and vivid colors fill the page!

Yes, you can certainly cut out assorted fancy letters from newspapers and magazines and then paste them letter-by-letter onto your sheet of paper, but that's usually done when you want to remain anonymous. How can you get Word 2000 to do the kind of stuff you'll be proud of? Sit back and enjoy; we'll break no laws (except perhaps those of good taste) on this subject of character formatting.

What Is Selected Text, and How Do You Select It?

This is a chapter about changing the basic look of your text. If the text is already in your document, you must choose exactly which text you want to change. This is called *selecting*. You must always select text before you can format it, move it, or get excited about it. Selected text typically doesn't stay selected for a long time. It's simply a middle step necessary for your decision to change something.

One at a time

You can select only one thing at a time in your document, but it can be any size and just about any shape.

You can select text several different ways, but no matter how it is done, selected text always looks the same. It usually appears in reverse-video on your screen, meaning if you usually see black letters on a white background, selected text will be white letters on a black background. That's how you know it's currently selected.

Selecting Text with Your Mouse

Most people find it's easiest to select text by using the mouse. Open any document containing some text, and move the mouse arrow until it hovers somewhere over some words in your document. Now click the left mouse button, hold it down, and drag your mouse in any direction. Let go of the mouse button. See what's there? Congratulations! You have just selected text!

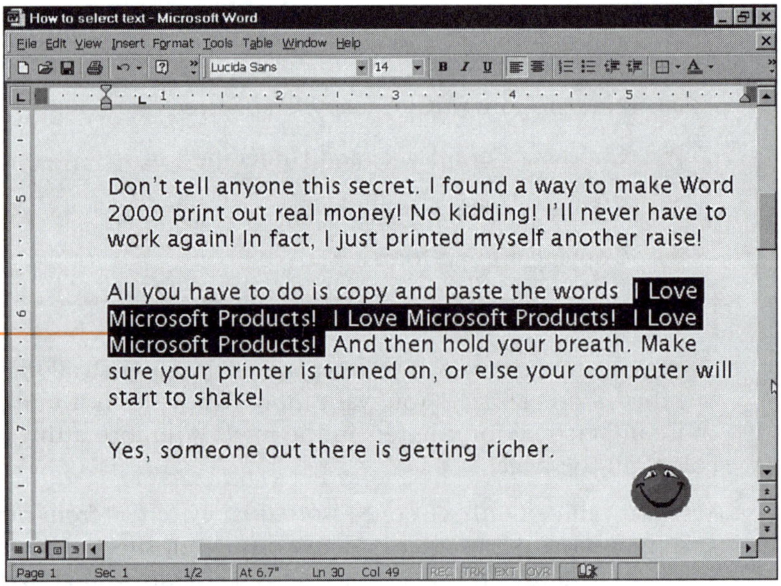

Figure 4.1: It's easy to see selected text.

This text is "selected" and ready for action.

Of course, to be useful, you have to be a good shot with your mouse. Aim well before clicking as you reach the end of your selection, or else you must start the whole selection process over again. There are other methods for selecting things, and some will be faster for you, depending on what you're selecting.

The Invisible Selection Bar Area

You can select an entire line with a single click if you know the trick. Take a closer look at the left border of your text screen. Can't see it, can you? That's because it's invisible, but trust me, it's still there. It's called the *selection bar*, and it always exists as a single thin strip on the left border of your entire document. By clicking in this area, you select everything on that line. Try it, because it's a very common and useful way to select multiple lines or paragraphs of text. Move your mouse pointer to the far left side of an opened document, as shown in the figure. The cursor will change to an arrow, which can be a helpful reminder that you are now inside the selection bar. Click while you're in this area to select an entire line, or click and drag (up and down in the selection bar) to select multiple lines at a time.

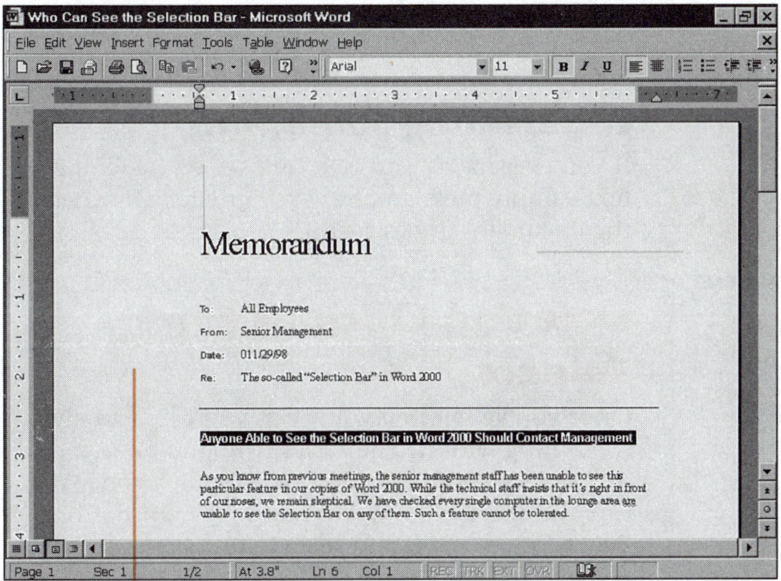

Click in this area for selecting entire lines at once.

Figure 4.2: Using the selection bar area.

Selection Quickies

If you find this method of selecting text a drag, here are some shortcuts you can use when selecting text with the mouse:

To Select This:	Do This:
Word	Double-click the word
Multiple Words	Double-click word and drag to grab more

continues

To Select This:	Do This:
Sentence	Press the **Ctrl** key and click anywhere in the sentence
Paragraph	Triple-click anywhere inside the paragraph
Multiple Paragraphs	Triple-click in one paragraph, then drag to select others
Line	Click in the selection bar next to the line
Multiple Lines	Click and drag in the selection bar next to the lines
Whole document	Open the **Edit** menu and choose the **Select All** command

Try the Shift and Arrow keys

You don't need the mouse to select text. Just hold down the **Shift** key and press any **Arrow** keys for instant selection. If you have only one hand available, you can first press the **F8** key, then the arrow keys to select. Want a quick way to select all text in your document? Hold down the **Ctrl** key and press the **A** key.

Unselecting Something

If you ever make a mistake and select the wrong text, simply press an arrow key or click anywhere in the document to deselect it.

Deleting Options for Selected Text

Once you've selected your text, you can actually do something with it. The easiest thing to do is get rid of it. Just press the **Delete** key. Bang! It's gone. You can also use the **Backspace** key or the **Cut** button. Don't forget that if you really didn't mean to kill the selected text, you can always click the **Undo** button to undo an inappropriate deletion and give your words a second chance at life. A right-click on selected text also displays the **Cut** command in the shortcut menu.

Another easy way to delete selected text is to simply start typing the replacement text. The first keyboard letter you press replaces the selected text, saving you the time and stress of finding and pressing the **Delete** key.

Cut, Copy, and Paste

If the term cut-copy-and-paste does nothing more for you than offer daydreams of happy times in kindergarten, you should sit up straight and pay attention! You need to know this before graduating to the fun stuff.

Copy Your Words to Use Them Again

Sometimes you write stuff that is so good you want to use it again. Once you've selected the part you like, click the **Copy** button on the Standard toolbar. Give it a try.

Hey, big deal; nothing happened, right? Wrong! That **Copy** command just notified millions of little computer nerds living inside your computer. They paid attention and wrote down exactly what you just selected. Your original text is copied into the clipboard and remains there safe and sound.

Now the nerds are waiting for you to tell them exactly where to put the text. Move your cursor (or click) to the area in your document where you want to place the copy. Don't worry if there isn't enough room; any existing things are pushed around to accommodate your copy.

Now click the **Paste** button. Magically, your selection is copied exactly as it was previously. The trick to copying and pasting is to remember that copying is only the first step. Then you must use the second step called pasting.

You Can Keep On Pasting, Keep On Pasting

Maybe your stuff is so good you want it sprinkled everywhere in your document. Do you have to keep going back to select a prior instance and copy it again? Heavens no. Just keep using the **Paste** command and a new copy continues to appear wherever your text cursor happens to be. By golly, you can even paste to completely different programs, like WordPerfect or an outgoing email note for the Internet!

Move Your Words with Cut and Paste

If your goal is to move text instead of copying it, save yourself some time and try the **Cut** button. You cut the selected text, which gets rid of it from the first place, and then paste it to a new location directly. This is how confident Windows experts live day-to-day, trusting that the cut text is safe and sound until it's pasted elsewhere. You can do it, too!

Any time you cut a selection, it's actually copied to the *clipboard*, which means it's still available to you. That's one of the advantages over the **Delete** key. If you delete a selection, it's gone; but if you cut a selection, you still have a chance to use it again somewhere else.

Shortcut Keys to the Rescue

Speed up changes using the shortcut keys for Cut (**Ctrl+X**), Copy (**Ctrl+C**), and Paste (**Ctrl+V**).

The Clipboard Now Holds a Dozen

The new **Office Clipboard** can hold up to 12 selections and keeps them handy and visible for you. You'll see the **Clipboard** toolbar appear the instant you make a second selection of anything. This figure displays the clipboard holding 12 items that can be identified by hovering the mouse pointer over the icons.

Why have so many selections? You may save time gathering all of your selections first, and then zip around your document depositing them wherever needed. Simply click the desired clipboard icon to paste the contents. And the selections stay in this clipboard until you click the **Clear Clipboard** icon.

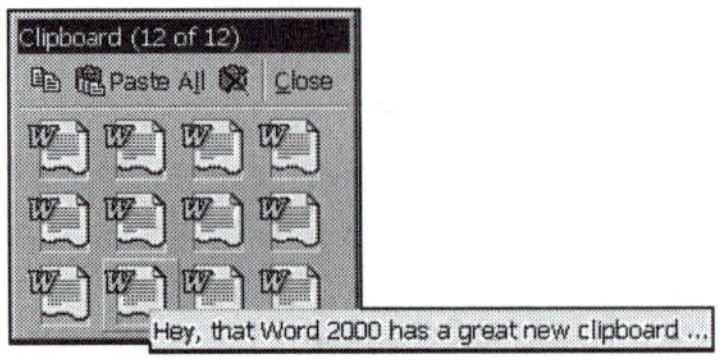

Figure 4.3: Store up to 12 selections in the clipboard.

Sentences Start and End Cleanly

When you copy, move, or drag entire sentences, Word automatically adds or removes extra spaces you may have selected accidentally—as long as the option **Smart Cut and Paste** is on. To check, open the **Tools** menu and choose **Options**. Click the **Edit** tab and make sure that **Use Smart Cut and Paste** is selected.

Drag Your Words Around

Try moving selected text another way. After you've selected text, move the mouse over it and the cursor changes to an arrow. Click anywhere inside the selection and hold down the left mouse button for a few moments. The cursor changes appearance slightly (a little box appears at the bottom of the arrow) to let you know it's ready. Now drag the whole thing to a new location. When you reach the new destination, let go of the left mouse button and watch the action. Your selection is moved automatically, and you may have saved some time over using the **Cut** and **Paste** buttons.

Please Undo What I Just Did

Undo has always been an important tool, especially when your computer doesn't listen to you. After you've done something (to your document) you've regretted, click the **Undo** button. If the action you want to undo occurred a few steps ago, you can click the little arrow attached to the **Undo** button and browse through a scrollable list of your last zillion activities. This helps you back up to precisely the point you want. When you undo an action, you also undo all actions above it in the list.

If you accidentally undo too far and want something put back the way it was, you can use the **Redo** button the same way. You'll find both of these buttons on the Standard toolbar.

You can undo almost anything, including typing, cutting and pasting, formatting, and so on, but not everything. The button label changes to **Can't Undo** if you cannot reverse the last action.

Try the Shortcut Menu

Word 2000 provides a convenient pop-up menu that appears when you press the right mouse button on selected text. Try it and you'll see the familiar **Cut**, **Copy**, and **Paste** commands at your fingertips.

Who's a Character, and What's Formatting?

Character is another computer term. It means a single letter of the alphabet (or a single number or symbol). The word antidisestablishmentarianism is made up of 28 characters.

Character formatting is the process of changing how a character looks. For example, through character formatting you can make a word bold, italic, or underlined. You can change the size of text (its point size), making it bigger or smaller. You can also change its style by choosing a different font.

Using Bold, Italic, and Underline

These are the three most famous formatting options, so each has been awarded its own button. To type characters that are either **Bold**, **Italic**, or **Underlined**, first click the button on the Formatting toolbar. From now on, anything you type is in that format—that is, of course, until you want to turn it off. It's not hard to do that, either. Simply click the button again!

Or, if you want to apply any of these formats to text that already exists, first select the text, then click any or all of the buttons. That's right, you can mix or match any combination of these three formats.

Returning to Normal (or Regular)

You can turn off all character formatting by pressing the **Ctrl+Spacebar** key combination. This also works on selected text containing any combination of character formatting. Simply select the range of text and press **Ctrl+Spacebar**. If you want to get rid of all character formatting, no matter what or where, select the entire document and then press **Ctrl+Shift+Z**. You'll be left with plain, unadulterated text (called *regular*) in the default font and size.

Uppercase and Lowercase Conversions

A neat trick available in Word 2000 is called the *case rotation*. It alternates letters between uppercase and lowercase in a chunk of selected text. The secret key combination is **Shift+F3**. The first rotation capitalizes the first letter in all words in the selection. Press **Shift+F3** again, and all letters are capitalized. Press it again, and they are all lowercase again.

Inserting Symbols to Suit You

Can't find what you need on the keyboard? Want to include one of those weird but useful symbols like a trademark, copyright, or fractions? All these symbols can be found by using the **Symbol** command in the **Insert** menu. It displays hundreds of symbols to choose from. You can double-click the symbol, and it appears in your document at the current insertion point. If the location isn't what you want, you can move it or cut-and-paste it to another location.

Fonts and Sizes: How the Other Half Lives

Hope you aren't tired yet, because we've only skimmed the surface of the vast character formatting jungle. Sure, the bold-italic-underline stuff helps, but the letters are still shaped the same way. That's called a font. You can change fonts whenever you want, and hundreds of fonts are available globally. When you installed Windows 95, 98, or Windows NT, you also installed many fonts. Installing Word 2000 gives you even more to play with. And if that's not enough, you can purchase additional fonts to install yourself. Ask your computer salesperson for more information on purchasing and installing additional fonts. What does a different font look like? Here's a sample:

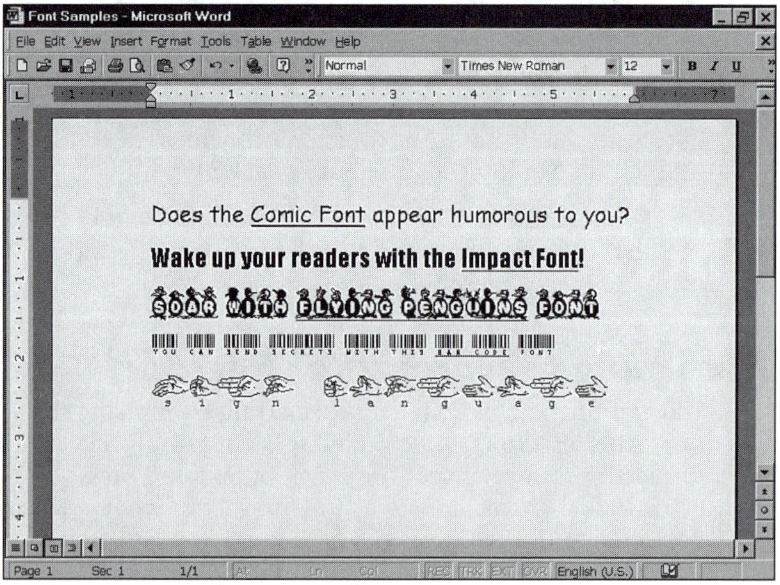

Figure 4.4: Sampling fonts from Word (first two) and the Web (last three).

Those first two fonts are included for you in Word 2000; the last three I've included as examples of fonts you can purchase to add to your repertoire of tools in Word 2000.

Changing Your Font

To change to a different font, click the down arrow in the font box on the formatting toolbar. A list of all available fonts drops down for you to view. The list is in alphabetical order, in case you know the name of the font you desire. Browse the list with your mouse or arrow keys and press **Enter,** or click the font you want. The font name you picked should now be displayed in the font box. Now start typing. Everything appears in the new font, and it should print as well.

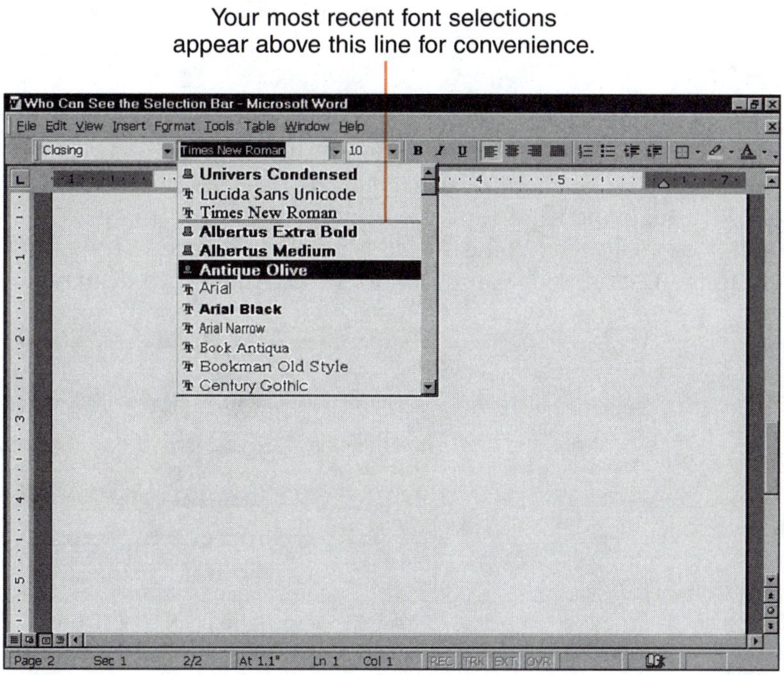

Figure 4.5: Squander years choosing between fonts!

You can also change the font of existing text by first selecting it. Next, choose a font from the font drop-down list on the formatting toolbar, and the selected text is changed to the new font. If more than one font is used in the selection, they are all converted to the single new font.

Want More Fonts?

Microsoft offers a convenient starting point in the search for fonts, both free and those you may purchase. To begin your hunt, just point your browser to `www.microsoft.com/typography/links` and enjoy! To install a new font after downloading it, open your Control Panel, open Fonts, click **File**, and choose **Install New Font**. Choose the font from your download folder.

If Size Is Important

You can make your text appear and print larger or smaller by changing the size of the current font, just as easily as you made it bold or italic, and you have many sizes from which to choose. To change the font size, click the **Font Size** box in the Formatting toolbar (scroll through the valid font size numbers). Choose a larger number to make it bigger, and vice versa. You can also type in sizes outside the displayed range (try 250 for fun), and your computer does its darnedest to display it.

Point Size

The correct way to refer to font size is to use the term *point*. The typical document now uses a 12-point font. A point is 1/72 inch. The larger the point size, the larger the letters will appear. Most fonts can be sized from 1 point to 1,638 points.

Take a Shortcut to Your Fonts!

You can also right-click to get the shortcut menu, which has the Font option conveniently located for your benefit. You can use this on selected text or at the beginning of an insertion point for new text.

The Whole Formatting Enchilada at Your Fingertips

There is yet another way to obtain all of the character formatting tips described in this chapter, and all of them are available in a single dialog box. It's called the **Font** dialog box, and you can get to it by opening the **Format** menu and then clicking the **Font** command.

One of the best reasons to use this method is the **Preview** box that displays your choice of formatting before you apply it. Take a peek:

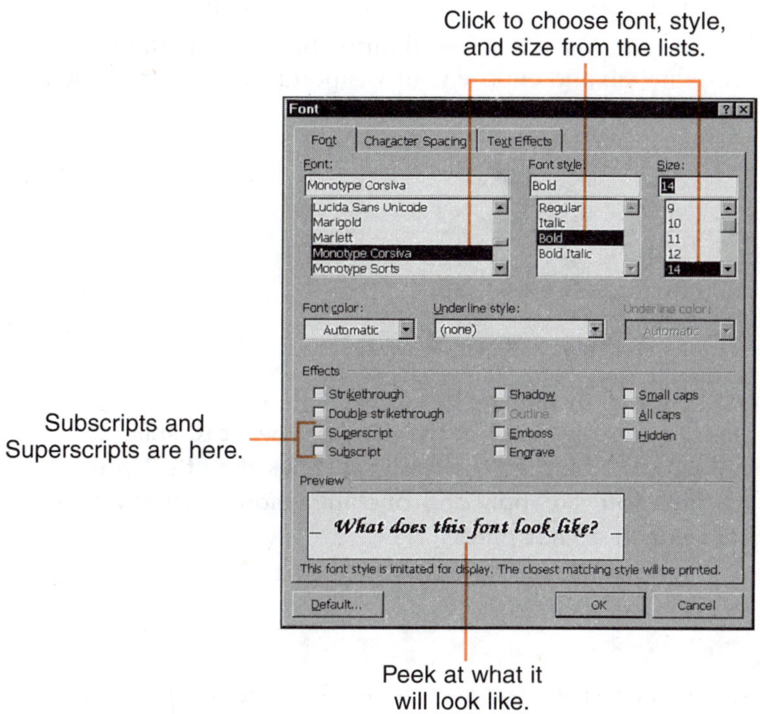

Figure 4.6: The Font dialog box has it all!

Another reason to use this dialog box is to set your default font to whatever combination you like best. Choose the font features you want, take a look at it in the preview box to be sure it's the way you like it, and then click the **Default** button.

You'll find plenty to wile away the hours while you're inside the **Font Dialog** box. Check out these features:

- **Shove your words Higher or Lower** *Superscript* text flies above any normal text, like a reference to a footnote, the degree symbol, or an exponent. *Subscript* text trudges along below normal text. Click the **Superscript** or **Subscript** check box in the **Formatting** dialog box to change selected text or start the insertion point. If the text appears too large, make it smaller by simply changing the Font size in this dialog box. Also, some fonts can't, or won't, appear on your screen as super- or subscript, but they do print out correctly. You have to experiment for yourself (try using Print Preview to see them before printing).
- **Character Spacing** Fanatics may want to adjust the spacing between their letters, like a capital T creeping over into little e's private space. It's called *kerning*, and if you want to try, click the **Character Spacing** tab in the **Font** dialog box.
- **Animate Your Words** You can make your word blink, buzz, and baffle your reader. Click the Animate tab and choose your weapon from the scrollable list.

Animate Your Words!

You can really liven up your text by making the words flash, move, and glisten. Select the text you want to animate, or click the word you want to animate. Open the **Font** dialog box and click the **Animation** tab. Click the effect you want in the **Animations** box. You can apply only one animation effect at a time. And no, these animated effects do not print.

Copy Good Formatting from Here to There

Suppose that you just finished choosing the most incredible combination of formatting options available and you want to apply it to existing text somewhere else. Is there a shortcut that can speed things up? You bet, and it's called the *Format Painter*.

 Even if you don't get around to it right away, you can still copy formatting from one place to another later. In your document, find the area of formatting you like and click anywhere inside of it. Click the **Format Painter** button on the Standard toolbar. Go to the text where you want the formatting to be applied and highlight (select) it. That's it; the formatting is applied automatically.

If you want to paint multiple sections, try double-clicking the **Format Painter** button, and then you can format as much as you want. Click this button again when you are finished to stop the process.

Viewing Format Codes

Perfectly normal people might worry at first that they can't see formatting codes to indicate the formatting details (like WordPerfect). Fret not, I say! To check the formats of a particular character or paragraph, click the **What's This?** command on the **Help** menu. When the mouse arrow changes into a flying question mark, hunt down and click the text you want to check. Word will display the formatting codes for the selected text. To get rid of this information when you are finished, press the **Esc** key.

The Least You Need to Know

Selecting and formatting text is a big deal. This skill deserves to be rewarded. Grab something tasty and ponder the importance of what you've learned.

- What's the fastest way to select text?

  If you are good with a mouse, just click and drag to select text. If you prefer the keyboard, hold down the **Shift** key and use the arrow keys. To get real fancy and select with only one hand, click **F8** first and then use the arrow keys.

- Why would anyone want to select text?

  To cut, copy, or paste it somewhere else, and Word gives you these three buttons (**Cut**, **Copy**, and **Paste**) on the Standard toolbar. You can also right-click selected text and see these three commands on the shortcut menu.

- What else can I do with selected text?

  You can quickly change the way it looks by clicking any of the buttons on the Formatting toolbar, including **Bold**, **Italic**, and **Underline**, and that's just for starters. Try clicking and changing the type of **Font**, or the **Font Size**, to spice up your document.

- How can I make lots of formatting changes at once?

  Aim for the **Font** dialog box. Open the **Format** menu and click **Font**. Choose everything you need, click OK, and start typing!

- Can I copy just the formatting features from one good area to another?

  Sure, but make sure you start by clicking anywhere inside of the "good" stuff. Next, click the **Format Painter** button on the Formatting toolbar. Finally, select the target text and the identical formatting will be applied immediately.

- My friend's document contains an interesting font. Can I find out what it's called?

  Yes. Word 2000 comes with a super-snooper for requests like this. Just open the **Help** menu, click the **What's This?** command, and then click the unsuspecting text. The details will be revealed!

Chapter 5

Proofing Tools (Spelling, Grammar and the Thesaurus)

In This Chapter

- Spell checking your document
- AutoText and AutoCorrect miracles
- Using the Thesaurus
- Getting to know the Grammar Checker

Once in a while, you do something that makes you feel like you've arrived in the future. Maybe it's your first jet ride, browsing your first Web page, or finding that first gray hair. Using the combined Spelling & Grammar Checker in Word 2000 does it for me. These tools, along with the improved Thesaurus, help you find better words and use them correctly.

Those Wavy Red Lines

Unless you're an expert speller, you may notice that several words you typed are underlined with a wavy red line. This tells you that these words are either misspelled, or they don't exist in Word's dictionary. Word 2000 has installed a little computer troll who lives under your keyboard and watches each word as you type it, ready to draw those wavy red lines. The instant you misspell a word, it jumps into action. The red wavy line doesn't print, and no formatting tool can get rid of it, but you can make it go away by correcting the spelling mistake.

How do you find the correct spelling? Right-click a misspelled word and you'll see a list of suggested spellings. Click the correct spelling from the list displayed.

Figure 5.1: Spell checking faster than you can misspell.

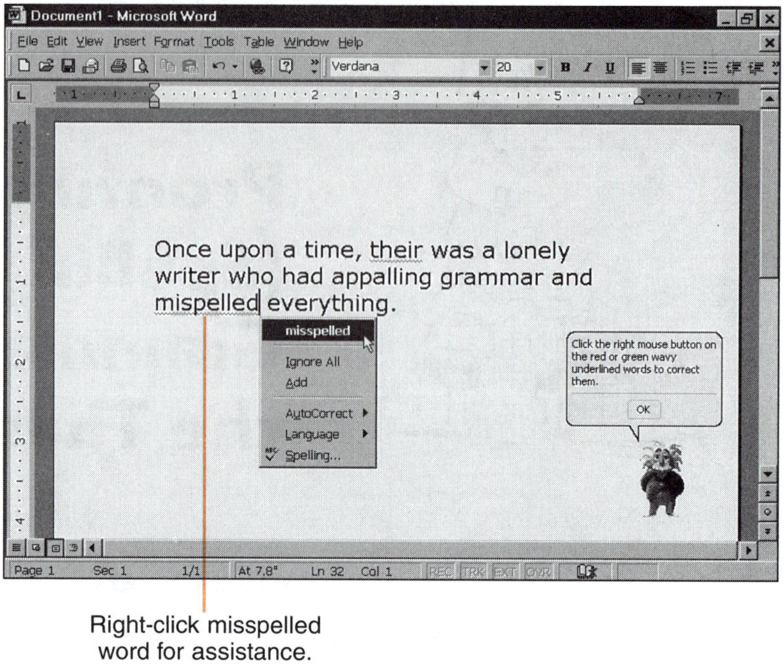

Turning Your Spell Checker On or Off

If you don't have any red wavy lines, you're either a great speller or someone has turned your Spell Checker off. To turn on the Spell Checker to check automatically while you type, open the **Tools** menu and select the **Options** command. Click the **Spelling** tab to bring it to the front. To have Word check spelling automatically as you type, select the **Check Spelling as You Type** check box (or clear the check box to turn automatic spell checking off). If you are allergic to the red wavy lines, click the **Hide Spelling Errors in this Document** option, and the lines disappear (and you'll be responsible for correcting your spelling errors, like in the old days). Press **OK** to return to your document.

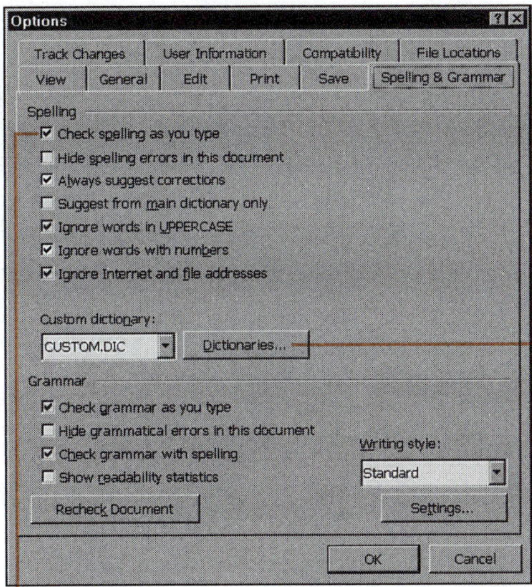

Figure 5.2: Spelling options available in Word 2000.

About Word's Spell Checker

When Word 2000 checks a document for spelling errors, it looks everywhere, including headers, footers, footnotes, and annotations. Also, if you repeat a word accidentally, or miscapitalize it, Word indicates this with that red wavy underline.

You can manually start spell checking your document by clicking the **Spelling and Grammar** button on the Standard toolbar. If everything is hunky-dory, nothing much happens, except that you see a message box telling you that Spell Checker has finished checking your document. If your fingers moved a little faster than your brain, however, you may have a few misspelled words. If so, you are presented with the **Spelling** dialog box.

Figure 5.3: Using the Spelling dialog box.

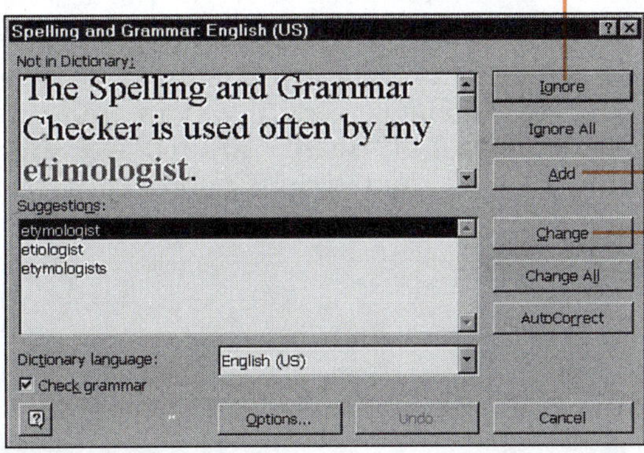

The **Spelling** dialog box displays the misspelled word and suggests alternate spellings. To correct the misspelling, select the correct word and click the **Change** button. If the word isn't in the list, you can type it in the **Change To** box. Or if the word is okay, you can click the **Ignore** button to skip over the word without making any changes. Word immediately moves to the next misspelled word, and you can continue the process until all misspellings have been corrected (or ignored). A dialog box appears when the process is finished, telling you that Spell Checker is finished. The following table gives you more information about what the options in the **Spelling** dialog box do.

Miscellaneous Corrections

There are some interesting miscellaneous items that Spell Checker finds. For instance, if two identical words are found next to each other, the second instance is underlined, indicating that one of them should be deleted. But Word also knows that "had had" is often correct and leaves them alone. (How about that?) Also, if any capital letters occur inside of a single word, the word is underlined for your inspection.

Table 5.1 Button Description for the Spelling Dialog Box

Button	Description
Correct the spelling of the word	If you agree with the selected word in the Suggestions box, just click the **Change** button. You can also type your own correction or select an alternative.
Ignore or Ignore All	Click this button if your word really is a word, such as names, acronyms, and products that often appear in documents. Word will no longer stop if it finds any more of these words existing in your document.
Change or Change All	Click here if you want to change every word that's spelled a certain way in your document. It acts just like search and replace, and it's helpful if you accidentally misspell or mistype some words often.

Add	There's nothing more annoying than Word always telling you a common word, like your name or street address, is misspelled. To make these words a permanent part of the dictionary in Word, click the **Add** button.
AutoCorrect	This tool fixes mistakes as soon as you make them, without wasting your time. If you have your own favorite misspellings, you can add them, along with the correct spelling to this list for instant changing.
Delete the repeated word	If a word is repeated twice and it shouldn't be, click the **Delete** button. You won't see this button unless Word encounters a repeated word.
Undo a previous correction	You can undo any of your last corrections in your document by clicking **Undo Last**. This is great in case you click the **Change** button only to realize that the last word was spelled correctly in the first place.

Wait! That Really Is a Word!

Many words you type are not included in the Word 2000 main dictionary, such as your name, address, abbreviations, or acronyms. This can give the troll another reason to draw that wavy line. If the words aren't recognized, Word lets you know. You can ignore these warnings and leave the word as it is, or you can add the word to the existing dictionary.

To add the word to the computer dictionary, click the **Add** button in the **Spelling** dialog box. You can also click the right mouse button on a misspelled word to add the word to the dictionary (choose the **Add** command from the pop-up menu). From now on, any occurrence of that word does not trigger a red wavy line or the **Spelling** dialog box. Be extra careful adding words to the dictionary so you don't accidentally enter a mistake.

Add can be found with a right-click!

When you right-click a misspelling, you'll find **Add** on the shortcut menu. Choose it to add this word to your dictionary and Word 2000 remembers it forever.

Creating Your Own Dictionary

Wondering where those words are stored when you click the **Add** button? It's known as the *standard supplemental dictionary*, and it's actually a separate file named CUSTOM.DIC. You can view this file by opening the **Tools** menu, clicking the **Options** command, pressing the **Spelling** tab to bring it to the front, and pressing the **Custom Dictionaries** button. Now click **Edit**. You'll see an alphabetical list of all words you have added.

Since Word lets you add more dictionaries, you might want to create one yourself. Create a new document and type a list of the words that you want to add to your dictionary (acronyms, your name, and so on). Be sure to press **Enter** after each word. Click the **Save** button, and save it as **Text Only**. Give it a name, such as **My Business Dictionary**. Now close it so Word can start using it. To use this new dictionary, you must click the **Add** button on the Custom Dictionaries dialog box, and find your new dictionary just below the **CUSTOM.DIC**. A check mark indicates all active dictionaries. Click **OK** to finish this operation.

Oh yes, you can follow this same procedure to edit either the **CUSTOM.DIC** or your new dictionaries in case you accidentally add an incorrect spelling of a word. Just click the **Edit** button while you are in the **Custom Dictionary** dialog box. Find the entries you wish to remove and delete them, then save the dictionary.

Skip Certain Text During Proofing

To speed up a spelling and grammar check, you can prevent Word 2000 from checking specialized text, such as a list of product names or text in another language.

First, select the text that you don't want to check. Open the **Tools** menu, point to **Language**, and then click **Set Language**. At the bottom of the **Language** box, check the box marked **Do Not Check Spelling Or Grammar**.

Check That Web Page

All of these proofing tools work just as well on Web pages you create in Word 2000. See Chapter 23, "Working with Web Frames and Other Tools," for details on creating your own Web pages.

The Magic of AutoCorrect

How many times do you mistype simple words? A common word is *the*, often mistyped as *teh*, or *and*, often typed *adn*. Technically, these aren't spelling errors because you know how to spell them; your fingers just got ahead of your computer. Word helps you by correcting these flaws on-the-fly using a feature called *AutoCorrect*. Plenty of entries have already been added for you (nearly 500 at last count).

To see what entries you already have stored in AutoCorrect, open the **Tools** menu and select the **AutoCorrect** command. Also notice that Word 2000 automatically expands many "symbols" into real symbol characters. For instance, typing (*tm*) automatically turns into the trademark symbol.

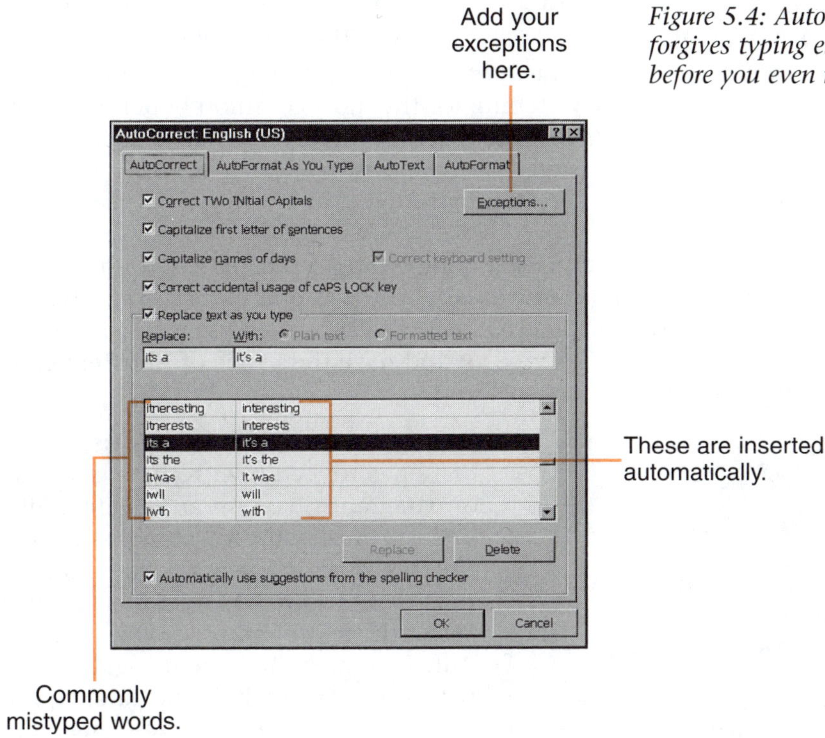

Figure 5.4: AutoCorrect forgives typing errors before you even notice.

Accidental usage of the Caps Lock key is automatically corrected with AutoCorrect. For example, when typing *tHIS* with the Caps Lock key depressed, Word automatically changes the typing to *This* and turns off the Caps Lock key.

AutoCorrect also supports an exception list for the "Capitalize First Letter of Sentence" rule. Word doesn't capitalize words that follow abbreviations from the exception list, and Word even watches as you type and automatically adds words to the list if you change an AutoCorrect action.

There's more. You also can add an AutoCorrect entry during a spelling check. When a word you often misspell or mistype is identified, enter the correct spelling in the **Change To** box. To add the misspelled word and its correct spelling to the list of words and phrases that are corrected automatically, click AutoCorrect.

AutoText Will Save You Time!

You can use shortcuts to quickly insert frequently used text or graphics in your documents:

- If you store text and graphics as AutoText entries, you can retrieve them by clicking a button or pressing **F3**.
- If you store them as AutoCorrect entries, Word inserts them automatically as you type, which you learned about in the last section.
- AutoComplete Tips (a feature of AutoText) moves you along faster when creating a letter by watching for the most common boilerplate words or phrases. You start to type *To W* and AutoComplete immediately suggests *To Whom It May Concern*. When the suggestion appears, you can press **Enter** or **F3** to accept the suggestion, or just keep typing to reject it.

AutoText is a helpful way to save time typing out repetitive (or just plain long and boring) words. What kind of words? If you're a pharmacist, you might get tired of typing the word for a bladder-controlling drug called pseudophonyhydroxidine. Wouldn't you much rather type **PP** and have the magic of AutoText expand it automatically to the correct spelling?

Try the AutoText Toolbar

You'll find an organized selection listing of common words and phrases used in writing letters in the new AutoText toolbar. Open the **View** menu, point to toolbars, and choose **AutoText**. The **All Entries** button displays the categories and entries, and there's an **AutoText** button that takes you to the **AutoCorrect** dialog box.

Before AutoText can be really useful to you, you first have to load it with the big words (or sentences or paragraphs) you use most often. Either find a document that already contains your big words or phrases, or start a new document and carefully type them in. Don't forget to spell them correctly. Select the text or graphics you want to store as an AutoText entry. To store paragraph formatting with the entry, include the paragraph mark in the selection. Open the **Insert** menu and choose the **AutoText** command. In the **Name** box, type the shortcut version you prefer, like *pp* or *baffle*. An AutoText name can have up to 32 characters, including spaces. Click the **Add** button and this entry is stored and ready to use.

By default, Word makes the AutoText entry available to all documents. If you want AutoText entries limited to particular documents, you can specify a template in which you want to store the entry by selecting a template name in the **Make AutoText Entry Available To** box. To put the AutoText entries to work, just start typing your document as you would normally. When it's time to add the big word or phrase, just type the shortcut you stored in AutoText (like pp or baffle) right in your document and then press the **F3** key. The shortcut word will be removed and replaced by the actual big word or phrase it represents. You can also print the list of AutoText entries. Open the **File** menu and choose **Print**. In the **Print What** box, choose **AutoText Entries**, then click **OK**.

Using Your Thesaurus

It's right on the tip of your tongue. I can see it. But you can't, which is why you need a Thesaurus. Using big words can help you appear smarter than you are, and it sure helps when doing a crossword puzzle. Improving vocabulary is a sign of higher intelligence in our species, so the next time you choose a word that doesn't exactly convey the meaning you want, try running it through the Thesaurus first.

To use the Thesaurus, just follow these simple steps. First select the word you want to look up, or move the insertion point anywhere inside the word. Then open the **Tools** menu, point to **Language**, and select the **Thesaurus** command (or press **Shift+F7**). Your word appears in the **Thesaurus** dialog box in the **Look Up** drop-down list.

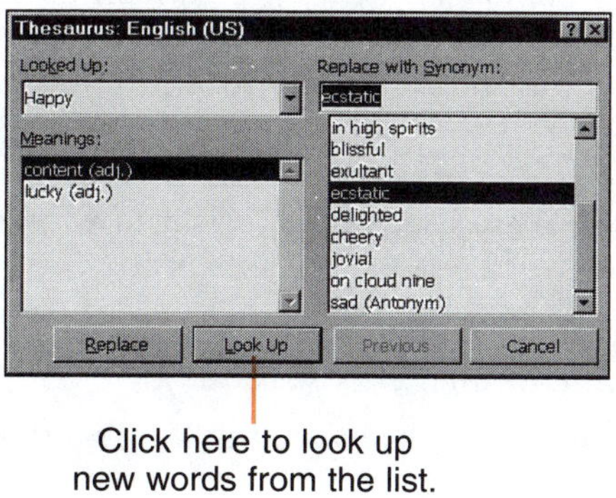

Figure 5.5: When you need help thinking of the right words...

Use the Thesaurus When You Can't Think of the Right Word

- ➤ If the word you selected is not found, enter an alternate word and click **Look Up**.
- ➤ Choose from the synonyms listed in the **Replace with Synonym** (or Antonym or Related Word) list box.

- To change the synonyms listed, choose from general variations of the selected word that appear in the **Meanings** box. If the **Related Words or Antonyms** options are listed under **Meanings**, select either one to display additional choices.
- Look up additional meanings for the word displayed in the **Replace with Synonym** box by clicking **Look Up**.
- Decide whether to replace the selected word. Click the **Replace** button to substitute the selected word with the word displayed in the **Replace with Synonym** box, or click **Cancel** to leave it alone.
- If one of the words in the left column is close but not exactly what you want, select it and click the **Look Up** button. The word's synonyms appear in the right column.
- If the word that you select has no synonyms, the Thesaurus displays an alphabetical list of words. Type a new, similar word or select **Cancel** to get back to your document.

Opposites Attract

Here's a tip for using the Thesaurus. On those rare occasions when you can't think of any words that mean what you want, don't give up! Try thinking of the complete opposite meaning. Quite often, the Thesaurus can take the opposite of what you mean and lead you back to what you really mean. (Work with me on this.)

The secret is in the word *antonym*, which we all learned at some point. It means the opposite, and it sometimes shows up as the last entry in the **Meanings** box. If you click **Antonyms**, you'll get a list of opposite meaning words. Now click one of those opposite meanings and press the **Look Up** button. Does it have the word antonym listed? That's your ticket. Selecting the antonym of an antonym of the word you want often discovers the word that works. It's like two wrongs making a right! It's even easier than it sounds. Here are a few examples:

- If you can't think up a single positive description of your boss, try stingy, lazy, cruel, or meatloaf, and then choose **Antonym**.
- There seem to be more words describing laziness than whatever the opposite is. Why is that?
- Flipping back and forth between opposite meanings helps you enrich your vocabulary by exposing you to many more words than you would otherwise see.

Grammar Checker

If you're a victim of poor grammar, cheer up. Word 2000 marks grammar errors with a green wavy line then suggest ways to correct them. Right-click any portion of the grammatical error and a shortcut menu appears offering the most likely corrections. If you don't agree with the choices or want to investigate further, click the bottom entry in the shortcut menu called **Grammar**, and you'll see the **Grammar** dialog box.

Grammatical Find and Replace

Word 2000 features new linguistic technology that understands the meaning of words and their different forms. You can now replace the word buy with the word sell, and you automatically replace all of the buying and bought with selling and sold automatically. For more details, see Chapter 8, "Can't Find It? Look Here!"

Pardon Me, May I Make a Suggestion?

From here, you have these options:

- Accept a suggestion by selecting one of those listed in the **Suggestions** box and clicking **Change**.
- Get more information about what's wrong by clicking the **Explain** button. Only certain grammatical errors have this option available. Otherwise, the description of the grammatical rules that have been broken appears in the **Suggestions** box.
- Make your own correction by clicking inside the document window and changing your text. To check the grammar in the rest of the document, click **Next Sentence**.
- Bypass the suggestion by clicking the **Ignore** button. You can bypass the entire sentence by clicking the **Next Sentence** button instead. You can tell Word to ignore this "grammatical faux pas" for the rest of the document by clicking **Ignore Rule**.

At the end of the grammar check, Word displays a short summary called **Readability Statistics**. It's like a final opinion, and it is very helpful. For instance, it can tell you how many sentences use the passive voice. They aren't wrong or bad, but passive sentences can be vague and confusing. Try to keep this number low (like zero). If you avoid criticism at all cost, you can choose not to display this information by clearing the **Show Readability Statistics** check box (in the **Grammar** options), but then you probably wouldn't start the Grammar Checker anyway.

What's Your Readability?

After Word completes a grammar check, readability statistics are displayed, telling you what kind of people should be able to figure out what the heck you just wrote. Mighty intelligent people wrote formulas to figure this out, and since no one knows which is best, you can choose from any of them.

Business or Casual?

Maybe you're a bit annoyed that the Grammar Checker doesn't like contractions. That's great for a report to your boss (it also gives you more words and fatter reports), but who cares in a letter to Mom? You can change the rules of your grammar checker to meet the occasion. You can even make up your own set of rules, but most people settle for choosing between the two most common sets of rules Standard and Casual.

Open the **Tools** menu and select the **Options** command. Click the **Spelling & Grammar** tab to bring it to the front. The lower half of the dialog box contains all available grammar options. In the **Writing Style** box, change the default from **Standard** to **Casual** by clicking it (you can also choose more critical styles like **Formal** or **Technical**). Don't forget to change back, following the same procedure, if you want a more strict Grammar Checker for future documents.

Figure 5.6: Changing the Grammar Settings.

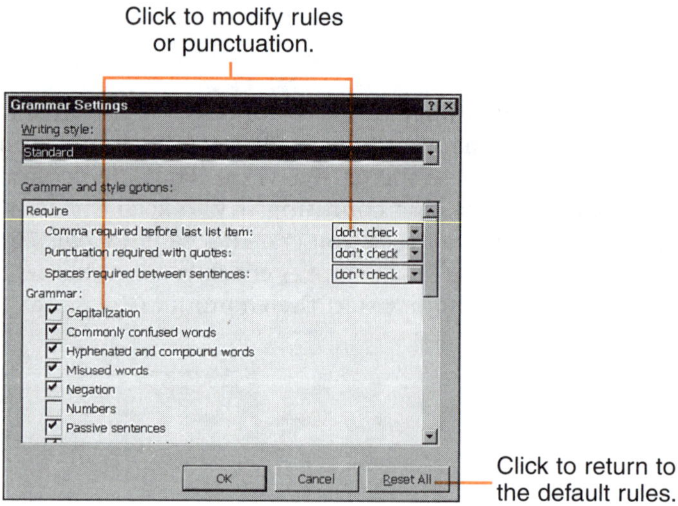

Customizing the Grammar Checker for Casual Use

If you're interested in digging further into the rules of grammar, click the **Settings** button located next to the **Writing Style** choice. This opens the **Grammar Settings** dialog box. You'll find each rule associated with that particular grammar style, and it's easy to customize by adding or clearing a check from the box of a rule. This means you can choose a general grammar style and also customize it to meet your exact requirements. For instance, you might choose a **Formal** grammar style, but want the Grammar Checker to forgive the use of contractions. Just clear the check mark from that specific rule.

Also, this dialog box contains three common punctuation rules at the bottom. These are rules about using a comma with the last item in a list, using punctuation inside or outside of quotes, and the number of spaces between sentences. Different people have very different opinions with these three rules, so Microsoft leaves it to you to decide which rules you plan to enforce.

The Least You Need to Know

Writing a letter or report is hard enough. You focus on content, and Word 2000 takes care of the spelling and grammar, even helping you find better words with the Thesaurus.

- What are those wavy lines all over my page?

  Wavy red lines identify misspelled words. Wavy green lines suggest your grammar is less than ideal. Both Spelling and Grammar Checking are automatic in Word 2000 (unless you turn them off).

- How do I get rid of them?

  Type better. Or, click the right mouse button on any red or green wavy-underlined words to see a shortcut menu with suggestions of improvement directly from the 150,000-word spelling dictionary and grammatical reference inside Word 2000.

- I can't misspell some words no matter how hard I try.

  Neat, huh? That's the AutoCorrect feature in action. It includes the most common misspellings of tons of words and automatically corrects them the moment you type, without bragging about it. If you sometimes fumble other words, you can just as easily add them to the list.

- How do I check just part of a document?

  Just select the text you want to check and click the **Spelling and Grammar** button on the Standard toolbar. You can check a single word, paragraph, or any part of a document.

- I use lots of big words. Can Word provide any help?

  Certainly! You can create shortcuts for typing long and difficult words or phrases by using AutoText. Add AutoText entries by selecting the big word or phrase, open the **Edit** menu, and choose the **AutoText** command. Give it a conveniently short name and press the **Add** button. Now, in any document, just type the short name and press **F3** and it is replaced with the real thing.

- Where did they hide the Thesaurus command?

  To look up an alternative for a selected word, press **Shift+F7**. You can also open the **Tools** menu, point to **Language**, and choose **Thesaurus**.

Chapter 6

If It's Worth Saving, Save It!

In This Chapter

- Naming and saving your documents
- New places to save in Word 2000
- Taking a document home with you
- Recovering from crashes with backups

You expect a computer to be smart enough to save all your work, every time, right? Well, sometimes it needs a little help from you. This chapter reviews the variety of saving options available inside Word 2000, so you'll never lose another word (or your patience).

Word Always Remembers Saved Documents

If you've ever accidentally kicked the power cables under your desk and had your computer go dead, you probably assumed anything you were working on was blasted to oblivion. If only you had considered one of the following options for saving your work:

- Take a Polaroid snapshot of each screen.
- Feverishly scribble a copy of what you've just typed.
- Attend a memory-enhancement class and practice until you can memorize your entire document.

- Hold thermal paper up to your screen and turn the brightness way up.
- Click the **Save** button on the Standard toolbar (you can also press the **Ctrl+S** key combination).

The final option is best. Use the **Save** function in Word. Once you officially save your work, you can always get it back.

How often should you save a document?

How often to save depends on how fast you work and how much trouble it would be to re-create your progress. Here are some rules to live by:

- Save immediately after thinking up brilliant prose or something really funny. Save anytime you think to yourself, "Wow! Did I do that?"
- Save before you print in case your printer jams and you turn off your computer before noticing.
- Save before you try some tricky functions in Word.
- Save right after a tricky function, if you like the results.

Saving a Document for the First Time

The first time you save any document is a little different from the rest because you must give your creation a name and a place (folder) it can call home. After that you just click **Save** as often as you need, typically every 5 or 10 minutes, or have Word do it automatically for you (described later). Save your document now by clicking the **Save** button on the standard toolbar. You are presented with the new **Save As** dialog box.

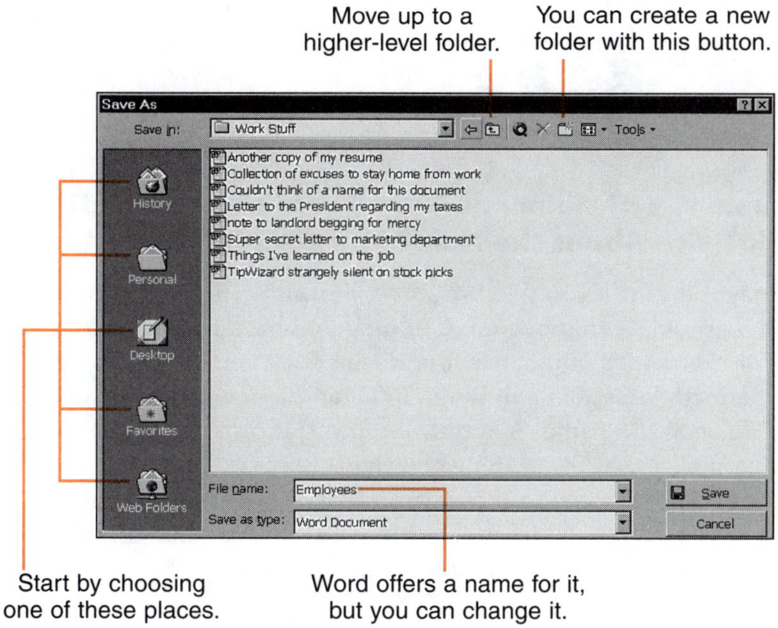

Figure 6.1: New places to save your documents.

Your document is stored in the folder shown in the **Save in** box. If you want to save your document in another folder, you can search for it using the **Previous Folder** button or by clicking folders in the Display area. You can also create a new folder at this time by clicking the **Create New Folder** button in the **Save As** dialog box. All new folders are closed when created, so be sure to open it first for saving your new document.

Give That Young Document a Proper Name

To make things easy, Word has already filled in a potential name for your document. Word just happened to grab the first few words of your document. Sometimes that's good enough, and you don't have to do anything more than press **Enter** (or click the **Save** button) to save your document. Or, you can type a better name in the File Name box. You can be as creative as you want in naming your file, which certainly helps you to identify it later.

Sharing a Document with Someone Who Doesn't Have Word? Think Twice About the Name You Give It!

Naming limitations may still exist if you need to share files with a friend who uses a very old computer and an old word processor. Old programs have a hard time with longer names. For example, if you name your document *Monthly Report for September*, which is perfectly acceptable in Word 2000, an older word processor may see only *MONTHL~1* as the name. A better name in this case might be *SEPT-REP* or something similar that fits in the eight-character DOS limitation. To find out the DOS equivalent of a document name that is longer than eight characters, right-click your document and choose the **Properties** command from the shortcut menu. It shows you the MS-DOS equivalent filename.

If at first you don't trust your computer or Word 2000, or both, you might find it reassuring to prove to yourself that your new document and changes have been saved. Simply open the document once again and look at it. It's easiest to find your document by choosing it from the selection of your last 15 documents. Click the **Start** button on your taskbar, point to **Documents**, and click the document you just saved (the list appears in alphabetical order). Word 2000 starts with this document opened, and it should prove to be exactly what you hoped for.

Where Should I Save It?

You want to be organized if you plan on creating zillions of documents, so you can find them later. Store your documents in folders, and name the folders so you'll recognize the contents. Create as many folders as you like, wherever you need them. The left side of the **Save As** dialog box now includes the **Places Bar**, granting convenient access to the following places:

- **History** Here you'll find the last 50 documents you've worked on, in date order, no matter where you've stored them.

Renaming Is Easier

You can also easily rename an existing document inside the **File Open** dialog box. Right-click the filename, choose the **Rename** command, and type a new name over the old one. Then press **Enter** to save it.

- **Personal** The default location, and a good place to keep all your stuff. Try adding folders here to keep things organized.
- **Desktop** Avoid storing here, because your Windows desktop soon becomes too cluttered with your documents.
- **Favorites** Another good place to store documents, and it's easy to remember. Create folders to keep things organized.
- **Web Folders** This may include your company file server, intranet, or the Web. A network administrator can help you set these up.

Click to open any of these places and find the folder you need, or create a new one by clicking the **Create New Folder** button. Then click the **Save** button to save your document and close the **Save As** dialog box.

Saving a Document the Second Time Is Easier, Unless...

After a document has been saved the first time, it has a name and it knows where it lives. If you make further changes to the document, you simply click the **Save** button on the Standard toolbar and everything is saved! No messy dialog boxes!

Saving documents this way simply updates the original document. However, you may need to preserve the original but also create a new, updated version. In this case you must use the **Save As** command, as you learned earlier, then give the document a new filename. In the end you have two separate documents—the original and the updated version.

> **Come Visit the Places Bar**
>
> Word 2000 introduces the **Places Bar**, granting quick access to common storage locations on your computer, file server, intranet, or Web page.

You've Got Options in Saving

There are many document-saving options that can make life easier for you. From the **Save As** dialog box, click the **Options** button to see the collection of saving options. To select an option, click it to add or remove the check mark. Here's the scoop on what all these options are for:

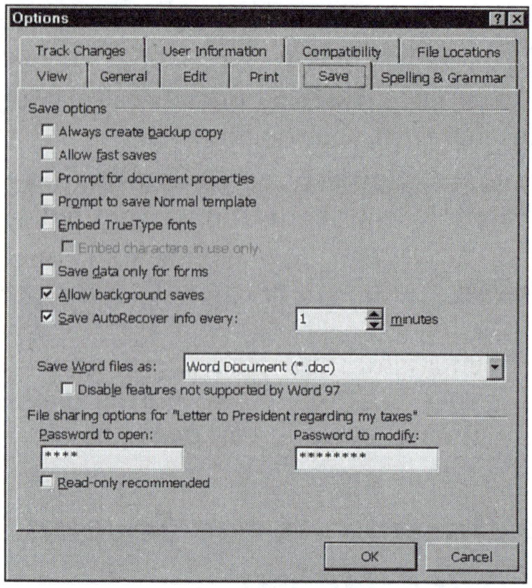

Figure 6.2: Options available to customize saving documents in Word.

- **Always create backup copy** If your location is disaster-prone (power failures, hurricanes, floods, and so on), select this option. A duplicate document with the extension .wbk is saved in the same folder as your original document.
- **Allow fast saves** This option saves only the changes to a file instead of the entire file. However, since computers have become so fast lately, you might want to disable this option, so you get a complete, full save of your entire document each time you save it.
- **Prompt for document properties** By selecting this option, you can make the Properties dialog box open automatically each time you perform a Save As to remind you to add optional information along with your document. For example, you can add keywords that can help you quickly find this document later.
- **Prompt to save Normal template** With this option on, you are prompted before changes are saved to the Normal template when you exit Word. You can find out more about templates and saving them in Chapter 19, "Templates, Themes, and Styles."
- **Embed True Type fonts** If you go through the hassle of purchasing special fonts, you may want to select this option to make sure those fonts are saved (embedded) in your documents, so anyone who doesn't have the fonts can still see them in your document.
- **Save data only for forms** If you are creating lots of forms with data fields, then you might turn this on to make your documents more compact.
- **Save AutoRecover info every: __ minutes** Highly recommended. Use this option to put Word 2000 saving on "automatic," and type the number of minutes you want Word to wait between automatic saves. You can enter any number between 1 and 120, and something around 10 minutes is recommended.

Protect Your Document with File-Sharing Options

Are your documents too secret for unauthorized eyes? Why not protect it with a password, which means no one can open or edit the document without knowing the password. These passwords are case-sensitive and can contain up to 15 characters, including letters, numerals, and symbols. Find these options near the bottom of the Save Options dialog box.

A Word About Fast Saves

Sure, things speed up a bit with fast saves. That's because only the latest changes are saved in a temporary file. But when you finish working in the document, clear the **Allow fast saves** check box so that you can save the complete document with a full save. This removes all the accumulated change files (often reducing the file size considerably) and gives you a nice, clean Word 2000 document.

- **Password to open** If you type a Password here, people must know the password before they can open and see your document. Viewing is all they can do, however, because the document opens as read-only. If someone opens your document as read-only and changes it, it must be saved with a different name. Guess what? If you forget or lose the password, you cannot open your document.
- **Password to modify** A password here requires your coworkers to know it before they are allowed to open your document for editing. If you forget or lose the password, you can only open your document as read-only.
- **Read-only recommended** If you don't want to set a password for your document, but you do want to alert your friends not to change it, choose this option. When the document opens, your friends see a recommendation to open the document as read-only. If they open the document as read-only and change it, it must be saved with a different name.

Recovering a Document After a Disaster

Stuff happens, what can I say? In the event of a disaster, such as a power failure, wait until the disaster is over, then restart Word 2000. All documents that were open at the time of the disaster appear for you. The only changes you may lose would be those made after the last AutoRecover.

You may want to verify that the recovery file contains the information you want before you replace the existing document (at the moment they have the same name), so open the existing document and compare the information. If it looks like you've got the latest and greatest document, go ahead and click the **Save** button. In the **File**

name box, type or select the filename of the existing document. Click the **Save** button. When you see a message asking whether you want to replace the existing document, click **Yes**. Be sure you review all documents, if more than one was opened at the time of the disaster. If you choose not to save any of the recovery files, they are deleted when you exit Word 2000.

What If It's Mangled and Mutilated?

If your computer locks up when you try to open a particular document, your document may be damaged. Restart your computer and restart Word 2000. This time, Word 2000 automatically uses a special file converter to recover the text. Hey, at least it's something. If you're lucky, the damaged document is repaired and appears on your screen. It's best to save it immediately and thank your lucky stars.

If you aren't as fortunate, and a stubborn file refuses to open, you can try another feature in Word 2000. It's an optional file converter you can use in such an emergency. Use it when you don't care so much for the lost formatting, but want to at least recover the words (the text) typed into any document. It also works on documents from ancient word processors where file converters no longer exist and even on those files not created with a word processor—like a database or spreadsheet—that still contain some bits and pieces of text you want to recover. Open the **Tools** menu, click **Options**, and then click the **General** tab. Find the option called **Confirm Conversion at Open** and be sure it's checked. Click **OK** to close the Options dialog box. Now you can click the Open button, and in the **Files of Type** box, click **Recover Text From Any File**. Now you're ready to open any kind of file whatsoever and drag the text out of it.

Saving a Document to Take Home with You

Feeling brave? Got a disk handy? Give this trick a try and see if you're not bragging about it around the water cooler tomorrow.

Use Word 2000 to create and save your document. Place an empty disk into your computer drive. Now click the **Open** button to see a dialog box with your document name listed. Right-click the document to see the shortcut menu. Choose the **Send To** command, select **3 1/2 Floppy (A)**, and then sit back and watch the fireworks. Your document is copied to disk.

Right-click any document to copy it to your disk.

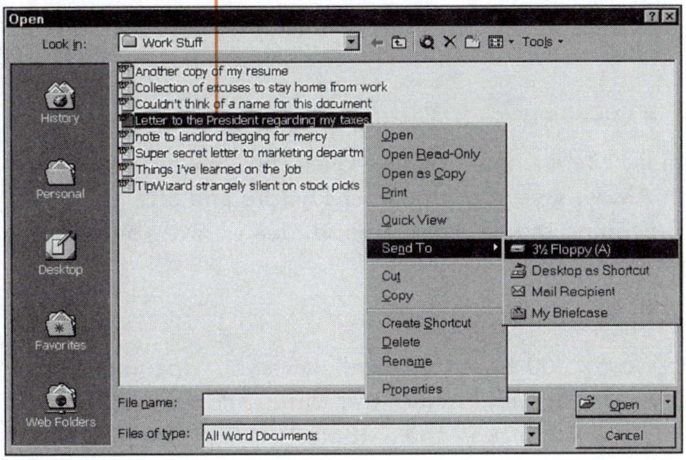

Figure 6.3: Take your work home with you, on disk.

Take this disk home with you and insert it into your computer. You can click to open and edit your work directly from the disk, or you can copy the contents of your disk to a folder on your home computer. Open Word 2000 and use the **File Open** dialog box to open your documents. If you need to bring the document back to work the next day, be sure to save the latest copy to your disk.

Closing Your Document and Going Home

It goes without saying, but not without writing, that it's a good habit to save and close your documents before turning off your computer and heading home. This is more important now than ever before, because your documents are always hanging around in memory. When you close Word 2000 and then close Windows, you guarantee that all of your documents are written to your hard drive and are now safe and sound. If you simply turn off your computer without closing Windows, there's a chance that a document didn't get written to disk and is now lost forever.

The proper way to keep your documents safe and sound is to close them. Also, if you are editing documents directly on floppy disk, be sure you don't remove the disk until you've closed your document. If changes have been made, you are alerted and granted time to decide on your saving options. Finally, you can close Word.

The Least You Need to Know

Prevent despair and anxiety by saving your work often. This chapter provided lots of tips on saving.

➤ How often should I save a document?

More often than you think. Life is unpredictable. Click the **Save** button on the Standard toolbar. Always save your document before and after any complicated word processing task. It's also a good idea to save your document prior to printing.

➤ I always forget to save. Can Word 2000 do it for me?

You're in luck. To set up Word 2000 to automatically save your document every few minutes, open the **Tools** menu, select the **Options** command, and choose the **Save** tab. Place a check in the automatic saving options you prefer.

➤ Can I give my document any name I want?

Yes, you can type long descriptive names, including spaces!

➤ I want to change a document but keep it the same, too.

It sounds like you want to do a **Save As** command. This enables you to open an existing document, make changes, and save it as a new document, keeping the old one intact. You just have to come up with a new name for your new document. The **Save As** command is found on the **File** menu.

➤ What's the fastest way to copy my document to a disk?

The fastest way to copy your saved document to a disk is to right-click its name in the **Open** dialog box, then point to Send To and choose the **3 1/2 Floppy (A)** command.

➤ How do I keep nosy people out of my documents?

Put a password on them. Without the correct password, the document cannot be opened. To find this option, open the **Tools** menu, select **Options**, and click the **Save** tab.

➤ Okay, I saved my document. How do I get it off the screen?

You can close a document to get it out of your way. Open the **File** menu and click the **Close** command.

Chapter 7

Previewing and Printing a Document

In This Chapter

- Fast ways to print your document
- Printing just part of the document
- Printing multiple document pages on a single sheet of paper
- Printing several documents or multiple copies at once
- Printing envelopes

In a truly paperless society, we humans will overcome our need to convert trees into newspaper and phone books, we'll distribute our communications electronically, and one can only guess what we'll do in the bathroom. But in a paperless society, what will we wrap the dishes with during a move?

That time is still far in the future, so for now you're going to have to print your documents for others to read. That means you still need a printer, some paper, and a connection between your computer and the printer. And you might need some patience. We've come a long way since Gutenberg—but he never had to worry about portrait versus landscape or printer memory overruns.

Printing Basics

 It's always a good idea to save a document before you print it, so click the **Save** button first. This way there is no chance of losing your latest changes in case you run into printer errors or other problems.

The Quickest and Easiest Way to Print a Document!

First, find the document you want to print using **Explorer**, **Find File**, or the Word 2000 **File Open** dialog box, but don't open the document. Just right-click it and choose the **Print** command from the pop-up menu. What could be easier?

Network Printer?

If you want to print to a network printer, you can save a few steps. Simply open your Network Neighborhood, find the printer, then double-click to choose it.

Printing the current document is easy if you want to print the whole thing and only want one copy of it. Just click the **Print** button on the Standard toolbar. The current document will start printing according to the print defaults (a "default" describes an option already chosen for you, options like which printer to use, the size of paper, the number of copies printed, and so on. Any of these defaults can be changed at any time).

If you want to print more than one copy (or less than the entire document), you'll need to open the **File** menu and choose the **Print** command (or press **Ctrl+P**) as described next.

Printing the Very First Time

If you've just installed Word 2000, you may get the error *"Printer Not Installed"* the first time you try to print. Don't panic; Word just wants to know what type of printer you'll be using. Click **Start**, **Settings**, **Printers**, and then double-click the **Add Printer** icon. You'll be asked for the brand and model number of your printer, and if it's on a network or attached directly to your computer. You only have to do this once.

Printing Only Part of a Document

Know anyone who prints another copy of a large document just because he found a spelling mistake on page 247? Help him save the forests by teaching the technique of single-page printing. You can have complete control over limiting what you print in a document. Here's what to do:

➤ Open the **File** menu and select the **Print** command. You will see the new and improved **Print** dialog box.

You can print only the current page by choosing **Current Page** in the **Print** dialog box. Be sure you've actually moved to that page, however, or it's likely to print the first page of your document.

Paper Shortage?

If the printer runs out of paper during the printing of your document, then a dialog box will appear and tell you so. Load more paper into your printer and then click the **Retry** button.

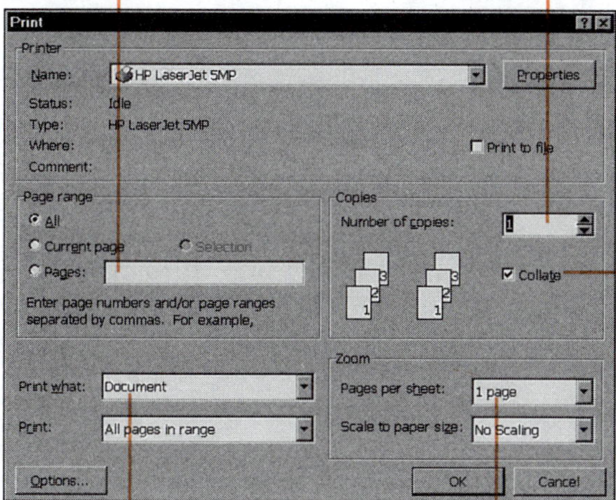

Figure 7.1: Printing more or less than a page.

If you want a few pages printed from a large document and they are scattered throughout your document, you can do so as long as you've got all of the page numbers in your head. In the **Page Range** area of the **Print** dialog box, click to select the **Pages** option, and type a single page number (such as 7), a page range (for example, 37-42), or a combination of the two separated by commas (for example, 7,18,23-37,95-98,117). When you are finished, click the **OK** button, and your selections will print in the order you've typed them. Once again, it's a great way to save paper and wear and tear on your printer.

Printing Multipage Documents on a Single Sheet of Paper

While we're on the subject of saving paper, allow Word to impress you by printing more than one document page per sheet of paper! This is great for reviewing rough drafts of documents. The page is split in two, four, eight, or *sixteen* sections, each containing an image of your whole document page. Sure, it's smaller, but lots of times you can still read each document page fine. Think of all the trees you'll save! You'll find this new option inside the **Print** dialog box.

Printing Even Less Than a Page (Selected Text)

If you need to print only part of a page or just a graphic, table, or drawing appearing on a page, Word 2000 will let you. You just have to remember to select what you want before bringing up that **Print** box. First, find the page containing the text or object you want to have printed and use your mouse to select the portion you want to print. Now, open the **File** menu and choose the **Print** command.

In the **Print** dialog box you'll find an option near the bottom called **Print What**. Click here; choose **Selected Text** and click **OK**, and only the selected text will be printed.

Printing Multiple Copies of Your Document

You can also print multiple copies by changing the number found in the **Number of Copies** box. When making several copies of a many-paged document, you'll probably want to click the **Collate** option. Collate means the printer will print the entire document, one after another, as many times as you desire. Without the collating option, the printer would print each page the specified number of times and then move on to the next page, leaving it up to you to organize, or collate, your document copies.

Two Ways to Print Multiple Copies

If you have a printer that allows you to select the number of copies to print by way of a control panel on the printer, then you may want to use that option instead of having Word print the extra copies for you. You may find your printer is faster than Word is at this task.

Choosing Your Paper Source

What if your printer has two paper bins, the top for letterhead and the bottom for regular paper—how do you choose your paper source? This setting is stored in the Page Setup for each document. Open the **File** menu, choose **Page Setup**, and click the **Paper Source** tab. The choices you see depend on the printer you have installed. Click to choose the source and then click **OK**.

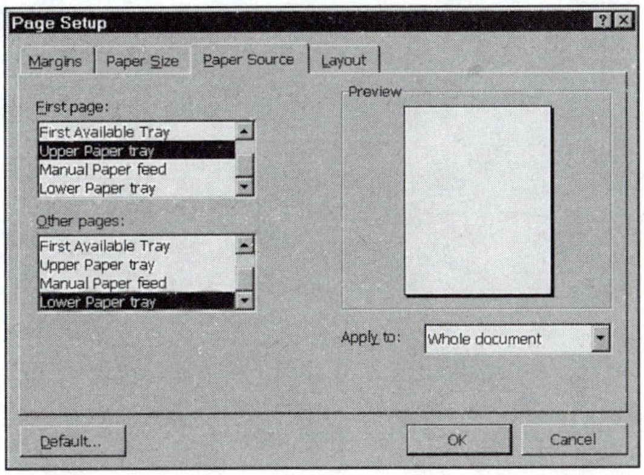

Figure 7.2: Choosing letterhead from another paper bin.

Look Before You Print: Using Print Preview

Before you print your document, you should look at it in either **Print Preview** mode or **Print Layout** view. These two viewing modes show you what your document will look like when printed, so you can be sure everything is the way you want it before you print. Use **Print Preview** for a quick peek of a completed document, or use **Print Layout** view to create or edit a document while it's displayed exactly as it will print.

To change to **Print Preview** mode, click the **Print Preview** button in the standard toolbar, or open the **File** menu and select the **Print Preview** command.

You can do lots of interesting things in **Print Preview**, as you can see by the following figure. To print, just click the **Print** button. To edit text, click on the tiny magnifying glass, then click within the document. After you zoom in on the area you clicked, press the **Magnifier** button again—the cursor changes into a regular mouse cursor, ready for editing. Edit until you are tired, then click on the **Magnifying** button again—and the text area again—to return to regular **Print Preview**.

Figure 7.3: Look at all the interesting things you can do in Print Preview!

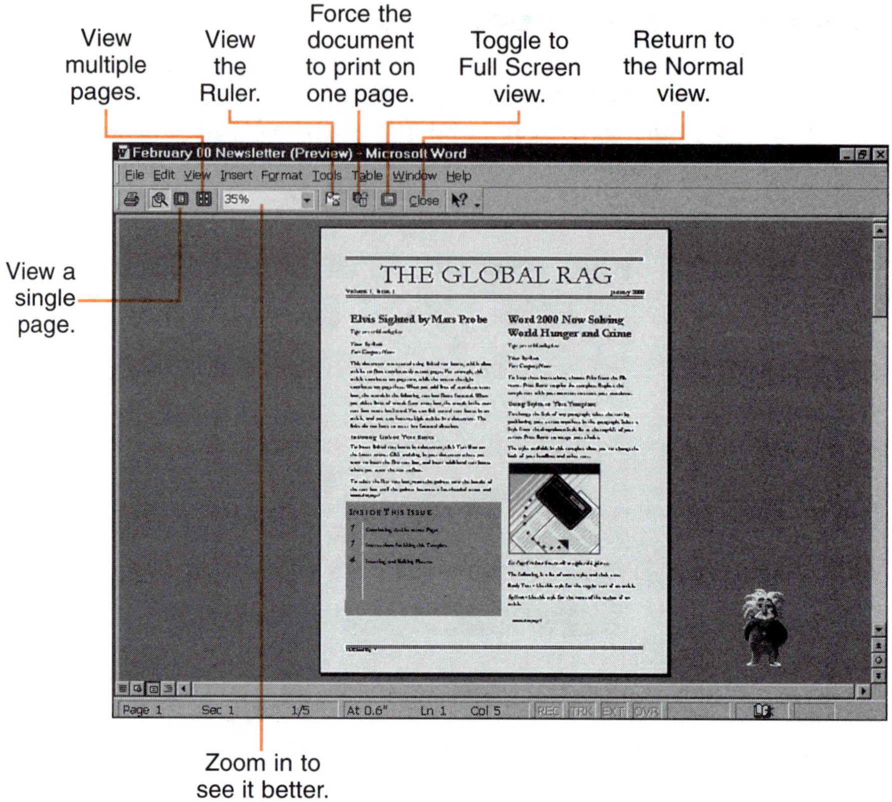

You Can Adjust Margins in Print Preview

If your margins need a slight adjustment, you can make it instantly and see the results before you print. Make sure the rulers are displayed. To move any margin, point to a margin boundary on the vertical or horizontal ruler. When the pointer changes to a double-headed arrow, drag the margin boundary back and forth a little. You will see the whole margin change on your screen. Drop the margin in the desired new location. Text will automatically flow on the page to accommodate the new space.

Printing Envelopes

Word makes it incredibly easy to prepare an envelope for a letter. But getting your printer to print the darned thing is another matter. First, the easy part.

1. From inside your completed letter or document, open the **Tools** menu and select the **Envelopes and Labels** command. When the **Envelopes and Labels** dialog box appears, type the delivery address in the **Delivery Address** box.

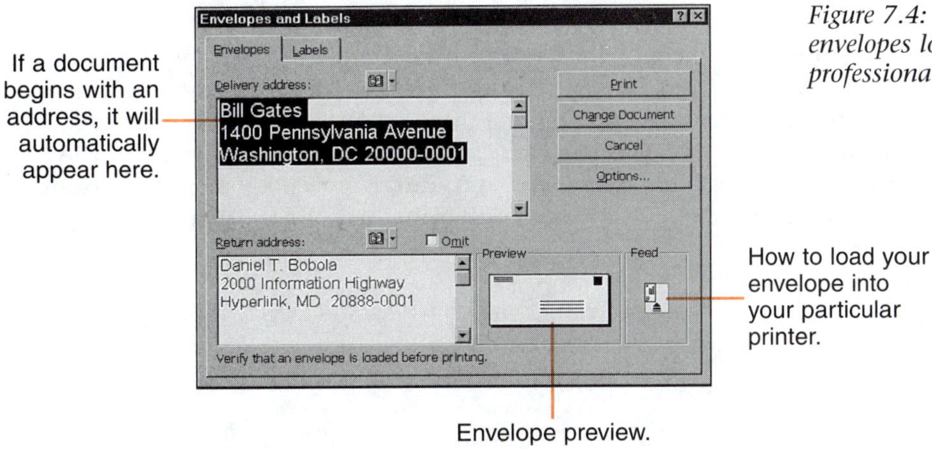

Figure 7.4: Printed envelopes look more professional.

2. Next, enter your return address by clicking in the **Return Address** box or by pressing **Tab**. The first time you use this option, Word will ask whether you want to save the return address. Click **Yes** or press **Enter** to save it. If you have special envelopes and you don't want to print a return address, use the **Omit** check box.

Addresses should appear automatically.

Word 2000 can fill in both delivery and return addresses automatically for your envelopes. Just be sure to apply the styles **Return Address** or **Delivery Address** where they are used in your document. Word 2000 will also assume that the first address in a document is the **Delivery Address**, if it's the first thing that appears in your document.

3. Before we print our envelope, let's check some of the options. Click the **Options** button and the **Envelope Options** dialog box appears.
   - ➤ If you want to, you can change the font for both the delivery and the return address. Click to select the desired options.
   - ➤ Check the envelope size. Make sure that the correct size is selected in the **Envelope Size** box. To change sizes, click the down arrow to open the list box. Select an envelope size by clicking on it. Then click OK to return to the **Envelopes and Labels** dialog box.
4. Now you can stick an envelope in your printer, a process called feeding. That word was probably coined shortly after a printer ate the first print job. Which way does the envelope go in? Follow the pictorial on the **Envelopes and Labels** dialog box. In the lower-right side, there's a box labeled **Feed**. There's a little picture showing the correct placement of feeding your envelope to your printer. If you still have trouble, refer to your printer manual or a local geek.

Figure 7.5: Options for specifying fonts and envelope sizes.

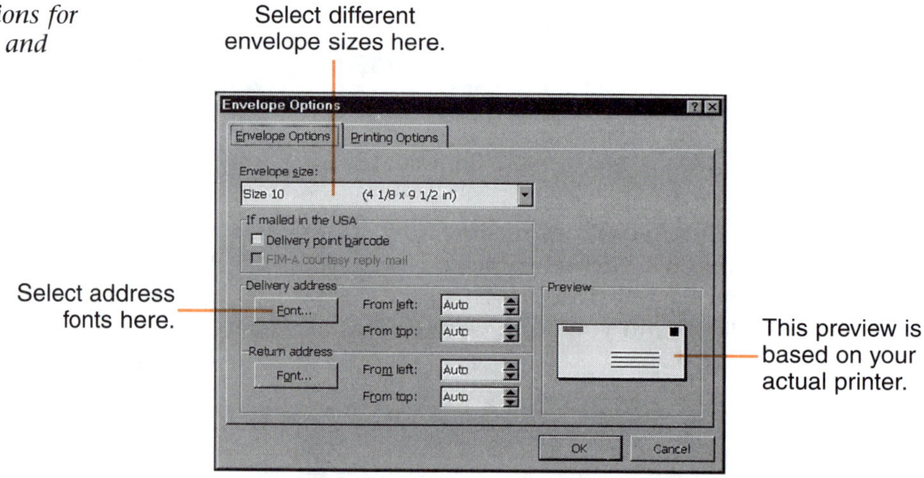

5. You can print the envelope now, by clicking the **Print** button, or you can print it later (usually when you print the document) by clicking the **Add to Document** button. To print only the envelope for this document, print page 0 (that's right, zero). Word 2000 stores the associated envelope for a document on page zero.

Quick Tips for Printing Envelopes

Everyone likes to receive mail in envelopes with clear and distinct addressing, but nobody likes to stick envelopes in a typewriter to create them. They get all curled up, and it's difficult to keep them straight. Your computer printer can help. Most printers today have the capability to print addresses on envelopes, as long as you follow the directions included with your printer and your word processor.

If you have a laser printer:

- If you print lots of envelopes, you'll benefit from having an addition to your printer called an envelope feeder. If you don't have one, check your printer manual for instructions on how to feed an envelope through the straightest possible path in your printer, to avoid excessive curling and twisting (maybe there's a side or back panel that opens up).
- Check out the little **Feed** icon in the **Envelopes and Labels** dialog box. It shows you how the envelope is supposed to be inserted into your printer—whether it should be centered or against one of the edges.
- Check for messages on your printer display. You may need to press the **Form Feed** button to get things started.
- Most important of all, don't skimp on quality. Buy envelopes that are made for a laser printer. Other envelopes practically melt from the heat and really gum up the works. And you'll find that the heat from the laser printer will sometimes seal the envelope before you've had time to insert your document.

Which Way Does the Envelope Go In?

If you need to verify the feed options (the methods used to insert the envelope in the printer), click the **Printing Options** tab in the **Envelope Options** dialog box. Select an appropriate option and click **OK**.

If you have a dot-matrix printer, you can print an envelope like this:

- Line up the left edge of the envelope against the left edge of the paper feed.
- Move the tractor feed so the top edge of the envelope is even with the print head. Word will move the envelope up about half an inch before it prints anything, so don't worry that your address will fall off the edge.

Bar Coding Your Envelopes May Save Postage Costs

If your printer can print graphics, Word can print two types of codes on an envelope. The POSTNET bar code is a machine-readable representation of a U.S. ZIP+4 code (the standardized geographic delivery route in the United States), and the FIM (Facing Identification Mark) code identifies the front of a courtesy reply envelope.

To print the POSTNET (Postal Numeric Encoding Technique) bar code, select the **Delivery Point Bar Code** check box in the **Envelope Options** dialog box. To print a Facing Identification Mark (FIM) in addition to the POSTNET bar code, select the **FIM-A Courtesy Reply Mail** check box. Please note that Word cannot print a Facing Identification Mark or POSTNET bar code if you use a daisy-wheel printer. It is expecting a laser printer.

What's a "Print Job"?

The term print job refers to the collection of bits and bytes sent to the printer. It's actually more than just the words and formatting of your document. It includes control information unique to the type of printer you own, including details on print options chosen at the time of printing.

Killing a Print Job (Make It Stop!)

Nobody ever prints a job accidentally, right? I do, and it's easy to send too much to the printer. For instance, maybe I don't hear the printer cranking up, so I click **Print** again and again, until I realize my printer isn't turned on. I turn on the printer and feel really dumb for about two seconds. Then I panic when I realize my printer is about to waste lots of paper printing those extra copies. There are several ways to delete those other undesired print jobs, and this section explains them.

Word 2000 spends just a few seconds processing your print job (you can see pages flowing out of the little printer icon in your status bar), sends it to your print folder, then waits for your printer to take it. While your print job sits in this folder, you have the opportunity to easily delete it if you wish.

To find and display your print folder, double-click the picture of the printer in your Task bar (it usually appears on the far right side, next to the clock). When the dialog box opens, you will see a list of all documents scheduled to print. Click to select the name of your print job (most of the time, there is only one document in this list anyway, so it's easy). You can delete this print job by pressing the **Delete** key.

If your printer has already started printing the document when you ask to delete it, Word will display a message on your screen. It warns that the job may be in progress. Click the **OK** button because you want to delete the job anyway, regardless of whether a few pages have already printed.

Kill That Print Job!

The trick to deleting a print job before it reaches your printer is finding it. After Word has finished preparing your document for the printer, Word temporarily stores it in a printer folder. To see this folder, double-click the picture of the printer in your Windows 95/98 or Windows NT Task bar (it shows up on the opposite end of Start when a print job is pending). When the dialog box opens, you can select your print job by clicking it and delete it by pressing the **Delete** key.

What? It's Still Printing?

Sometimes the print job slips away and makes it to the printer before you get the chance to delete it. You can still delete it, but do it the right way. Don't simply turn off your printer, or you'll probably be left with a printer jam, loose toner, and dirty fingers.

Here's the best way to stop printing in progress. Find the Online button and press it to take the printer offline. Wait patiently as the few pages in process flush out. When it stops printing, turn the printer off. This erases your print job from the printer's memory. Check to be sure that the job has really been deleted from your print folder. Now go ahead and turn on the printer, and you should be back in business.

The Least You Need to Know

Sometimes getting your document to print can be annoying, but the whole process will go a bit smoother if you remember tips from this chapter.

- What happens when I click the **Print** button on the Standard toolbar?

  You will print one copy of all pages of the current document.

- What if I want more printing options?

  Use the **Print** command on the **File** menu to print selected text or individual pages, choose a different printer or paper bin, or print multiple copies of the document. It's always a good idea to save your document before printing.

- Before I waste paper, can I see what it will look like?

  Good idea. You can see exactly how your document will look printed. Open the **File** menu and choose **Print Preview**. Click **Close** when you are finished previewing it.

- Is it difficult to print an envelope?

  The hardest part about printing envelopes is making sure the proper side of the envelope gets printed. The envelope feature of Word 2000 will automatically pick up address information from your document, so you won't have to retype it. Open the **Tools** menu and click **Envelopes and Labels**. You'll even find directions on how to properly load your envelope into your printer!

- Oops! How do I cancel that print job?

  If you want to cancel a print job or change the priority of a print job, use the new **Print Manager** in Windows 95/98 or Windows NT. Click the printer icon in the system tray, choose your job, and press the **Delete** key to cancel the job.

Part 2

Fine-tuning That Masterpiece

Does your document look like something you ripped out of the telephone book? Is it…well …boring? Of course, neither you nor what you've typed is boring, so it must be something else. Liven it up! It's called formatting! Start small; experiment with letters or small words, then work up to sentences and paragraphs, and soon you'll be competing with magazine advertisements.

Not feeling too artistic? Let Word 2000 take charge while you sit back, sip coffee, and watch automated tools bring your document to life. Now why can't other things in life be this easy?

Chapter 8

Can't Find It? Look Here!

In This Chapter

- Finding words in a document
- Using Find and Replace to quickly update a document
- Changing the past, present, and future forms of a word
- Getting rid of things with Find and Delete

You've just finished that big marketing document minutes before meeting your new client, but learn they've just changed their name from Bud's Cheese Shop to Cheese Products International. Panic? Not at all; you've got features in Word 2000 able to update your document in seconds, making you look sharp in your meeting with the Big Cheese.

Finding Something Inside Your Opened Document

No matter what it might be if it's in your document, you can find it. Just open the **Edit** menu and select the **Find** command. You can also click the **Select Browse** button found inside your vertical scrollbar, then click the **Find** button. Either way, the dialog box shown here appears:

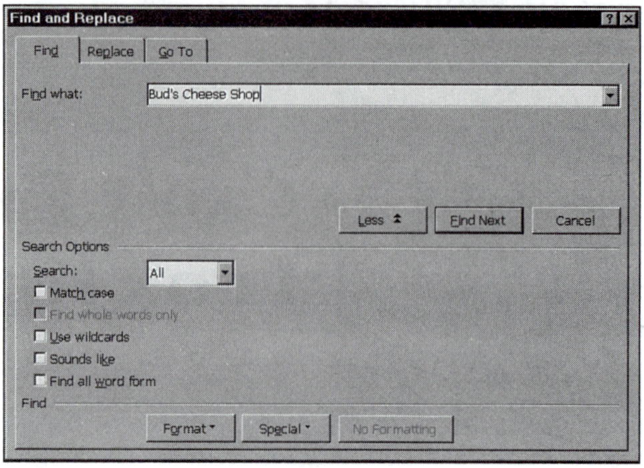

Figure 8.1: If it's in there, you can find it.

The **Find** dialog box lets you type the word or phrase you're looking for in the **Find What** text box. Here are some handy options you can choose from:

- To locate only the word you typed, and not words that include it as a part (for example, you want to find `search` but not `searching`), use the **Find Whole Words Only** check box.
- To match upper- or lowercase letters in your search (for example, `Word` but not `word`), use the **Match Case** check box.
- If you want to search backward, open the **Search** list and select the **Up** option.
- If you want to search for a word with particular formatting, click **Format**, select **Font**, **Paragraph**, **Language**, or **Style**, and make the selections you want.
- To search for a special mark, such as a page break or a tab, click on **Special**, then select an item from the list.

Shorten Up That Search

Word 2000 finds any matching text in your document. It can find things so well, however, that it might drive you crazy. Search for the word `me` and you could be bombarded with all the words containing the letters `m` and `e`, such as home, tame, meander, and remedial. To make Word 2000 more precise—to locate only the whole word `me`, for example—select the **Find Whole Word Only** check box in the **Find** dialog box.

When you have selected all the options you want, click **Find Next**. Word 2000 begins the search from the current location in the document and then automatically continues the search at the beginning of your document, so nothing is missed.

After finding the first occurrence, you can continue looking by clicking **Find Next**. To stop the searching and return to your document, click **Cancel**. You can continue your search any time by pressing **Shift+F4**.

Finding Special Characters

Want to find something strange, like the next tab marker located in a document? Try typing a tab in the **Find What** text box and you'll be bounced right out. Same with the **Enter** key, and many others. To find these special characters, click the **Special** button in the **Find and Replace** dialog box. The pop-up list appears of all the various characters that Word 2000 can search for but you aren't able to type. Click the character you want, and a symbol representing it appears in the **Find What** box, ready for the search. You also see a symbol next to it called a *caret* (^) that has to be there, but you can ignore it.

Try the Select Browse Object

The Select Browse Object is used to display a pop-up table of the best browsing methods from which you can choose your favorite. The icon is found on your vertical scrollbar.

Finding and Replacing Things in Your Document

Finding something isn't always a happy reunion. Most people usually want to find something in a document so they can get rid of it or at least change it to something else. Word 2000 has a special feature to help you with this, and it's called **Replace**.

The **Replace** feature is incredibly powerful. Sure, it searches your entire document for a particular word (or words) and replaces them with whatever you want, maintaining the format. But it's also flexible enough to enable creative searching. Like swapping a font from one type to another, or wiping out any bold or italic highlighting. Or, it just plain wipes out anything you like.

Replacing Plain Old Text

The text you replace doesn't have to be plain or old, and what you replace it with can be just about anything. You can even search for combinations of letters inside words (for instance, acronyms), making updates easy when the names change. Open the **Edit** menu and choose the **Replace** command, or take a shortcut and press **Ctrl+H**. In the **Replace** dialog box, type the text you want to find in the **Find What** box and press **Tab** to move to the next box (incidentally, if you already opened the **Find** dialog box, you can click the **Replace** button to turn it into the **Replace** dialog box). In the **Replace With** box, type your replacement text. The **Find Next** button searches for the next occurrence, and the dialog box stays with you as the search travels through your document. Press the **Replace** button to replace the text, or skip it and move to the next occurrence by pressing **Find Next** again.

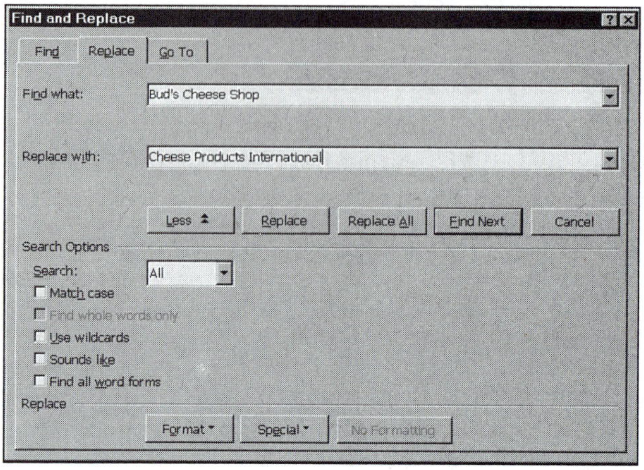

Figure 8.2: You can replace what you find automatically.

If you are brave and daring (or just impatient), go ahead and try the **Replace All** button. No holds are barred with this button; it blasts through your document replacing every occurrence before you can scream "OH NO!" Don't panic. Just remember the **Undo** button (or **Ctrl+Z**), which works well at restoring the previous state of your document, and possibly your health.

It's A Good Idea to Always Type Something in the Replace With Box

If you don't type anything in the **Replace With** box, the **Replace** command systematically deletes all of the Find Whats. It's great to use on imported text files where each line ends with a paragraph symbol. This process can quickly blow them all away (although you might prefer replacing them with a single space key). It's less productive to blow away, for example, all of the words `the` in a document, but you might come across a word that deserves it. You might also try using it to remove all words of a particular size or font by searching for character formats instead of words.

Replacing Formatted Text

You can also search for words that are formatted in a particular way. For example, you may want to tone down a document by replacing every bold **No** with normal text. Or, you can take normal words and replace them with formatted versions of the same thing, and the formatting is limited only by your imagination. You can also search for words in different fonts and sizes and replace them with yet another font or size. Here's a simple example to get started.

Perhaps you decide to replace every bold **No** in your document with a quieter plain `No`, no bold needed.

1. Open the **Edit** menu and choose the **Find** command. Type the text you want to find in the **Find What** text box, and apply the formatting you want to find (for instance, click **Bold** button and type the word **No**).
2. Indicate the formatting of the replacement text in the **Replace With** box (same example, type `No` without any formatting). You can use any combination of the formatting options for your search or replace.
3. Now click **Find Next** to begin your search. The dialog box remains on the screen as it displays the found words in your document (you usually see enough of the surrounding text to confirm that you really want to replace it; if not, just move the dialog box around the screen by dragging the Title bar of its window).
4. To replace the text, click **Replace**. To move to the next occurrence, press the **Find Next** button. Continue this process until you return to the beginning of your document. Click **Close** when you are finished.

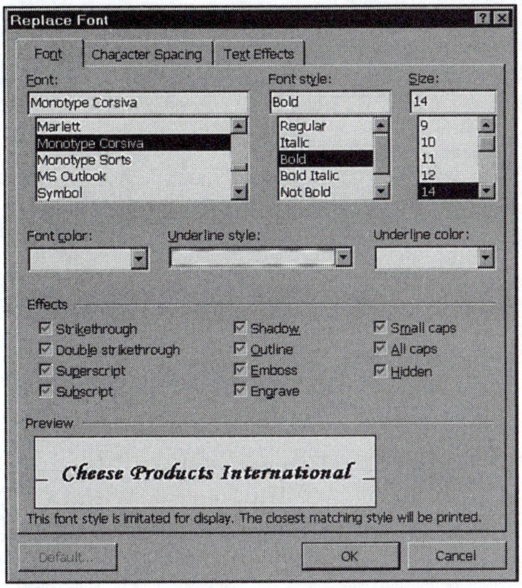

Figure 8.3: Replace enables you to find fonts, attributes, and other symbols.

Replace the Formatting Only

Sometimes you don't care about the words, only the formatting. You can search for and replace all occurrences of any specific formatting, regardless of the text. For example, try to delete any and all words in your document that are bold. Don't get rid of the words, just get rid of the bold. Or change any words in 10-point Courier font to 12-point Times New Roman. You get the idea. Open the **Edit** menu and choose the **Replace** command. Delete any text in the **Find What** box and the **Replace With** box that might be lingering from a previous search or replace. To specify the formats you want to find and replace, click the Format button and choose the formats you wish to replace. Click **Bold**, for instance, and the word Bold appears just below the text box as the description of the search. Do the same after clicking in the **Replace With** box. Look for **Not Bold**, which is fairly descriptive. The description below reads **Not Bold**. Click **Find Next** and you are on your way. Each and every entry of bold text appears in order on your screen, and you have the option of changing them to normal text by clicking **Replace** or leaving them alone by clicking the **Find Next** button.

Figure 8.4: An example of replacing a format throughout your document.

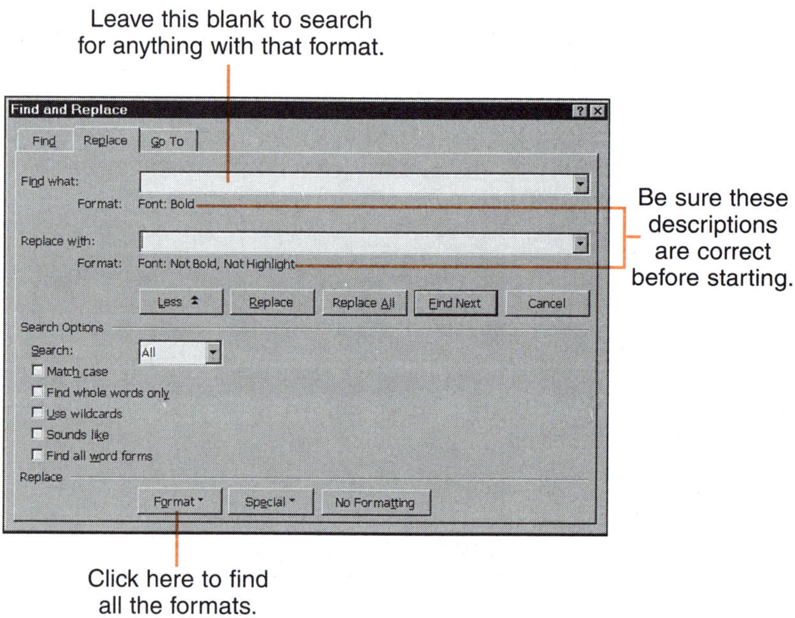

Word even enables you to totally destroy a document by, for instance, replacing all normal text with nothing. Just leave the **Replace With** box completely empty. I can't think of a practical reason to do this, but it serves as a good warning to you. Be sure you know what is in your **Replace With** box before starting one of these experiments.

Finding and Replacing Graphics, Fields, and Annotations

If you use lots of graphics in your document, you may be happy to know you can find and replace any of them (or get rid of them all with one click). And, if you create templates or create annotation comments, you may find it helpful to search either fields or the inserted annotations.

To find these special items in the **Find or Replace** dialog box, click the **Special** button (it's labeled **Special**). Now click **Graphic**, **Field**, or **Annotation Mark**. If you are replacing something, type what you want to use as a replacement in the **Replace With** box (or leave it blank to remove them). They can also be replaced with text, graphics, annotations. Now start your search by pressing the **Find Next**, **Replace**, or **Replace All** buttons.

Special Characters You Can Find and Replace

Word has preloaded almost all of the control characters enabling you to search for them. If you happen to know the key combination for the special character, you can just type it in the **Find What** box. Otherwise, click the **Special** button and choose the description of the symbol you want to find. The key combination for the symbol appears in the **Find What** box, though it may not look as expected. Word uses these codes to find what you're looking for.

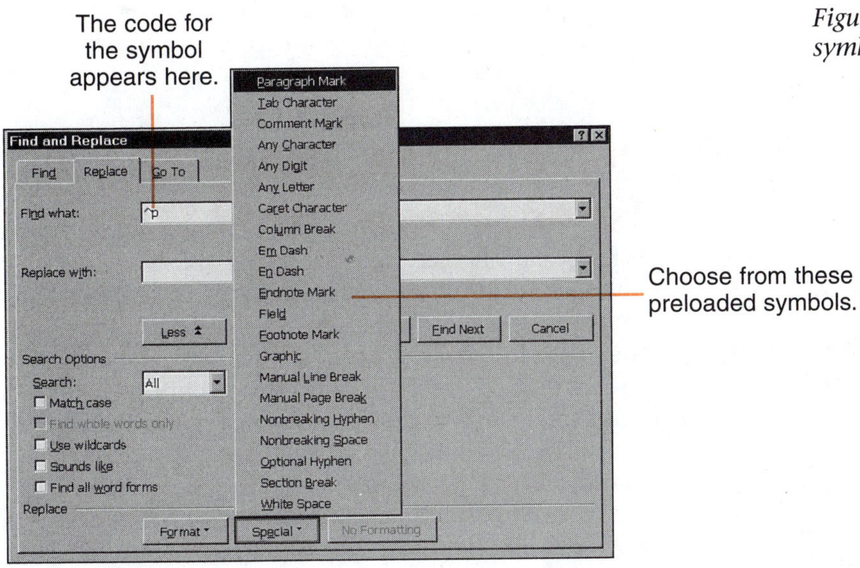

Figure 8.5: Even the secret symbols can't hide.

White Space?

That last option on the **Special** character button may have you wondering what's included in this thing called *white space*. After all, isn't the background considered white space? Not all of it. White space includes any number and combination of normal and nonbreaking spaces, tab characters, and paragraph and section formatting.

What more can you search for? Spaces are a popular item. They end up a lot more than they should at the end of sentences, like twice as much. A single space between sentences is now considered correct, not the two most people prefer to type. You can get rid of that second space by typing two spaces into the **Find What** box, and only a single space in the **Replace With** box. Pretty simple, huh? Since you probably don't want two spaces in a row appearing anywhere in your document, you can press the **Replace All** button to save yourself some time. (Hint: You may want to run this multiple times in a row until there are no replacements made. This takes care of any instances of three or more spaces in a row that you would want to reduce to one space.)

Replace Past, Present, and Future Words All At Once

What a pain it used to be worrying about all the different forms of a word during a word replace. Marketing folks and politicians complained that they couldn't, for example, change all the words `go` with the word `leave`, because they might also have additional steps to find occurrences of `going` or `gone`. These people pushed their weight around Microsoft and got them to include some pretty fancy innards in this version. Accurate replacement of words usually means painstakingly determining the different word forms, or tense, and finding and replacing them. It works, and it's fun. You can also change the entire gist of a letter by replacing words with ones of opposite meaning (called *antonyms*). To

Don't Get Too Crazy with Word Forms

This intelligence of replacing word forms is powerful, but it can't change the underlying structure of your sentence. It won't replace all forms of a verb with a noun, for example, or vice versa, but why would anyone try that anyway?

invoke this new wonder, open the **Edit** menu and choose either **Find** or **Replace**; it works for both functions as well. In the dialog box, click to check the **Find All Word Forms**. Now all your searches include the past, present, and future tenses with the press of a single button.

Buy, Buying, Bought

Word 2000 now features linguistic technology to understand the meaning of words and their different forms. For example, if you want to replace the word buy with the word `sell` throughout your document, Word applies some smarts and changes not only `buy` to `sell`, but also `buying` to `selling`, and `bought` to `sold`. Now you can send form letters to your stockbroker.

I Don't Know, but It Sounds Like...

Did you experience the parental spelling paradox as a child? Ask how a word was spelled and the answer was "go look it up." It usually meant go outside and play, because how can anyone look up a word in a dictionary when you don't know how to spell it in the first place?

This paradox no longer frustrates the youth, or the elderly for that matter, with the **Sounds Like** feature in **Find** and **Replace**. Just spell it the best you can, and let Word 2000 look it up for you. In a split second it returns with the closest matches. The better your attempt at guessing, the more accurate your results become. To try it, check this option on either the **Find** or **Replace** dialog boxes. Don't be so bold as to click the **Replace All** button here unless you are completely familiar with the **Undo** button.

The Least You Need to Know

- Where is the **Find** and **Replace** feature hiding?

  Either click to open the **Select Browse Object** in your scrollbar and choose the **Find** icon, or open the **Edit** menu and choose either **Find**, **Replace**, or **Go To**.

- I've used the words go, going, and gone throughout my document. Can I replace them all at once and maintain the proper tense?

  Yes, and you need only find the single word go. The other two related word forms can also be changed (while maintaining proper tense) by choosing **Find All Word Forms** in the **Replace** dialog box.

- Is it possible to get rid of all italics in a document? Or change only a specific font size?

  Certainly; you have complete control of finding and replacing formatting options as easy as words. Just click the **Format** button on the **Find and Replace** dialog box and choose the formatting targets.

- Can you replace all double tabs with single tabs, leaving everything else alone?

  Yes, the **Special** button on the **Find and Replace** dialog box lists all the special characters you don't normally see in a document, like tabs, paragraph symbols, page breaks, and so on. You can find and replace these as easily as words.

- It's a big document and I'm a lousy speller. I have to find a word but I can't spell it. How can I search for it?

  Don't expect miracles, but Word has another trick up its sleeve. Do the best you can, spelling it the way it sounds, and click the **Sounds Like** box in the **Find and Replace** dialog box. Word takes you to everything that comes close, and perhaps you'll find what you need.

Chapter 9

Enhancing Your Paragraphs & Pages with Formatting Options

In This Chapter

- Aligning paragraphs
- Changing a paragraph's indents
- Creating bullets and numbered lists
- Setting and working with tabs
- Centering a page on the paper
- When and how to create sections in your document

String a few good sentences together and you've got a report, letter, memo, short story, and so on. Now you'll want to provide your words with the best possible environment, for nurturing growth. Clean and centered on the page, with crisp paragraphs and pleasing spacing. Maybe dignify it with some bulleted lists, or better yet, sophisticated numbered lists. This chapter describes how you can enhance the formatting of paragraphs, pages, and complete documents, so you can be proud of your creation.

Paragraph Basics: First Things First

In Word 2000, a paragraph is nothing more than a collection of words that ends when you press the **Enter** key. This includes single-line paragraphs, such as chapter titles, section headings, and captions for charts and other figures. When you press the **Enter** key, you are marking the end of a paragraph (and the start of a new one).

Paragraph Format Continues

When you press **Enter** to create a new paragraph, the formatting of that paragraph continues to the next paragraph. Once you make changes to a paragraph (such as changing its margin settings), those changes are effective until you change them again.

At the end of each paragraph, Word inserts a paragraph mark that is normally invisible, and for good reason—they're ugly and sometimes get in your way. However, you may want to see them sometimes to make sure they are where they belong and nowhere else (such as at the end of a line in the middle of a paragraph). To see your paragraph marks, click the **Show/Hide** button on the Standard toolbar. This button is a toggle, so you can click it again when you've finished to make them disappear.

So who cares, you ask? Well, have you ever cut and pasted text and had the whole darned thing change its formatting? This paragraph mark is the culprit. These critters hold all the formatting options contained in the paragraph (such as font, size, indenting, margins, and so on). So if you don't normally see it and forget it's there, you may forget to include it during your copy. Without it, your words forget what formatting they should have and resort to the formatting of where they are placed.

Soft or Hard Return?

If you need to move to the next line without creating a new paragraph (as in a list or an address at the top of a letter), press **Shift+Enter**. This inserts a "soft return" marking the end of a line, as opposed to a "hard return," which marks the end of a paragraph.

Also, if you ever accidentally delete a paragraph mark and cause the formatting of your paragraphs to change unexpectedly, don't panic. The best thing to do is click the **Undo** button, which returns the original formatting to your paragraph.

Center Lines and Paragraphs on Your Page

To create a new paragraph equally distant from the left and right margins, click the **Center** button on the Formatting toolbar. The insertion point moves to the center of the page. Start typing, and you notice that the words spread out from the center of the page. Press **Enter** when you're done, and you have a completely centered paragraph. You can also center any existing paragraph by clicking anywhere inside the paragraph and pressing the **Center** button.

To change a centered paragraph back to the normal alignment (aligned with the left margin), click anywhere inside the paragraph, then click the **Align Left** button on the formatting toolbar. Paragraph alignment is usually independent; just click inside any of them and align them the way you like.

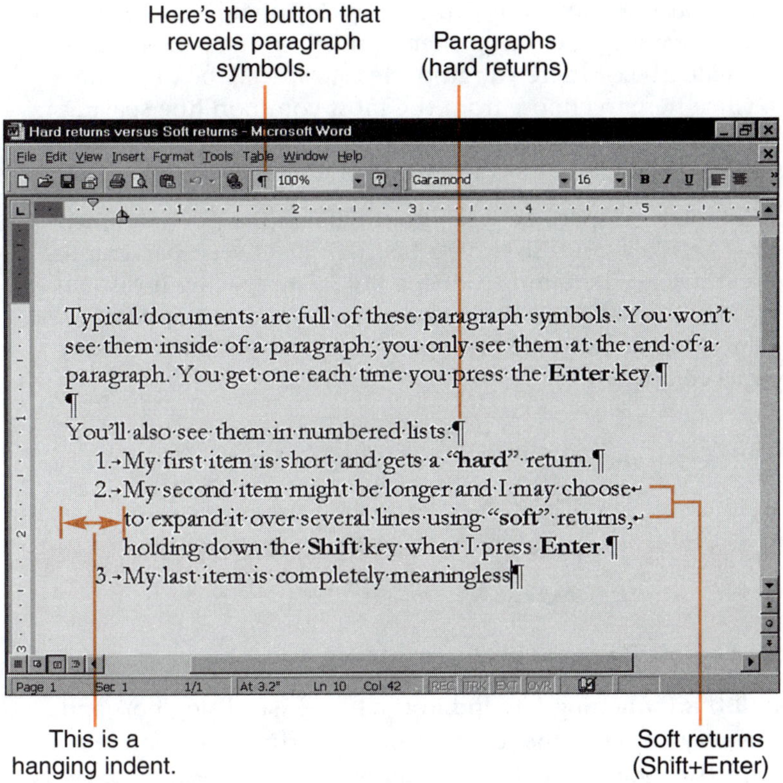

Figure 9.1: Displaying the normally hidden paragraph symbol.

Aligning Text Right or Left

Use the Alignment buttons to change where your text lines up. Most documents are prepared with the text aligned left, with each line starting at the left margin. It can just as easily be aligned right for things like dates that you want to appear at the top right side of your page.

A Quick Date on the Right

It's common to place the date at the top right as the first step in writing a letter. Word 2000 makes this easy. Just click the **Align Right** button, open **Insert** and choose **Date and Time**, and press **Enter**. Click **Align Left** to get back to familiar territory.

Changing Line and Paragraph Spacing

Someday your boss may ask you to read between the lines, and your vision may not be so good. You can increase the distance between lines in your Word 2000 document.

Normally, all lines are single-spaced. However, you can quickly change the line spacing of any paragraph by opening the **Format** menu and choosing **Paragraph**. This opens the **Paragraph** dialog box, where you find the **Line Spacing** box (on the **Indents and Spacing** tab). Click here to choose from the most common line spacing alternatives, including Single, Double, and something exactly between those two (1.5 lines spacing).

Next, you can adjust the amount of space between your paragraphs. For example, maybe you always hit the **Enter** key twice to leave a blank line between paragraphs. Why not just adjust the extra space here in this dialog box? The spacing measured in points is displayed in the **Before** or **After** boxes, which you can change. Most people enter a value in only one, usually the **After** box. That's all you need to keep your paragraphs neatly spaced apart.

Quick Paragraph Formatting

The headquarters for all this formatting is found in the **Paragraph** dialog box, and there's a quick and easy way to get it opened. Place the insertion point inside a paragraph and click with the right mouse button. Choose the **Paragraph** command to open the **Paragraph** dialog box, and you have access to all of the features described in this chapter.

Indenting a Paragraph

 Regular paragraphs are indented by using the **Tab** key to indent the first line. That's fine, but sometimes you just have to call attention to an entire paragraph by indenting the whole thing, not just the first line.

To indent an entire paragraph, place the insertion point anywhere in the paragraph and click the **Increase Indent** button on the Formatting toolbar. To return an indented paragraph to the original margin, click the **Decrease Indent** button.

Incidentally, if the first indent wasn't far enough for your tastes, you can go farther. To indent to each next tab stop, just click the **Increase Indent** button again and again until the indented paragraph is placed where you want it.

If you want to indent both right and left sides, use the method called *double-indenting*. Click to select any existing paragraph (or start a new one), open the **Format** menu and choose **Paragraph**. In the **Paragraph** dialog box, choose the **Indents and**

Spacing tab to bring it to the front. Now, click the **Left** box and enter something like .5 (one-half inch), or simply play with the up/down arrows and pick a number. Click the **Right** box and enter .5 again. You should keep each side the same, but no one will arrest you if you don't. Click **OK** and start typing. Your text is double-indented.

Making a Hanging Indent

For some reason, certain people like to do exactly the opposite of what you expect. That's what the hanging indent looks like. Instead of the first line starting comfortably inside the paragraph, the hanging indent sticks out (to the left) from the rest of the paragraph. It looks backward—but it can be put to good use, such as in numbered lists described in the next section.

To create a hanging indent, click anywhere in an existing paragraph (or start a new one), open the **Paragraph** dialog box, and place a negative number in the **Left Indention** box by clicking the down arrow next to it. A sample display of text responds to your adjustment, so you know when the text hangs "out" the preferred distance from the rest of the paragraph.

Hanging Around Numbered and Bulleted Lists

A special kind of hanging indent is a numbered or bulleted list. This kind of list is special because a number or symbol (that sometimes looks like a bullet) is placed to the left of all the other lines in the paragraph.

 You've seen bulleted lists used throughout these chapters to:

- Create snazzy lists like this one.
- Highlight what's coming up.
- Summarize the important points that were covered.

 Numbered lists are especially helpful when you want to explain the specific steps for doing something, such as step 1, step 2, and so on. Ready to number or bullet? Here's what to do.

Click the **Bullets** button on the Formatting toolbar, and then start typing. What you type becomes a bullet on a list. If you press **Enter**, you start a new bullet. You can stop the bullets from appearing by clicking the **Bullets** button again. Similarly, when you click the **Numbering** bullet, each time you press **Enter**, the number is increased by one. You can interrupt a numbered list by clicking the right mouse button and selecting **Skip Numbering** from the shortcut menu. To resume numbering later in your document, click the **Numbering** button on the Formatting toolbar.

Doesn't Look Like a Bullet?

If you want to create different bullets or numbering, use the **Bullets and Numbering** command on the **Format** menu. You can change the type and size of bullets, the numbering system (letters, Roman numerals, or decimal numbers), and the amount of space between the number or bullet and the rest of the paragraph.

Using Tabs

Tabs are a way to align text within paragraphs consistently. Press the **Tab** key, and you move in one tab stop. Normal tab stops are set every half-inch. Word 2000 also includes a few different types of tabs you may want to try, including a centering tab marker to align the decimal points in a column of numbers.

You can change the distance between tab stops, or change the type of tab marker you want to use, but you need to do something weird first. Click to the left of where you want to add the desired tab stop (this prevents existing text, and you, from getting confused when the change occurs). Take a look at the ruler near the top of your page. (If you don't see your ruler, or aren't sure, open the **View** menu and choose the **Ruler** command so that a check mark appears next to it.) At the far left of the ruler is a box with a strange symbol inside; it looks like an L unless you've already clicked the button. This button toggles through the available tab markers as you click it. Select the type of tab you want to apply to the paragraph, and then click anywhere in the **Ruler** where you want the tab marker to appear. A little marker appears, indicating a tab stop location. You can change the tab stop location by dragging it with your mouse to the left or right. You can get rid of tab stops by dragging them off the ruler.

Tab Markers

Word 2000 uses four different types of tabs which can be viewed on the **Ruler**.

- **Left Tab** The most common tab is the left tab, which operates just like a typewriter.
- **Right Tab** The right tab causes text to line up right-justified at that tab stop. This can help create interesting titles, which are, of course, single-line paragraphs.

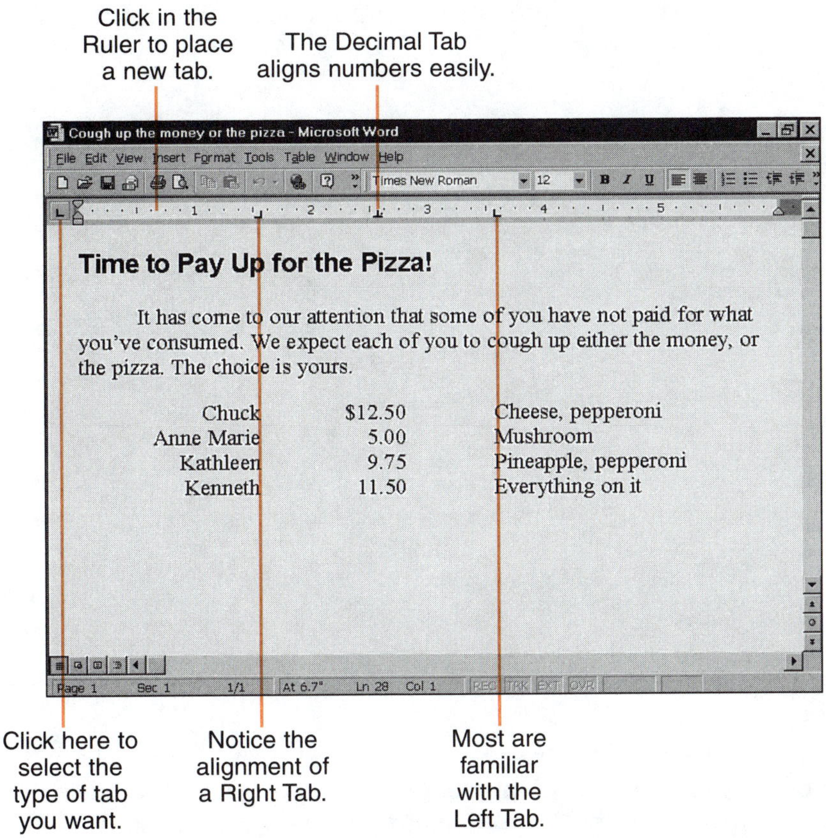

Figure 9.2: Manage your tabs for fast alignments.

- **Center Tab** This is great for one-word columns of text. The center tab lines all the words up in the center, left-justified.
- **Decimal Tab** Place this tab where you want to align numbers by their decimal point. The number is right-justified before you press the period key and then left-justified on the decimal.
- **Bar** This tab creates a vertical bar symbol. If you continue it for several lines, the bars connect and draw a vertical line. It's great for creating divided lists.

Using Leader Tabs

Sometimes tabs can be used to provide interesting effects in your document. For instance, have you ever wondered how they get that line of dots that extend out to the page number in a table of contents? Me neither. But it just so happens that you can use something called a *leader tab* to get the job done.

Figure 9.3: Samples of tab leaders that can help organize your page.

In this example, leaders and text alignment have been applied to this tab.

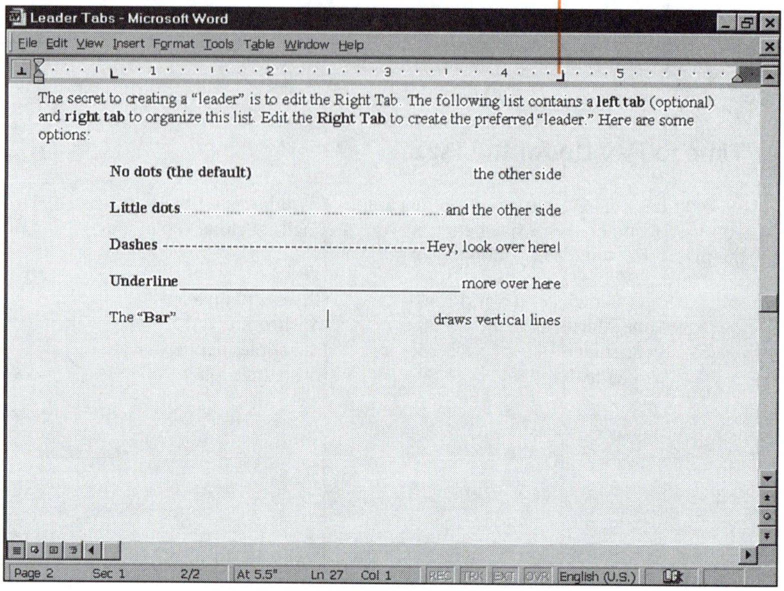

Leaders appear to the *left* of a given tab. So first choose (or create) the tab that will contain the leader. It's typically a **Right Tab** on the right side of the page (with the text right-justified). All of this can be set in the **Tabs** dialog box. Open it by either double-clicking this tab in the ruler or opening the **Format** menu and choosing **Tabs**.

Figure 9.4: Take control of your Tabs.

Insert the distance where you want the leader to end.

Choose your leader for the selected tab.

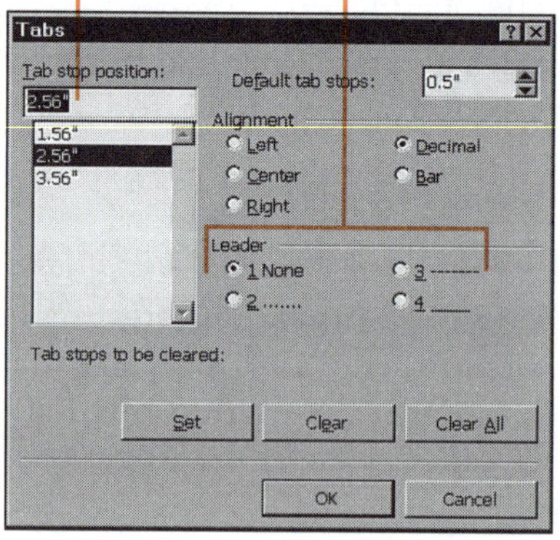

Click to select the style of leader you prefer and then press the **OK** button.

Now start typing. Type the text to appear in front of the tab stop. Press the **Tab** key. Bingo! The leader appears, and all you are left with is to decide what to type at the other end. Press the **Enter** key to end each line containing a leader tab.

The Paragraph Dialog Box

Yes, the paragraph is so important that it has its own dialog box inside Word 2000. All of the features and procedures described in this chapter (and a whole bunch more!) can also be performed from this dialog box. You can find it by opening the **Format** menu and choosing the **Paragraph** command. You can also right-click any paragraph to see the formatting shortcut menu, and choose the **Paragraph** command.

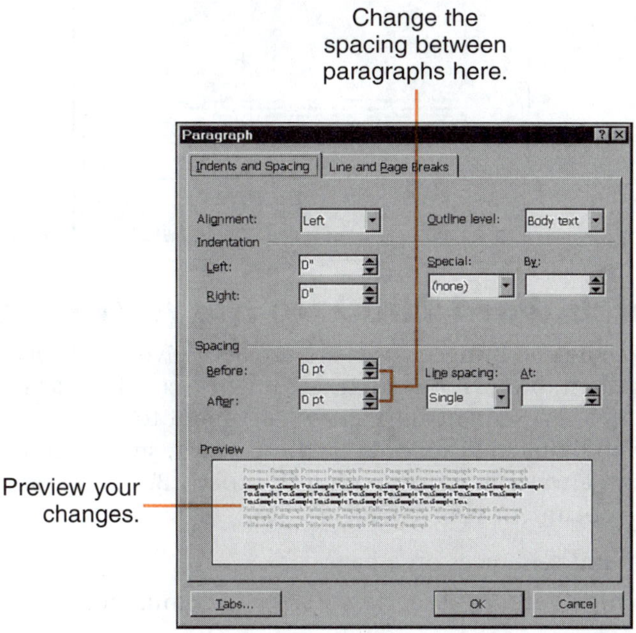

Figure 9.5: Identify paragraph formatting.

The remaining paragraph formatting functions can be found by clicking the **Line and Page Breaks** tab to bring it to the front. Here, you find lesser-known features like the **Widow/Orphan** option, which prevents single lines of a paragraph from appearing at the bottom or top of a page. To prevent a page break between paragraphs, check this box. You can also access all the **Tab** and **Tab Leader** options by clicking the **Tabs** button at the bottom of the dialog box.

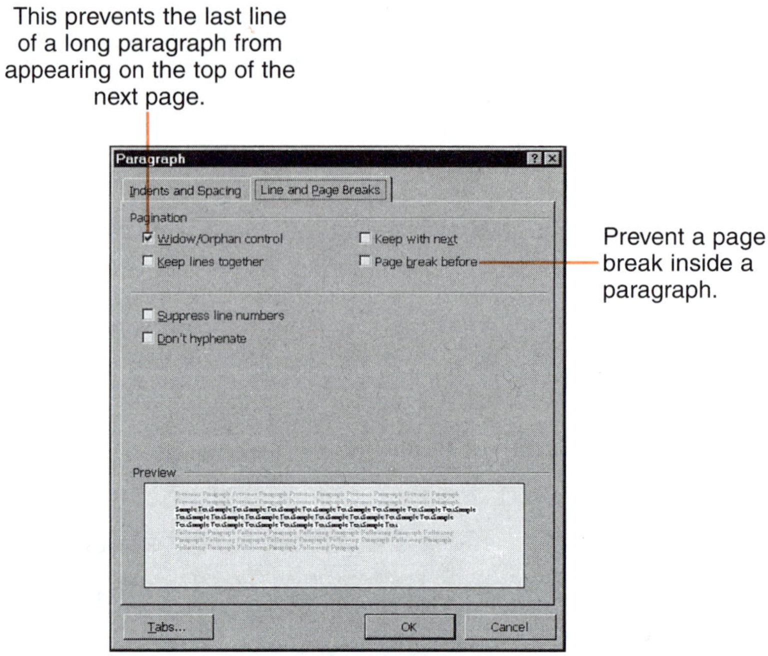

Figure 9.6: Keep your paragraphs from breaking up.

Sit Back and Watch Word 2000 Do the AutoFormat

If you are feeling daring and no bungee cords are at hand, give *AutoFormatting* a try. No, not on a real document, but just a scratch document (scratch means you can live without it). Type up a few sentences in a new document to test out this feature. It's supposed to help you by taking care of everything—lock, stock, and barrel. Unfortunately, it doesn't always do what you might expect. But don't take my word for it; test it on a document yourself. Here's how:

1. Type some words and sentences on a page.
2. Open the **Format** menu and choose the **AutoFormat** command.
3. Click the **Options** button to have a look at what interesting things might happen.
4. Click **OK** to run the beast.
5. Don't like what you see? Click **Reject Changes**, and everything returns to normal so you can do this process manually.

AutoFormat works great if the document is consistent in its layout (indents, tabs, spaces, and so on). But if you pay that much attention to the way you type, you might as well control the formatting yourself. Give it a try and see what you think.

Large imported text files are ideal documents to AutoFormat because these documents typically have no formatting at all (and therefore look very boring).

Break Up Your Document into Sections

A section is a portion of a Word document that has formatting settings different from the rest. These settings might include margins, paper size, headers, footers, columns, and page numbering. A section can be of any length: several pages, several paragraphs, or even a single line (such as a major heading). You can include as many sections as you want in a document. There are a lot of good reasons to include sections in your document, such as:

- To create multiple chapters in a long report. Each chapter would have its own chapter titles (called headers), and it is even easier to have Word generate a table of contents or an index for the whole document.
- For legal documents that require line numbering in some sections but not in others.
- To create a company newsletter with various formats. You could create a section just for the front-page heading so that it reaches from margin to margin on a single line. Underneath, you could change to a three-column format for the text of the newsletter.
- For business reports printed in portrait orientation (for example, 8 1/2- by 11 inches) with a chart that's printed in landscape orientation (11- by 8 1/2 inches).
- In a small manual, where each section has its own page numbers. The table of contents section could use Roman numerals (I, ii, and so on) for page numbers. Each section after the Table of Contents could start with page 1. Because the title page wouldn't need a page number, you could suppress page numbering on just that page.
- To include text in two different languages (for example, a human resources memorandum). The document could be divided into paired sections—one section for English and the other for Spanish.

Before you create your first section break in a document, do yourself a favor: Set the most common document formatting options first. For example, if you want most pages to have two newspaper columns, go ahead and set them up before you start dividing your document into sections. Otherwise, you'd be left to duplicate the common options within each section, and you have better things to do with your time.

When you're ready to start dividing your document into sections, place the insertion point at the desired divider, open the **Insert** menu, and choose the **Break** command.

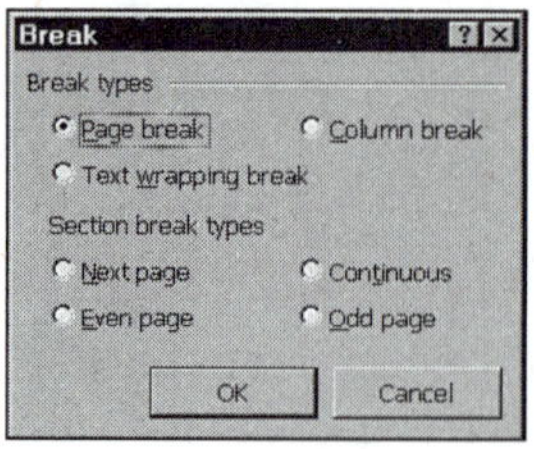

Figure 9.7: Choosing a break in your document.

Under **Section Break Types**, choose from these available options:

Next Page	The section starts at the top of the next page.
Continuous	The section starts right after the previous section, even if it's in the middle of the page.
Odd Page	The section starts on the next odd-numbered page. That's typically the next right-hand page.
Even Page	Yes, the section starts on the next even-numbered page, which is typically the next left-hand page.

When you have made your selection, click the **OK** button to close the **Section** dialog box, and you're done!

So Now That I Have a Section, What Do I Do with It?

These are some of the changes you can make that affect just a section of a document, instead of the whole document:

Margins. You learned how to change the margins of a document from the **Print Preview** window earlier in this chapter. If you decide to create different sections in your document, you can change the margins within each section separately. You'll learn to do this later in this chapter.

Paper Size and Page Orientation. You can choose from lots of paper sizes (such as 8 1/2-by-11 inches and 11-by-14 inches), and even change the paper size by section (but that could cause printing delays if a paper tray is empty or not supported by your printer). Certain sections may look better with a different orientation (landscape versus portrait). I'll tell you more about page orientation later in this chapter.

Headers and Footers. A header is stuff that's printed at the top of the page, such as a chapter title or date, and a footer is stuff (such as page numbers, filename, and so on) printed at the bottom. You'll learn how to create these in Chapter 10, "What's That in the Margins?" but you get the idea that these are ideal candidates for section use in a document.

Page Numbers. These are usually included as part of a header or footer. You can change the page-numbering system from the default of 1, 2, 3 to something else, such as I, ii, iii or A, B, C. You can change the page-numbering system within a document by creating sections and using different numbering schemes for each section.

Newspaper-style Columns. You can create columns in your document that appear like those you find in a newspaper or a magazine. If you ever want to vary the number of columns inside the same document, you are required to set up a new section. You will learn how to set up columns of text in Chapter 17, "Using More Word 2000 Tools."

Deleting a Section Break

To delete a section break, just select the section break symbol with your mouse, and then press the **Delete** key. Be careful! When you delete a section break, you also delete the section formatting for the text above it. That text above becomes part of the following section, so it picks up the formatting of the text below it. If you really didn't want to do this, click the **Undo** button on the Standard toolbar.

Copying the Formatting Between Sections

When a document has more than one section, you can copy section formatting by copying the section break. When you paste the section break into a new location, the text above the section break automatically picks up the formatting of the new section break.

Formatting in the Last Section

You may notice that the last section of your document has no section break. That's because the section formatting for the last section in a document is contained in the final paragraph mark of the document. To copy the formatting of the last section to any other section in your document, click **Show/Hide** to reveal the paragraph symbols, then replace any existing paragraph mark with the last paragraph mark by using the **Copy** and **Paste** commands on the **Edit** menu.

Centering Your Page on the Paper

If your document doesn't fill up a single page, you have empty space near the bottom. If that bothers you, why not center what text you have, with equal spacing from the top and bottom edges of the page? Even inside a large document, you may want the effect of having some important text centered from top-to-bottom in the middle of a page by itself. Word 2000 provides an easy way to do this.

Easy stuff first: Here's an example of a single-page document, with just a few sentences or paragraphs wanting to be centered, between top and bottom, on the printed page. Open the **File** menu and choose the **Page Setup** command. When you see the **Page Setup** dialog box, click the tab that says **Layout** to bring it to the front. Near the bottom of this box there is the **Vertical Alignment** label. That's it! Click it to pull down the choices, and in this case, choose **Center**. Click the **OK** button; Word centers your text on the page.

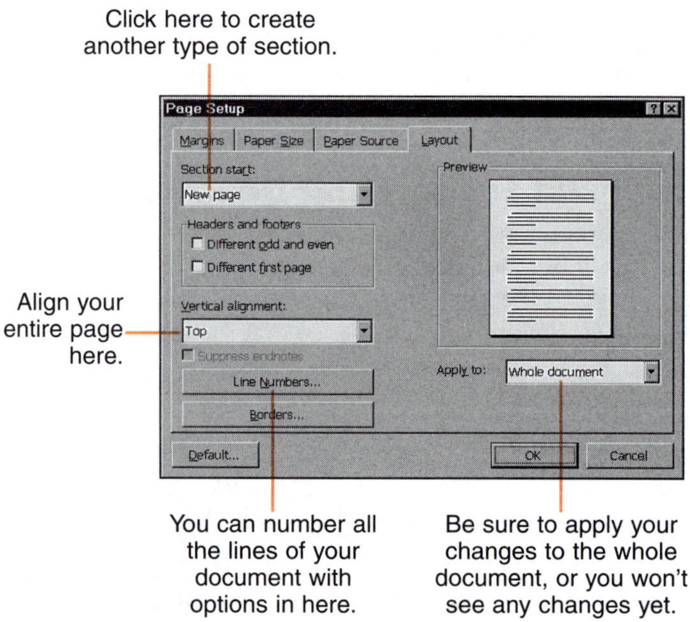

Figure 9.8: Page formatting details revealed in Page Setup.

Centering an Entire Page Inside a Large Document

Centering one page inside a large document is a little trickier. You see, the page settings are things that affect all pages in a document. If you jump to the middle and try to center one page using the **Page Setup** command, you'll mistakenly change the alignment of your entire document.

To do this correctly, find the page containing the text you want to center. Insert a page break at the top of the page and choose **Next Page** as the type of break. Add a page break before and after the actual text you want to center. Now you've safely isolated that page, and you can center it quickly with the **Page Setup** command.

If you have existing text you want to center, and it happens to appear in the middle of your document, you can take a shortcut. Simply select the text you want to have centered, open the **Page Setup** dialog box from the **File** menu, and choose **Center** in the **Vertical Alignment** text box. Word 2000 automatically inserts section breaks before and after the selected text to isolate the centered formatting.

Setting the Page Size

Although you probably plan to print on standard, 8 1/2- by 11-inch paper, Word 2000 will enable you to change the paper size to anything you want. Start by placing the insertion point at the beginning of the document or the top of the page. Open the **File** menu and choose the **Page Setup** command. Click on the **Paper Size** tab to bring it to the front. When you click on the **Paper Size** drop-down list, you see the paper sizes offered by Word. Make your selection and prepare to click the **OK** button.

Wait! There's the **Apply To** box again. You must decide if you are changing paper for your entire document or if you really want a mixed bag of different paper sizes making up this single document (probably not). Since that's unlikely, don't wait; just click the **OK** button to change the size for the entire document.

Deciding Between Landscape and Portrait Mode

If you think of pictures hanging on a wall, you get the idea. Portraits (pictures of people) are usually taller than they are wide. Scenery or landscape shots are usually wider than they are tall. Documents are easier to hold and read in **Portrait** mode. Spreadsheets are easier to follow in **Landscape** mode. Presentations are usually created in Landscape for the same reason. Landscape is also called sideways printing.

To change your document to **Landscape** mode, open the **File** menu and press the **Page Setup** command. Click the **Paper Size** tab to bring it to the front. Choose either **Portrait** or **Landscape** and watch the sample document rotate in the **Orientation** area to demonstrate the effects of your selection. Click the **OK** button, and the change is applied to your document.

The Least You Need to Know

Now you can have your paragraph and format it, too. Here are the tips and reminders about paragraph formatting.

- When does a sentence become a paragraph?

  In Word 2000, when you press the **Enter** key. That creates a paragraph symbol, and all formatting for the paragraph is stored with that symbol.

- What's the easiest way to change paragraph formatting?

  Click the buttons! Try the **Align Left**, **Align Center**, **Increase Indent**, **Bullets**, and **Numbering**. They can be applied to any paragraph.

- How can I tweak the spacing on a single paragraph in my document?

  You can change the spacing before, after, and within paragraphs using the **Paragraph** command on the **Format** menu.

- Why can't I apply more than one type of page formatting in my document?

  You can, but page formatting is contained with section breaks. Create a section break with the **Break** command on the **Insert** menu. You can now apply new page formatting after the section break.

Chapter 10

What's That in the Margins?

In This Chapter

- Making your page look more interesting
- Setting margins
- Creating and editing headers and footers
- Easy page numbering

You may not be satisfied with the constraints of a normal page of text in Word 2000. If you are interested in journeying beyond the normal confines of a typical document, this chapter gives you the know-how to create elements that appear in the margins—the famous headers and footers. In fact, we'll even adjust those margins for you.

Natural Extensions to Your Pages

Look closely at a page from a textbook or novel and you'll notice there is a lot more information than just the words on the page. You also find page numbers at the top or bottom of each page, either in the corner or centered. By convention, the top of the left page of an open book contains information such as the book title or section name, whereas the top of the right page includes the name of the current chapter or the title of the article. These bits of helpful information are referred to as headers if they are located at the top of the page, and footers if at the bottom.

If you attempted to add these professional touches to your own documents by staying inside the margins, you would quickly notice a substantial loss of writing space. Luckily, you can add all of these features to your documents in space that otherwise wouldn't be used—the margins.

Laser Printers Can't Print Here

Remember not to set your margins less than 0.25 inch on the left or right side if you plan to print using a laser printer. Most laser printers are designed to ignore any text within a quarter-inch of the paper edge.

Look Good with Three-Holed Paper

If you plan to print using three-holed paper, set the left margin to 2 inches. This setting enables comfortable viewing of your text even if the pages are placed in a tight three-ring binder.

Adjusting Margins Using Page Setup

Word 2000 automatically sets your margins at one inch from the top and bottom, and 1.25 inches from the right and left sides. If you aren't happy with these default settings, you can change them. And you can choose to either change the margins on your entire document or just on selected text. Open the **File** menu and choose the **Page Setup** command. In the **Page Setup** dialog box, click on the **Margins** tab if it isn't in front. The actual margin settings are listed near the top left of this box, and you can change them easily by typing over the value (you can leave off the inch symbol) or by clicking the increase/decrease arrow buttons for any item.

Don't forget to look in the **Preview** box. The sample document demonstrates the effect of your changes immediately. This is a live picture of a sample document that changes as you choose different margin values.

Now look at the **Apply To** drop-down list near the bottom of the **Page Setup** dialog box. Now it's big decision time. If you happen to be in the middle of your document and you are changing your margins, you must decide if you want them changed starting at this point, or changed throughout your entire document. Choose either **Whole Document** or **This Point Forward**.

Click the **OK** button, and your new margins are applied to your document. Automatic formatting occurs to adjust any existing text, columns, or pictures.

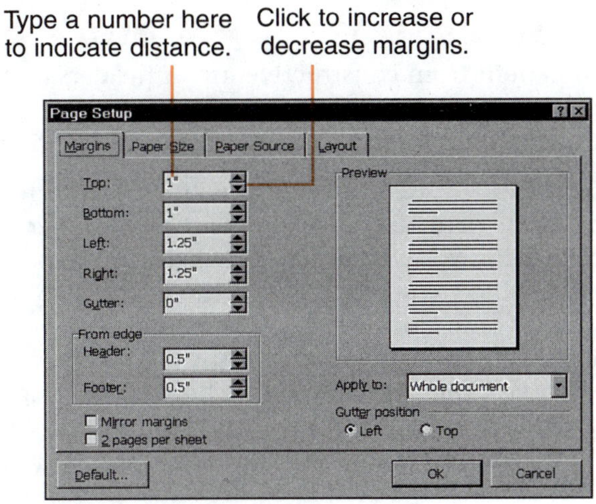

Figure 10.1: Changing your margins in the Page Setup box.

Adding a Header or Footer

You can make your document more interesting by creating your own headers and footers, and placing whatever information helps to clarify your document to your reader.

To make your document even more interesting, you can use a unique header or footer on the first page only of the document or each section, or omit a header or footer on the first page of the document or section. And for anyone creating a document with printing on both sides of individual pages, to be fastened or bound like a book, you can use different headers and footers on odd and even pages or for each section in a document.

Headers and Footers

A *header* is information that can be printed in the top margin of a page, either on every page, every odd page, every even page, or just the first page. Typical information included in a header includes book titles, chapter headings, and sometimes page numbers. A *footer* contains information such as page numbers and footnotes and is printed at the bottom of the page, in the bottom margin.

Putting Useful Things in Headers and Footers

Large documents really benefit from constructive use of headers and footers. An open document lying on your desktop can be instantly identified with the title or subject of discussion, and the page number provides a relative location within the document.

But don't waste toner; always put useful things in your header or footer! Include good information such as the date, document name, page number, title, and other information that helps identify your document or where you happen to be within the document. And understand that certain conventions apply to where you place information. For instance, if your document will be bound, you will have right- and left-hand pages. Book titles usually appear on the left-hand page header, while chapter or section titles are on the right-hand page header. Although Word doesn't provide a way to automatically insert book titles and section headings into headers, they aren't that hard to create. What does Word provide? Handy and helpful information like the date or time, the author, or the name of the document. Headers and footers like these are simple enough to make, so let's get started.

To create a header or footer, open the **View** menu and choose the **Header and Footer** command. You'll see the Header and Footer toolbar. If needed, click inside the header area to establish the insertion point, and begin typing the desired text. Press the **Tab** key one time to center this text and twice to right-align it. You can add character formatting, such as bold or italic, by clicking on the appropriate buttons on the Formatting toolbar. If you'd rather be in the footer box, click the **Switch Between Header and Footer** button.

Just in case you tried, you cannot edit text and graphics in the main document while the header or footer areas are visible.

In the Header and Footer toolbar, there are several buttons for creating the header and footer information you want. Here's a rundown on what they do:

Insert AutoText. Choose from the most common items for your header and footer, such as filename, author, date last printed, and so on.

Insert Page Number. Inserts the current page number of your document. Provides a single number—the total number of pages in your document.

Insert Number of Pages. (Although it's easier to use "Page X of Y" found in Insert AutoText).

Format Page Number. Change the font to match your page text (helpful, since the default is Times New Roman).

Date. Inserts today's date into your header/footer.

Time. Provides a current time stamp to your document.

Page Setup. Brings up the Page Setup dialog box.

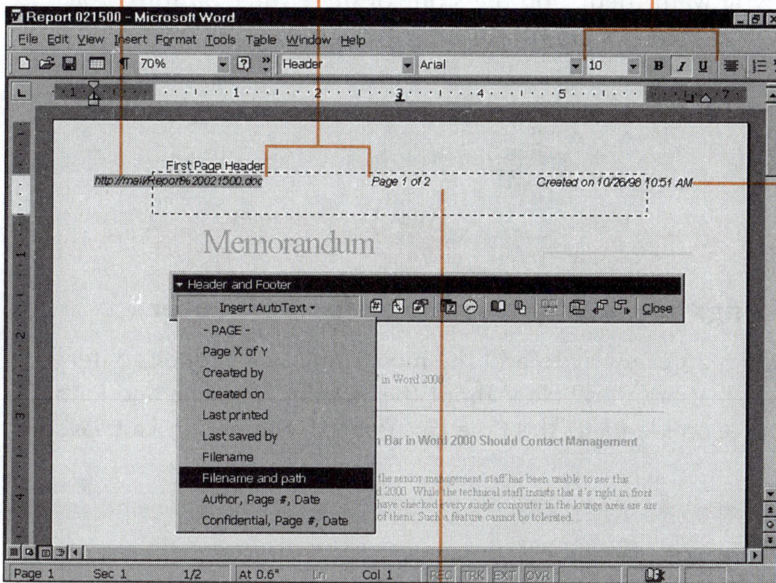

Figure 10.2: Putting useful things in your headers and footers.

Show/Hide Document Text. Helps you concentrate on the header/footer by hiding your document temporarily (until you press it again).

Same as Previous. Copy the previous one to this location. Useful to match up even and odd pages.

Switch Between Header/Footer. This moves you quickly between the two.

Show Previous. Take a look at the previous page header/footer.

Show Next. If you're in the middle of a document, take a peek at the header/footer on the next page.

Close. Returns you to your document, saving the header/footer changes.

You can type whatever you want to have appear, such as a title or heading, or you can choose from a whole list of the most commonly requested header/footer items provided by Word 2000. The list provided by Word 2000 is found by clicking the **Insert AutoText** button on the Headers and Footers toolbar. Some of these header and footer things are pretty smart, because they can display information that can change, such as the date or time, or things unique to the document, like the title or author. The instant you place these in your document, they change to become the name or value of what they represent. The three bits of information most commonly used in headers and footers—Page Numbers, Date, and Time—are included right on the Headers and Footers toolbar. Just place the insertion point at the location in the header or footer where you want them, and press one of these three buttons. You can mix or match any combination of them in the same header or footer.

Finally! Things You Really Need in a Header/Footer

Word 2000 now provides an easy way to add the most commonly requested items in a header or footer. What are they? How about the Author, Filename and Path, Page X of Y, the word "Confidential," the time Last Printed, the person Last Saved By, and a few more.

How easy is it? Just view the Headers and Footers toolbar and click the **AutoText** button on this newly designed toolbar. Pick what you want from this list! You can place as many as you like in either header or footer.

Formatting Those Page Numbers Is Easier

Because there's now a **Format Page Number** button on the Headers and Footers Toolbar, just click this button and you'll have the correct selection of your page number, waiting for you to choose a different font, size, color, and so on.

Using Different Headers/Footers on the First Page

You can use a unique header or footer that appears only on the first page of the document, like a special title. You can also get rid of a header or footer on the first page of the document or section. Word also provides the capability to put a header or footer only on odd or even pages, and you can also limit your headers and footers to appearing in only a particular section of your document.

By clicking on the **Page Setup** button on the Header and Footer toolbar, you can select special options, such as **Different First Page** (for a header that's different on the title page, for example) and **Different Odd and Even** pages (for headers that are different for the left- and right-hand pages). If you want, you can also change the placement of the header or footer in relation to the edge of the page.

Check to alternate headers/footers by page.

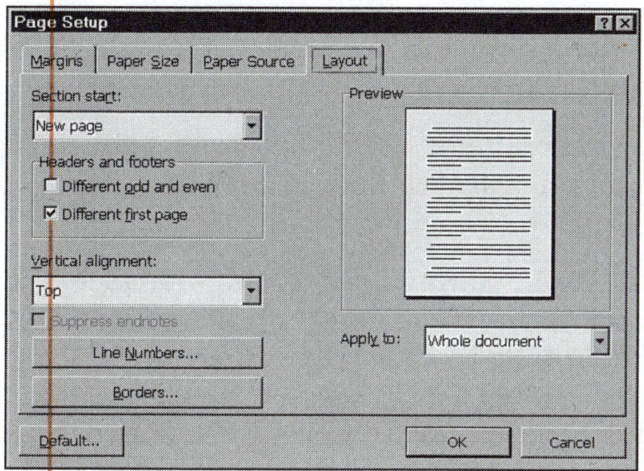

Check to use unique headers/footers on first page only.

Figure 10.3: Customize pages on which headers/footers appear.

Want Only Page Numbers? There's an Easier Way

You don't have to create headers and footers just to add the page number to every page in your document. Instead, you can open the **Insert** menu and select the **Page Number** command. Under **Position**, select either **Top of Page** or **Bottom of Page**, and also choose alignment. Click **OK**, and you've got page numbers!

Viewing Headers and Footers

So where are they, you ask? You certainly created them, and you may swear to this fact, but they disappeared from view when you clicked the **Close** button. Don't panic, unless you have doctor's orders—then it's okay. The headers and footers are really there, trust me. Of course, you could print your document to see them, but in the interest of saving paper, you can also view the headers and footers if your document is in the **Print Layout** view. Open the **View** menu and choose the **Print Layout** command. Your normal editing view is replaced with a more accurate rendering of what your pages really look like. The headers and footers in the margins are printed in a slightly lighter color on your screen so you don't confuse what they are.

Editing Headers and Footers

To edit an existing header or footer, go to the page it's on, open the View menu and select the **Header and Footer** command. An area opens enabling you to edit the header. If it was the footer you were after, click **Switch Between Header and Footer**.

Now edit the changes you require by typing over what's there. Or use any of the editing tools; they all work just as well here as anywhere else. When finished, click the **Close** button on the Header and Footer toolbar.

You can also take a shortcut in editing headers and footers if you're using **Print Layout** view. You can actually see them, although they appear faded. All you need to do is double-click in this area and the Headers and Footers toolbar appears.

The Least You Need to Know

Things can hide in the margins of our documents. Headers (at the top) and footers (at the bottom) are natural extensions to our documents. There's no reason to avoid them when you have useful information to provide.

- So what exactly is a header or a footer?

  These refer to helpful bits of text or graphics placed at the top or bottom of a page, beyond the confines of your document text. The best example of a header is the page number; you don't notice it or think of it as being part of your document until it is printed.

- What kinds of things can I put in a header or footer?

  Besides basic text you can include dates, filenames, page numbers, titles, and even small graphics.

- What's the best way to view headers and footers?

  Editing and viewing a header or footer are easiest when you are in the **Print Layout** view. Simply double-click any header or footer and the editing box will be activated.

- It looks as if my footer is being squished. What can be done?

  You can change margins to give your headers and footers more breathing room. Open the **File** menu and click the **Page Setup** command. Here you can adjust the margins and view the results at the same time.

Chapter 11

Decorating Your Document with Pictures

In This Chapter

- Placing clip art graphics in your document
- Where to find zillions of clip art graphics (hint: the Web)
- Wrapping your words around your graphics
- Adding borders, callouts, and captions

A picture may be worth a thousand words, as long as it's legal and no one gets hurt. Think of how much typing you'll save! Even if your picture isn't worth a thousand words, illustrating your document with pictures or graphics can make your pages more appealing and help convey meaning much faster to your readers—assuming you pick the right graphic and put it in the right place. You pick the graphic and the location, and we'll show you what to do.

Tell Me About Pictures and Graphics

We need to come to terms with our terms. Everyone knows what a picture is, and a picture by any other name looks as sweet. Shakespeare would have told Microsoft that the word *graphic* is an adjective, but in the modern computer world, it is also the term used for anything resembling a picture.

Graphic or Picture?

Many people use these terms interchangeably, but the term *graphic* usually refers to clip art, and *picture* usually refers to scanned images or photos.

You have a lot of freedom working with graphics. The freedom starts by finding or creating any possible graphic you can think of, and you have lots of sources and tools to help you. Next, you get to choose how and where you want to place the graphic in your document. Finally, you have the ability to adjust and manipulate the graphic in unlimited ways.

Where Can You Find a Good Graphic?

Because we live in the digital age, the hunt for existing graphics is relatively easy. Most computer programs, like Word 2000, come packaged with a lot of graphics ready for your use. These simple graphics are called *clip art images*.

If that's not enough, you can purchase additional clip art at any computer store (or the Web) containing graphics categorized by subject. The topics range from *Aquatic Animals* to *Zinnias and Zoysia*, with prices ranging from cheap to mortgage-your-house expensive.

You can also search for free graphics on the Web. Search using words like pictures, graphics, clip art, bitmaps, PIX, GIF, PCX, JPEG, and TIFF. Be forewarned that many graphics contain mature themes, with content that may shock and offend you. With some patience you're likely to find what you need.

Who Owns That Graphic?

Many graphic images (especially popular images) are copyrighted material in most countries. That means you can't copy them or scan them and then use them as your own in your own document; you are required to obtain permission from the author or owner of the graphic, and even reference the source in your document.

Also, you can't just take a picture of someone and use it without his or her permission. It's a privacy issue, and a legal one as well. Avoid such problems and look for graphics that are considered in the *public domain*, which essentially means they are free to copy and distribute as you like. The graphics that come with Word 2000 are free for you to use in any way you like.

However, if you are an artist, you may want to create your own graphics with the Drawing tool (see Chapter 17, "Using More Word 2000 Tools"), or you can use even more sophisticated drawing programs available for purchase at your local computer store. And, if you've got a scanner, you can even draw your graphic on a piece of paper, and then scan it. A scanner converts a picture on paper into an electronic file (graphic) that is ready for your use.

All these graphics have file formats associated with them, and the most common have extensions, such as PCX, BMP, GIF, TIF, JPG, and WMF. Who cares? You should, if you want to use the graphic in your document. Make sure the graphic is in one of these common forms that you can work with, or you won't even be able to get started. Most Web documents usually prefer to include JPG or GIF formats, because they require the least amount of space. The TIF format is used when you need excellent image quality; the file sizes are much larger in this format.

Graphic Formats Word 2000 Can Use

Word 2000 provides lots of graphic converters, called filters, to allow your graphic to become a part of your Word document. Some graphics, like bitmap images, don't even need a filter. If a particular filter hasn't been installed yet, Word 2000 installs it as needed. If the format isn't recognized by any of the filters, you may be required to browse the Microsoft Web site for new filters, or you may need to purchase them.

- AutoCAD Format 2D (.dxf)
- Computer Graphics Metafile (.cgm)
- CorelDRAW! 3.0 (.cdr) file
- Encapsulated PostScript (.eps) file
- Enhanced Windows Metafile (.emf)
- Graphics Interchange Format (.gif)
- JPEG File Interchange Format (.jpg or .jpeg)
- Kodak Photo CD (.pcd) file
- Macintosh PICT (.pct) file
- Micrografx Designer/Draw (.drw) file
- PC Paintbrush (.pcx) file
- Portable Network Graphics (.png) file
- Tagged Image File Format (.tif)
- Targa (.tga) file
- Windows Bitmap (.bmp, .rle, .dib)
- Windows Metafile (.wmf)
- WordPerfect Graphics (.wpg) file

Adding a Graphic to Your Document

You now know where to find graphics and what kind of graphics Word 2000 can use. The next big question is how to insert graphics into your document. Based on where you find your clip art, here are the ways to insert it into your Word document:

> Version NEW! 2000
>
> **Searching for graphics?**
>
> Hate sorting through zillions of clip-art images? Find one similar to what you are looking for, and then click the new option **Find More Like This**. The Gallery displays only the graphics that match the categories of your original.

- **From the Word 2000 Clip Art Gallery**. Open the **Insert** menu, point to **Picture**, and choose **Clip Art**. The **Clip Art Gallery** dialog box appears from which you can choose from hundreds of graphic clip-art images. Find the clip art you want and click to select it. Then click the **Insert** button to paste the graphic at the current location in your document.
- **From Another Software Program**. Just open the **Insert** menu, point to **Picture**, and choose **From File**. You'll find the **Insert Picture** dialog box. Then click the **Insert** button to insert the graphic at the insertion point in your document.
- **Draw Your Own**. You can also draw your own pictures by using tools on the new Drawing toolbar. Interested? Turn to Chapter 17, where the Drawing toolbar and tools are covered in detail.

Figure 11.1: Choose from hundreds of clip-art images included in Word 2000.

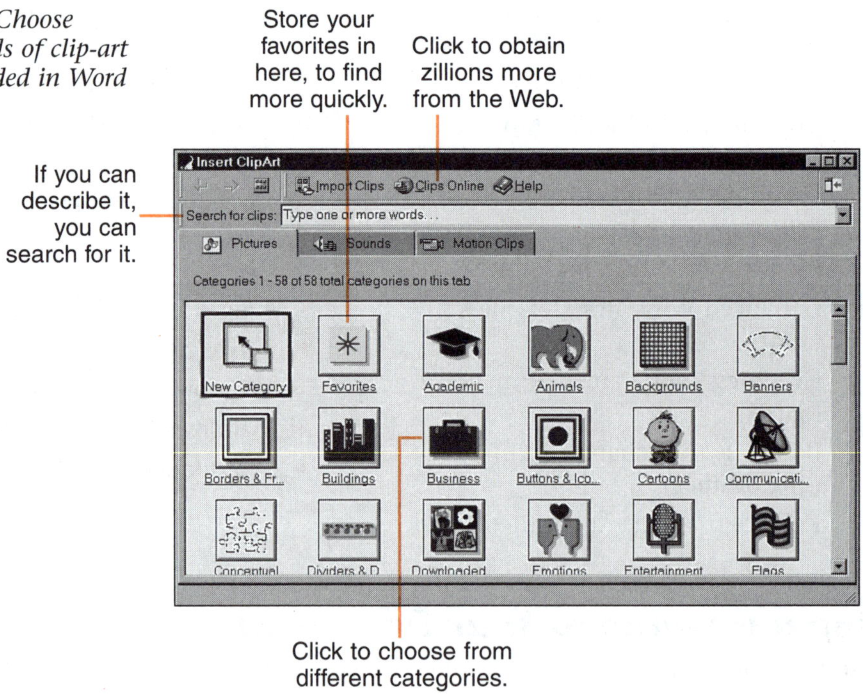

Place Graphics Anywhere!

Because inserting graphics is this simple, you may try to reach new levels of artistic expression. How about placing graphics directly into special parts of your document, like a table, or a header, footer, or footnote? Basically, Word 2000 enables you to put a graphic just about anywhere your heart desires. Whether you or your audience for the document will be able to recognize and interpret it is based on the size, quality, and location of the graphic you choose. You can also crop the picture, add a border to it, or adjust its brightness and contrast. The Picture toolbar helps you complete those tasks.

Version NEW! 2000

Drag and Drop Your Clip Art

The Clip Art Gallery now lets you drag and drop right from the Gallery into your document. And the Gallery stays open, making it a lot faster to add additional graphics.

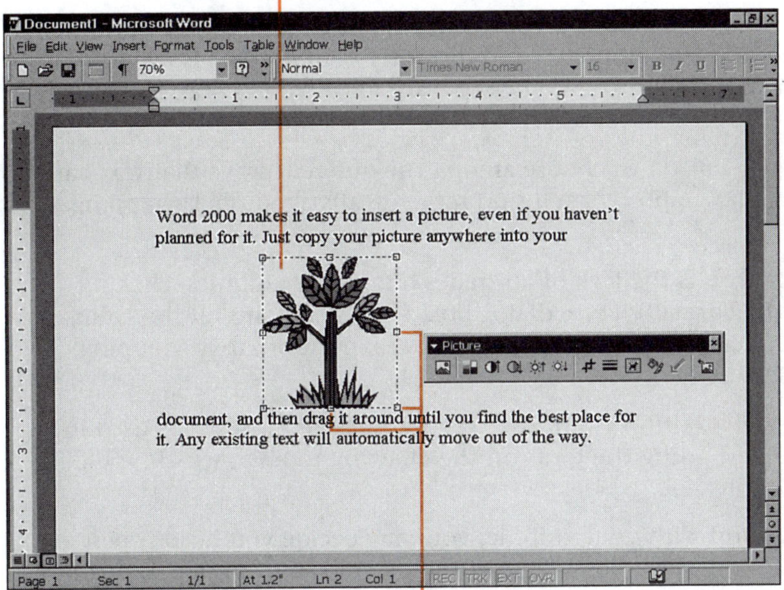

Figure 11.2: Instant pictures can liven up your document.

Make Life Easy with the Picture Toolbar

Each time you click a graphic, the Picture toolbar appears. This is a handy feature because it has everything you need to adjust and fine-tune your graphic to perfection. Spend a minute or two and see what power is packed into this new toolbar.

You can add new graphics right here by clicking the **Insert Picture** button.

To convert your color image to black and white, or shades of gray, click the **Image Control** button.

Just like the knob on your video display, you can click the **Contrast** buttons and adjust the contrast inside a graphic. Use it to reduce or enhance the visual details of your graphic. Use the **More** or **Less** buttons to find the balance you require.

And just like the other knob on your video display, you can click the **Brightness** buttons and adjust the visual impact of your graphic relative to the rest of your document. You use a **More** and **Less** button to adjust the brightness.

To cut away unnecessary parts of your graphic, use the **Crop** button. After clicking the **Crop** button, position the pointer over the graphic handle nearest the offending portion, and drag the handle until you see only what you want. You crop from the outside to the inside, and you can choose any or all of the sides to crop.

To quickly place a line border around your graphic, click the **Line Style** button. Choose the thickness of border you prefer, and instantly your graphic is framed with a border. To change the border thickness, click **Line Style** again and choose a different thickness.

Click the **Text Wrapping** button to choose among the different ways that text can flow around your particular graphic. You'll find more details about text wrapping later in the chapter.

The **Format Picture** button is the jack-of-all-trades button for graphics; clicking this button brings up the Format Picture dialog box, which contains all the color, brightness, contrast, and cropping tools, along with size, position, text wrapping, and line bordering adjustments.

The **Set Transparent Color** button is not used on graphics you insert. It's used for pictures you draw freehand, using the tools on the Drawing toolbar, which you'll learn more about in Chapter 17.

After monkeying around with your graphic, you may decide you liked it best at the beginning. To remove all the adjustments of the previous buttons, click the **Reset Picture** button. The graphic appears as it was when first inserted.

Improved Microsoft Clip Gallery

The Clip Gallery holds hundreds of art clips that are categorized and easy to browse. You can search and find exactly what you need with the **Gallery Find** button. You can edit the categories, and add (import) additional clip art into your gallery. You can even click a **Magnify** button to see more of the details before inserting the art into your document. Finally, to save disk space, the entire collection can be run from the Word 2000 CD-ROM.

Clip Gallery Is Now Tied to the Web!

You'll see a button near the top of your Clip Gallery dialog box. It's called **Clips Online** (Connect to Web for Additional Clips), and if you're into clip art, this is the nirvana button. If you have access to the World Wide Web, you'll connect to a special Web page that lets you choose from a vast array of clip art, and the ones you choose are automatically added to your own Clip Gallery.

Break Up That Graphic

Most clip art is in *metafile* format. One benefit of this format is that you can convert clip art to a drawing object, and then edit it. Try it yourself by selecting it, and then click **Ungroup** on the **Draw** menu. You can then modify it just as you can any other object you draw. For example, you might insert a clip-art image of a building, ungroup it, edit the shape to make it appear closer to your own, and even save the modified image as a new clip-art image.

The Gallery Now Includes AutoShapes

It's getting closer to one-stop shopping for graphics with the Clip Art Gallery. Now **AutoShapes** is included here to save you some steps.

Flow Text Around Your Graphic for a More Professional Result

You can make text flow gracefully around your graphic by using the new Wrapping tools in Word 2000. After you choose the wrapping style for a given graphic, you can move the graphic around, and text will flow naturally around it.

Right-click the graphic you want text to flow around. Choose **Format Picture** on the shortcut menu that appears. In the **Format Object** dialog box, click the **Wrapping** tab to bring its contents to the front. The top row displays the five different text-wrapping styles. The default is **Top & Bottom**, which is why lines of text in our first example stopped abruptly above and below wherever we placed the graphic. Try choosing **Tight**; it works well for most odd-shaped clip art. The other options include flowing text inside your graphic, and allowing text to flow on top of your graphic.

Figure 11.3: Right-click your picture and choose Format Object to see these options.

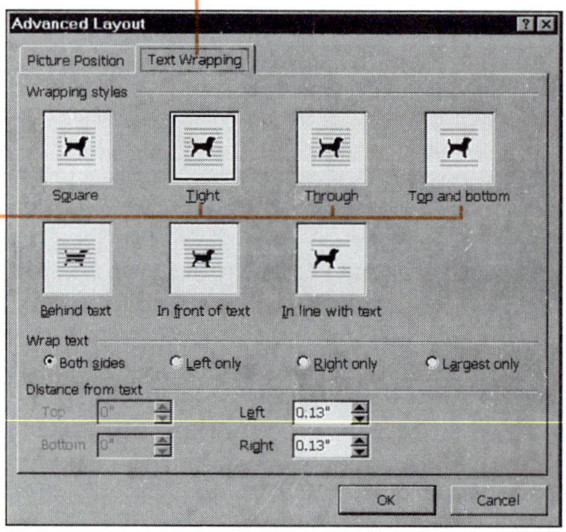

The **Wrapping Styles** in the second row give you additional ways to wrap text around a graphic. This set of options is particularly useful when you must wrap text around a large graphic, which makes the text difficult to follow from one side of the graphic to the other.

Your text can flow smoothly around any shapes.

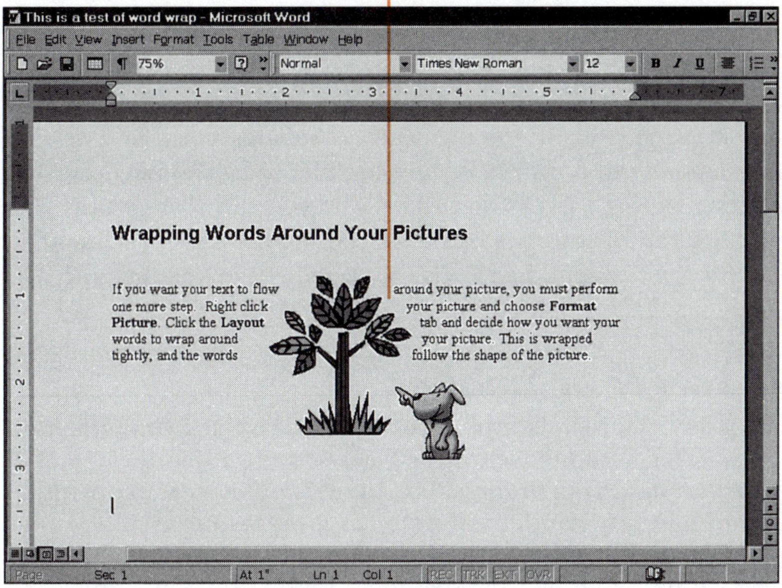

Figure 11.4: That's a wrap!

Deleting a Graphic

To get rid of any graphic, just click to select it. Now press the **Delete** key. It's gone without a trace.

Editing Graphic Images Inside Your Document

Now that the original graphic has become a part of your document, you can manipulate the graphic by squishing, stretching, elongating, enlarging, shrinking, and moving it all around. And when you select a picture, the Picture toolbar appears with tools you can use to crop the picture, add a border to it, and adjust its brightness and contrast.

Moving Graphics Around

After you've placed a graphic in your document, it can be moved anywhere inside your document. Click the graphic to select it, and then use the left mouse button to drag the graphic around your document. Don't worry about the underlying text on the page—it is moved automatically and flows around the new graphic location.

Word 2000 doesn't allow you to split a graphic between two pages, so anything extending beyond the bottom margin is pushed to the next page. The same goes for the sides—Word doesn't allow a graphic to spill over the edge of your paper.

Move 'em and Size 'em in Here

You can also resize and move graphics in the **Format Picture** dialog box. (Find it by clicking the **Format Picture** button on the Picture toolbar, or by choosing the **Format** menu and selecting **Picture**.) Click the **Size** tab and you can change the values for the height and width of your graphic. Click the **Position** tab if you want to use actual distances for the horizontal and vertical placement of your graphic.

Making a Graphic Larger or Smaller

You can change the size of any graphic placed in your document. Click your graphic to reveal its object handles, which are the eight little black boxes on the sides and corners of the box surrounding your graphic. Use these handles to grab on and size your graphic. Click and drag any handle and watch as it resizes the graphic automatically. The top and bottom handles make a graphic taller or shorter, and the side handles make it skinnier or fatter. Corners can do both at the same time.

Improving Image Quality

If your graphic is too light or dark, is the wrong color, needs better contrast, or should be cropped (did we miss anything?), you'll be thankful for the **Format Object** dialog and the **Picture** tab, to be exact. Right-click your graphic and choose **Format Object** on the shortcut menu. Click the **Picture** tab and you'll find slider bars for all these adjustments. You can also crop your picture by setting the measurements in the crop boxes at the top of the dialog box. If you don't like any of your changes, you can click the **Reset** button on this dialog box to restore the graphic as it was.

Putting a Border Around Your Picture

Some graphics look better with a border. If the graphic did not come with a border, you can create one. Borders can be placed around any graphic, whether it has been placed inside a frame (although Word 2000 doesn't require frames, it still supports them, in case you happen to be working with documents saved in earlier file formats). Right-click your graphic to expose the **Shortcut** menu, designed for all your formatting and editing needs. Click the **Format Picture** command to arrive at the same **Format Picture** dialog box in a snap.

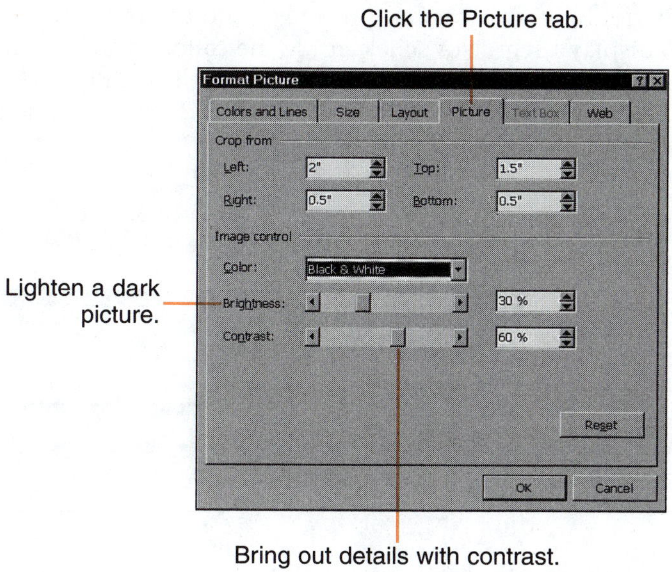

Figure 11.5: Adjust any picture to your liking.

Click the **Colors and Lines** tab to design your border. Choose the thickness of the border by clicking in the **Line Color** text box and choosing either a color, or one of the Patterned Lines displayed when you click this option. You can also provide a background color or texture to your graphic by clicking in the **Fill Color** text box. Choose a fill color from the palette, or click **More Colors** for a wider variety. To experiment with different textures and effects, click the **Fill Effects** option and try the options on any of the **Gradient**, **Texture**, **Pattern**, or **Picture** tabs.

Like shadows? Click to choose your graphic, and then click the **Shadow** button on the Drawing toolbar. Click the shadow type you prefer from the selection provided, and the effect is applied to your graphic. To change the length of the shadow, click **Shadow Settings,** choose one of the four **Nudge Shadow** buttons, and watch your shadow grow or shrink to your command.

Adding a Callout to a Detail in Your Graphic

A callout is that text-in-a-balloon stuff you see in the Sunday comics. Callouts can be helpful in clarifying details in your pictures or graphics, and are easy to apply because they just lie on top of your graphic. You can edit and shape the callout using tools on the new Drawing toolbar. Let's put a callout on our graphic.

If the Drawing toolbar isn't showing itself, open the **View** menu, point to **Toolbars** and choose the **Drawing** toolbar. After you have the toolbar near your graphic, click the **AutoShapes** button and point to **Callouts**. Choose the style and shape of the callout you prefer, and it appears as a floating object on your document. You can immediately start typing text into it, but it's better to drag it into position first, and then make it larger by dragging the callout handles. This is better because the default callout size usually only holds a few letters of typed text, and the rest is hidden until the callout is resized to display them. Now click inside the callout and type anything you want. To start a new line, press **Enter**. You can also format this callout text using any of the formatting features in Word. When you are finished, click outside the callout area.

Callouts can be applied to pictures, text, or anything.

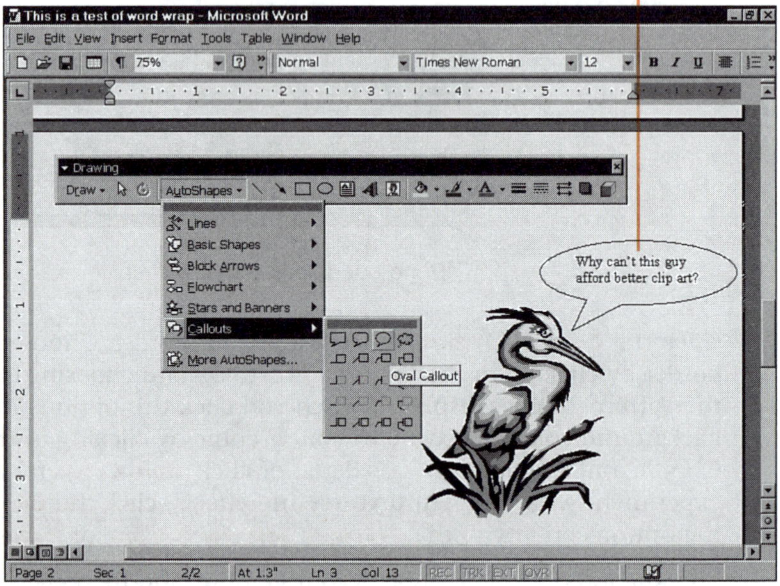

Figure 11.6: Hundreds of options on the Drawing toolbar.

Adding Captions to Things

You may need to do some explaining on certain pictures. Try adding descriptive titles to objects such as graphics, tables, figures, equations, and so on. These titles are called *captions*, and Word 2000 provides an easy new way to apply them. You can automatically add a caption to an object when you insert it. Or you can manually add a caption to an item in a document that already exists.

Placing a Caption on an Existing Object

If you have a graphic, table, or other object that requires a caption, first select the object. Then open the **Insert** menu and choose the **Caption** command. The **Caption** dialog box allows you to select from existing caption names (like *Figure* or *Table*), but you can also create your own by typing in the **New Caption** box.

You can also select the position of the caption by clicking and choosing from the list of options presented in the **Position** pull-down list. You can choose from above or below your object.

Adding Captions Automatically

If you plan to add several graphics to a document, and want a caption for each, make it easy on yourself by turning on **AutoCaptions**. If you set this up while placing your first graphic, you'll save tedious steps for the rest—the captions are placed automatically. You can automatically add a caption to a table, figure, equation, slide, video, spreadsheet, sound recording, and just about anything else you can think of.

Open the **Insert** menu and select the **Caption** command. In the **Caption** dialog box, click the **AutoCaption** box. Select the options you want to be captioned automatically when you insert them in a document. Captions are inserted automatically when you add the type of item selected in the **AutoCaption** dialog box. Better yet, they can be consecutively numbered to your specifications if you prefer, so you won't have to remember the last number you used.

Linking Up

Linking means you make a connection between a graphic (or any object) in your document and the original source of the object. That way, if the original object is ever updated or changed, even if the owner forgets to tell you, your document can have the latest update appear automatically.

To create a link to the selected picture rather than embedding it, open the **Insert** menu, point to **Picture**, and choose **From File**. Now select the **Link To File** check box in the **Insert Picture** dialog box. The picture appears just as it did before. The only difference is that each time you open this document, Word automatically updates the picture with the linked source, and you see the latest updated version of the picture. Of course, this requires that the linked source be available when you open this document (no problem if it's linked to another location on your computer's drive, but it might slow you down if linked to another location on your network, or the Internet).

The Least You Need to Know

Anyone can place quality pictures into their documents because Word 2000 already comes packaged with a great selection of Clip Art.

- What's the fastest way to stick a picture into my document?

  You can quickly place a picture (a graphic) into your document by opening the **Insert** menu, pointing to the **Picture** command, and choosing **Clip Art**. Find the graphic you want, click **OK**, and the graphic is included in your document.

- I'm bored with the clip art on my computer. Is there any more?

  Boatloads. If you ever need more than the hundreds of clip-art images that come with Word 2000, click **Connect To Web For Additional Clips** and say hello to zillions of them.

- My graphic is too big for my document. How can I make it smaller?

  All graphics can be shaped and resized by selecting them (that is, clicking them) to reveal their handles, and then clicking and dragging any of the handles in the direction needed for the desired size.

- I have a lot of graphics and need a simple caption to appear under each. What's the best way to do it?

  Open the **Insert** menu and choose **Caption**. Click the **AutoCaption** button and select the style and words you prefer. Now insert the captions in your document. They will maintain a consistent format and be consecutively numbered automatically.

- I want a balloon with text inside my graphic, just like in the comics. What should I do?

  You need a callout (that's what it's called). Locate your Drawing toolbar, click the **AutoShapes** button, and point to **Callouts**. Choose the style and shape and it appears on your document. Drag it into place and then click to type inside.

Chapter 12

Make Your Documents Sing & Dance (Using Mutimedia Features)

In This Chapter

- Spicing up your document with voice clips and sound recordings
- Adding video clips to your document
- Editing sound and video clips inside your document
- Animating text and other effects

Think your document is too boring to send to your audience? Want to knock their socks off by adding real sounds and video recordings? It's no longer considered rocket science to add these multimedia effects to your document, especially since Word 2000 provides all the help. Blast off today with sounds and videos by following along in this chapter.

Tell Me Again, What's Multimedia?

The term multimedia has evolved into the description for any or all of the objects that make you take notice in a document. It might be a sound effect, a voice, animated objects, or video segments. This was once a big-time technical event that you could sell tickets to, but almost all computers now have the power to make it an everyday event. There's no reason you can't add some to your own documents.

Give Me Some Examples!

Here are some examples of multimedia paving the way to riches and glory in today's world, and you can be a part of it:

- Add sound effects, such as applause or breaking glass, to an instructional document to help guide the reader to a conclusion.
- Supplement a training document with short video segments that demonstrate the key ideas.
- Include speeches or conversation so the reader (listener) can hear the inflection and other nuances that provide additional meaning.
- Leave voice messages in everyday announcement documents, such as cafeteria menus or daily bulletins.
- Dictate a letter directly into your computer's microphone, then send it to your secretary to have the thing typed up into a document.
- Speak your mind and record your words as part of your status reports to your boss.

Multimedia Effects Are Great for Web Pages!

Stored videos, speeches, and other recordings are great for your Web documents. You can add them as described in Chapter 22, "Creating a Web Page in Word 2000."

What Do I Need to Get Started?

If you've purchased your computer in the last year or so, it most likely contains everything you need to get started in multimedia.

A sound card. This enables you to play back recorded sounds in your documents. Sound cards also include the capability to record sounds, but first you'll need a microphone with the correct connector to plug into your sound card. A sound card by itself produces enough sound to be heard using headphones, which can plug directly into the sound card. If you want to hear the sound without wearing headphones, you'll need speakers.

Speakers. But not that little one that beeps inside your computer. Speech and music sounds require real speakers, usually connected outside your computer case, but sometimes they are integrated into the case (often in laptops) or even on the sides of your computer display. Nothing fancy is needed, and a good small pair (two provide stereo sound) won't cost much more than dinner for one in the city (less than $30). Speakers plug right into your sound card, and also require electrical power in the form of batteries or an AC-adapter that plugs into a wall outlet.

A capable video card. Multimedia includes graphics animation and video, and the video can slow down your computer if it's not prepared to handle it. The way to speed things up is to get a fast video card with lots of video memory.

A microphone. If you want to record your own voice, you'll need a microphone. Most sound cards come with a microphone that gets the job done, but you can spend lots more money if you want.

A CD-ROM player. A multimedia computer can play your music CDs in the background while you work on other things. Most software, clip art, and computer games are now purchased on CD-ROM, so this investment is almost a necessity.

If you don't have any of this, all the components are readily available at your local computer store or dealer. If you are handy with a screwdriver, you can probably install all of them yourself. Or, your computer store can install them for you at a reasonably small fee.

Want to watch real video or animations on your computer screen? You'll need a media player program. By a stroke of incredible luck, you have purchased Microsoft Word 2000, which includes the incredible Media Player that gets the job done nicely. You'll learn more about the Media Player program later in this chapter.

Want to record your own video? You need either a digital camera that connects to your computer, or an adapter for a common VCR camera that connects it to your computer. These can get a little more expensive, into the hundreds of dollars, but the prices are coming down every day.

Upgrading Your PC?

If you discover that your PC is just not up to snuff, and you need a little help figuring out what it takes to bring it up to a multimedia machine, check out Que's *The Complete Idiot's Guide to PCs, 4th Edition,* by Joe Kraynak.

Adding Sound Clips or Video Clips That Already Exist

If you don't have a microphone to record your speech, it doesn't mean your documents have to be silent. You can add sounds that have been prerecorded. It's becoming more common to find sound files in places all over the Internet, but you don't have to look that far. The Word 2000 (and Office 2000) CD-ROM comes with lots of categorized prerecorded sound bites that you can use in your documents.

Sample sound clips (and video clips also) are available from the Microsoft Clip Gallery. The easiest way to get there is to open the **Insert** menu, choose the **Object** command, then find and select the **Microsoft Clip Gallery** in the **Object Type** selection box. The **Clip Gallery** dialog box opens and the CD-ROM is accessed automatically to display additional clip art pictures, sounds, and video clips.

Figure 12.1: The Clip Gallery also provides sounds and videos.

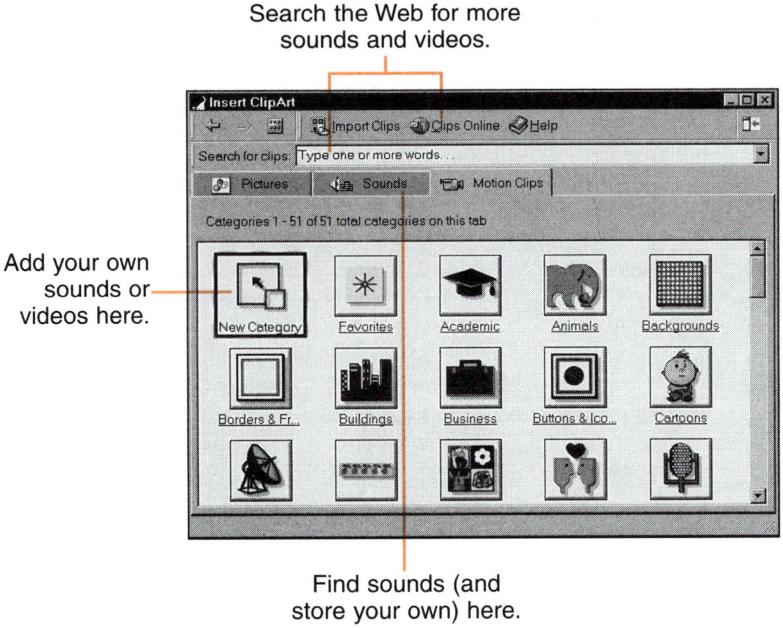

See the tabs for **Pictures**, **Sounds**, and **Motion Clips**? Word 2000 considers sound clips and video clips to be just another object you can add to your document, like a graphic. Click the **Sounds** tab to bring it to the front, and make sure **All Categories** is selected in the list of categories on the left. You see several sample sound clips, each with a descriptive name and a time duration. After you find a sample sound clip you want to include in your document, click to select it, and then click the **Insert** button. The sound clip gets inserted into your document at the cursor position.

Want more? Click the new **Clips Online** to connect you to preprogrammed Web sites containing thousands of more samples of clip art, sound recordings, and video clips.

What if you've been given a sound or video file on a disk? Try inserting it into your document as a Media Clip. After placing the insertion point in your document at the desired location for the sound, open the **Insert** menu and choose **Object**. In the **Object** dialog box choose **Media Clip** from the **Object** type list. Now locate the sound file you want to add and click the **Insert** button.

You can use this **Media Clip** object whenever you want to insert sound, video, voice recording, and other multimedia effects.

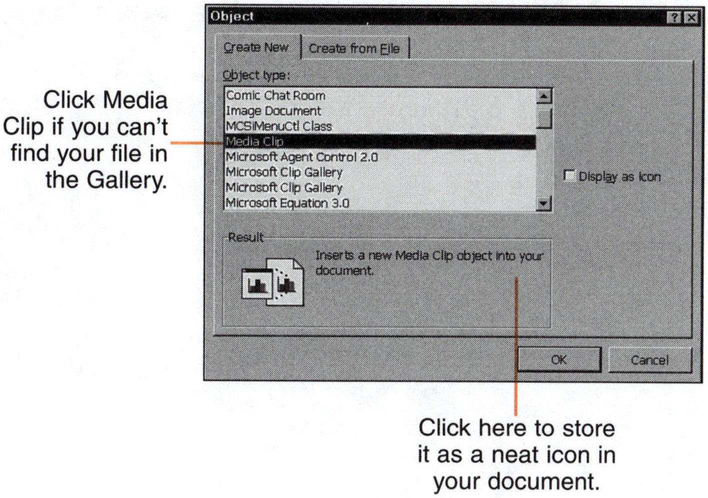

Figure 12.2: Adding Media Clips through the Insert Object dialog box.

Add All Your Sounds and Videos to the Clip Gallery

You can save steps later by adding your additional sound and video files to the Clip Gallery. Click the **Import Clips** or **Clips Online** button on the **Clip Gallery** dialog box and locate your file. You'll be able to give it a title and place it in a category. The next time you need this file, you'll know exactly where to look!

Let's Hear Those Sound Clips

After the sound is inserted in your document, it appears as a small media icon. To play the sound, just double-click the icon. The sound starts automatically. When it's finished, you can hear it again by clicking the **Play** button, or by double-clicking the icon.

Figure 12.3: Shhh! Let's hear the speech!

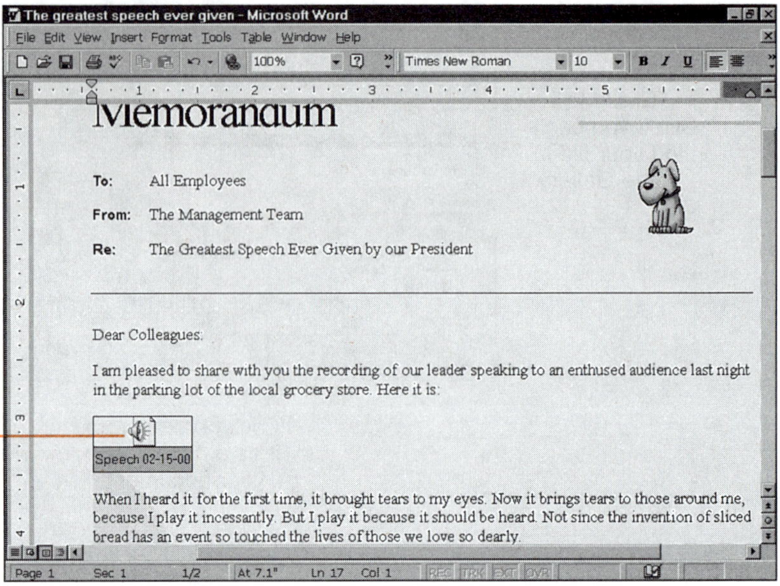

Here's the icon that alerts your reader.

Inserting Voice Comments While Revising a Document

You can attach voice recordings as a part of revising a Word 2000 document. To listen to your voice comments (these were called annotations in earlier versions of Word), your audience must have a sound card installed on their computer. To record comments, you must also have a microphone.

This might sound confusing at first, but Word 2000 offers two different and distinct methods to record voice comments in a document. The previous part of this chapter showed you how to add sounds using the Clip Gallery and the Media Object. Here we discuss the second alternative called the Comment, which is inserted in a similar way. When would you use a Comment over a Sound Clip? Comments are usually used by multiple people during a document revision, because it provides an additional window on the screen to help identify and organize the comments of the reviewers. To insert a voice comment, open the **Insert** menu and click **Comment**. The bottom of the screen splits into the Comments pane, where your voice comment can be recorded. Click the **Insert Sound Object** button and record your voice comment. If Word displays a message asking whether you want to update the sound object, click **Yes**. After recording the comment, click the **Close** button.

To test your recorded comment, right-click the **Sound** icon in the Comments pane and choose **Play** from the shortcut menu. If you don't like what you hear, you can click the **Cut** button or press the **Delete** key to remove this comment, then record another. Once the comment meets your approval, you can save your document and the sound will remain as part of the document. To close the Comment pane, click the **Close** button.

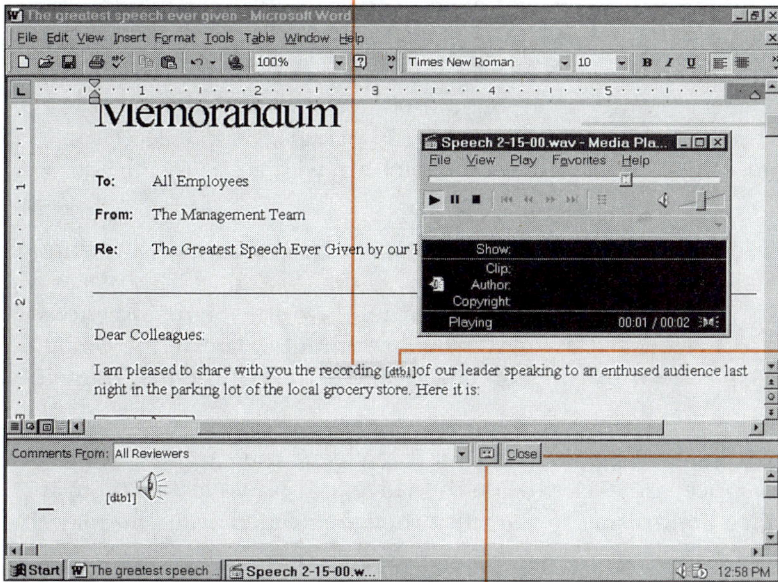

Figure 12.4: Record a voice comment inside your document.

Listening to Comments in Your Document

When a friend opens your document and wants to listen to your comment, they simply double-click the sound icon and the Media Player appears. Click the **Play** button in the Media Player and the comment is played back. Click the **Close** button (the upper right corner of the window) to close the Media Player when you are finished listening to the comment.

Launch Options for Multimedia

As a listener to comments, you can choose when a media clip plays. This can happen either when you double-click it, or as soon as the document is opened, or as a customized event (bring up **Media Player**, but wait for me to click the **Play** button). You can choose one of these settings in your Media Player. Open the **Tools** menu and click **Animations Settings Object**. Place a check in the option you prefer.

Adding Video to Your Documents

Inserting a video (now called a *motion clip*) is just as simple. For inserting prerecorded video clips that come with your Word 2000 (or Office 2000) CD-ROM, place the CD-ROM in your computer, open the **Insert** menu, point to **Object**, and choose the **Clip Gallery**. Click the **Motion Clips** tab to bring the samples to the front. Click in the desired category, select the video clip of your choice, and click the **Insert** button. The video clip is inserted in your document. To play back the video clip, double-click it with your mouse. To close the clip, click anywhere else inside your document.

To insert a recorded video clip from another source, open the **Insert** menu and choose **Object**. In the **Insert Object** dialog box, choose the **Microsoft Media Clip**. This places a small media clip icon in your document. Now open the **Insert Clip** menu and choose between the supported formats that may exist on your computer. Locate the actual video file and click the **Open** button. The icon changes to a view of the first frame of your video.

All the controls for playing your video are now on the screen. You can play, rewind, fast-forward, and so on. Once you click outside the video and on your document in the background, the video controls disappear until they are needed again. To play the video again, just double-click the media icon.

More on the new Media Player

The easiest tool to use with multimedia is the Media Player, and it's included in Word 2000. The Media Player application enables you to embed video clips, animation clips, MIDI (Musical Instrument Digital Interface) sequences, and sound clips in your Word 2000 document.

To open and learn more about your Media Player, click the Windows 95 or Windows NT **Start** button, point to **Programs**, then point to **Accessories**, next to **Multimedia**, and finally choose the **Media Player** icon. Whew! Want an easier way to open it? Just find a supported multimedia file and double-click. The Media Player opens automatically in preparation for playing the file.

With the Media Player open, notice the **Device** menu. Click to open it and you find the list of all categories of supported multimedia files, including videos, sound, and audio CDs. By choosing each device, you get a file open dialog box that views only those files of the proper type for that device (choose **Sound** and you see only sound files, and so on). When the Media Player is opened by double-clicking a multimedia file, the proper device is automatically chosen for you.

The other very important command on this **Device** menu is the **Volume Control**. Choose it to adjust the volume and balance (between the right and left of your stereo speakers) for each of your multimedia devices.

The Media Player includes all the buttons you typically see on a tape recorder or VCR. You can play, stop, pause, rewind, and fast-forward to arrive at any point inside your sound or video clip. Here are some tips on using the buttons in the Media Player:

- **Rewind** or **Fastforward**. To rewind the recorded sound or video, drag the slider to the left (rewind) or right (fast forward). You can also click one of the following buttons to rewind to a specific spot.
- **Rewind automatically**. To have your multimedia file rewind automatically when it's finished playing, open the **Edit** menu and click **Options**. Click to choose either **Auto Rewind** or **Auto Repeat**.
- **Change the Scales on Your Media Player**. Depending on the type of file you are playing, you can choose a scale that represents time in seconds, frames in the video or animation file, or tracks on the CD. With the multimedia file opened, click to open the **Scale** menu. Now choose the type of scale you want to display.

Play It Back Quick!

A fast way to play back most multimedia files is to use the right mouse button. Simply right-click the media icon and choose the appropriate command from the shortcut menu that appears.

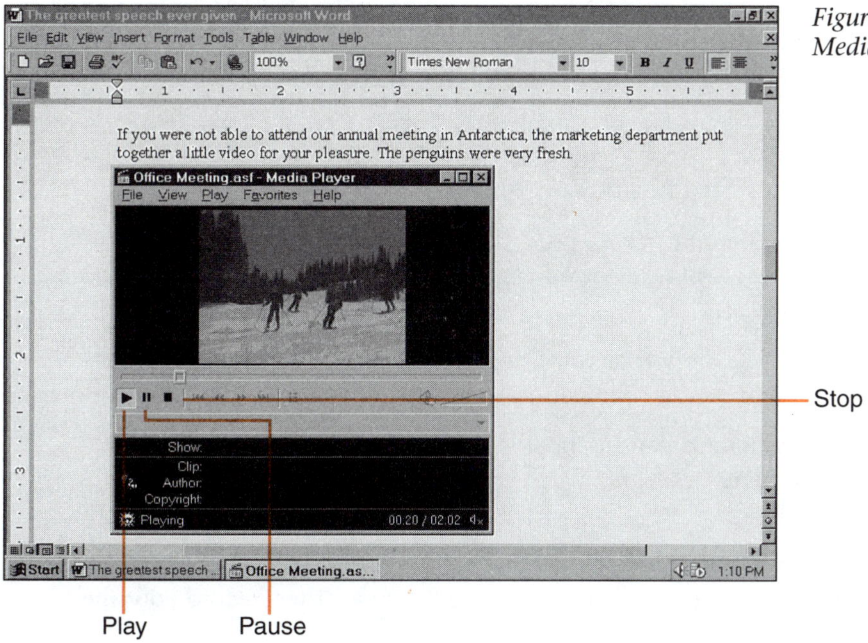

Figure 12.5: Running the Media Player.

Link Sound Files to Your Document

When a sound (or video) file is linked, the new document is updated automatically if the information in the original recording changes. If you want to edit the linked recording, double-click it. The toolbars and menus from the program that was used to create the information appear.

When to Link a Large Multimedia File Instead

Because multimedia files (like sound, but especially video) are so large, they are often stored with others like them in a shared area on a central server (perhaps a file server at your business, but it could be a folder on your computer). Instead of inserting these large files into your document, making your document very huge, you can point to them instead. You do this by linking a multimedia file to your document. An added benefit to linking multimedia files to your document is that if anyone updates the original multimedia file, your document points to the update automatically. All you need do is double-click the multimedia icon to get the updated version.

To try linking for yourself, open the **File** menu, click **Open**, and then find and double-click the multimedia file you want to link. Open the Word 2000 document you want to link the file to, and then click where you want it to appear. On the **Edit** menu, click **Paste Special**. Click the format you want to use, and then click **Paste Link**. It sounds like a lot of steps, but you benefit by having a document that's much smaller in size (because the media file is stored separately), and if the media file ever changes, your document is updated automatically.

The Least You Need to Know

Your documents may benefit from a prudent use of multimedia effects such as sound and video. This chapter reviewed the methods used to place multimedia in your documents, such as:

- Look in the Clip Gallery that came with Word 2000. You find lots of prerecorded sound and video files, and automatic links to the Web to get more.
- Quick voice comments can be included in a document by opening the **Insert** menu and choosing **Comment**. Click the **Insert Sound Object** button and record your message.
- Record your own audio clips by inserting a **Media Clip** icon in your document. Then open the icon and select a format, then record your file.
- Editing sound and video clips inside your document is easy when you use the Media Controls.

Chapter 13

Your Table Is Being Prepared

In This Chapter

- Important and unexpected uses of tables
- Creating a table to organize your information
- Making your table look nicer with borders and shading
- Moving around inside a table
- Making changes to an existing table
- Getting rid of tables you hate

Who cares about tables besides accountants and restaurant owners? You should, because Word 2000 can make your document-formatting life much easier. Using a table is a good way to line up information neatly (like a résumé). And just because it's a table doesn't mean it has to be a box with gridlines separating your words or figures, either. Tables can be subtle, even invisible, and still have the power to control the placement of your information.

Setting the Table

Tables present information in rows and columns. They're great for organizing information in your faxes, letters, memos, and reports. You can use tables to show lists of data, personnel rosters, financial information, scripts, and procedural steps. A reader usually finds it easier to locate and understand detailed information when it is presented in a table. You will discover that you can place just about anything in a table, including pictures, and then format the content of the table using all of the features you learned in the past few chapters.

Table Definitions

A *table* is a collection of rows and columns, just like a simple spreadsheet. Each row and column inside a table is made up of units called *cells*. A single cell is where a row and a column intersect. A cell is where you type a table entry. The smallest table consists of a single cell (not very useful), while the largest can contain thousands of cells, spanning as many pages as is necessary. Entire documents can be created inside a table.

A common résumé is one of the best examples of a document that's easier to create and edit using a table rather than tabs or margins. You might not think it at first, until you generalize that tables are nothing more than text lined up neatly in columns. A résumé has dates or companies lined up on the left, and experiences described to the right. A perfect match for a table. Tables are also an easy way to align paragraphs side by side. What about table lines, you ask? Well, tables don't always require lines or borders, which aren't always needed or wanted. Let's table any further discussion until we review the basics.

When to Create a Table in your Document

I bet you have used the Tab key in the past to create simple (or complicated) tables. There's nothing wrong with that at all. In fact, a very small table with two columns and short words can still be created easily using nothing but the Tab key. But, if your table requirements include any of the following, you may find that tabs just don't make the grade when it comes to controlling the appearance of your tables:

- The need to hold more than a column or two of information
- The desire to line up paragraphs side by side
- The desire to use the length of tables that will extend beyond a single page
- The desire to apply special formats to individual rows or columns
- The desire to add gridlines and borders to show off your table

Any or all of these requirements point you to using the Word's Table feature, which can be as easy or as sophisticated as you want to make it.

The Cool Way to Create a Table

By far the easiest way to create a perfect table in Word 2000 is using the Table feature and your mouse. Decide where you want the table to exist in your document, and click to place the insertion point there. Did I mention it's always a good habit to save a document before going on vacation or trying a stunt like this? Now click the **Insert Table** button on the Standard toolbar.

The table grid drops down, presenting the most popular table sizes. Picture in your mind the size of the table you want, and then use your mouse to select it. Drag the mouse down and to the right to highlight the size of table you desire. As you drag the mouse pointer, the grid expands to create rows and columns like a miniature table. The resulting table size is displayed at the bottom of this grid. When you release the mouse button, your table is created precisely the way you sized it. An empty table is instantly created in your document, waiting to be filled with your wisdom. How's that for simplicity?

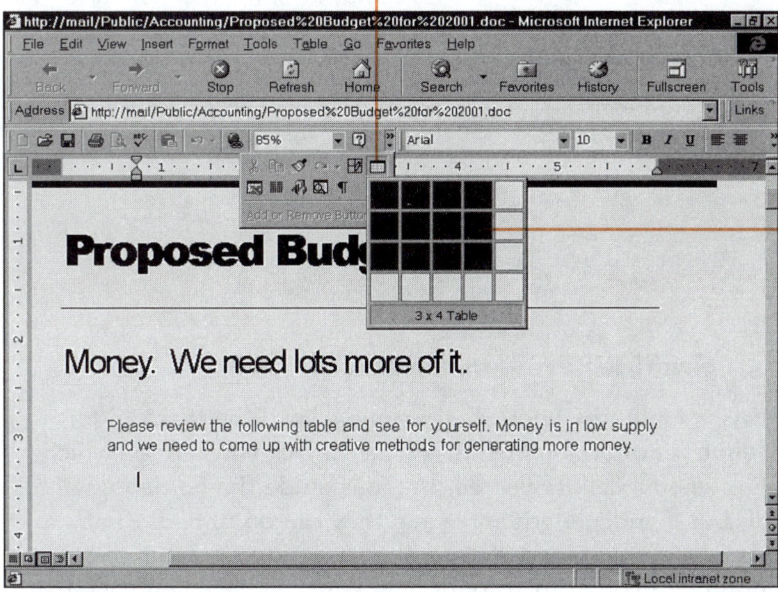

Figure 13.1: The easiest way to create a quick table.

Still Another Method of Preparing Your Table

If your mouse died, you can still create a table using the keyboard. Word actually offers more options this way, but there are more steps to follow. Once again, make sure you have the document you want opened and saved. Place the insertion point where you want the table to be created. Now open the **Table** menu and select the **Insert Table** command. The **Insert Table** dialog box appears.

Enter the number of columns in the first box. Press the **Tab** key to move to the second box (or click it with the mouse button). Enter the number of rows in the second box. You don't have to be exact at this point because you can easily change the shape after the table is created. Leave Column Width set to Auto to let Word manage them (if you type more, the column automatically gets bigger). Of course, you can set your Column Width now if you know the size you need. Now click **OK** to create your table.

There you go—a table built to your specifications. But it's empty, and empty tables serve little purpose in a document (unless you are creating graph paper), so now it's time to fill it in.

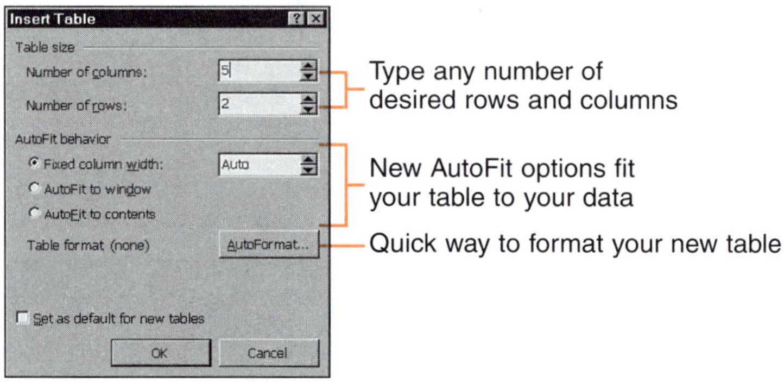

Figure 13.2: Table manners improve with this dialog box.

Gridlines Prevent Gridlock

If you have trouble staying inside the lines when coloring, you'll be thankful for table *gridlines*. Word displays dotted gridlines in a table so that you can see which cell you are working in. When a cell is selected, the area inside the bordering gridlines is highlighted. But if gridlines get annoying, they can be turned off at any time by opening the **Table** menu and clicking the **Hide Gridlines** command. Gridlines cannot be printed. If you want to print lines between cells, you have to add *borders* to the table, which is covered later in this chapter.

Drawing Your Tables by Hand

Now you can use a new drawing feature of Word 2000 to draw tables similar to the way you use a pencil to draw a table. Just substitute the mouse for the pencil.

Ready to try? Click the **Tables And Borders** button on the Standard toolbar and you see the Tables And Borders toolbar.

By default, the **Draw Table** button is already selected when you open the Tables And Borders toolbar. Notice that the mouse pointer now appears as the icon of a small pencil on the drawing space of your document. If you don't see the pencil, be sure to click the **Draw Table** button on the Tables and Borders toolbar.

To start drawing, just click and drag with the left mouse button. The fastest way to draw a table is to create the outside border first, and then the lines inside. To draw the outside border, click where you want the top-left corner to start, then drag to the desired spot for the bottom-right corner. No matter how nervous you are, a perfect rectangle is drawn to your general requirements.

Now draw the row and column lines. Don't worry if the lines aren't even; Word 2000 has tools to straighten them out later. The drawing tool helps by drawing only straight lines. Start by dragging inside your table where you would normally sketch a row or column to appear. Connecting each line to the edge of your table happens automatically as you approach the edge with your drag.

If you make a drawing mistake, you can erase it with the **Eraser** button. Erase the same way you draw, by clicking and dragging the left mouse button over the mistake. You can erase entire lines this way, or just parts of lines. The eraser works only on lines you draw with the Draw Table, so don't try using it to edit footnotes in your document.

Maybe you've had a rough day and your row lines aren't evenly distributed. To spread them out perfectly, select the rows and then click the **Distribute Rows Evenly** button. They'll be perfect in no time.

Likewise, you can select your columns and click **Distribute Columns Evenly** to balance the width and line them up perfectly.

If you lose your creative spirit, you can always click the **Table AutoFormat** button on this Tables and Borders toolbar, and choose a predesigned table to suit your needs.

That's all you need to create a great table, with the feeling of accomplishment that you drew it all yourself. You'll find that sometimes this is the only way to draw complex tables that have combined row headings in multiple areas or mixed-width columns.

Converting Existing Text to Tables

If you've already got text in your document and you'd like to see it entered into a table, why not try a new feature of Word 2000? It's called **Convert Text To Table**, and it works quite well on text or numbers that are already aligned in your document using tabs or commas. This might include a list of names or numbers in your document, or it could be the result of an import of information from a spreadsheet or database, which is often delimited (separated) by a tab or comma.

Give this a try by selecting the entire range of text you want to include, then open the **Table** menu and point to the **Convert** command. You see the **Convert Text to Table** command that attempts to create the most appropriate shape of table based on the selected text. If the result doesn't satisfy you, click the **Undo** button and try something else, such as setting the available row, column, and format options yourself.

You can also perform the reverse of this command, taking a table from your document and converting it to plain text. This might be something you try when you want to break down a large table into smaller pieces. Select the table, then open the **Table** menu and choose the **Convert Table to Text** command. All table lines, borders, shading, and special effects are removed, and you are left with the collection of text or numbers that once appeared in the table cells.

Filling In Your Table with Useful Stuff

After a table has been created, it's a straightforward process to fill it in. If your insertion point isn't already in the first table cell, you can get it there by clicking anywhere inside the cell. Once inside, just start typing. The cell automatically adjusts to accommodate what you type. You can type in words or numbers, or even place pictures in a cell. And Word 2000 actually enables you to create a whole table inside of a table cell, if that interests you (it could come in handy when creating Web pages).

Pressing the **Enter** key inside a cell puts a new paragraph in the same cell. Think of each cell as its own little document, which means the rules of editing and formatting apply.

After filling in the first cell, you can move to the next cell by pressing the **Tab** key. If the insertion point is in the last cell of a table, pressing Tab adds a new row. To move backward to a previous key, press the combination **Shift+Tab** keys. You can also use the Arrow keys to move around between cells inside your table, but the Tab key is faster. Here are a few more navigational tips summed up in, what else, a table:

Table 13.1 Navigating Your Table

To....	Press...
Move to the next cell	Tab
Move to the previous cell	Shift+Tab
Move to the previous or next row	Up or Down arrow keys
Move to the first cell in the row	Alt+Home, or Alt+7 on the numeric keypad
Move to the last cell in the row	Alt+End, or Alt+1 on the numeric keypad

Move to the first cell in the column	Alt+Page Up, or Alt+9 on the numeric keypad
Move to the last cell in the column	Alt+Page Down, or Alt+3 on the numeric keypad
Start a new paragraph	Enter key
Add a new row at the bottom of the table	Tab at the end of the last row
To add text before a table at the beginning of a document	Press Enter at the beginning of the first cell

Formatting Tables Is Easy

After you enter information into your table you may be so excited that you'll print your document to see it for real. Surprise! Not what you expected, I bet. No gridlines, no box around it, in fact, except for lining up your information, it doesn't look like a table at all!

We can fix that. This section explains several ways to improve the look of your tables. We'll start with the automated tools that format an entire table at once, and then move into the tactical tools for formatting individual pieces of a table.

The Magic of Table AutoFormat

The easiest way to make a table fancy is by using another miracle of Word 2000 called *Table AutoFormat*. Just click inside your table anywhere; it doesn't matter where. Now open the **Table** menu and choose the **Table AutoFormat** command. This is the dialog box you see, and it's full of ideas for making your table the best it can be.

Scroll up or down this listing of preformatted sample tables using your Up or Down arrow keys. Watch the Preview box to see if any choices come close to what you want. Don't worry if your table is a different size; the formatting applies to the size of your table. If the table you're planning is much smaller than the samples, however, you may not get the heading or column format shown in the Preview screen. If you can't decide between a few of them, try them all…one at a time, of course. You can always click the **Undo** button on the Standard toolbar to get rid of an end table that doesn't match the rest of the furniture in your document.

If, at a later date, you decide you prefer another style of table, go get it! The information you have already stored in your table is preserved and placed in the new table format. Select your existing table, open the **Table** menu, and run the **Table AutoFormat** command. Choose a new table format from the list and press the **OK** button.

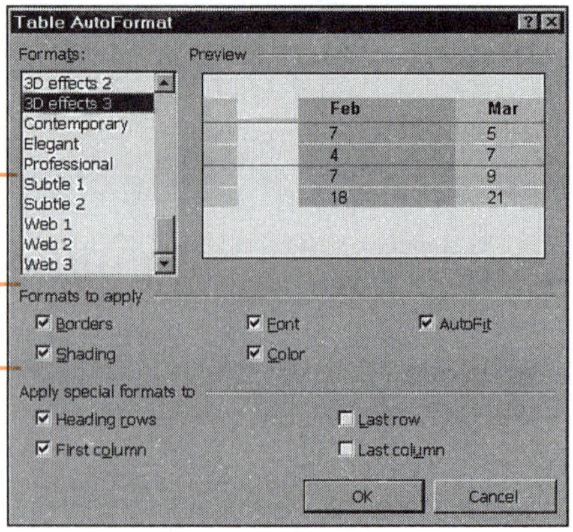

Scroll this list to view different designs.

Add or remove these options for even more variety.

Figure 13.3: Fancy tables await you in the AutoFormat.

Creating Custom Table Borders and Shading Manually

If you're a perfectionist, you may not like any of the table format choices in Table AutoFormat. Whether your table already has a border you don't like, or no border at all, you can create your own custom border (or shading) for it. Start by selecting the entire table (to add borders and shading to only specific cells, select only those cells, including the end-of-cell mark). Open the **Format** menu and choose the **Borders and Shading** command. Click the **Border** tab to make sure it's in front. The easiest way to border your table is to click the **Grid** box, and optionally change to a heavier line width by clicking a fatter line on the right side of the dialog box. When you press the **OK** button, the custom border is applied to your table.

Shading can provide emphasis for important cells in your table. One or more cells can stand out from the rest by giving them a background shading, color, or pattern. To give it a try, select the cells, then open the **Format** menu and choose the **Borders and Shading** command. Click the **Shading** tab to bring the options to the front. In the Fill area, click a shade of gray or a color to appear as the background color. You can also choose to have a background pattern for the selected cells by clicking and choosing the Style and Color boxes in the Patterns area and choosing from the palette that appears. The Preview box gives you an idea of what it looks like. Click **OK** to apply the shading selections to your table.

Using the Tables and Borders Toolbar

Most tables you see in books and magazines are surrounded by crisply detailed lines called borders. Adding a border to your table can help call attention to it on a page. Borders are so common, in fact, that Word 2000 includes an entire toolbar dedicated to creating these borders, the Tables and Borders toolbar. Just right-click any toolbar and choose Tables and Borders. Here are the buttons that control line style and thickness, colors, shading, and more.

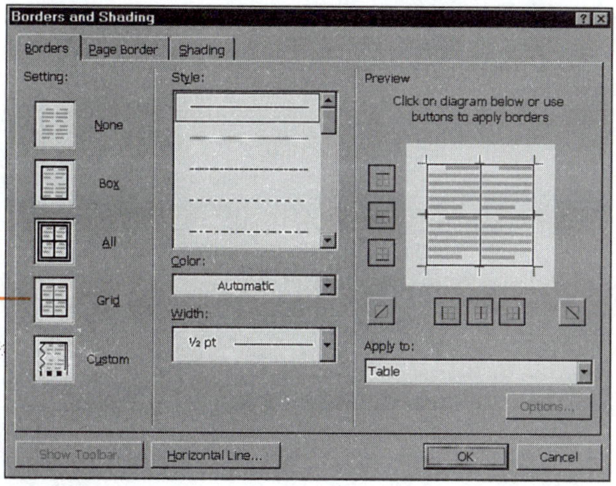

Figure 13.4: Adding a custom border to any table.

For the quickest border, click **Grid** and then **OK**.

Removing Borders and Shading from Your Table

Regardless of how the border was applied to your table, there's an easy way to get rid of it. First, select the table by clicking anywhere inside it. Open the **Table** menu and choose the **Table AutoFormat** command (even if you created the border using the Tables and Border toolbar or the **Borders and Shading** dialog box). In the **Formats** box, click **None**. Click **OK** to close the dialog box, and the borders have disappeared from your table.

Formatting the Contents of Cells

Once your table is formatted, you may still wish to format the individual contents of cells, or even whole rows or columns. No problem, just click and drag to select the portion of the table you wish to change. Anything you can type in a cell is fair game for the formatting tools of Word. You can apply any of the character-formatting options to any cell, group of cells, entire row, entire column, or the entire table.

When in doubt, you can also select rows, columns, or the entire table by clicking in the table and using the **Select** commands on the **Table** menu, or by using keyboard shortcuts.

And Borders Aren't Limited to Tables

Once you learn the method of placing a border on a table, you'll find that it also works for words, paragraphs, and entire pages.

Once the cells are selected, you can apply any of the tools on the Formatting toolbar. Maybe the Bold, Italic, and Underline are growing old. Try changing the font or font size, or arrange the contents with the Center or Right Justify button, or even create a numbered list inside a single cell.

Rotate That Text!

A helpful tool for fitting more text into your tables is the **Change Text Direction** button. If there's not enough room for the text in your table cells, rotate the text and fit it in vertically! You'll find this button on the Tables and Borders toolbar. Just right-click inside any toolbar and choose **Tables and Borders** from the pop-up menu. Select the text in your table, click this button, and rotate the text instantly.

Merging and Splitting Cells

Some tables look better with a heading on the top row. But with multiple columns in a typical table, you always have those column dividers preventing a nicely centered title. You can get rid of column dividers on any given row using the **Merge Cells** command. To create a heading for your table, select the entire first row. Open the **Table** menu and choose the **Merge Cells** command (the **Merge Cells** button also exists on the **Tables and Borders** toolbar). The multiple cells will be merged into one cell across the width of a table. Now you can enter and format your title in this new cell.

On the other hand, sometimes you need to create two cells where only one exists. Select the cell you want to split and then click the **Split Cells** button on the **Tables and Borders** toolbar. You'll see the **Split Cells** dialog box, in which you can choose the ways you want to slice your cell. Type in or click to increment either the columns or rows, or both, then click **OK**. Your table cell is now split into the number of rows and columns you chose.

Editing an Existing Table

Tables hold information, and information changes. Good thing that Word 2000 is packed with features and functions that assist you in your editing process. You can add, delete, or move information from one part of your table to another, adjust the size or number of your rows or columns, and even sort the contents of those cells after you make a change.

Can't See Text in a Cell?

Sometimes you can't see some or all of the text in a cell. What should you do? Give it more room with the new AutoFit options! Click on your table, open the **Table** menu and point to **AutoFit**. You can fit your table to match your data or the room on the page. You'll save lots of time because your data will be made immediately visible. Sure beats the old way!

Moving Information from Cell to Cell

If you need to move a cell's contents, select the contents by clicking in the middle of the cell. Drag the cell to its new location. You copy the contents of one cell to another with a similar technique. To copy a cell, hold down the **Ctrl** key as you drag.

Deleting Information in a Table

If you don't like the contents of any cell in your table, you can get rid of it easily. Your best bet for deleting a cell is to select it, then open the **Table** menu and choose the **Delete Cell** command. This opens a dialog box that provides you with deletion options. If you do not want to leave a cell in the middle of your table blank, you have the option of shifting the cells around it to fill the space. Another available option is to delete either the entire row or entire column.

To remove a larger amount of information in your table, you can delete one or more rows or columns at a time. Click and drag to select an entire row (or rows) and open the **Table** menu. You'll see that the **Delete Cell** command has now changed into the **Delete Rows** command. Choose this command and the row is deleted, and the remaining portion of the table shift to fill the empty space. Likewise, to remove one or more columns, select the columns and choose the **Delete Columns** command; the table shifts to fill the empty space.

If you don't see the command you want on the **Table** menu, it probably means you haven't selected the row or column completely. Try again, or use the command **Select Column** to help you.

Changing the Inner Dimensions of Your Table

A quick way to change the width of any column in your table is to drag either column's edge to a new location. If you want to let Word adjust the widths of columns automatically, you can double-click either edge of a column.

Unless you specify otherwise, the height of each row in a table depends on two things: the contents of the cells in that row and the paragraph spacing you add before or after text. The AutoFit feature has been expanded in Word 2000, and it's time to try it. Click to open the **Table** menu and point to **AutoFit**. Here you can choose to fit your table to match the contents, the window, or simply space rows and columns evenly.

More Headroom in a Table

You can also change row height by using the vertical ruler in **Print Layout** view. On the **View** menu, click **Print Layout**. On the vertical ruler, drag a row mark to the location that adjusts the size to your taste.

Adding Columns and Rows

To add more rows or columns to your table, click to select the area closest to where you want the new row or column placed, then choose either the **Insert Columns** or **Insert Rows** command from the **Table** menu. The new table addition will be added, and the table size will be adjusted to accommodate the new size. You can easily make a table bigger by moving the insertion point to the last cell (the bottom right) and pressing the **Tab** key. A new row of cells will be added.

Numbering Anything in Your Table

Here's an easy method for numbering the cells in your table. First, select the range of cells you want to number. Or, to number the beginning of each row, select only the first column in the table. Click the **Numbering** button on the Formatting toolbar, and the cells (or rows) are automatically numbered. You may have to adjust the size of the column or row to accommodate the new numbering additions.

Sorting Table Information Automatically

Do you get the shakes when you need to prepare a table in alphabetical or numerical order? Shake no more, my friend, and say hello to the powerful sorting features of Word 2000 that remove the pain of sorting—any sorting—in any kind of table, including sorts by date.

For important reasons known by logicians and the people who create the phone book, it's always a good idea to select your entire table, not just a single column, when performing a sort. Selecting only a single column in other word processors, including previous versions of Word, can cause misalignment of other related information in your table. By selecting the entire table, all related information contained in a row gets sorted at the same time, so it all stays together nicely.

Sort This and Sum That

You'll notice that the Tables And Borders toolbar now includes **Sort Ascending** and **Sort Descending**.

As you edit your table, you may find these buttons helpful in sorting the contents. To use them properly, first select the range you wish to sort, then choose either ascending or descending. The cells don't have to be numeric—you can sort alphabetically just as easily.

And to turn your table into a fancy worksheet, the **AutoSum** button is at your service. Let's say you want to sum all the values of a column and put the total at the bottom. Just click in the bottom cell of the column (add an extra row if needed) and click the **AutoSum** button. The cell now contains the sum value of the column.

Select your table and open the **Table** menu. Choose the **Sort** command, which opens the **Sort** dialog box. You can choose to sort on any column by clicking and selecting the column heading in the **Sort By** text box. The default is the first column, which is usually what you want anyway. Click the **OK** button, and a-sorting it will go. If the results look good the first time, save your work and quit while you're ahead. If not, click the **Undo** button and try again.

Calculating Your Information

You can also perform calculations in a table. To add a column of numbers, for example, click the cell below the column you want to add, and then click **AutoSum** on the Tables and Borders toolbar. The result appears in the cell you clicked. For other calculations, use the **Formula** command on the **Table** menu.

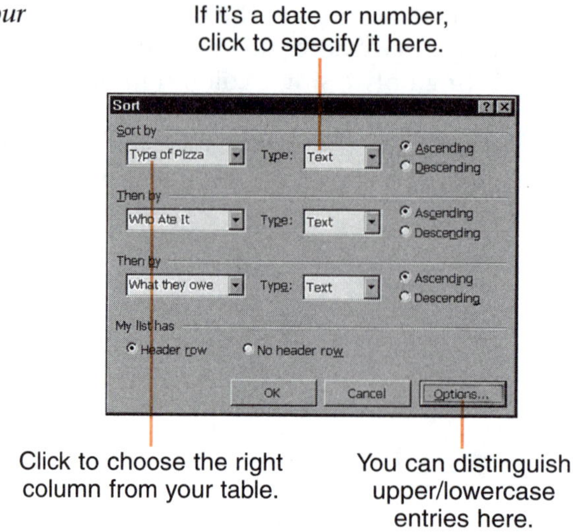

Figure 13.5: Sort your table in any way imaginable.

Dealing with Tables That Spread over Multiple Pages

There's nothing worse than table headings appearing at the bottom of a page, with rows and columns of unlabeled data appearing at the top of the next page. Word provides protection from this sort of thing either by preventing smaller tables from being broken up in the first place, or by providing table headings on every page for large tables.

If Your Table Extends Beyond a Single Page

To break a table across pages, click the row you want to appear on the next page. Press **Ctrl+Enter**, and the table is conveniently split between pages, including formatting and borders that may have been applied.

Preventing a Table from Breaking Across Pages

If your table fits comfortably on a single page and you want to keep it that way, you can tell Word to take care of it. Then, if text editing ever pushes or pulls your table toward a natural page break, Word pushes your table in its entirety to the next page.

To protect your table from ever splitting, first select it by clicking it. Open the **Table** menu and choose **Table Properties**. Now click the **Row** tab to bring it to the front. Clear the **Allow Row To Break Across Pages** check box. Click the **OK** button, and your table is forever protected (until you decide to fill that check box again).

Putting a Table Heading on Each Page

Big tables that run multiple pages usually need the same top rows to appear on each page (so you don't have to keep looking back). Word 2000 assists with a new option called Heading Rows Repeat, and it's intuitive. First, select the rows of text, including the first row, that you want to use as a table heading. Then open the **Table** menu and click the **Heading Rows Repeat** command. Word automatically repeats table headings only for tables that are split with automatic page breaks. Word does not repeat a heading if you insert a manual page break within a table. These repeated table headings are visible only in **Print Layout** view.

Messing Up a Table with Margins

If you change your margins with an existing table, notice that the table isn't affected at all. It's stuck right where you put it. That's because existing tables are not affected by changes to the page margins. If you want to maintain the same relationship between table width and page margins after changing the margins, you have to adjust the table width manually.

But Word helps you out a bit with the AutoFit feature. Click to select your table, open the **Table** menu, and point to **AutoFit**. Choose **AutoFit to Window** and the columns automatically adjust to the new page margins. Don't forget that you can also change the width of a column by dragging the column boundaries in the table itself or by dragging the column markers on the horizontal ruler. To display column-width measurements, point to the horizontal ruler, and then hold down **Alt** while you click the mouse button. The table markers appear in the Ruler.

Completely Blasting Away a Table

There is still no "delete the whole table" button in Word 2000, which is bad news if you create lots of bad tables. You can still get rid of them however, but it takes an extra step.

To completely eliminate a table, click anywhere inside it, open the **Table** menu, and choose **Select Table**. The whole thing should be selected. Now open the **Table** menu again and choose the **Delete Rows** command. It's gone forever, unless you want to bring it back with the magic **Undo** button. But why would you?

The Least You Need to Know

Tables are the best way to organize and present multicolumned lists of information in your document.

- Show me the fastest way to create a table in my document.

  Click the **Insert Table** button on the Standard toolbar and drag it to the size and shape you need. When you release the mouse button, the table appears, designed to your order.

- Where are the tools to edit my table?

  All the tools you ever need to edit a table can be found on the Tables and Borders toolbar, including alignment, merging, splitting, drawing, erasing, rotating, and formatting.

- How do I move data from one part of my table to another?

  If you need to move a cell's contents, select it by clicking in the cell, then drag the cell to its new location. If you want to copy it instead, hold down the **Ctrl** key as you drag.

- I goofed. My table's too short. How do I make it longer?

  To add either more rows or more columns, select the area inside the table nearest to where you want it extended, then choose either the **Insert Columns** or **Insert Rows** command from the **Table** menu.

- Okay, but my words are squished in the table cells. How can I give them more room?

  You can add more space between the rows of a table by increasing the value found in the **Cell Height and Width** command on the **Table** menu.

- Can I place a title that spans all my columns?

  Sure, but first merge the cells across the width of a table by using the **Merge Cells** command from the **Table** menu. Then insert your heading and center it as needed.

Chapter 14

Importing a Fine Piece of Text

In This Chapter

- Loading and saving non-Word documents
- Grabbing words from the Web
- Copying existing work from another application
- Saving documents in other formats

Although most new documents are now created using Microsoft Word, you may be in the process of converting from another program like WordPerfect or Lotus WordPro. Or perhaps you find information from the Web to include in your document. To your computer, these things are like foreign languages. And computers have trouble understanding files that aren't stored in their repertoire of languages. So before you share a document with a friend who is using a different word processor or a different type of computer, you might want to review these helpful tips on file formats.

Opening a Non-Word Document in Word 2000

Most computer programs store their files in a unique way, trying to be better than the competitors. The default file format for Word is different from the file format in WordPerfect, as you might expect. This sounds like it could lead to utter chaos in the world of computers, especially if you have to share documents between word processors. But amazingly, it works! The miracle is called a *converter* (sometimes called a *filter*, although filters are usually associated with graphics). Converters change a document from one format to another. For example, the WordPerfect 6.1 converter in Word 2000 converts WordPerfect files into Word documents.

The good news for you is that Word does all the work! So the next time someone hands you a disk with a document on it, you can feel reasonably confident that Word can open it.

Looking for Files on Disk

A friend gives you a disk containing a document that describes how to make money while you sleep. You rush to your desk and pop the disk into your computer and start Word 2000, hoping to double your salary by morning. Click the **Open** button and then click the **Look In** box. Locate the icon of a disk labeled "3 1/2 Floppy" and click to select it. All the files stored on the disk should be displayed, right? So why is it blank?

Figure 14.1: Using the file converters in Word.

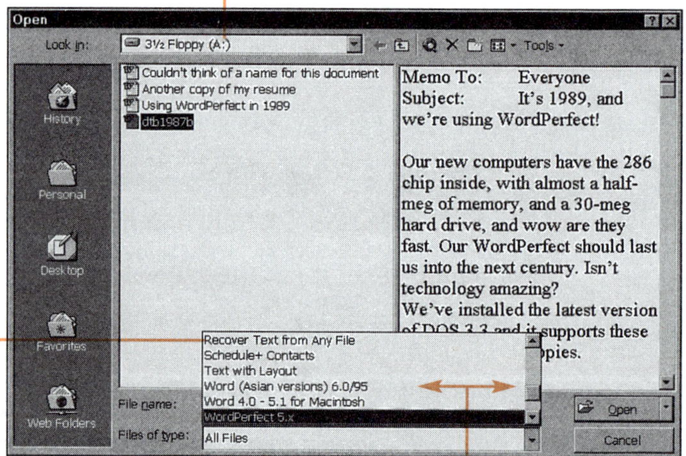

What If You Can't See It?

Don't be discouraged if you don't see anything at first. It doesn't mean a disk is empty. Word is expecting Word documents, so if the file on the disk is in another format, Word doesn't display it. You'll have to manually invoke one or all of the conversion filters. You will find them at the bottom of the **File Open** dialog box in the **Files of type** field.

Open the **Files of type** drop-down box by clicking it once. The drop-down box lists the available word processor products; find yours and click to select it. If you aren't sure or you want to see all the files on the disk anyway, select the **All Files (*.*)** entry. This option allows you to view all the files on your disk (and also your hard drive), not just the Word 2000 documents.

When you find the file you want, click the **OK** button and Word 2000 kicks into conversion action. Word attempts to maintain the contents and formatting of the original file, but if it can't, Word gives you an informational message describing the problem.

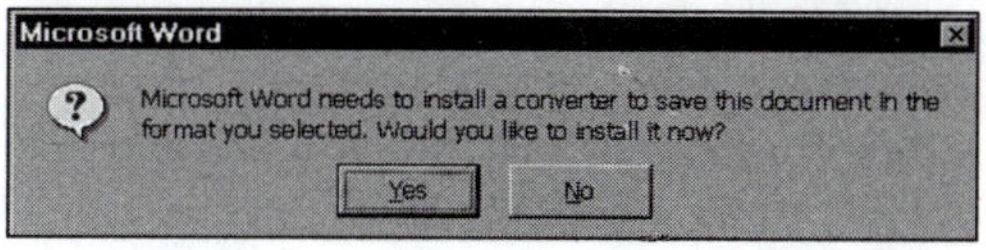

Figure 14.2: Word may ask permission to install the required converter.

Sometimes an external style file may be required, and you can either ask for the style from the person who gave you the document, or try to continue by clicking the Ignore button (it may not look great, but at least the words show up).

Now that the document is open, you can enrich it by using all the features of Word 2000. You don't have to know a lick about the original word processor product. For now, it's considered a Word document, and sooner or later, you will want to save it.

Saving and Closing Non-Word Documents

You can save your document at any time during the editing of a non-Word document (just click the **Save** button on the Standard toolbar); the **Save As** dialog box appears. Word knows you've been working with a different type of file format, so it needs to know how you want to save the file—in Word format or the other word processor format. Select the format you need from the options in the dialog box. Remember that if you added any fancy formatting to this document while in Word, those items may not translate back to the other word processor format. Follow these tips to decide how to save your document:

- If you will be using Word to edit this document in the future, save it as a Word document.
- If you want to apply Word formatting to this document, you're better off saving it as a Word document.
- If the document has to be used again with the other word processor, avoid using any special formatting inside Word, and save the document in the other word processor format.
- If you haven't a clue, click **No** or **Cancel** and ask someone for help.

If you are returning the file to your friend using WordPerfect or Lotus WordPro, you can do your friend a favor by choosing the original format. Otherwise, he or she might not have a file converter for Word 2000 documents and won't be able to open your document.

Decide on the format you want, click the **Save** button on the Standard toolbar, and you'll see a dialog box similar to the one shown here:

Figure 14.3: You decide on the format based on who uses it next.

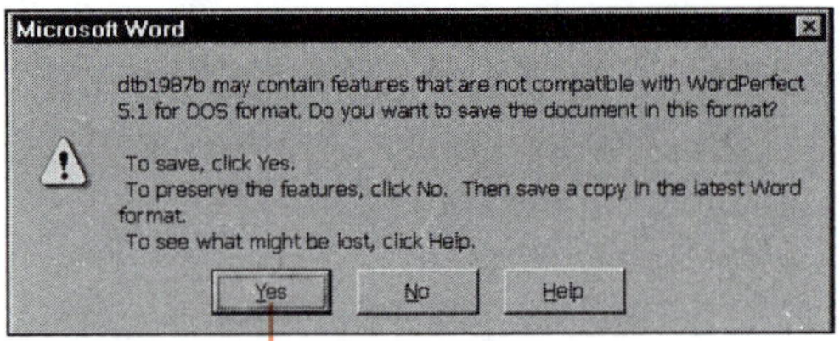

Word Keeps Track of the Original Format, So You Don't Have To

Click either the **Yes** or **No** button, and the file is saved. When it's time to close the file, Word asks if you want to save your changes. Just remember that Word considers any open document a Word document (except for some plain text files), so you may be asked to save changes even when you didn't make any. That's Word asking one last time if you want to keep it as a Word document. If it's a WordPerfect document, for example, and you haven't made any further changes, you can click the **Cancel** button to prevent Word from replacing it in Word format.

Inserting a Whole File into a Word Document

What's the difference between opening and inserting a file? Glad you asked, because you can save yourself editing time if you choose correctly. *Inserting* is taking the contents (some or all) of one file and placing it inside a Word document.

With your Word document open, click where you want the text to be inserted. Open the **Insert** menu and select the **File** command. Locate the file you want, highlight it, and click the **OK** button. The file will be imported, which means the words and formatting will be automatically converted to Word 2000 format and become a permanent part of your document. You may need to do some cleanup using Word's formatting tools, but the result is much improved over previous versions of Word. Remember to save your work when finished.

If you're unhappy with the inserted file, you can quickly remove it by clicking the **Undo** button. Maybe you inserted the wrong file. Try again.

Lots of Formats to Choose From

In the earlier example, you used the **Files of type** drop-down box in the **File Open** dialog box to see the selection of available word processing formats. If you can't find the converter you need, it may have been deleted or moved or is not yet installed. Word 2000 lets you know and automatically installs the appropriate converter when you try to open the file.

Have You Been Converted?

A converter is used to take the text and formatting of a document created in one program and make it appear as similar as possible in another program. Microsoft Word 2000 comes with converters for over 20 different programs, making it easy to convert documents created in those programs into Word 2000 documents.

Strange Sights in Converted Documents

Nothing is perfect in life, and you may find that the file converter you used created a document that looks different from the original. For instance, an original font may be replaced with something else. Or a margin setting may be lost, causing heading locations and page counts to change. You may find that everything looks different including characters, headers, and footers. In all these cases of formatting changes, you need to make adjustments to produce the document you want.

Handling Graphics

If graphics are a part of the file you are inserting, you might have to kiss them goodbye. Although text is usually successful, graphics don't often make it through a file conversion. If yours didn't, don't give up hope; just look for a different way. If the graphic was stored as a separate file, you can use the graphic import files described in Chapter 11, "Decorating Your Document with Pictures." Or maybe it's clip art stored on another disk or CD-ROM, and you can copy it directly from the original source. Or you can copy and paste it from the original computer into another Windows program that might have better success, like Paint or another graphics program. Then you can store the graphic in a format you can insert using the **Picture** command on the **Insert** menu. Finally, if all hope seems lost, you can always print the graphic from the original computer and scan it in as a new graphic.

Inserting Only Portions of Text from Other Sources

Sometimes the information you want to insert is only a small part of a larger document that was created in other Windows or non-Windows programs. This is no problem for Word 2000. You don't have to waste time or risk making mistakes by retyping these sections. Just follow these tips to easily insert the information into your document.

You Can't Beat Cut and Paste

Because you are running Word 2000 using Windows 95, 98, or NT/2000, you can do many things at once. Just as you can copy and paste between two opened Word documents, you can copy text from another program into your Word document (and vice versa).

First, get your programs running and the documents or files opened in each. You don't have to tile and view all windows at the same time. The task bar makes it easy to switch between running applications. You can select and copy text in one full-screen program, choose another program from the taskbar, and paste the text into that full-screen program. In fact, your computer remembers what you select and copy from any program, even after you close that program, so it's not absolutely necessary to have both programs running at the same time—it's just easier to explain and prevent mistakes.

If the other program happens to be a Windows program, you'll be happy to know that your copy and paste keys usually work the same. Select the text in the other program and click the familiar **Copy** button to copy the text (or you can use the menu commands from that other program). The same guidelines apply to non-Windows programs, but you may have to hunt for the **Copy** command (it's often found on the **Control** menu; the top-left icon in your window). Only *copy* text from non-Windows programs—never cut text—to prevent losing it in case of an accident.

Don't Cut Out on This Lesson

Yes, the **Cut** button also provides the Cutting function, but don't use it; it's not worth the risk. It's like throwing a bag of food to a friend on the other side of a raging river. If your pal catches it, that's great; if not, your dinner's gone down the river.

After you switch back to Word 2000, place the insertion point where you want the text pasted and click the **Paste** button. The text is pasted into your document.

If the pasted text looks good, congratulate yourself and then save your Word document for safekeeping. If the pasted text looks different than you expected, you may have to do some adjusting, or click **Undo** to remove it.

Grabbing Text from the Web and the Rest of the Internet

The Internet is a great place to find just about anything you can imagine. You can download text files from newsgroups, recorded chats, email from friends, and text from countless other sources. Find a friend who has experience downloading files from the Internet if you want to explore this subject further, or buy one of the many books available on the subject, such as Que's *Complete Idiot's Guide to Downloading*.

Your browser has built-in Cut, Copy, and Paste functions. You can capture chats you have with other people, copy contents of email messages and paste them into your document, and search bulletin boards and subject categories for things that are interesting or helpful in your work.

Just click and drag to select text from a Web page, open the **Edit** menu on your browser and click **Copy**. Return to Word 2000 and click the **Paste** button to place the text into an opened document.

Click **Copy** in your browser, and then...

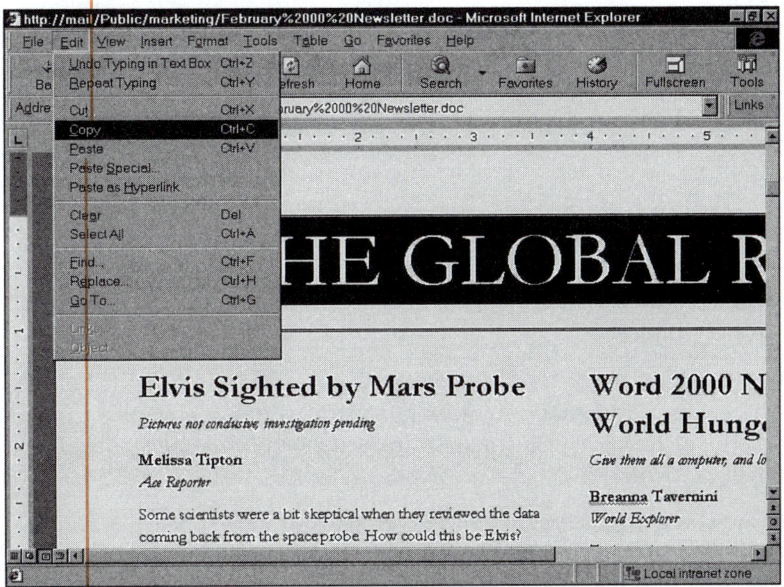

switch to Word and **Paste** the selection.

Figure 14.4: Grabbing text from the Web.

Salvaging Text from Older Files

If the file you need still exists on a disk or an older computer, you may be able to recover at least some of the text contained in it. Copy the file to a disk, bring it to your computer, and then review these quick tips:

- Try opening the file with the new Word 2000 converter called **Recover text from any file**. Regardless of the format of your file, this converter tries to grab any text, and it might find what you need.
- You can convert files stored on 5.25-inch disks to 3.5-inch disks using a computer that has both types of drives; copy from one drive to the other.
- If you have only a 5.25-inch drive, you can still connect your computer to a modem and email the file as an attachment to yourself. Then download the file to a computer with a 3.5-inch disk drive.

- If the file you need exists on an older computer, use the application stored on that computer to open it. If it opens, save it in a format you can import, such as DOS text (or ASCII file).
- When a file exists on a minicomputer or mainframe at work, contact the support staff and request the file. They can usually provide the file you need on a disk in ASCII format. Or you can copy and paste from your terminal session.

Scanning In Your Own Text from Any Source

The sky's the limit. Well, actually the copyright laws are the limit. You can take any piece of paper containing almost any kind of text and get those words into Word 2000. This can be a real lifesaver if your computer crashes and the only remaining copy of your 500-page thesis is a draft you printed last week. Use this technique when the alternative—retyping all those pages—is interminable hell.

The solution is called *scanning*. A scanner is a machine that comes in many shapes and sizes, with costs to match. It's usually attached to a computer. A scanner takes a paper document and turns it into a computer file. Think of it like a printer in reverse. You may not have to buy a scanner; you probably already have access to one or at least have a friend who does. Many offices have scanners, and many computer stores offer scanning services for a small fee.

Here's the routine: You walk up to a scanner with your report and blank disk in hand, feed the scanner your document, and place the disk into the attached computer. You press a button or two on the computer (ask for help if necessary), and the scanner stores the file on your disk.

Sound too easy? You knew there was a catch—and there is—because the scanner just takes a picture of your paper document, which might contain rips, folded corners, pictures, smudges, grape jelly, and so on. That's why most scanners also come with a software program called OCR (Optical Character Recognition). The OCR looks at the scanned picture of your page, determines if there's any text on it, and attempts to read only the text. So the single file saved to your disk is only the text found on all the pages (no pictures or jelly). OCR isn't always perfect, and smudges and folds reduce the accuracy of the file, so it's always important to quality-check your file before using it.

When you scan pages of text and the OCR is complete, your file is usually stored in plain text format, which is easily opened in Word. Some scanning packages even try to capture the formatting and save the document in Word format, saving you even more time. Don't push your luck, and remember the real value in scanning is saving the time of retyping. Do the rest yourself.

Support for Your Scanner

Yes, if you've got a scanner attached to your computer, Word 2000 allows you to insert a picture directly from the scanner! Place the picture in your scanner, click to place your insertion point in your document, and start the engines. Open the **Insert** menu, point to **Picture**, and choose **From Scanner**. Your scanned image is placed in your document automatically. After it's inserted, you can move it, crop it, and resize it (and all the other editing features) just like any other graphic in your document.

All that's left is to take the disk back to your computer and import the file into Word. Again, remember to check this new document for errors before using it. Word helps you catch many errors by using the Spelling and Grammar Checker. See Chapter 5, "Proofing Tools (Spelling, Grammar, and the Thesaurus)," for more information on proofing a document.

Saving Documents for Use in Other Word Processors

You have the document that other people want, and you've created it in Word 2000. But you discover that not everyone on the planet has converted to Word yet, or may be a version or two behind. A friend using another word processor like WordPerfect or WordPro may get an error trying to open your document, and the error message will be "`unrecognizable file format.`" Before they become ex-friends, try converting your Word document to the type your friends require. Open the **File** menu, click **Save As**, and locate the converter you require from the **Save As Type** box.

Not Converting? Turn Off Fast Saves

If you are using **Fast Saves** in Word, turn them off before you forward a document to someone to use in another program, such as desktop publishing. Other programs often have problems understanding the Fast Save format of Word 2000.

More Word File Converters Available

If you've browsed through the list of converters in Word 2000 and don't see the one you need, don't give up hope! Try searching for the latest converters on the Microsoft Web site using the search words *converter* and *Word*.

Saving Your Document as a Text File

If you want a reason to save your Word document as a text file, I've got one. Over a billion computers exist on our planet, and who knows how many on other planets, and they can all understand a simple text file! That means you could take the file anywhere, even in the foreseeable future, and feel confident that your words will be recognized. A text file is considered the lowest common denominator of file formats.

Open the **File** menu and select the **Save As** command. You cannot use the plain Save command for this. Now change the format, which appears in the **Save file as type** box. Click it to see the drop-down list of choices. Click the **Text Only** option and press the **Enter** key. Now click the **File Name** box and name the file. Because this will be an ordinary text file, you should follow DOS naming conventions, which are really restrictions. The name must fit in eight letters, with no spaces or fancy symbols. Now click the **OK** button, and your file is saved to disk.

What Gets Lost When You Save as a Text File?

All the formatting is lost (including fonts, bullets, centering, page numbers, pictures, and margins) when you save a file as a text file. Hey, that's everything! Yes, basically, all the neat features of Word 2000 that you choose to use are applied on top of a basic text file. So if you want the plain text file, you have to rip away all the Word features. All word processors are like this, including WordPerfect, Lotus WordPro, Write, WordPad, and countless others.

The Least You Need to Know

Converting files and importing text is the way Word 2000 acts like a language translator. You may become fluent at performing these tasks by reviewing the highlights of this chapter.

- Why can't I see a WordPerfect document on my disk?

  Word 2000 can easily open documents created in other programs. Click the **Open** button and be sure to change the file type to **All Files (*.*)** to allow you to view the names of non-Word files.

- How can I grab just a small part of another document for use in my current document?

  If you need only a few sentences or paragraphs from another document, it's often easiest to open that document, select the text you want, click the **Copy** button, return to your Word document, and click **Paste**.

- How can I send a document to a client who doesn't have Word 2000?

  You're always safe saving it as a text file, but it's better to ask your client which product they use. Then you can open the **File** menu, select **Save As**, and choose the appropriate file converter.

- What if I don't know what program my reader might use to view my document?

  Remember that Word 2000 offers the Save As option called Text File, that guarantees that your reader will be able to view it no matter what product they use.

Chapter 15

Working with Multiple Documents

In This Chapter

- Viewing multiple documents at once
- Viewing multiple parts of the same document
- Saving multiple documents at once
- Mail Merge for mere mortals

Sometimes one document just isn't enough. Sure, it's open on your screen and you're comfortable with all the controls, but you're sure there's more to life. You need more than this document. You probably need additional information stored in another document, and you want them both open at the same time.

If that's how you feel, this chapter shows you how to get not one, not two, but up to a gazillion documents open on your screen at once (if you have enough memory). You'll also learn how to copy or move information (or yourself) between them. And to keep things interesting, you'll also learn how to create your own form letters for fun and for profit.

Opening Documents

Why would anyone want to have more than one document open at the same time? An informal poll of the entire human population was taken last week, and here are the preliminary results:

- It's the easiest way to cut, copy, and paste between them.
- It's quick when you need multiple reference documents available fast.
- It's easy to move graphics and text back and forth.
- It makes your boss think you're doing more work.
- It's the best way to slow down really fast computers.

Whatever your reason, having multiple opened documents on your screen is as simple as opening one document, and then opening another, and so on. Word 2000 now gives each opened document a button on your Task bar. To move between any of your opened documents, just click the button for it on your Task bar.

Figure 15.1: Each button is now an opened Word document.

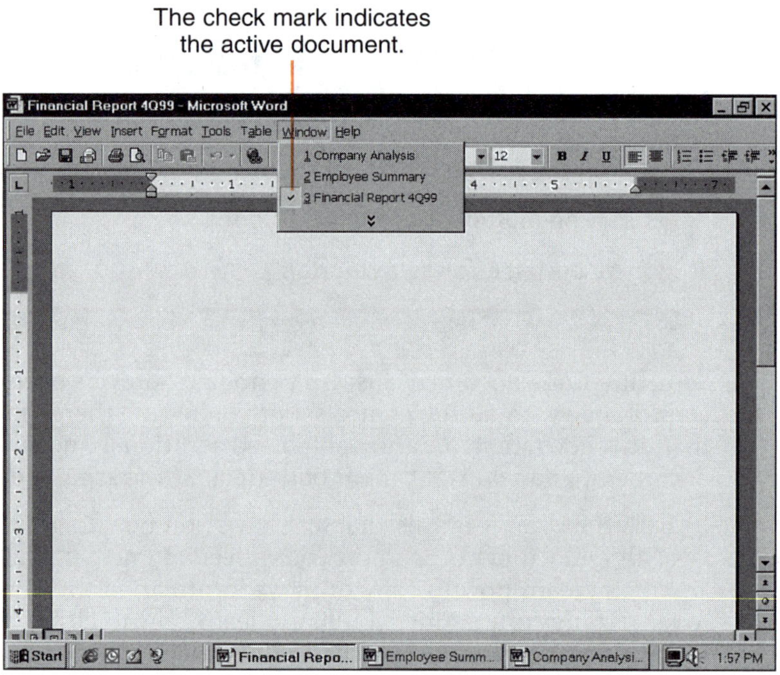

Figure 15.2: You can also track open documents in the Window menu.

Opening Many Documents at the Same Time

You know how to open one document, but do you know the secret to opening lots of documents at once? Try to save some time next time. Open the **File** menu, choose **Open**, and click to select the first file you need. Now hold the **Ctrl** key down and click another file. They're both highlighted, and ready to open simultaneously! You can keep clicking on files to open, as long as you hold down that **Ctrl** key. You can even browse around to other folders. When you're ready, click the **Open** button and they all open at once.

The old Window Menu still works, too

You can still see the list of all open documents the old-fashioned way—by clicking the **Window** menu. If you have more than nine opened documents, you see the last entry as **More Windows** which, if selected, takes you to a dialog box containing the complete list of all your opened documents.

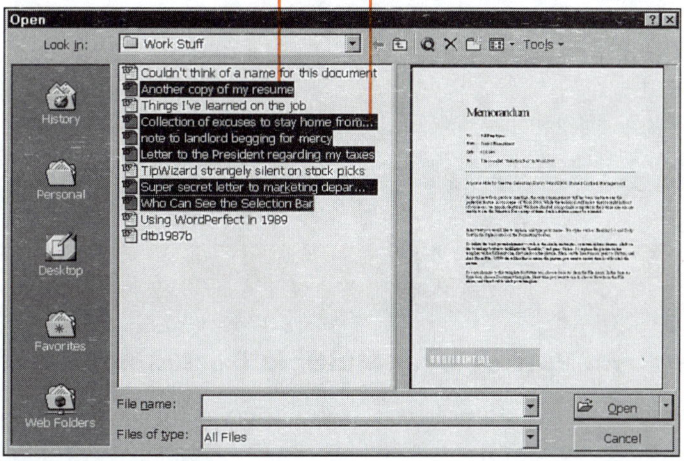

Figure 15.3: Opening several documents at once.

You Opened Them, but Where Are They?

You're fairly certain you just opened 16 documents, but only one is staring you in the face. Where are the rest? In Word 2000, each document uses the entire screen, so a single document is all you see at the moment. But the others are there as well, for each document is represented as a button on your Task bar. And to help you remember what they are, the name on the Task bar button happens to be the name of your document.

Allergic to mouse devices? You can also switch between open documents by pressing **Ctrl+Shift+F6**, which takes you to the next Word document on your Task bar. It's even easier to press **Ctrl+F6** to go to the previous document, since most people just keep switching documents until they find the one they want.

Limited Only by Your Memory

Word 2000 enables you to open as many documents as you want, as long as your computer has enough memory to support all of them.

So What Can You Do with Two Open Documents?

Probably the best thing you can do with multiple opened documents is to easily cut, copy, and paste anything between them, and it can be anything stored in any of the documents. Just select the portion of text, figures, or objects you want to cut or copy from any document and click the **Copy** button. Now find the spot in any document you want to copy to, click once to pinpoint the spot, and click the **Paste** button for instant gratification. The **Cut** button also works fine for moving selected text or graphics across multiple documents.

Word 2000 handles each window independently, in case you were wondering why only one document prints when you press the Print button. Each command affects only the current document, which is the one you're looking at. Spell-checking, formatting commands, and printing are examples of tasks that are performed only on the current document.

Cutting and Pasting over Multiple Documents

Incidentally, multiple documents do not have to be open at the same time in order for you to cut, copy, and paste between them. You can select and copy from one document, close it, open another document, and paste it just fine. But fewer steps are required when both documents are opened.

Viewing Multiple Documents at Once

Instead of seeing a single document on the screen at a time, you may decide you want to see more than one, or all documents. Just open the **Window** menu and choose the **Arrange All** command. All opened documents are placed on your screen, each in its own smaller window. This works best for two or three documents because each window has to share space on your screen, and too many open windows make it difficult to work on any single document.

Although you can see more than one document on your screen at a time, only one is currently active. You can tell by looking at it (the Title bar is bold) but it's easier just to click on the one you want to make it active. You can also toggle through them by pressing the **Ctrl+F6** keys.

Clicking the Maximize title bar button on your active document causes that document to be maximized, taking over your entire screen again. The remaining documents are still there, just covered up at the moment. You can get to them again by clicking the Task bar buttons, pressing **Ctrl+F6**, or by minimizing or restoring the current window (press the Minimize or Restore Title bar button). Don't forget, you can also resize any window and move them around wherever you want.

Viewing Multiple Parts of the Same Document

If you like working on two things at once, even if the two things are in a single document, then you'll love this screen manipulation. You can view different parts of a large document at the same time, in different windows on your screen.

Open the document you want to work with. Open the **Window** menu and choose the **New Window** command. This creates another window on your screen where you find another copy of the same document. These aren't two different copies—just two different views of the same document. Make a change in one, and it's instantly updated in the other view also. Your documents are also labeled in the Title bar with something extra—a colon and a number after the filename—which helps you identify the views. For example, you may have Report:1 in one window and Report:2 in the title bar of the second window.

See Multiple, Use One

It's easier to find the active window when you have many windows open. Word 2000 places the Title bar buttons (Minimize, Maximize, Restore, and Close) on only the active window. This makes it much less confusing on a busy screen.

What's this dual view good for? It's great for cutting and pasting in very long documents. Display the text or graphics you want to move or copy in one window and the destination in the other window, and then drag the text or graphics between the two. Instant success and feedback. What a concept.

When you are finished editing either part of this document, save it and close it by opening the **File** menu and choosing the **Close** command. You have to do this only once because closing one closes both.

Splitting Your Viewing Screen

You can save some space on your viewing screen and still have two views of the same document by using a slightly different feature of Word 2000 called *screen splitting*. To view two parts of an open document simultaneously, open the **Window** menu and choose the **Split** command. A horizontal bar appears about halfway down your screen. Now just click your mouse button to plant the split and you have a split screen. The bottom window contains an exact duplicate of your document. Try clicking in this new window and scroll around. The other window remains still, enabling you to see different parts of the same document at the same time. When you get tired of this split bar, open the **Window** menu and choose **Remove Split**.

Saving Multiple Documents at Once

You can save all open documents at once by opening the **File** menu and selecting the **Save All** command. Any document containing any new changes since it was last saved are now saved. Of course, if you are going to be away from your computer for more than a few minutes, it's best to close all your documents.

Closing All Documents at the Same Time

Press and hold down the **Shift** key (either one) and use the mouse to open the **File** menu. Surprise! There's now a **Close All** command, and by selecting it, all of your documents are closed. Of course, if any documents have changes not yet saved, Word stops before closing them and asks if you want to save the changes. These dynamically changing menus may have you wondering what else might change if you hold down a key and open a menu.

Mail Merge

You may not know what mail merge is, but every time you receive junk mail with your name listed as possible winner of $1,000,000, you have experienced a mail merge.

If it's done well, a mail merge is ideal for communicating more personally to a large number of people, such as your friends during the holidays, the customers of your business, or the tax base of your country.

What Is a Merge?

Mail merge is the process of taking one document and mixing it with another, usually a name and address list, to create an almost identical bunch of new documents. Each new document is customized with one name and address from your list. First, some Word 2000 definitions. The document that contains the names, addresses, phone numbers, and so on is called the *data source*. The file that contains the form letter is called the *main document*.

Now the process. Start by creating the **main document** (your form letter), complete with formatting. But leave blank the places you would normally enter a name or address, or anything else you want to change. In these blank spaces, you add something called a *field*. Each field is replaced with a real name or address during a merge.

Next you find or create a **data source**. The data source is a document that contains a collection of the names and addresses (or anything else) that you want. Unlike a regular document, however, this one is created in a different format called a database. For example, this could be a database of all your customer names and addresses. Got it? One database file, many names and addresses. Each combination of name, address, and other information in this data source is called a *record*.

When you say go, Word 2000 creates a bunch of customized documents (as many as you have records in your data source), one form letter for each customer in your database. It's very easy to print all of these custom documents as a final step, without the need for saving all of them (or you can save them all—in fact, you can email them all if the names came from your address book provided with Word 2000).

Using the Mail Merge Command

This won't be so bad, I promise. The easiest way to explain mail merge is to use an example. You just had a birthday and got lots of presents. You know you'll keep getting presents in the future if you send a personal thank-you note to everyone. But that's a lot of work. You decide to send the same note to everyone because they all live in different parts of the country. Only the names and addresses will change.

What's first? Building the basic thank-you note. Start by opening the **Tools** menu and choose the **Mail Merge** command. You see the **Mail Merge Helper** dialog box. The large numbers 1, 2, and 3 make you guess you'll be finished in a snap. Guess again! This example goes on for pages! See the **Create** button? Click it. Now select **Form Letter** from the list. You can press **New Main Document** next, to begin the creation of your form letter.

After pressing the **New Main Document** button, two new buttons appear—an **Edit** button and a **Get Data** button. Now you're ready to gather the names and addresses of the friends who will be getting this letter. You can either gather these names from an existing electronic address book or create a new list from scratch.

Grabbing the Names from Your Address Book

Press the **Get Data** button to reveal the pull-down listing of potential sources of data. Choose **From Address Book** (if you don't have an address book, you can create your own list now by clicking **Create Data Source** building one from scratch).

Choose the type of address book you are using. If it's Outlook, this is called your *Contacts*, but you can also have what is called the Outlook *Personal Address Book*. Once you've decided which to use, select it from the list. In some cases, you may be asked to provide the location of this address book file.

If you want to include every name from your address book, you don't have to do anything else. They've all been selected and are ready to go. But because your address book may contain more names than you want to include for this merge, you can click to select the names individually. When you've finished, click **OK** to continue with the merge process.

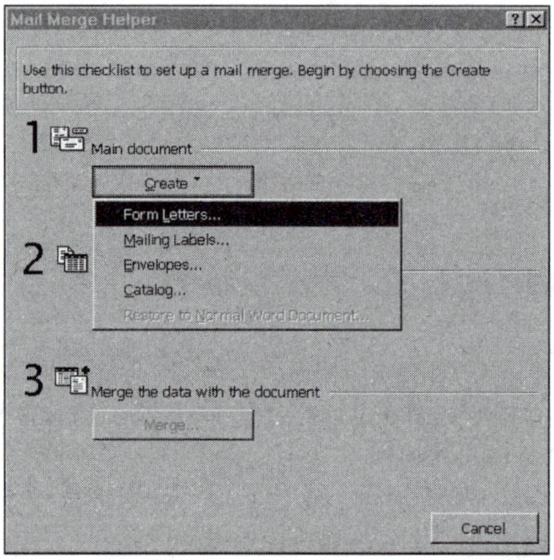

Figure 15.4: Mail Merge steps you through the process.

Merge it Easy! Use Your Address Book!

If you already have your friends' names and addresses stored in your computer, you can use that file as your *data source* for a mail merge. If you don't, it's still smarter to first add those names to an address book such as Outlook, instead of creating a new data source here. Merge automatically accepts entries from the Outlook Contacts list or Outlook Personal Address Book (and several other third-party address books), and you are able to use them again in the future. You can also open address list files created in Microsoft Excel or Microsoft Access.

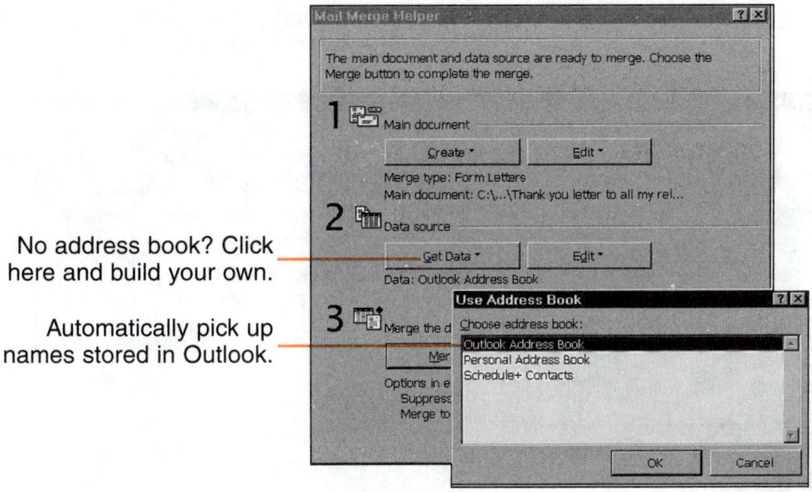

Figure 15.5: Quick mail merges using your address book.

Creating Your Form Letter

Now be creative as you compose a generic thank-you note. When it's time to add something personal, such as a first name after Dear so-and-so, click that **Insert Merge Field** button on your Mail Merge toolbar (the Mail Merge toolbar appears automatically when you choose Mail Merge from the Tools menu). Choose **First Name** from the list of fields. This ties directly back to the names in your address book.

Don't worry about the formatting, those silly <<things>> are replaced later (they're just placeholders for the real information stored in your address book or database). Keep on creating the thank-you note.

Merging at Last

You're so close to the end of this example, you should be able to taste it. Open the **Tools** menu and press **Mail Merge** for the third (and final) time. Click the **Merge** button to see the **Merge** dialog box. The most common defaults are already selected in this dialog box, such as the option to merge to a new document. You can also choose to merge directly to your printer, or even email, by clicking the **Merge To** pull-down arrow and choosing another destination.

Now click the **Merge** button to finally start the merging process. You may be surprised how quickly your computer can accomplish this merging, and you will want to inspect the results to make sure the proper merging took place. If the merge was less than spectacular, you can press **Ctrl+Z** to undo the previous step, or simply delete the merged results (by closing them without saving) and trying again. All of the tedious merging steps have been saved, so you are taken to the very last step to try again.

Figure 15.6: A generic thank-you note ready to be merged.

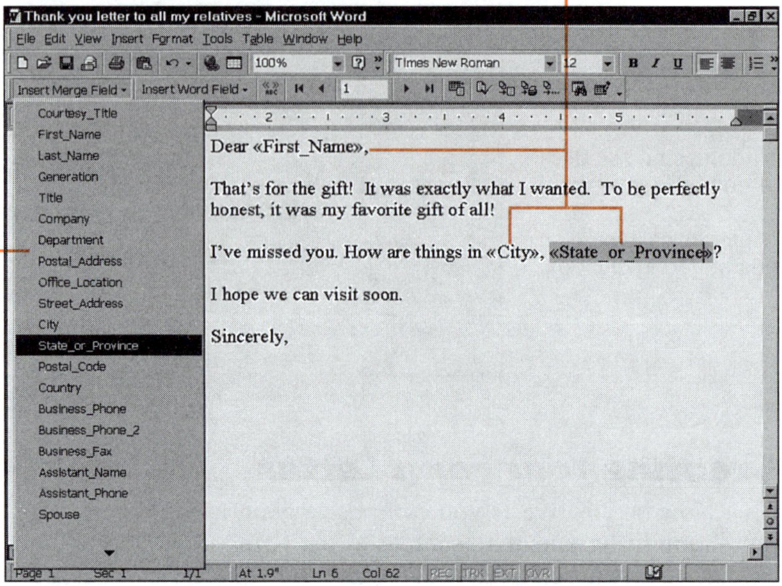

Figure 15.7: The finished product, ready to print or email!

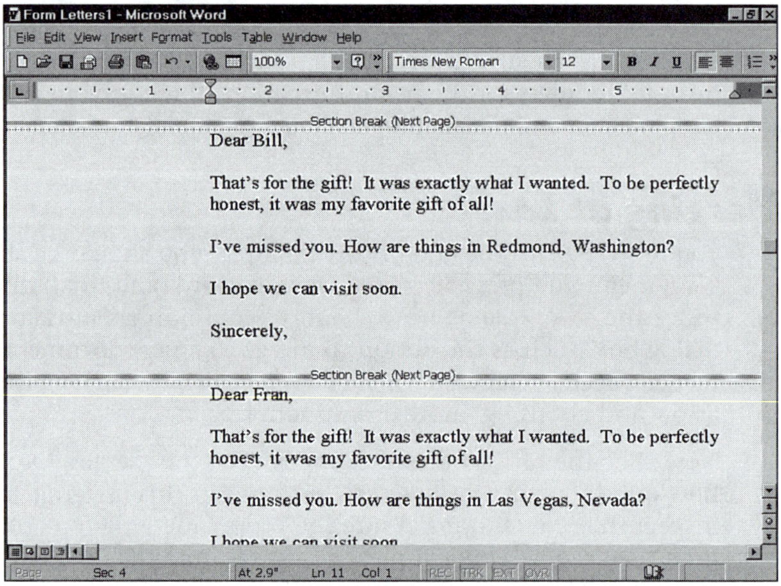

The Least You Need to Know

Humans have no problem doing 50 things at once. Now our documents can keep up with us. This chapter reviewed ideas on using multiple documents.

➤ How many documents can be open at the same time in Word 2000?

As many as you require. You'll run out of space long before Word 2000 runs out of gas. Open as many documents as your heart desires and track them as buttons on your Task bar.

➤ I've opened two documents but I can't see them at the same time. What should I do?

You can view two (or more) opened documents at once by opening the **Windows** menu and choosing the **Arrange All** command.

➤ I need to see two different parts of the same document at the same time. Am I crazy?

Not at all. You can work on two sections of the same document by splitting the window into panes. Double-click on the **Split Box** or open the **Window** menu and select the **Split** command. Click in each pane as needed to control that area.

➤ What's the easiest way to send the same letter to lots of people?

A mail merge takes a single master document and mixes it with another (usually an address list) to create many new documents (also known as "form letters"). Find the Mail Merge feature of Word 2000 under the **Tools** menu.

Part 3

Pushing Word 2000 to the Limit

It's never to late to learn a new tool. Especially if you need it to survive. Once in a while you have to take a chance and see what technology can do for you. Look what we accomplished with fire.

So if your survival depends on Word 2000, find another climate. Or, review some of these chapters on evolutionary features, and adapt to better ways to accomplish your work.

Chapter 16

Sharing Your Word 2000 Documents

In This Chapter

- Using online collaboration features
- Starting a discussion
- Subscribing for email notification when changes occur
- Tracking different versions of a document
- Comparing documents for changes
- Protecting documents before sharing them with others

One person usually has enough problems keeping an important document up-to-date; imagine sharing and updating the same document with others! Collaboration is supposed to make us more productive, right? Relax, you've got Word 2000 and this book. You'll learn to use the new online collaboration features, including *discussions* and *subscribing* to changes. Then you can spend all your time discussing your documents with others.

Online Collaboration is Here!

Yes, we have all been told that collaboration is good for us. With good collaboration, our work teams can

- Share ideas and get feedback quickly
- Easily distribute information

- Access company business information
- Eliminate problems with different file formats and platforms
- Eliminate problems associated with differing languages

So, how does all this work in Word 2000? First, you must make yourself available for the collaboration by subscribing to that document. Here's how it's done.

Figure 16.1: Let's discuss this, shall we?

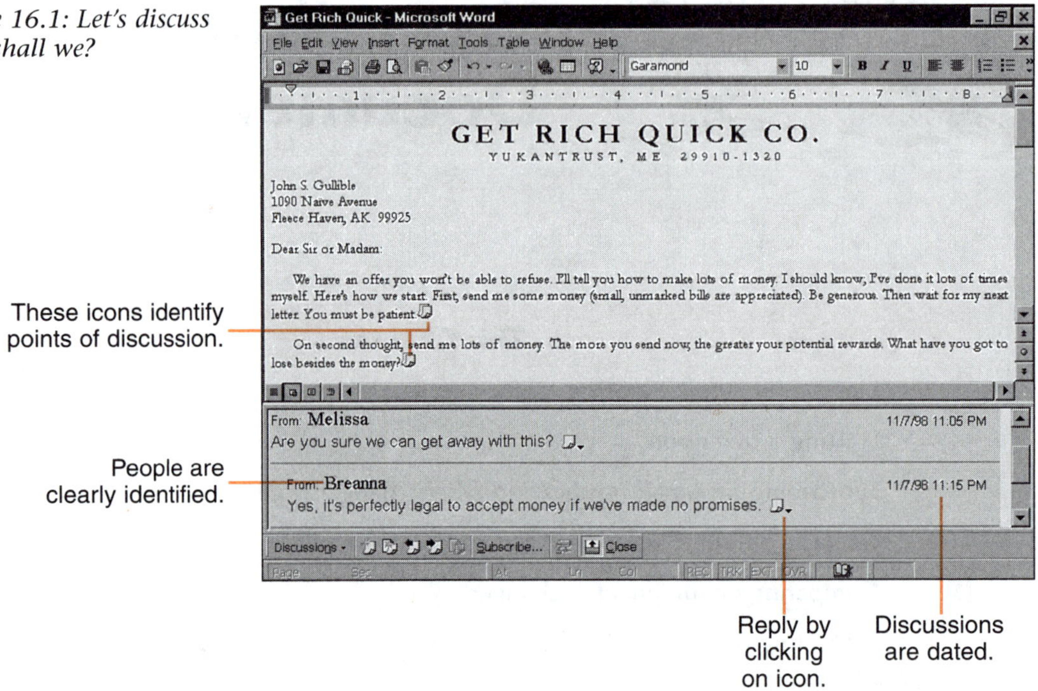

Subscribing to a document or folder for discussion

Want to try that yourself? Let's make sure your computer is ready for it. Before you can use discussions in a document, you must first *subscribe* to that document.

You may need to get your system administrator involved. The administrator is usually responsible for loading the required *Microsoft Office Server Extensions* on your Web server in order to support these online collaborations. Most important, the administrator must provide you with the correct name of your Web server.

To subscribe to a document, have it opened on your screen, then open the **Tools** menu, point to **Online Collaboration** and choose **Web Discussions**. This opens the Discussions toolbar at the bottom. Click **Discussions** and choose **Discussion Options**. Now click **Add** and add the Web address in **Type the Name of the Discussion Server your Administrator has Provided**. You can include a personal name for your server (such as My Server) and click **OK** and then **OK** again to save everything.

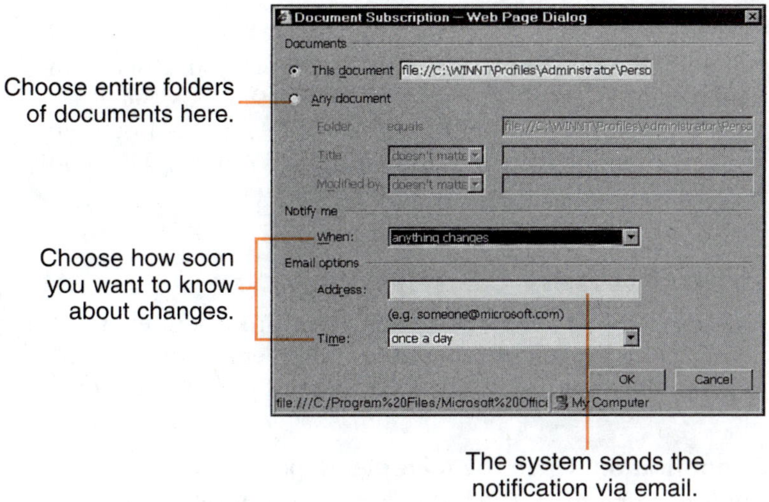

Figure 16.2: Receive email notification if your document ever changes.

Starting a Discussion

Now that you've subscribed to a document, you can start a discussion about it. You get two choices for initiating a discussion. You can create either a *General* discussion, regarding the entire document, or an *Inline* document, specific to a word, paragraph, table, or picture.

After you've decided, open the **Tools** menu, point to **Online Collaboration** and choose **Web Discussions**. Click in the document anywhere you want to start the discussion. Click the **Insert Discussion In the Document** button (or for a general discussion, choose **Insert Discussion About the Document**). Type a **Subject** and **Discussion Text**, then click **OK**. Your new discussion appears near the bottom.

Once you start seeing discussions in your document, you can read them and reply to them, and your reply is inserted as the next discussion item. To reply to a discussion, click the **Discussion** icon and click **Reply** on the shortcut menu.

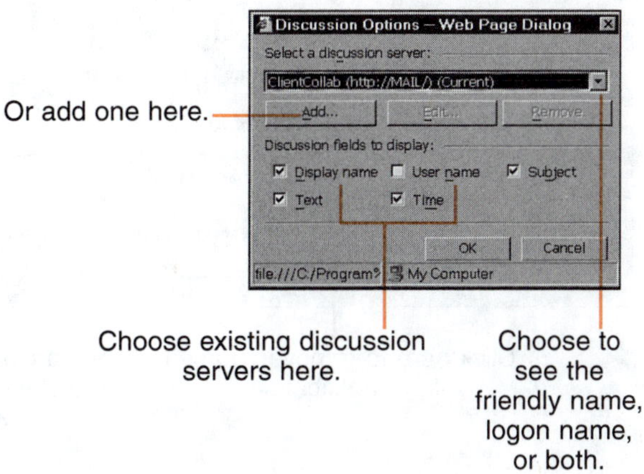

Figure 16.3: Start an interactive discussion regarding your document.

Deleting Your Discussions

If you've thought twice about what you wrote and want to retract your discussion, that's okay. Click the appropriate **Discussion** icon and then click **Show a Menu of Actions**. Here you find the Delete button. No matter how strong you are, however, you are not able to delete a discussion created by someone else. You can delete only your own discussions and replies.

Get Notified via Email When Changes Occur

The best reason to subscribe to a folder is obvious when you think about email. When someone adds a new file to the folder, the system sends you an email announcing the event and also gives you an instant link to the new file! Just click it and you are there!

Set yourself up for email notification. Open the **Tools** menu, point to **Online Collaborations**, and choose **Web Discussions**. Click the **Discussions** button and choose **Discussion Options**. Type in your email address and choose how soon you want to be notified after any change is made, and click **OK** to save your settings. The following figure shows what you see if someone changes one of your subscribed documents.

Figure 16.4: The system warns you when a document has been changed.

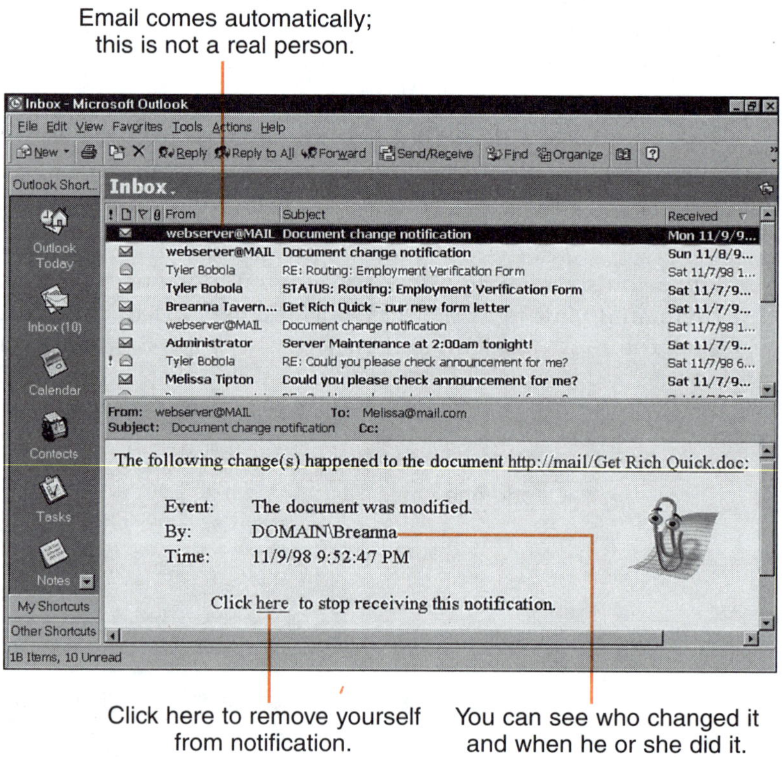

When you no longer want to be notified of any changes for this document, wait for the next email notification, and read it. Near the bottom of the message is a notice asking you to "Click <u>*here*</u> to stop receiving this notification." It is processed immediately and the disruptions cease.

Keeping Track of Changes in Shared Documents

Let's say you and a friend must work on the same document, but you don't have any of the previously described online collaboration tools. You're given enough time to finish the task, so you plan to share a disk with the stored document. Each of you builds and edits the document, while trading the disk back and forth. It's important for each of you to know what the other person has done, especially if there's a lot of moving and deleting of text. Otherwise, suspicion and tension may arise, wars may begin, and hunger and famine may spread.

Luckily for you, Microsoft Word 2000 provides several options for tracking, incorporating, and keeping a record of all these changes. Let's start with simple and common ways to track changes.

Highlighting Text in Color

An easy way to identify a change is to highlight it. Click the **Highlight** button on the Formatting toolbar, and then click and drag to select any text you want to highlight (you can also highlight graphics).

You can highlight in one of 15 different colors, even more than the famous marking pens. To change the highlighter color, click the arrow next to the **Highlight** button, click the color you want, and then select the text or graphic you want to highlight. When you highlight parts of a document that you intend to print, be sure to use a light color for best results on laser and dot matrix printers.

Anyone opening your document immediately sees your highlighted text. If it bothers him, he can switch it off without removing it. Open the **Tools** menu, click **Options**, and click the **View** tab to bring it to the front. To display or hide highlighting (but not the text itself) on the screen and in the printed document, set or clear the **Highlight** check box. Want to try something faster? Right-click the **TRK** that appears in your status bar, and choose **Highlight**.

Find Those Highlights Fast

Want to focus your reviewer on the key sections only? Tell him to open the **Edit** menu, click **Find**, and click **Highlight** in the Format box. Now he can browse the document, stopping only at your highlights.

Please Leave Your Message at the Tone...

Yes, voice comments are a reality in today's multimedia world, and you can add them to your Word 2000 documents with ease. Chapter 12 provides all the details about sound cards and microphones to get you started. Once you're up and talking, you can talk to your document and it listens.

To put voice comments in your document, click where you want to add a comment. Open the **Insert** menu and choose the **Comment** command. Click the **Insert Sound Object** button and talk away! Click the **Close** button to save it, and a small set of initials appears, representing the person creating the comment.

Incidentally, you don't have to have sound to put Comments to great use. You can type your message in the **Comment** pane and click the **Close** button to save it. The very same set of small initials appears, representing the initials of the person creating the comment.

To get rid of comments in your document, the preferred method is to select them first (don't just backup over them with the backspace—the comment remains, even though it's empty) and then delete them with the **Cut** button or the **Delete** key. You can also click in the **Comment** pane and delete your message there.

Wrong Initials or Name?

If the initials are not set correctly on your reviewer's computer, have him open the **Tools** menu and select the **Options** command. Click the **User Info** tab to bring it to the front. Correct the user initials in the text box, and click **OK** to save the changes and close the **Options** dialog box.

Is This the Latest Version?

Instead of filling a document with comments or highlights, you may prefer to work with documents as if they were in final form. You just reconcile changes by calling each new updated document a new version of the same document. Yes, Word 2000 makes this easy using the Version feature. This enables you to save different versions of a document as a separate file.

To turn on the Version feature for a document at any time, open the **File** menu and click **Versions**. In the **Version** dialog box, you see the history of saved versions for this document. Click **Save Now** and you are asked to comment on this particular version. These comments help you further identify a version if you need it in the future. You also have the exact time, date, and name of the person who last saved a version of this document. After typing a comment, click **Save**. Provide a name for this document and a folder to store it in.

 Each time you want to save another version of this document, just click the **Save Version** button on the Versions toolbar. You can also open the **File** menu, click **Save As**, click the **Tools** button and click **Save Version**.

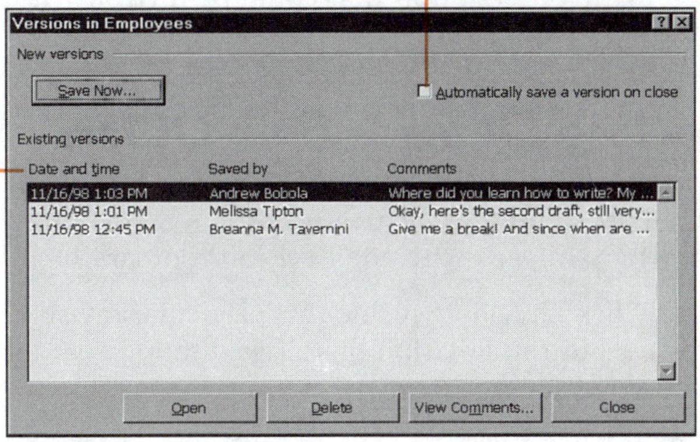

Figure 16.5: What version of my document do you want?

You can also set up versioning to automatically save a version each time the document is closed, which can provide a great audit trail for paranoid schizophrenics. Open the **File** menu and click **Versions**. Select the **Automatically save a version on close** check box. Click **Close** and sleep peacefully.

Adding, Editing, Reviewing Comments in a Document

Word 2000 enables you to save versions of your growing document along the way. Each version is a complete copy of your document as it existed at some point in time. It's a great feature to use when collaborating because you can always fall back on any earlier version if the content ever strays too far or if something is accidentally rearranged or erased.

Start the revision process on an opened document by clicking the **Track Changes** button on the Revising toolbar. Now make the changes you want by inserting, deleting, or moving text or graphics. With each change, you see revision markings like bars in the margins, text color changes, and lined-out text. These make it easy to find and understand changes.

- All changes are identified by a bar in the margin to help you quickly find them.
- Inserted text is a different color.
- Deleted text is lined out, but still visible and readable.
- Moved text is lined out in the old location, and a different color in the new location.
- All formatting changes may not be noticeable but are still identified by a bar in the margin.

If you don't like any or all of these revision formats, you can change them. Open the **Tools** menu and click **Options**. In the **Options** dialog box, click **Track Changes** and you see all the revision format options. Change them as you like, then click **OK** to save your changes in the current document.

Remember, you can add comments to help clarify any changes you might be making. Comments are a much better way to communicate changes to a document. You don't clutter the actual change with a description that could be misconstrued as part of the change.

Accepting or Rejecting Changes from Others

After your friend returns a revised document, you'll be ready to negotiate the changes. Revisions can either stand as they are, or become merged into your document. You control what happens with the Revision toolbar.

Like a particular change? Click anywhere inside this particular revision marking and click the **Accept Change** button. Revision markings disappear and the change is smoothly integrated into your document.

Don't agree with a change? Click the **Reject Change** button and the change is returned to its previous state. Revision markings disappear.

Likewise, comments can be added, edited, and deleted using the Comments portion of the Revision toolbar (you can even cut and paste comment text into the document). And you can speed through a document using only the **Next** or **Previous Change** buttons. At any time during the process you might decide it's time to call this document a new version by clicking the **Version** button.

Comparing Different Versions for Changes

What if colleagues forgot to turn on Revision markings before they made changes to your document? Do they run and hide as you hunt them down? Give them a break and test your wits with the Compare feature. Just find an earlier copy of the same document (go hunt it down) and compare the two. Any differences between the documents will be the most current revisions, right?

Make sure that the documents you are comparing have different filenames by renaming one of them (or, if you insist on the documents having the same name, make sure they are in different folders). Start by opening the latest version of your document. To start comparing, open the **Tools** menu, point to **Track Changes**, and choose **Compare Documents**.

Now find the other document you want to compare and double-click the name of the document to start the comparison process. Comparisons can take many seconds, even minutes, so be patient. When the comparison is completed, you see a single document on your screen with all differences between the two documents fully identified. You can save this as a new document, or discard it after reviewing the changes. Lawyers often use features such as this to determine if any changes have been made to a contract.

Protecting Your Work Before You Share

If you plan to share your document with lots of people, on a network for example, you may want to protect your document to prevent unauthorized changes. This section describes the different levels of security available to you.

Passwords Can Protect Your Secret Files

Word 2000 provides multiple ways to restrict access to your document. You find all of them by opening the **File** menu and choosing **Save As**. Click the **Tools** command and choose the **General Options** button and examine your **File Sharing Options** near the bottom. You can do any of the following:

- Assign a password to open the document, which prevents unauthorized users from opening the document.
- Assign a password to modify the document, which enables others to open the document but not to save changes without the password. If someone opens the document without the password to modify and changes the document, that person can save the document only by giving it a different filename.
- Recommend that others open the document as a read-only file. If someone opens the document as a read-only file and changes it, that person can save the document only by giving it a different filename. If someone opens the document as a read-write file and changes it, the document can be saved with its original filename.
- Assign a password when you route a document for review, which prevents any changes except for comments or tracked changes.

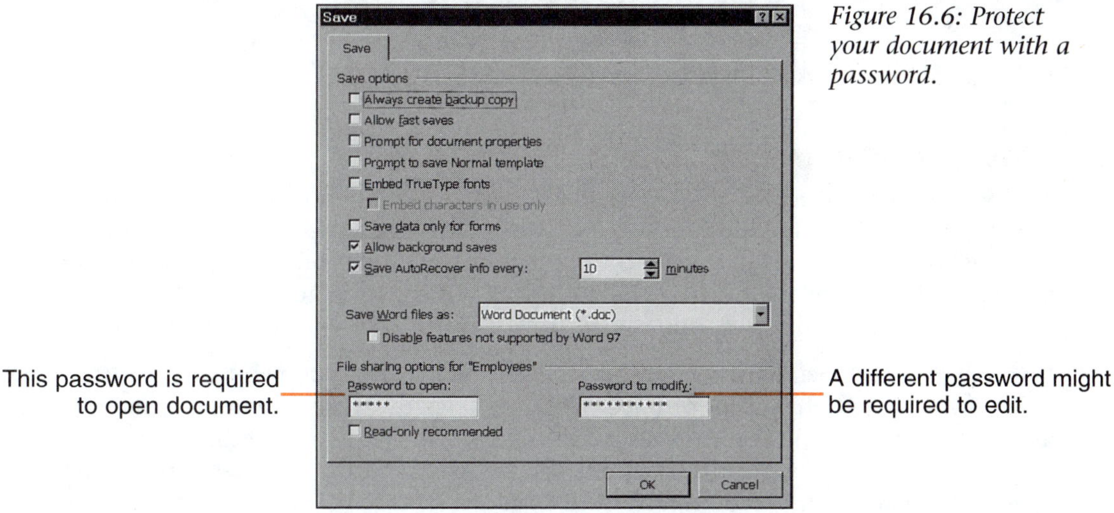

Figure 16.6: Protect your document with a password.

What If You Forget the Password?

If you assign password protection to a document and then forget the password, you can't open the document, remove protection from it, or even recover data from it. Pretty bad, huh? It's a good idea to keep a list of your passwords and their corresponding document names in a safe place, so you can refer to them at a time like this.

Preventing Virus Attacks

Be certain to protect yourself from "macro viruses." These may be hiding inside documents you receive from friend or foe, and once unleashed, they can do damage such as erasing information stored on your computer. Word 2000 offers some built-in protection: It can warn you about the presence of a macro in a document before it is opened. You get the chance to disable any macros and still open the document.

To make sure this level of virus protection is turned on, open the **Tools** menu, point to **Macros**, and click **Security**. Choose between High, Medium, and Low, depending on the level of security you need. Click **OK** to save this setting.

It's also a good idea to invest in a full-featured antivirus program such as McAfee VirusScan or Norton AntiVirus to protect all of your programs from the wide range of virus threats.

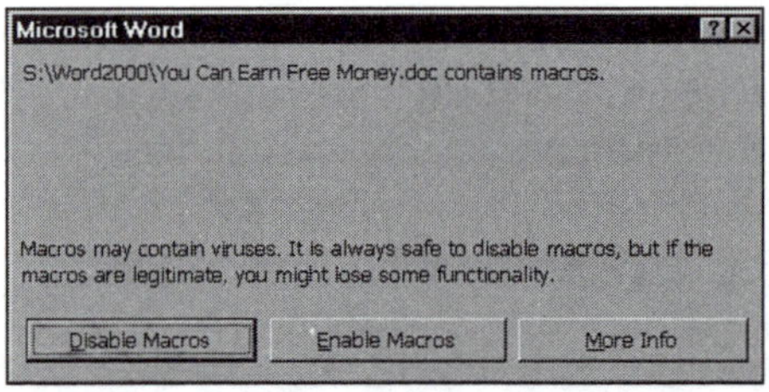

Figure 16.7: Word 2000 can warn you about potential viruses.

Sharing Documents on a Network

Now we're ready to share our document with just about anyone, because we know how to use revision markings and we can protect our document from unauthorized changes using passwords. It's time to trust technology and send your document off to be poked and prodded by your assortment of bosses, secretaries, and other work associates, until one day it finally returns to the warmth of your loving computer.

If you want your document reviewed by several people and you want final control over which changes to accept or reject, you can prepare a copy of your document and distribute it to others for revision editing. Instead of the old method of passing a single disk from one person to the next, you might try putting the network to work. Here are two alternatives you might want to try.

You can place the document in a shared location on network and have your team members access it one at a time. Each reviewer can take turns opening and revising the document as needed, and all changes are tracked automatically. When team members complete their reviews, the document is up-to-date.

Or, you can route a single document through your email system so each team member can open and revise the document, and then forwards it to the next person on the distribution list. After reaching each member, the document is then returned to you for review of all extraneous reviewers' changes and comments.

Setting Up Your Document for Sharing on the Network

Open the document you want set up as a shared document. For best results, make sure the document doesn't have multiple versions (or else your reviewers might open previous versions) by clicking **Versions** on the **File** menu. If multiple versions exist, save the current version as a separate document with a different name, and use this copy as the review copy. If this happens to be a newly created document, save it before performing these steps.

Can Two People Edit the Same Document at the Same Time?

In Word 2000, it's possible to have two people concurrently working on the same document, using a feature called *NetMeeting*. However, you may find it too awkward to be useful, because only one person can control the screen at a time.

But don't give up hope. A document can still be opened and edited while someone else has it opened, but the second person to open a document must save the changes using **Save As**, and provide a different name for the document. The result is two documents that may have to be merged manually, or you can use the compare feature (described earlier in this chapter) and merge them automatically.

It's almost a given that you'll want to have reviewers' changes and comments automatically appear as tracked changes, so turn on revision marks by opening the **Tools** menu and choose **Protect Document**. Click **Tracked Changes**. To let reviewers insert only comments but not change the contents of the document, click **Comments**.

Now place a copy of this document on a shared network drive where your team members have appropriate network access. Your network administrator can help with this, but generally it's a drive letter and a directory, or a folder, where users have read and write access. Now each team member can open and revise the document, and revisions are identified with the initials of the reviewer.

If a team member opens the document while another has it open, Word alerts him that it is currently opened by another user. Only one person can revise a document at a time, so this member can try to access it again later, when the document might be available. Or, if this person just wants to view, not edit, the document, he can click the **Open As Read-Only Copy** button. This enables full viewing of the document currently opened by someone else.

Figure 16.8: A dead giveaway that someone else has your document open.

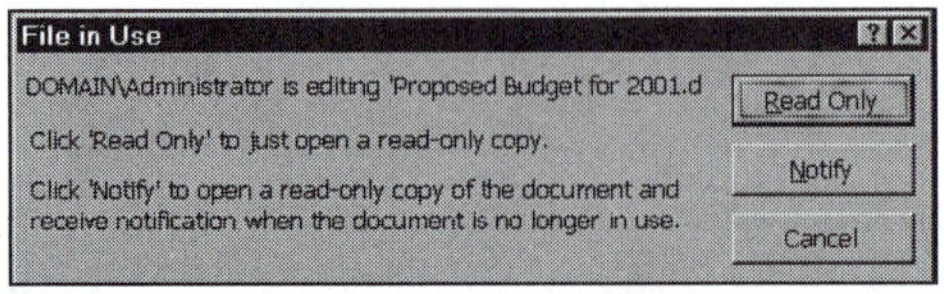

Sending Shared Documents by Email

The best method of routing a document to each member of the team for revisions is to use the email capabilities of your network. Instead of sending the document to all team members at once, you should route the document to each member, one at a time. You can accomplish this by including a note telling the reviewer to send it to the next team member when his revisions are complete, or you can use the automatic routing capabilities built into many email packages. After all of the recipients have reviewed the document, it should be returned to you with the accumulated revisions made by all team members.

To email your document to one or more people, just click the **Send to Mail Recipient** button on the Revision toolbar, or use the following options found in the **File** menu:

- **Email a document to another person.** Open the document you want to mail. Open the **File** menu, point to **Send To**, and click **Mail Recipient**. Address and send the mail message to whomever you want to receive the document, then click **Send**.
- **Route a document to multiple people.** Open the document you want to route. Open the **File** menu, point to **Send To**, and click **Routing Recipient**. To select your recipients for routing, click **Address**. In the **Type Name Or Select From** list box, type a recipient's name, and then click **To**. After you enter the last recipient's name in the To box, click **OK**. Select any other routing options you want, and then click **Route**.

The Least You Need to Know

Word 2000 offers several features to help you share your documents with others. You just have to learn how to use them. Some of the better ones are reviewed in this chapter.

➤ I want Web-style discussions for my team. Can I also get an automatic email notification if anyone ever touches my document?

Yes. Use the new online collaboration tools of Word 2000. Click **Tools**, **Online Collaboration**, and choose **Web Discussions**. Just subscribe to the important document, and ask the server to notify you of any changes.

➤ How can I control updates from several people on a single document?

Open the **Tools** menu and turn on **Track Changes** to initiate revision controls for that document. After that, all changes to a document are easily visible, manageable, and traceable to the originator.

➤ How can I protect my document from unauthorized personnel?

Protect it with a password. Nosy people won't be able to open or edit your document without the password.

➤ Is there an easy method to route this document during the revision process?

You can use email to conveniently send or route shared documents during the revision process. You'll find the **Send to Mail Recipient** button on the Revision toolbar.

➤ My yellow highlighter dried out last week. Am I out of luck?

Not if you use the **Highlight** button on the Formatting toolbar. You can quickly highlight a document with a click and drag of the mouse. If you need a different color, click the **Highlight color option** button right next to it and choose one of the color options.

Chapter 17

Using More Word 2000 Tools

In This Chapter

- Using AutoFormat and AutoSummarize tools
- Working with footnotes and endnotes
- Using Word as your email editor
- Adding a table of contents to your document
- Using Word 2000 Document Search features

Here's the place where you'll find the leftovers. But some of these powerful Word 2000 tools could be the main course to help you solve difficult formatting problems, or make life easier with automated correction of errors. Bon appétit!

A Hands-On Introduction to AutoFormat

If you are new to the whole subject of formatting styles, there's a quick way to jump in and immerse yourself. It's called the **AutoFormat** command. It sounds like a miracle worker—garbage in, beautiful document out, right? Not so, my friend. A better suited phrase for AutoFormat is garbage in, garbage out. And that's good enough, because it gets rid of the garbage most of us (who don't use styles) put into our documents as we create them.

Take a look at your **Style** box in the **Formatting** toolbar. Does it say *Normal*? Does it always say Normal? If so, then you aren't making use of styles. The **Normal** selection is the epitome of boring text. Now let's find the garbage produced by using nothing but the Normal style.

How do you separate paragraphs to make them look better on your page? Many people press **Enter** twice. Here in Utopia, that second **Enter** is considered useless, and therefore, garbage. How do you indent the first line of your paragraph? Even the Tab key is considered unnecessary (garbage) when using styles. Do you create numbered or bullet lists manually? Do you always center the page heading on the page, and make it bold or underlined? All of these formatting tasks needlessly chew up your valuable time.

Training Wheels: AutoFormat While You Type and Watch

During an AutoFormat, Word 2000 analyzes each paragraph within your document (even as you create it) to determine its purpose (such as a heading, a bullet or number list, regular text, and so on), and then applies an appropriate style from the current template.

Open the **Format** menu and choose the **AutoFormat** command. Click the **Options** button. Click to select the **AutoFormat As You Type** tab. Here you'll find_the automatic options. Go ahead and click to select the **Headings** box, to discover a fast way to create a document with consistent heading formats. Now start a new document and have some fun.

Figure 17.1: Save time with these AutoFormat features.

Try applying heading formats automatically with this.

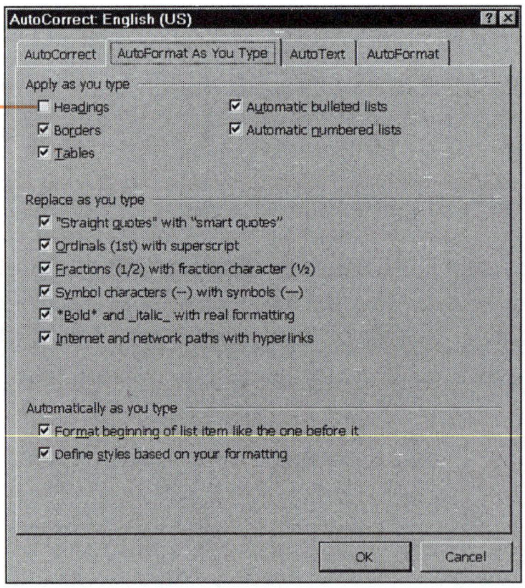

Type the title at the top of your page, and press **Enter** twice. How about that? Word watches you press Enter twice, determines the text is important enough to become a *style heading*, and picks a style called **Heading 1**. It also gets rid of the spare blank line above your insertion point.

Now press three underline symbols (_) and press **Enter**. An instant underline appears across the entire page! Actually, you always have this feature regardless of AutoFormat, and it even works with the equals symbol (=) and the hyphen (-) as well. Try using the **Tab** key to begin your second short sentence and press **Enter** twice. AutoFormat kicks in again, and you are pleasantly surprised with a **Heading 2** style applied (you must be using a Tab stop on your ruler for this one to work).

Keep going. Start a list by typing something like: *1) My first option* and press **Enter**. Instant numbered lists! AutoFormat presumes you want a *2)* next and gives it to you. It also removes any spaces or tabs you might have included between the number and your text. Not a bad way to create numbered lists in a hurry. As long as you include a closed parenthesis or a period (some form of punctuation) after the first number, AutoFormat kicks in and both adds new numbers and applies an appropriate style for you. To make it stop, just press **Enter** again, and you return to normal text.

You can also create quick bulleted lists this same way. Type an asterisk (*) or the letter *o* (you know, the one after *n*) and a space. Type some text and press **Enter** once. The asterisk or letter o is converted to a bullet symbol automatically.

Automatically Summarize Any Document

Got lots of large documents that you need to read, but you don't have the time? Feeling wild and crazy? How about letting Word 2000 automatically read those documents for you, and present you with a brief summary of the most important information. Sound like science fiction? Well, sometimes it borders on humor, but the new AutoSummarize tool is worth a look.

Keep in mind that AutoSummarize works best on well-structured documents, such as reports, articles, and scientific papers. And for the best-quality summaries, AutoSummarize recognizes and uses past, present, and future tenses of words in making its judgment as to what belongs in the summary.

Okay, the first time you try this you might laugh yourself silly, because maybe the summary isn't quite what you expected. Remember that AutoSummarize is only a tool, and you should review the accuracy of any summary because it is, after all, just a summary or your entire document.

AutoSummarize

A tool that might save you lots of time summarizing large documents is AutoSummarize. It analyzes and summarizes any document automatically.

Build Large Web Sites Faster

AutoSummarize can be a great help in building large Web sites, when you've got oodles of large documents that need to be condensed to provide abstracts and hyperlinks from the home page. Give this tool the first stab at it, then check it for accuracy, and edit as needed.

Got the New Mouse with the Wheel?

If you're using the new Microsoft IntelliMouse, you can use it to adjust the level of detail displayed in AutoSummarize view. To display more or less detail in five-percent increments, hold down the Shift key as you rotate the wheel forward or backward.

Create Your Abstract Automatically

Don't forget to save your document before trying this at home. Open the document you wish to analyze, then open the **Tools** menu and click **AutoSummarize**. When it's finished (longer documents may take a few seconds), in the **Type Of Summary** area click one of the four ways you can view the summary of the document.

- **Highlight Key Points**. This view maintains the original layout of your document, but highlights the words and sentences that express the major themes of the document.
- **Create A New Document and Put the Summary There**. This view leaves your original document untouched, but copies and consolidates the major themes of the document into a single summary, which is then placed in a newly created document, completely separate from your original document.
- **Insert an Executive Summary or Abstract at the Top of the Document**. Choose this to insert the automatic summary at the beginning of your document, where you can edit or save it as part of your document.
- **Hide Everything But the Summary Without Leaving the Original Document**. When you choose this option, only the summary text is displayed. All other text is hidden.

With each of these options, you can control the amount of summary information you receive. To adjust the level of detail, drag the yellow **Percent of original** slider (or click the arrows) in the AutoSummarize toolbar. This level is expressed as a percentage of your document, so if you choose 25 percent for the summary length of a four-page document, your summary is one page long. To switch between displaying only the key points or highlighting them within your document, click the **Highlight/Show Only Summary** button on this same toolbar.

Now click **OK**. You see the basic summary screen (prepared according to the option you've chosen), and the AutoSummarize toolbar. Spend a few moments to analyze it yourself. This summary text is nothing more than a "rough draft" and you should treat it as such. Make sure it covers the key points in your document. If it doesn't, click the **Undo** button to delete the summary, and then repeat the process, but this time choose a higher percentage of the original document. You can also keep a rough summary and modify it yourself later.

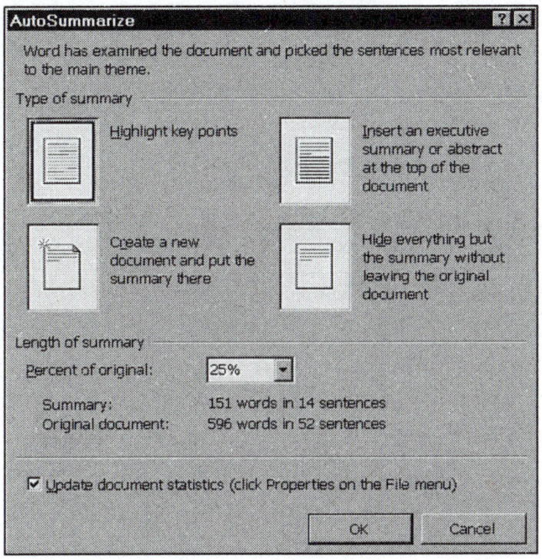

Figure 17.2: Need a quick summary of a long document?

How Does AutoSummarize Really Work?

AutoSummarize searches the document for keywords and sentences that represent the most frequently discussed topics. It then assigns a score to each sentence in your document. It gives a higher score to sentences that contain words used frequently in the document. When it completes, you decide what percentage of the highest-scoring sentences to display in the summary.

AutoSummarize then copies the keywords and sentences to the Keywords and Comments boxes on the Summary tab. To see this, open the **File** menu and click **Properties**. With this information stored here, you can easily locate the document by searching for the keywords or comments it contains. If you don't want AutoSummarize to replace your existing keywords and comments, clear the **Update document statistics** check box in the AutoSummarize dialog box.

Creating Footnotes

You remember footnotes from high school or college. At least you remember those little numbers in the text that always go with them. These are strategically placed to interrupt your reading and to send subliminal messages urging you to look down to the bottom of the page to see what was so important.

Well, if you really want to impress your boss, try placing footnotes in your status reports, referencing conversations you've secretly recorded. It's easy to make simple documents look impressively professional by following these tips on creating footnotes.

Your First Footnote Is the Hardest

If you have trouble making decisions in life, stick with the defaults, and you won't go wrong. This philosophy also applies to footnotes because the hardest part about creating them, besides writing them, is deciding where they should appear on your page. Some people like them at the bottom of the page (the default), some prefer just below the current paragraph, still others at the bottom of a table or the end of a document (but technically, that's called an endnote); the rest of us don't bother with footnotes.

Don't Confuse Footers with Footnotes

Yes, they're both at the bottom of your page, but serve different purposes. Footers appear at the bottom of *every* page (in the margin), regardless of the content of that page (see Chapter 10, "What's That in the Margins?").

Footnotes are easy to recognize by the little superscript number that identifies its reference point on that particular page. These are used as extended explanations of some detail in your writing, when you don't care to distract with too many details.

You can have several footnotes per page, and you can have both footnotes and footer on a page.

When you're ready to create a footnote, start by placing the insertion point where you want the footnote to be referenced. For a word, place the insertion point at the end of the word, and Word automatically places the footnote mark in the conventional location—slightly raised and to the right of the word. If you want to footnote an entire sentence, place the insertion point at the end of the last word of the sentence. Open the **Insert** menu and select the **Footnote** command. You see the **Footnote and Endnote** dialog box.

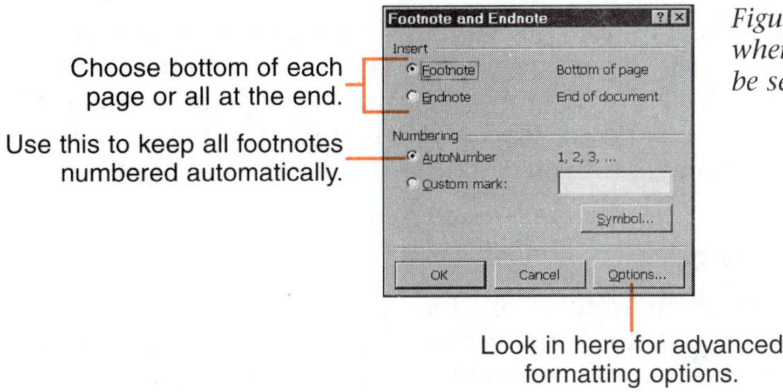

Figure 17.3: Deciding where footnotes should be seen.

Make sure you leave **AutoNumber** selected so your footnotes are correctly numbered and organized. You may also want to try the **Options** button, which helps adjust the placement of notes, sets note numbering and formatting options, and converts notes to footnotes or endnotes (or vice versa). And if you would prefer to use a different symbol as a custom note reference mark, click the **Symbol** button.

When you click **OK**, you are transported to the footnote area at the bottom of the page. You normally don't see this part of your page when your view is set to Normal. If you insert a footnote while in Normal view, the window splits and the cursor is transported to a footnote editor. Working in **Print Layout** view moves the cursor to the bottom of the page, where the footnotes are located.

Now start typing your footnote. You can place almost anything in a footnote, including text, pictures, and charts (and even sounds and video for multimedia buffs). Footnotes can be long, and can exceed a page in length. Don't fret, because Word 2000 takes care of the formatting.

Graphics in Footnotes?

If you're serious about sticking things such as pictures, charts, or graphs in your headers, footers, or footnotes, you need to see a doctor soon. In the meantime, you can review Chapter 14, "Importing a Fine Piece of Text," which shows you how to add pictures just about anywhere, including in footnotes.

When you are finished typing, click the **Close** button. If you happen to be in **Print Layout** view, you don't need to do anything—you're finished. Now admire your work. Little numbers appear properly, and the page is adjusted to fit the footnote.

The good news is that once you've set your footnote options, you don't have to come back to this dialog box each time you add another footnote or endnote.

Spewing Forth Footnotes

After the first footnote has been placed, the rest are easy to create—even if you have to place one earlier in your document. Click where you need it and select the **Footnote** command from the **Insert** menu. You are now in the footnote editing area. Type away and click **Close** when finished. No more menus to worry about, and the numbering is taken care of for you.

Editing Footnotes

If you need to change the wording of a footnote or two, they can easily be edited. Just double-click the little footnote number and the handy footnote editing window appears, with the cursor already at the start of the footnote text. Or, if your aim is not so good on those little numbers, you can switch to **Print Layout** view and see the footnotes directly. Either way, once you are inside the footnote area you can edit your footnote directly. After editing the footnote, click the **Close** button, or simply click in the main body of your document to return to it.

Deleting Footnotes

Now here's a demonstration of Word 2000 doing something really helpful for you. Let's say you've got 27 footnotes in your research document on the livers of aquatic emus, and you just realize the first one is incorrect and has to be deleted. Word not only blasts it away and reformats the entire document, but more importantly renumbers and re-references the remaining footnotes automatically. Now that's what you bought a computer for.

To delete a footnote, you must go to the footnote number in your document, not the header and footer area. You don't have to be in Print Layout view when you delete a footnote. Select the footnote's number in your document (it appears highlighted) and press the **Delete** key.

To delete all automatically numbered footnotes or endnotes, open the **Edit** menu and choose the **Replace** command. Click **Special** and then click **Endnote Mark** or **Footnote Mark**. Make sure the **Replace With** box is empty, and then click **Replace All**. You cannot delete all custom footnote marks at one time.

Cutting, Copying, and Pasting Footnotes

Even geeks are amazed that you can cut and paste a footnote from one area to another if needed. Select the footnote and click the **Cut** button. Find the proper location for the footnote and click the **Paste** button. If you pass another footnote during the move, everything is renumbered automatically and referenced correctly for you.

Copying is just as easy for those popular *ibid's*, *op. cit.'s*, or plain old *See Footnote #1's*. Select the footnote and click **Copy**, and go find the next location. Click the **Paste** button and you've got a newly numbered visitor here to stay.

Try Microsoft Office Email

What's this? Email in my word processor? Not just any email editor, mind you, but Word itself tuned especially for email, and now called *Microsoft Office Email*. Yes, when you installed Word 2000, the Office Email component is installed by default as one of its features. Lots of you have been clamoring for this (keep it down) because you wanted full formatting capabilities (and new *Personal Stationery*) in your email. Office Email works in conjunction with your email system and enables you to create mail messages with all the formatting capabilities of Word 2000.

Send an email from inside Word. Click **File**, **Send To**, and choose **Mail Recipient**. The top part of your screen morphs into an email header, complete with address book and priority buttons! These should be tied to your email package, of course, or else they won't do much. Compose your mail and send!

Start Office Email from Your Web Browser!

Any recent version of Web browser, including the Microsoft Internet Explorer and Netscape Navigator, includes access to email through a button or menu command. Choosing this command automatically starts Office Email. If it doesn't start automatically, check the options for setting the default email editor inside your browser.

Improve the Look of Your Email Messages

Word 2000 includes several email templates to help you compose your email when you use Office Email as your email editor. Each template has a different theme. For example, you might use the urgent theme template to compose an urgent mail message. Click the **Format** menu and choose **Theme**, then choose one and click **OK**.

In addition, Word automatically formats headings and lists in your plain text messages when you open them. You can easily distinguish the current message from the previous messages in the email conversation.

Word 2000 as Your Outlook Email Editor

Open Microsoft Outlook 2000, click **Options** on the **Tools** menu, and then click the **Mail Format** tab. To turn on Word 2000 as your email editor, click to put a check in the **Use Microsoft Word To Edit Email Messages** check box. To turn off Word as your email editor, clear this check box.

Automatically Format Your Office Email Messages

Want to format the email coming in, to clean it up from its Internet journey? To automatically format your Office Email messages, open the **Format** menu, click **AutoFormat**, and click the **Options** button. Under **Always AutoFormat**, select the **Plain Text Office Email Documents** check box. When you select this option, Word 2000 automatically formats unformatted email messages that you open using Office Email. To help you even more, Word automatically formats all Internet addresses in your Email messages as hyperlinks. That means you can click on the hyperlink and jump right to that destination.

Figure 17.4: Personal Stationery creates impressive email solutions.

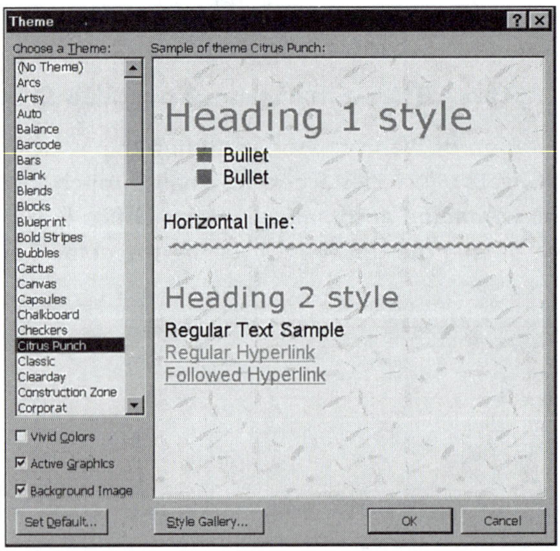

Several Office Email formatting features don't appear in other email programs. If recipients of your messages aren't using Word as their email editor, then borders, highlighted text, numbered lists, and floating drawings in your messages may not appear. Also, other editors may display tables as tab-delimited text and reduce all fancy bullets to plain round bullets.

Fancy Email Formatting

Word 2000 offers a couple of new features to brighten your email adventures. The first is called *Personal Stationery*, and it's a huge set of email templates already designed for special occasions or just day-to-day use. Just click **Format** and choose **Apply Stationery** in the Mail Header toolbar. Click to choose the style you like, and then customize to your heart's content. Send them anywhere, even over the Internet, and the formatting is supposed to stay with it. Don't go overboard, however, since even simple formatting can make an email grow to very large sizes.

Tired of typing your initials at the end of each email? Now you can send your signature! Actually, it's a picture of your signature, saved as a small graphic file, in the new feature called Email AutoSignature. Basically, you sign anything and scan it in (if you're artistic, try the Drawing toolbar and scribble one yourself). Save it in a personal folder, and call it up during email creation. Click the **Tools** menu and choose **AutoSignature**, and choose this saved file. Quite impressive.

Adding a Table of Contents Automatically

If you've paid your dues, then you can reap your rewards, and the automatic *Table of Contents* generator in Word 2000 is a big reward. The only dues required are consistent use of heading Styles throughout your document. For example, use Heading 1 for the big chapters, Heading 2 for sections in those chapters, and so on (even including a heading for tables or figures if you like). You'll get a great-looking document anyway, even if you don't use the TOC function.

Once your document has Heading styles for all the important parts, you can generate a table of contents. Start with a click in your document telling it exactly where to place this table of contents (usually up front). Open the **Insert** menu, click **Index and Tables**, and then click the **Table of Contents** tab.

Click to choose from the different appearances available for your table of contents. Also decide how many levels, and which levels, you want to include in your table of contents. For example, maybe your document title is the only Heading 1; you might choose to ignore that heading. Or maybe skip other headings to keep the size down, but perhaps leave in a lowly heading that you've used for figures or tables, because you'd like to include them. Experiment! You can always delete a table of contents and try again.

Afraid to try a TOC because you forgot to use styles, and you think it's too hard to apply them now? Try this tip when no one is looking—have Word 2000 automatically format your document with AutoFormat. The result might be close enough to a result that allows for a decent table of contents. If not, you can also **Undo** an AutoFormat.

Figure 17.5: Generating a table of contents for your document automatically.

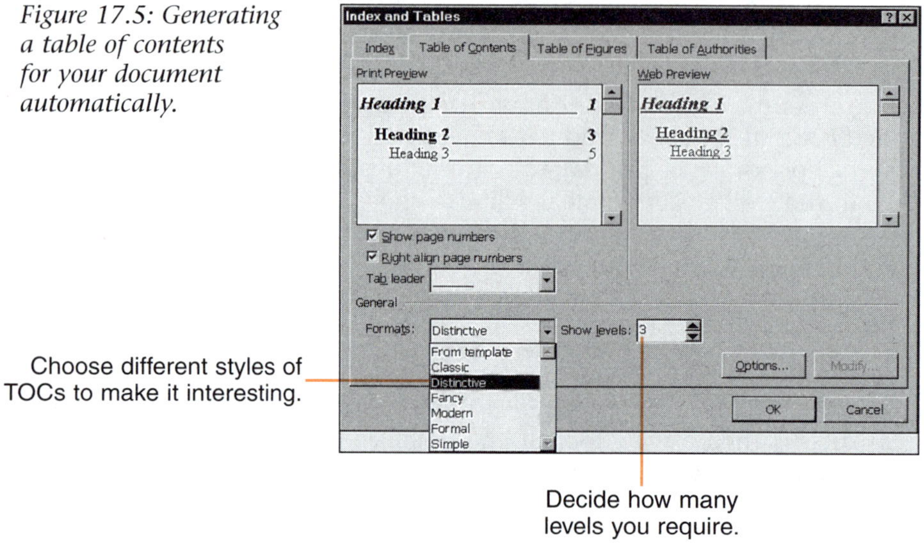

Using Word 2000 Document Searching Tools

It's tough enough to find your car keys in this day and age—you don't need the extra headache of a complicated search for a particular document. Thank goodness Word 2000 provides the kind of searching tools we've been asking for since the Industrial Age began. Too bad it can't also find car keys.

Where to Look

To begin your search for a document, click **Open** (or open the **File** menu and choose the **Open** command). The start of a search for any document usually begins with the **Look In** box at the top of the **Open** dialog box. Click it to reveal a list containing all the possible places your computer can search for your documents. By double-clicking any of these icons, you can dig deeper into the folder levels to find your documents. For example, double-clicking Desktop displays My Computer, and double-clicking My Computer reveals all the folders at the very top level of the computer's hard disk.

Up One Level

A folder can contain documents and other subfolders. When you double-click a folder, you go down into it, and see the documents and folders that might be stored inside. To move to a parent folder, click the **Up One Level** button. Click it once and you move up a folder level. Click it again and you move up another, and so on, until you are at the top level of your computer. You can also click the **Backspace** key, which has the same function as Up One Level. Prefer browser buttons? Click the new **Previous** button to view the previous folder, wherever it may be.

Your Favorite Hiding Spot

Another new button in the **Open** dialog box can help you store and find documents: the **Favorites** button. The Favorites folder could become your favorite place to store the documents you create.

Click **Favorites** to search this area for documents. You can also create folders inside Favorites, and you probably should if you plan to store more than a handful of documents here. Organize your documents by storing them in several logical folders, and name the folders so you recognize them, such as Weekly Reports, or Client Contracts, and so on. It will be much easier to find what you're looking for in the future.

Search the Web

If you need to find a source of information on the Internet, click the **Search the Web** button to open the search page of your Internet browser.

Looking on Disks

Lots of people save their documents to disk—with good reason. There's a lot of comfort in the fact that you can carry the documents wherever you go, on a single disk that's easy to protect. Word 2000 can find your documents on disk as well. Open the **File** menu and choose the **Open** command. Near the top of the dialog box, click to open the **Look In** text box. Click the **3 1/2 Floppy (A)** to display the contents of your disk.

If you don't see any documents, it could mean that the files stored on disk were not created with Word; in that case, your best bet is to view all possible file formats on the disk. Click the **Files of Type** box near the bottom left of the **Open** dialog box. In the drop-down box that appears, scroll to the top of the list and choose **All Files**. This option enables you to see the name of any type of file, no matter what program may have created it.

Searching All Over for Your Documents

A fast way to find documents isn't part of Word at all, but you should know about it. Click the **Start** button, point to **Find**, and choose **Files or Folders**. Use the search capabilities found on any of these three tabs, in any combination.

- **Name and Location**. Type as much or as little of the name as you can remember. You can also include words found inside your document, even if you can't remember the filename, by typing them in **Containing Text**.
- **Date**. If you have an inkling of when something was created, say a date range or the month of June, you can include that information here, and find those documents.
- **Advanced**. Not as useful unless you happen to know the size of what you're looking for.

Confirm the appropriate drive and folder exists in the **Look In** box, and be sure **Include Subfolders** is checked. Click **Find Now** and you'll obtain a listing of all documents that meet these criteria.

Still can't find your document? It's time to get creative and unleash the detective powers of Word 2000. To get started, open the **File** menu and choose **Open**. In the **Open** dialog box, click the **Tools** menu and choose the **Find** command. You see a slightly different **Find** dialog box than the one we saw in Chapter 8, as shown in the following figure.

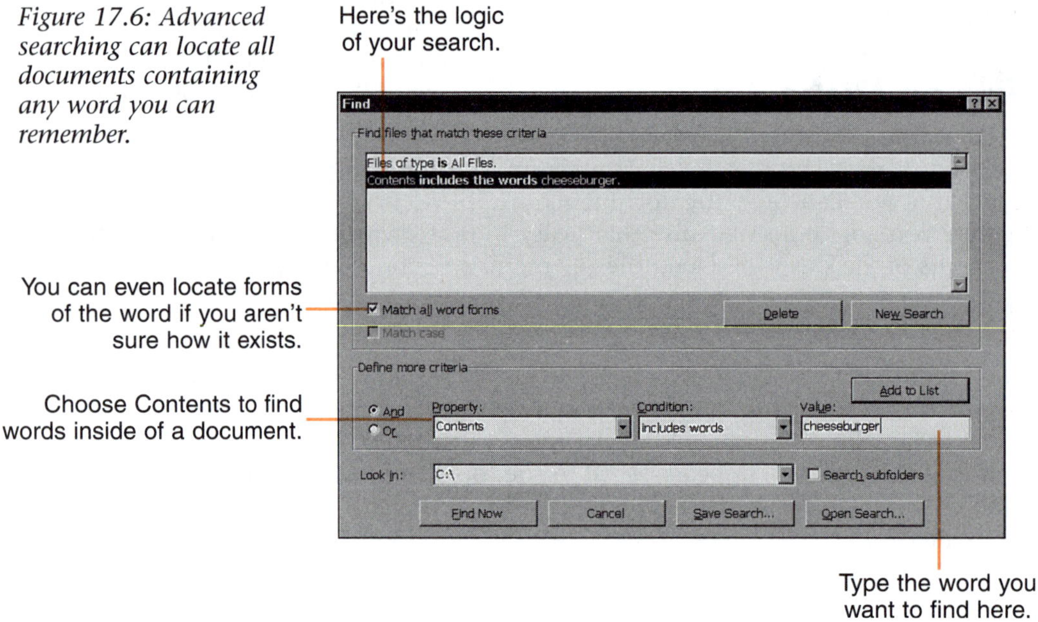

Figure 17.6: Advanced searching can locate all documents containing any word you can remember.

This dialog box may look intimidating, but it's worth the investment in learning a powerful search tool. The top area lists your current search statements (you can have more than one). You create these statements by choosing a value in each of the three boxes in the **Define More Criteria** area:

- **Property**. Choose what you want to find.
- **Condition**. Choose the operator (usually "begins with," or "contains").
- **Value**. Type your own search words here.

When all three line up to create a meaningful search, like "*Contents - includes words – Cheeseburger*," click the **Add to List** button and this search statement appears in the top area. To execute this search, click the **Find Now** button.

After a successful search, you may want to save your searching parameters for the next time you need to search. You can save your search criteria by clicking the **Save Search** button and providing a name for your search.

The Least You Need to Know

At last, if you couldn't find it in the rest of the book, you probably found it here.

- I need to add a footnote in this exact location. What do I do?

  Create a footnote easily by first clicking where you need it, then open the **Insert** menu, and choose **Footnote**. To move or copy a footnote, use the **Cut**, **Copy**, and **Paste** buttons. Footnotes renumber automatically.

- I'm a real beginner and my document looks boring. What can I do?

  Use the AutoFormat features of Word 2000 to improve the appearance of your document and to correct typos on-the-fly. Open the **Format** menu and choose **AutoFormat**.

- This document is huge and I'd like to summarize it. Are there any features hiding in Word 2000 that might help me?

  The **AutoSummarize** feature can help you analyze a document even before you read it—by automatically creating an abstract, or summary report. Try it by clicking **AutoSummarize** on the **Tools** menu.

- My email package lacks a decent editor. Can I use Word instead?

  Microsoft Office Email is a helpful tool that provides full formatting features as you compose email. It's automatically installed with Word 2000, and is waiting to be your email editor of choice. Just open the **File** menu, click **Send To**, and choose **Mail Recipient**.

- When is it best to add a table of contents?

  Most people wait until a document is complete before adding the table of contents. Open the **Insert** menu and choose the **Index and Tables** command. An index or table of contents can be generated automatically. If you've used Style Headings consistently in your document, your new index or table of contents may achieve a status of perfection.

- I've lost my document. What kind of search tools are available?

  Powerful searching capabilities are built into the **File Open** features of Word 2000. You can search your entire computer for details about your document, such as date ranges that may have been created, words that may be in the document name, or even text that may be inside the document.

Chapter 18

Desktop Publishing Techniques

In This Chapter

- Fast and easy newsletters
- Creating columns like a newspaper
- Flowing text from one location to another
- Using WordArt
- How to create a drop cap

Read all about it! All the tips that are fit to print (the ones related to newsletters, anyway) are located in this chapter. And these features aren't just for newspapers alone—you'll find uses for some of these features in all your documents, especially formatting your text into columns, flowing text around graphics, and using some unusual character-formatting tools.

Instant Newsletter Guaranteed!

You can't go wrong with a wizard on your side. Although this entire chapter covers details about creating your own newsletter, here's an example that might be enough to satisfy your requirements. Word 2000 comes with a Newsletter Wizard that walks you through the creation of something good enough to sell on the street corner.

Can't find your Newsletter Wizard?

If you can't find your Newsletter Wizard, try checking the Microsoft Office Update Web site at `officeupdate.microsoft.com`, where you'll find the latest enhancements to your copy of Word 2000.

Start a new document by opening the **File** menu and choosing the **New** command. You must use the menu, and not the **New** button on the Standard toolbar, to find the Wizard. In the **File New** dialog box, click the **Publications** tab to bring it to the front. Double-click on the **Newsletter Wizard**.

Figure 18.1: Instant newsletter success using the wizard.

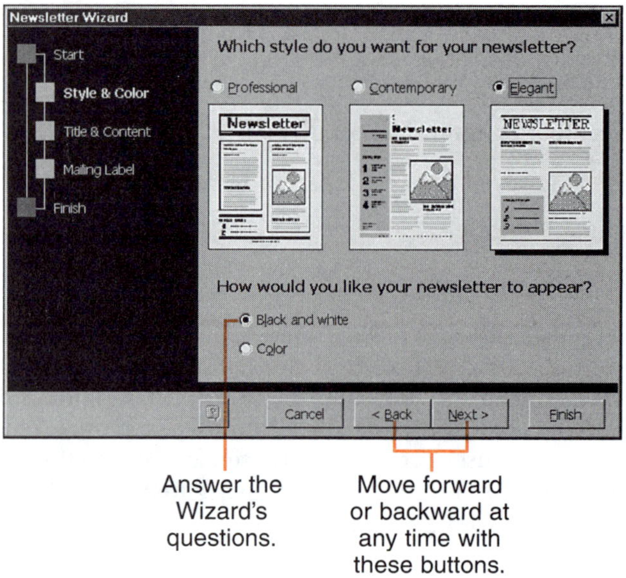

When the wizard starts, you see an attractive finished newsletter in the **Preview** box. Your first decision is to choose among the three styles shown. Click the **Next** button to continue to the next question. That's all there is to talking to your wizard.

Continue answering the following questions. Notice that a default appears in all of them, so you can easily get through the process by pressing nothing more than the **Next** button.

- How many columns do you want?
- What's the name of the newsletter?

- How many pages do you think it will be?
- Would you like any of these options—Table of Contents, Fancy First Letters, Date, Volume and Issue?

When you click the **Finish** button on the last Wizard dialog box, a completely formatted professional-looking newsletter appears on your screen.

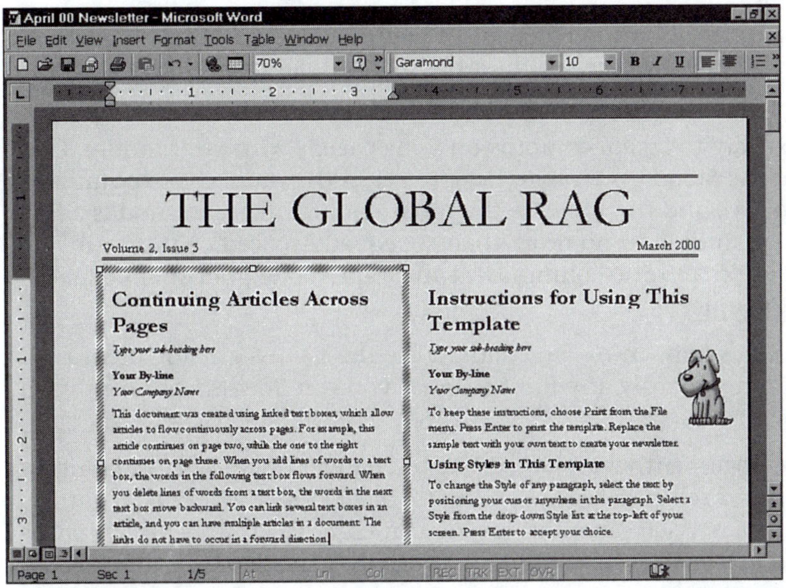

Figure 18.2: Time to add articles to your newsletter.

With the formatting completed, you are left with filling in the contents of your newsletter articles. You can click directly in the heading of a column and type your headline, then click in the text area to type your news article. You never have to worry about paragraph formatting because it has already been created for you.

When you save your newsletter, it is saved as a regular document, albeit one with loads of formatting. The point is that it's no longer related to the wizard that created it. You can use the wizard over and over again to create different newsletters.

If you always choose the same options in the Newsletter Wizard, you can save even more time by opening a previously created newsletter and saving it with a new name. Then you can simply make changes to it. Or, if you want to get fancy, you can create your own custom newsletter template. The details for creating your own template are found in Chapter 19, "Templates, Themes, and Styles."

Doing Columns

Which would you rather read, a supermarket tabloid claiming that the "President is Bigfoot," or the novel *War and Peace*? Probably the tabloid, but not for the reasons you might think (the president just isn't that big and hairy). Newspapers in general, along with magazines and newsletters, align their text in multiple columns on a page. Why? It's easier to read that way. You don't have to move your eyes as much, or turn your head, shoulders, or entire body to keep up with the text running across the pages of a book.

Creating Columns

Believe it or not, you are already using columns in your documents. It just happens to be one large column that stretches the width of the margins. So much for trivia. But, you can add multiple columns anytime you need them.

The absolute fastest way to create columns on your page is with your mouse. Click the **Columns** button on the Standard toolbar. Drag to select the number of columns you want (from two to six), and then release the mouse button. This method is a bit restrictive because you're limited to no more than six equally spaced columns (in Portrait mode or no more than nine columns in Landscape mode), but that's usually good enough for most people.

To learn more about what's happening, you should use the **Columns** dialog box to create your columns. There's hardly any limit to what you can do with columns when you create them this way.

Start by clicking in the document where you'd like to change the number of columns. Open the **Format** menu and select **Columns**. Select any of the preset column patterns by clicking on the examples. As an alternative, you can enter the number of columns you want in the **Number of Columns** text box. If you need to create a section break so you don't affect earlier text, select the number of columns you want and then choose **This Point Forward** in the **Apply To** list box. You'll see a preview of your choices in the Preview screen. When you are finished, press **OK** and return to your document, now formatted in columns.

When you add columns to a document, the width of the columns is adjusted automatically so they fit between the margins. For instance, if you add three columns, the width of your paper is divided into three equal parts. You can also decide to create column widths that are unequal, if you want a different effect.

If you want to try creating columns of different widths, remove the check from the **Equal Column Width** check box by clicking on it. Now you can enter the width and spacing desired for each column. The numbers you enter are in the default unit of measure, in this case, inches. Try entering different numbers and watch the effect in the Preview box.

Editing Columns (Making Them Bigger or Smaller)

Your columns should be wide enough to have at least a few words (4 or 5 minimum) on each line for readability. If you find you're averaging one or less, you have a problem. To change the width of your columns using your mouse, first expose your horizontal ruler. If your ruler isn't visible, open the **View** menu and make sure the **Ruler** is checked by clicking on it. To change the width of a column, drag the column marker on the horizontal ruler to the right or left, until the column meets your approval.

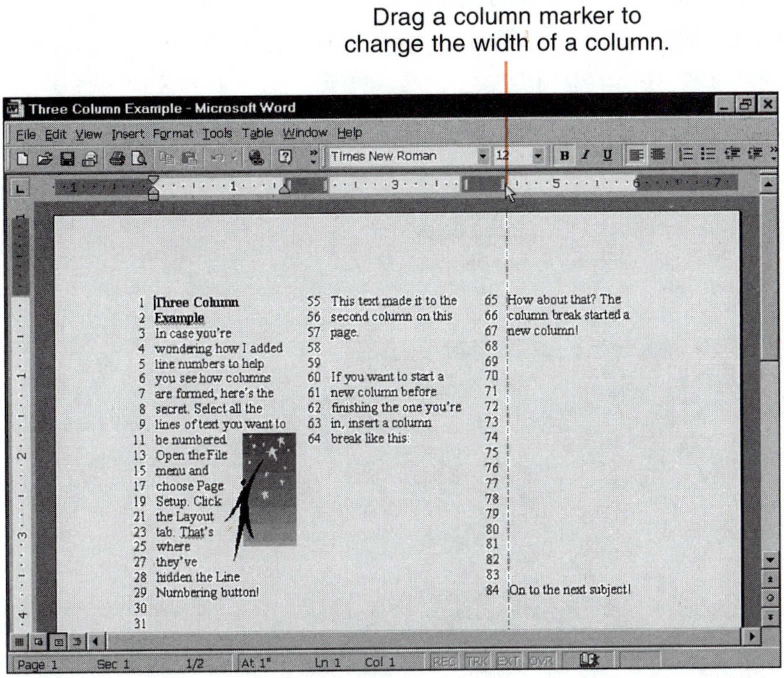

Figure 18.3: Controlling the width of your columns.

To make precise changes to your columns, open the **Format** menu and choose the **Columns** command. Enter a new measurement in the **Width** box. If column widths are even, the other columns adjust automatically. If you are using uneven columns, enter new measurements for each column. You can also change the spacing between columns.

Viewing Your Columns

Each viewing mode displays columns a little differently, with each view offering its own advantages. At least when it comes to columns, the Normal view (most common all-purpose view) doesn't do a good job of displaying columns. Try the **Print Layout** View, which can be found by clicking its button on the Horizontal scrollbar.

To make things even better, you can zoom in to get a closer look at text or zoom out to get a bigger overall picture of your work. Just click the **Zoom** box down arrow on the Standard toolbar and select a magnification from the drop-down list box. You can also zoom by opening the **View** menu and choosing the **Zoom** command.

Dividing Your Columns with Lines

Sometimes it helps to keep those eyes where they belong. Truckers call it white line fever when you start hugging the middle of the road. Reading can be boring sometimes, just like driving, but instead of blasting the radio to stay awake (or improving your writing), you can draw lines between your columns of text to help contain them. It's especially helpful when your columns are close together.

Remember that you should be in **Print Layout View** when working with columns, and especially when creating these lines. Open the **Format** menu and choose **Columns**. Then click the **Line Between** check box. Using the **Apply To** box, select how much of the document you want the line to appear in.

Figure 18.4: Vertical lines make columns easier to read.

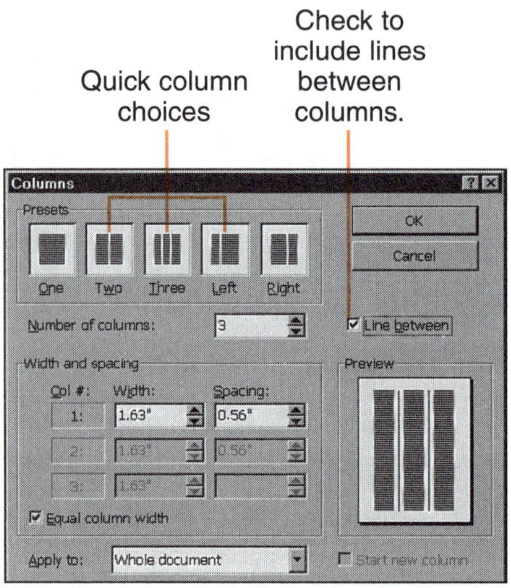

Other Ways to Draw Lines

The **Line Between** option places lines between all the columns in that section. There is no way to place a line between only two columns in a three-column section using this option. You can always create a line yourself by using the Drawing toolbar and then place it between two of the columns.

Straightening Out the End of Those Columns

Take a look at the last page of your newly columned document. When real newspapers or magazines can't fill a page, at least they balance the remaining text across the multiple columns. You can, too—and it's easy. Just insert a section break at the end of the document. Open the **Insert** menu and select **Break**. Under Section Breaks, choose **Continuous**, and then click the **OK** button.

You Want to Add Pictures in Your Column?

Sure you want to add pictures to your newsletter or columns. They would be boring without them. Chapter 11, "Decorating Your Document with Pictures," provides all the details about how to insert pictures and scanned photographs (called imported art or graphics) from other programs. To insert a picture or clip art, open the **Insert** menu, point to **Picture**, and then click the type of picture you are inserting. Once the picture is in your document, you can use the Picture toolbar to crop the picture, add a border to it, and adjust its brightness and contrast.

You might also be wondering how to get text to flow around a picture or graphic. That's in Chapter 11 also. There's no secret to this skill; just right-click your graphic, choose **Format Picture**, and click the **Wrapping** tab. The top row displays five different wrapping styles; click the one you prefer. The next row provides options for side margins of wrapping. Use these with larger graphics to keep text flowing on one side only.

Flowing Text to Another Part of Your Document

Want to make that story from page one finish in a column on page three, skipping page two altogether? You can make text flow in a continuous story from one location in your document to the next by creating text boxes. You place your text in these boxes and then create text box links throughout your document, even if the locations aren't adjacent.

When you add lines of text to a linked text box, the text flows forward into the next text box. When you delete lines of text from a text box, the text in the next text box moves backward. It's a neat trick. You can link several text boxes in a document, and you can have multiple sets of linked text boxes. The links can flow forward or backward through your document.

Creating Text Boxes for Flowing Text

Open the **Insert** menu and click **Text Box**. Click or drag in your document where you want to insert the first text box. The instant you create your first text box, the Text Box toolbar appears. Now click and drag your second text box, where you want the text to flow. Click the first text box to start the linking process. On the Text

Box toolbar, click **Create Text Box Link**. Now click in the text box that you want the text to flow to. The text boxes are now linked. To link to more text boxes, continue these same steps to create the box and then link them. In the first text box, type text that you want. As the text box fills, the text flows into the other text boxes that you've linked. The text box that you link to must be empty (and not previously linked somewhere else). To use the Text Box shortcut menu, move the pointer over the border of the text box until the pointer becomes a four-headed arrow, and then right-click the border.

Figure 18.5: Text boxes let you flow your words anywhere.

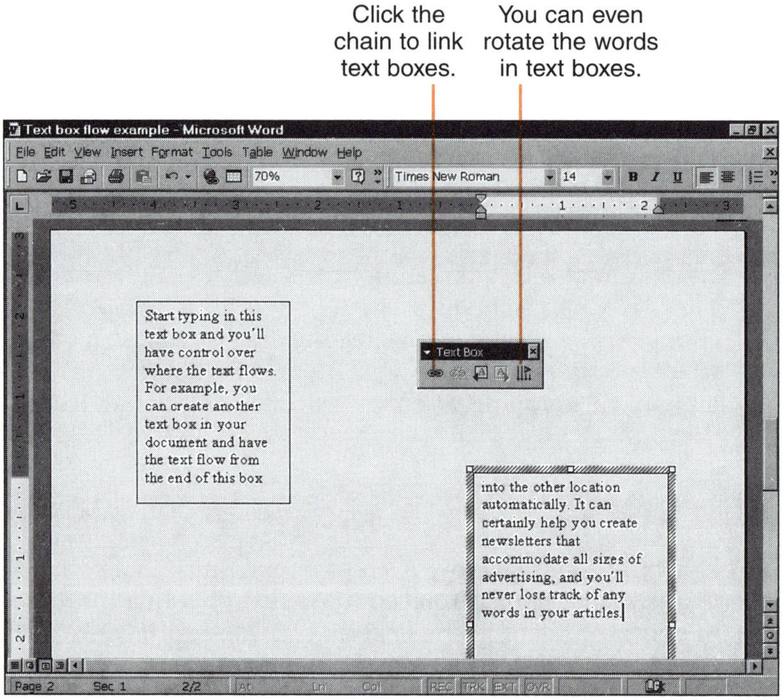

How Do I Stop This Thing?

If you click **Create Text Box Link** and then decide you don't want to link to another text box, press the **Esc** key to cancel the linking process.

To restore the Text Box toolbar if you accidentally close it, click a text box in your document, point to **Toolbars** on the **View** menu, and then click **Text Box**. (Your document must contain a text box for this toolbar to be available on the list.)

If you want to make your text box more interesting, you can remove the borders, change borders, or add background colors or textures. First, select the text box, then click the **Text Box** command on the **Format** menu (it appears only if a text box is selected).

Creating Flowing Text to an AutoShape

It's just as easy to create text box links between different shapes, such as circles, diamonds, flowchart shapes, even stars and banners. First, create your drawing object, then right-click the shape. Click **Add Text** on the shortcut menu. Now, select the first text box or drawing object containing the text you want to flow. On the Text Box toolbar, click **Create Text Box Link**. Finally, click in your drawing object (when you move the upright pitcher over a text box that can receive the link, the pitcher turns into a pouring pitcher) and the text flows.

Deleting a Linked Text Box Without Deleting the Text

If you need to delete a linked text box but you want to save the text inside, click the text box to see the border handles. Carefully move the pointer over the border of the text box until the pointer becomes a four-headed arrow, and then click the border. Press the **Delete** key and the text box vanishes. The text, however, is stuffed back into the previously linked text box.

Playing with Your Words (Special Character Formatting)

Work hard. Play hard. Sleep in. Being the life of the party is hard work—so is coming up with ideas to make your words more interesting. The tools to accomplish this task, however, are easy to use and work quite well in Word 2000. You'll now learn how to take your best stuff and make it even better.

Dropping Your Caps

You've seen them all over the place, in magazines, books, and newspapers. Big letters. Really big. But only one, and it's the first letter of the first word of the reading. They have a name for this kind of thing. It's called a *drop cap*.

The drop cap used to be a special effect reserved for highly talented artists, editors, and monks. Now with Word 2000, mere mortals can create them in a fraction of the time once required. Not much to learn here except how to choose the **Drop Cap** command from the **Format** menu.

To create a drop cap, move to the paragraph where you want to place it, then open the **Format** menu and choose the **Drop Cap** command. In the **Drop Cap** dialog box, you can change the font and point size in the text boxes provided. Choose whether you want it **Dropped** or **In Margin**. You can also change the number of lines to drop by clicking **Lines to Drop**. This determines the size of the drop cap letter. You can even change the distance between the drop cap and the paragraph text by clicking on **Distance from Text**. Click the **OK** button (or **Enter**) to close the dialog box.

Staying Young and Playful with WordArt

WordArt is a tool enabling you to manipulate words artistically, and it goes beyond the normal text attributes you learned about in Chapter 9, "Enhancing Your Paragraphs & Pages with Formatting Options." Take a look at some examples, and you will agree that they could have a place in your newsletter:

Figure 18.6: Fast and easy examples of WordArt.

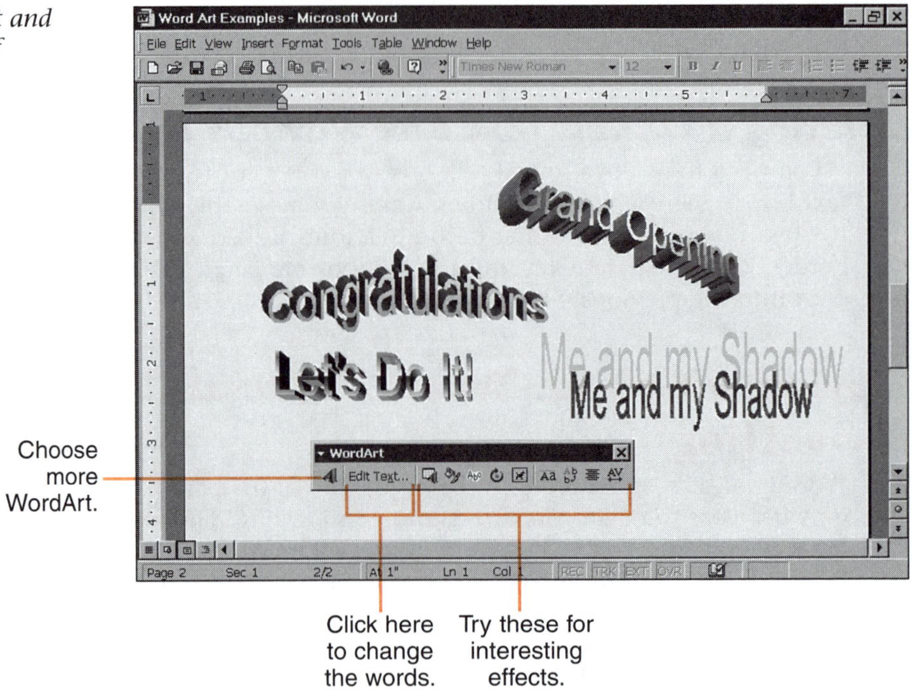

To give WordArt a try, click where you want the creation. Open the **Insert** menu, point to **Picture**, and choose **WordArt**. Here are actual WordArt samples; you just select the one you like and click the **OK** button. You see the **Edit WordArt Text** dialog box waiting for you to type in the words you want to display as art. Type some text, then click the **OK** button. The text you've entered is converted to WordArt and is placed in your document, along with the new WordArt toolbar, in case you want to customize it further. Click the **Edit Text** button on the WordArt toolbar if you need to change this text. That's all it takes!

Because your new WordArt is a graphic, you can change the size and shape by clicking and dragging the handles that appear when the graphic is selected.

The WordArt toolbar contains helpful buttons to assist you even more, by letting you twist, rotate, color, fill, and more. It's easier to experience than to describe, so give them all a chance to impress you. If something happens that you don't like, you can always click the **Undo** button.

Boxing Your Words and Shading Them Well

Warning labels had trouble in the 1950s and 1960s. Nobody was reading them. Dying continued to be the major cause of death around the world. But then, almost like magic, someone decided to draw a box around a warning label. People started reading them. Lives were saved. And now you can do the same in Word 2000 (draw a box, that is—not save lives).

You can draw a box around anything. It calls attention to whatever is inside the box. Need more attention? Shade your box, or else wear baggy lime-green pants and cluck like a chicken.

Drawing a Box Around Your Words

Start easy. Write some words first. Then box them up. You won't find the word "box" anywhere, however, because Word refers to them as *borders*. Borders are lines placed on any (or all) of the four sides of a text paragraph, the cells in a table, or a graphic such as a picture or a chart.

Easier Than Ever to Border Your Work!

Horizontal borders can now be created quickly with a shortcut in Word 2000. Just press three or more special characters in a row and then press the **Enter** key, and a perfect horizontal border appears. The special symbols are === (equal), --- (dash), or ___ (underline). Each provides a slightly different version of horizontal border, so you should want to try all three and see for yourself.

Placing a border around text or a graphic is fairly easy. Start by selecting the text or table cells. A graphic (a picture or a chart) can be selected by clicking on it.

After making your selection, open the **Format** menu and select **Borders and Shading**. On the left side of the dialog box, you see a make-believe page with two paragraphs. The choices you make in this box are reflected in this little page as a sample. If you want to add a box (a border around all four sides), click one of the styles provided. To get rid of a box, click **None**. Really upscale boxes have a shadow effect, giving your words a three-dimensional appearance. You can try it by clicking **Shadow**.

The Tables and Border Toolbar

If you want to apply borders and shading to a lot of areas within your document, use the Tables and Borders toolbar. To display the tool bar, open the **View** menu, select **Toolbars**, and then select **Tables and Borders**. You can also click the right mouse button while pointing to any displayed toolbar, and select **Tables and Borders** from the list.

Shading Really Important Boxes

You should avoid having too many boxes in your document. If you really need to have several, and still want to call special attention to one or more of them, try shading. In fact, forget about how many boxes you may have; shading is so great that you can do it anywhere!

It's important to understand that shading is the background color of your text. You'll want to know that in case you plan to include a picture or two because any picture existing in a shaded area disappears on you. It's still there, of course; it's just hidden behind the shading.

Carefully select the text or table cells you want to shade. The shading occurs exactly where you highlight (unlike boxes, which were still square, even if a paragraph was indented). Open the **Format** menu and select **Borders and Shading**. Click the **Shading** tab to bring Shading to the front.

Use the Shading box to select the percentage of gray that you want. If your letters are small, choose a lighter percentage, such as 10 percent. Larger letters can withstand larger percentages to become more striking and yet remain visible. The result is really determined by the type of printer you have and how well it handles shading; therefore, you might need to experiment until you get the results you like. Use a font with clean, crisp lettering, such as Arial, or apply bold formatting for better results. Now click **OK** to return to your document and witness the shading of your selection.

Get Rid of the Border Fast!

If you want to remove a border completely, select the same text or graphic, open the **Format** menu, and select **Borders and Shading**. Click **None**, and then click **OK**.

Headlining with Fancy Titles

It's probably time to put a banner on this thing and go home. A banner is a headline or a major title across the top of a page. It's usually on the first page of your document. If you already tried this on a multiple-column section, you may have been frustrated if you couldn't figure out how to spread the title over the multiple columns. Don't worry, here is the secret.

Banners should be fancy. If you haven't used any of the fancy character-formatting capabilities of Word yet, now is the time. How else do you capture the attention of your audience, unless they see a startling and teasing title, such as "Elvis Seen with Mars Probe" or "Pumpkin Crushes Building"?

Type the words first. Short and interesting. This becomes your heading text, which can span multiple columns. Now, change to **Print Layout** view (open the **View** menu and choose the **Print Layout** command). Select the heading text, using your favorite selecting technique learned in Chapter 5, "Proofing Tools (Spelling, Grammar, and the Thesaurus)." Click the **Columns** button on the Standard toolbar and drag to select a single column. The result is your heading centered in what's basically a single column above multiple columns.

Next, click the **Font Size** box, also on the Formatting toolbar (in fact, all of these tools are found on the Formatting toolbar, so you get to know them well). Pick a large number, like 26 or so. If the text flows to the next line, it's too big; try something smaller. Although you can justify this text to spread evenly across the page (using the **Justify** button), it's better to choose the proper size with natural font spacing.

Oh, yes; next is the choice of the actual font. Click the **Font** box to see the many fonts you can choose from. Scroll down the list and try different fonts to see what's available. Make sure your text is selected before trying this, or else you won't see much. You should be able to find a font that matches your mood or style. Don't forget the basic font attributes of Bold and Italic that can also help the appearance. You might even want to shade the background, put a border around it, or both, using the skills you learned earlier in this chapter.

The Least You Need to Know

If a newsletter is what you need, this chapter covered the features to make yours the best.

- What's the quickest way to create an entire newsletter from scratch?

  Use the Newsletter Wizard. Open the **File** menu and click **New**. Click the **Publications** tab and double-click this wizard to get started.

- How can I quickly create three columns in my document?

  Click the **Columns** button on the Standard toolbar and drag to select the number of columns you desire.

- What tools should I use to create special effects?

  For some snazzy special effects with text, use **WordArt**, which is available as a button on the Standard toolbar.

- Can I put a fancy box around some of my words?

  Sure, but call them borders, because that's what you need to use in Word 2000. Select the text you want to contain, open the **Format** menu, and choose **Borders and Shading**. Click any of the box styles or customizing features and click **OK**. You'll like it.

Chapter 19

Templates, Themes, and Styles

In This Chapter

- What is a template, and why you should care
- Creating, editing, and saving your own templates
- Applying a Theme to your document
- When a custom style can help you
- Understand the Normal template, since you use it every day

Your computer earns its keep by making your life easier. Well, at least it should. Word 2000 adds templates, wizards, and themes guaranteed to make you happy. That is, of course, if creating beautiful documents in a fraction of the time (so you can get home earlier) makes you happy.

What Is a Template?

Creating any document takes time, especially if you want it to look good. There are lots of tedious steps. You type the date, enter the addresses and the salutation, and maybe create headers and footers (such as a company logo or a page number). Maybe you change the margins, paragraph formatting, or add borders or lines to improve the appearance. But when you use a *template*, most of this groundwork is already done for you. Think of a template as a blueprint for the text, graphics, and formatting of a document. Templates in Word 2000 are predesigned, ready-to-use documents into which you put your own information. Those tedious details, like margins, dates, headings, and so on, are already there. All you do is type the words of your memo or report. When you finish and it's time to save your work, provide a name and your creation is stored as a regular document. The original template remains unchanged and is ready to help you whenever you need it.

Nice Documents Word Can Create for You

Appearing in alphabetical order, here are some of the more popular categories that already exist to help you create common documents with the least amount of work:

- **Letters & Faxes** Business letters in several styles, fax cover sheets, mailing labels, and an envelope wizard.
- **Memos** Three different styles of memorandums.
- **Other Documents** Agendas for meetings, a calendar maker, different résumé styles, and converter for entire folders of documents.
- **Publications** Brochures, directories of names and addresses, manuals, newsletters, and theses.
- **Reports** Three different styles of casual and professional reports.
- **Web Pages** Choices of web page designs, FAQ's page, table of contents, and web page wizard.

These templates can be changed if necessary, and completely new templates can also be created. You really should consider taking your most common document type and saving it as a template to make your life easier the next time. Before we get too daring, let's test drive an existing template.

Using a Template for the First Time

See the template choices by opening the **File** menu and choosing the **New** command (unfortunately, clicking the **New** button on the toolbar will not display the **New** dialog box. That's just a fast way to create a new document using the normal template). With the **New** dialog box open, notice the list of tab titles across the top. This is how Word organizes the templates so you can find the one you want faster. Click the **Letters & Faxes** tab to bring it to the front. What you see are all templates, waiting to be chosen.

Be sure that **Document** is selected in the **Create New** box near the bottom. Double-click the **Contemporary Letter** to start using it. Your screen fills with an interesting preformatted letter just waiting for you to fill in with your own information.

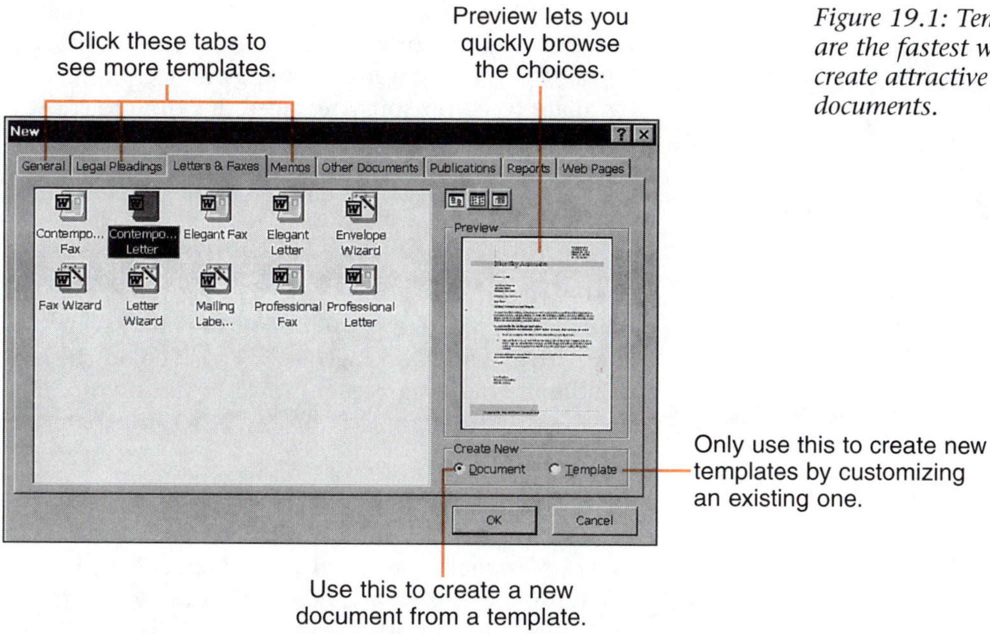

Figure 19.1: Templates are the fastest way to create attractive documents.

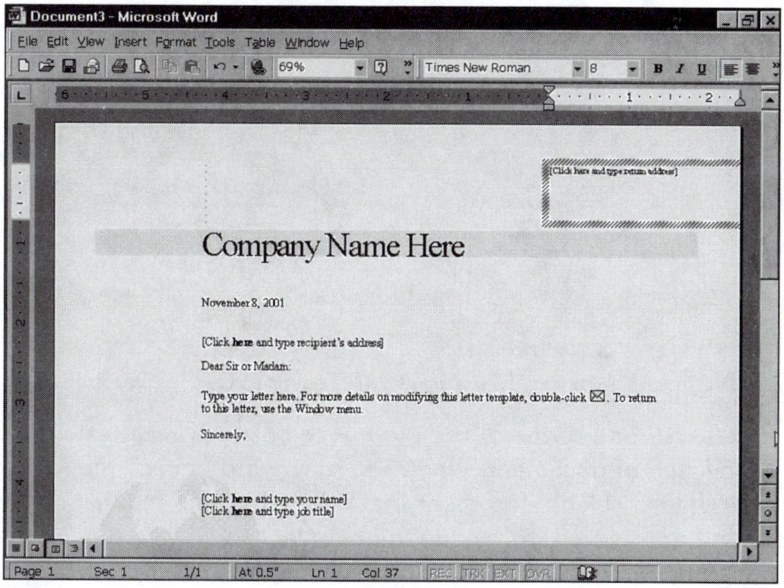

Figure 19.2: Templates guide you to perfectly formatted documents.

Click in any of the areas you would like to fill out, and start typing. The text you enter is formatted automatically for that part of the letter. Click your way through the rest of these text fields to complete the letter. When you're finished, click the **Save** button. You now save this completed letter as a regular document—it's no longer a template.

Easier Web Pages from a Template

Another great use for a template is in helping you create Web pages. Word 2000 includes lots of Web Page templates and the Web Page Wizard to get your Web site filled fast. Find out more about these in Chapter 22, "Creating a Web Page in Word 2000."

So remember, creating a document with a template won't change the original template. On the other hand, if you really want to change an existing template to better suit your need, it's time to show you how.

Modify an Existing Word 2000 Template

Like that Newsletter template? Wish it had your company's name and logo on it, to save you the trouble of changing it each time? It can, by modifying the original template (or any other, for that matter).

Open the **File** menu and choose the **New** command. Be sure to click **Template**, not Document, in the **Create New** area (lower right on your screen). Find the template you want to modify, click to select it, and click the **OK** button.

Now go ahead and make changes. Change any of the template's text and graphics, styles, formatting, macros, AutoText entries, toolbars, menu settings, and shortcut keys. When you finish, click the **Save** button. Provide a name you recognize in the future. The template is saved with your changes, ready to provide customized service in the future.

What's Normal About My Normal Template?

Everyone using Word 2000 has one of these. The Normal template is a general-purpose template for any type of document. When you start Word or click the **New** button, Word creates a new blank document that is based on the Normal template. It's possible, but not advised, to modify this template to change the default document formatting or content. Word also uses the Normal template to store the AutoText entries, macros, toolbars, and custom menu settings and shortcut keys you routinely use. Should you customize any of these elements and store them in the Normal template, they become available for use with any document.

Creating Your Own Customized Template

You probably have documents you already use as unofficial "templates." Maybe it's a weekly report that you open and change a few words, then save it as a new document. Whenever you open, copy, and adapt the contents of an existing document, you're using that document as a template. Protect your time investment by formally saving these documents as templates.

The easiest way to create a new template is by saving an existing document as a template. Locate and open the document you want. Add the text and graphics you want to appear in all new documents that you base on this template, and delete any items you don't want to appear. Don't forget to make the changes you want to the margin settings, page size and orientation, styles, and other formats. Now, save it as a template. Open the **File** menu and choose **Save As**. In the **File Name** box, type a name for the new template. In the **Save As Type** box, click **Document Template**, and your template is stored automatically in the Templates folder (or, if you want to store your template elsewhere, locate that folder). Now click **OK**. Congratulations! A new template exists.

Protect Your Originals

If you happen to click any of the templates in the **New** dialog box with the right mouse button, be careful not to choose the **Open** command. The original template is opened for modification, and you might accidentally change the original. Always use the **New** command to create new documents based on templates.

Where Should You Store Your Templates?

The easiest place to save your new templates is in standard **Word Template** folder, which is the default location that appears when you click the **Save As Type** box and choose **Document Template**. Your new template appears in the **General** tab in the **File New** dialog box.

If you choose to store your template anywhere else, you can, and it still works and acts as a template. But, to use it next time, you have to remember where you put it.

Create Your Own Tab in the New Dialog Box

Why not organize your life and add your own folder for your custom templates, and create a fancy new tab to store them? When you first save the template, click the **Create New Folder** button and type the name of a new folder. This name appears as a new tab heading in the **File New** dialog box. Now store your custom templates in this folder, and you should never have a problem finding them in the future.

Themes Paint a More Colorful Document

Word 2000 finally makes it easy to improve the appearance of any new or existing document. To do so, simply apply a predesigned collection of formats, each called a *theme*.

To discover your themes, open the **Format** menu and choose **Theme**. You'll see a list on the left and a preview on the right. Don't forget to look below to see different options that can be applied to each theme.

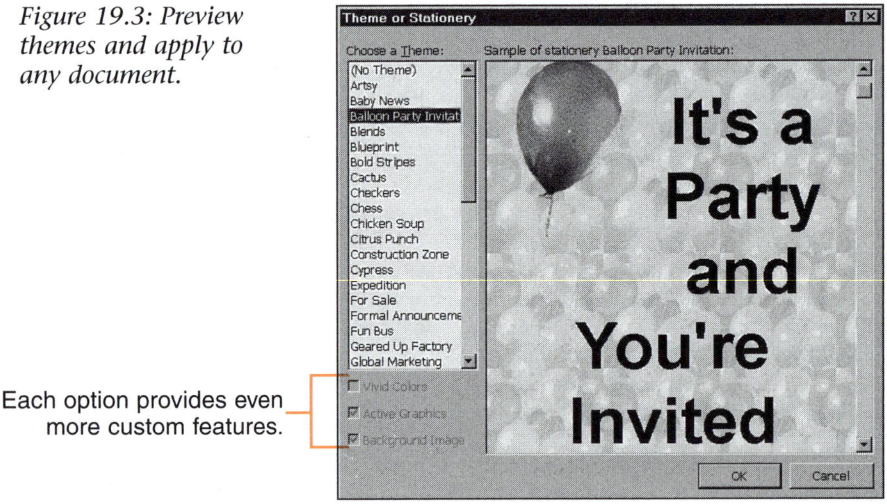

Figure 19.3: Preview themes and apply to any document.

After you choose a theme, your document is converted to the theme appearance. Notice your view changes to **Web Layout View**, making it easy to create custom web pages from existing documents. You can tweak and adjust anywhere using the **Style** box or changing the heading styles. If you don't like that theme, choose another (only one theme can be applied to a document).

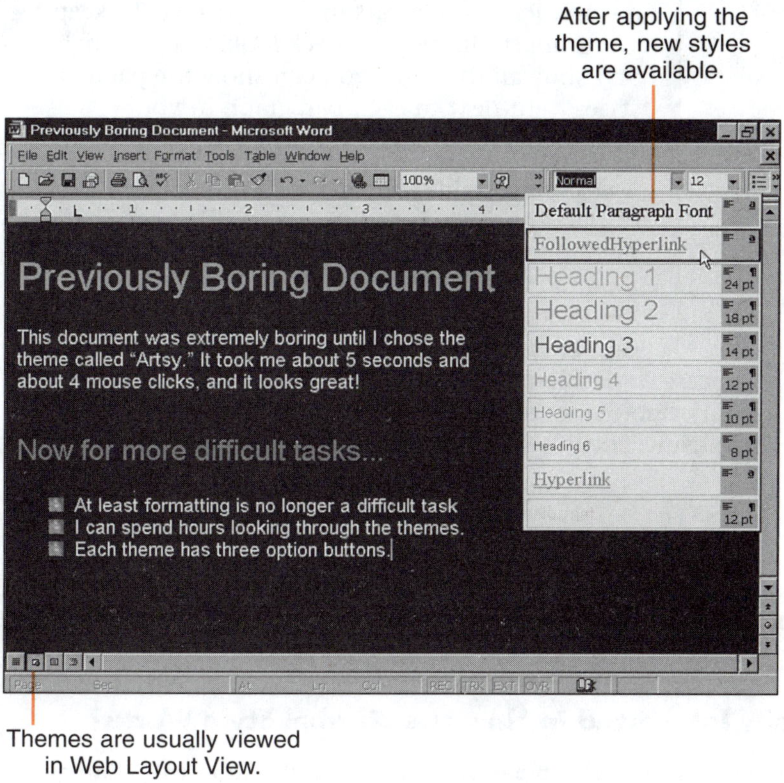

Figure 19.4: Apply a theme to your most boring documents.

Styles: What Templates Are Made Of

Before leaving the subject of templates and themes, you should know about *styles*, because if a whole template won't do the trick, maybe a style will. Styles are combinations of character, paragraph, and other formatting all saved in one easy-to-remember name. This goes beyond the bold, italic, or underline formatting that you give to individual words. Think of styles as a broader collection of interesting details brought together to become the default formatting of what you type.

Is It a Style or a Template?

What is the difference between a style and a template? Basically, a template is made up of several styles. A single style is a collection of paragraph and character formatting used in a document. A collection of styles can be saved as a template.

Exposing the Styles on Your Screen

When you click inside a paragraph, the style you are currently using appears in the **Style** box on the Formatting toolbar. If a character style is applied to a word, its style appears in the **Style** box. To keep you from straining your neck looking up at that Style box all the time, you can show the paragraph styles right next to each paragraph in your document. To do this, turn on the **Style Area**.

You should be in Normal view for this trick. To display the Style Area on your screen, open the **Tools** menu and choose the **Options** command. Click the **View** tab to bring it to the front. Look for the **Style Area Width** box and replace that zero with a positive decimal number. You can just type over it, or click the up/down arrows to increase or decrease the width. A number like **1** (inch) will do just fine; this is temporary (remember to change this back to zero after you've experienced the Style Area). Now, click the **OK** button and look at your screen.

Are You Really Interested in How the Normal Style Works?

Up until now, every paragraph you've typed probably starts its life in the Normal style: Times New Roman 12-point font (the new default size in Word 2000) in a left-aligned paragraph. These are the attributes stored in the Normal Template. If you hate Times New Roman font, all you have to do is modify the Normal style to use some other font.

But be aware that changing your Normal style can, and often does, change the rest of your styles. That's because most built-in Word styles are based on the Normal style. So, if you tweak an attribute in the Normal style, expect to see the change in other styles, too.

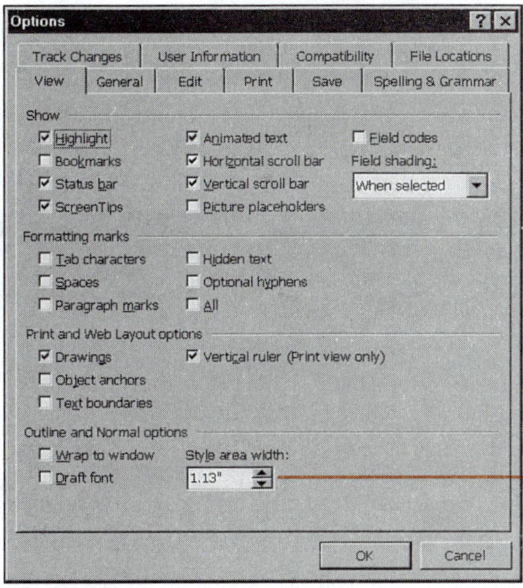

Figure 19.5: Exposing the secrets of styles.

The extra margin to the left now displays the style applied to each paragraph on the screen. You can see that templates can be made up of many different styles, each serving a useful purpose. Remember the names of styles you like, because you can apply them to your own paragraphs whenever you wish.

Applying Styles to Paragraphs

With that introduction out of the way, and before you think styles are too complicated, let's apply a style to a paragraph.

Find a boring paragraph and click anywhere inside the paragraph. Click the down arrow in the **Style** box on the Formatting toolbar. All of the currently available styles can be seen and selected from this drop-down scroll box. Click one of them, such as the **Heading 1**, and watch your paragraph jump into action and transform itself into something that looks like a major heading of a magazine article.

I Want More Styles!

If a style you want to use isn't listed, press the **Shift** key, then click the same down arrow. A box appears displaying all of Word's built-in styles, instead of the mere sampling you usually see.

Try another style. Click the **Style** list again and choose **Heading 2**, and then **Heading 3**, for example. Keep trying different styles to get a feel for how styles convert your paragraph into impressive, consistent formats that can improve the look and feel of your document.

Now click the **Undo** button and watch your paragraph change to the previous style. You can always undo an applied style, so don't be afraid of experimenting with them!

Figure 19.6: Styles finally exposed on the left.

You can also double-click in here to edit styles.

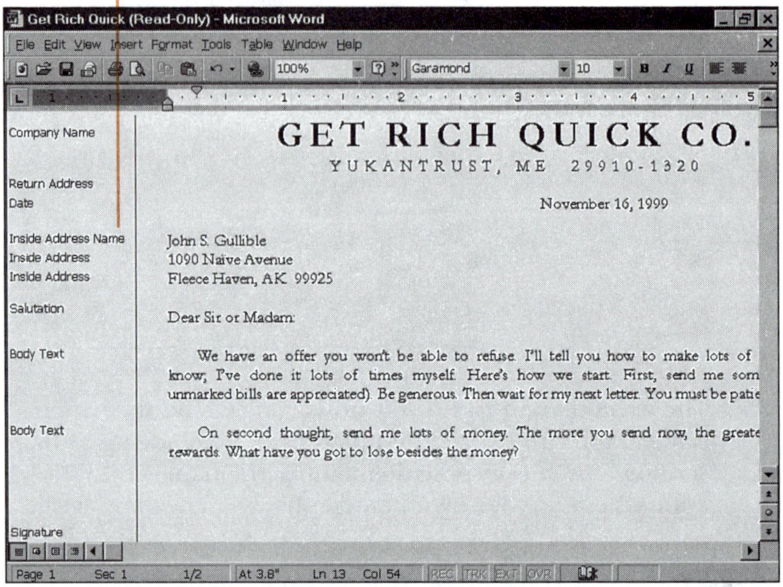

Copying Styles from One Paragraph to Another

If you have a paragraph that looks really good and you want to copy the style (the formatting) to another paragraph inside your document, you can use a helpful feature of Word 2000. It's called the *Format Painter*. Click anywhere in the preferred paragraph and then click the **Format Painter** button on the Standard toolbar. Now be careful, because the next thing you click is modified to this preferred formatting. Find the target paragraph and select it (it's usually easiest to use the selection bar on the left). That's it. The formatting is copied to the target paragraph.

When you click the **Format Painter** once, it works once. To copy style formatting to several paragraphs, double-click the **Format Painter** button. Now, you can click as many paragraphs as you wish, and they all have your preferred style applied to them. When you want to stop this activity, press the **Esc** (Escape) key to end the repetitive style applications.

What's a Global Template?

Global templates are templates whose styles and other settings are available to all open documents. They make it easy to have a custom set of macros, styles, AutoText entries, and even custom toolbar, menu, and shortcut key settings available for your convenience.

The Normal template happens to be a global template, as customized items you store in the Normal template are available to all documents. But, you can also create more global templates in order to create different environments for different work. Open the **Tools** menu and choose **Templates and Add-Ins**. Click the **Add** button, browse and add the desired template, then click **OK**. Your new global template is available and remains that way until you close Word. The next time you restart Word, the template is listed in the Global templates and Add-Ins scroll box, but you need to click its check box to make it active again.

Using the Style Dialog Box

You can also create and modify existing styles using the **Style** dialog box, which contains every possible paragraph formatting function under the sun. It's useful to take a peek at it to give you an idea of the wealth of formatting options available. Open the **Format** menu and choose the **Style** command to see the **Style** dialog box.

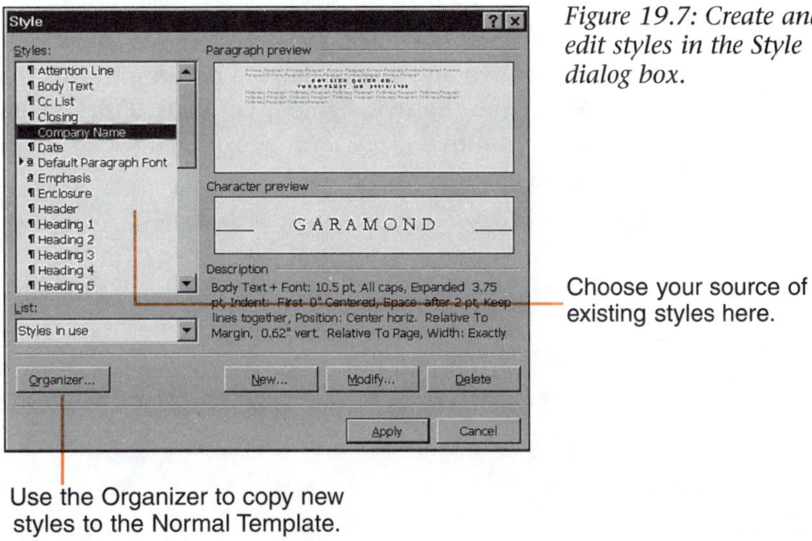

Figure 19.7: Create and edit styles in the Style dialog box.

The Least You Need to Know

Templates, themes, and styles can make your life a whole lot easier. You can write home about some of these template and style tips learned in this chapter.

- I'm afraid of messing up a template. Any advice?

  Don't worry. Templates are hard to mess up. After using a template, click the **Save** button. Give it a name, click **OK**, and your work is saved as a new *document*. Your changes won't affect the template.

- This document is good. Can I make it a template?

  Yes, you can create a template based on your document by opening the **File** menu and choosing the **Save As** command. Type a name for your new template, then select **Document Template** under **Save File As Type**.

- I want something even simpler than a template to make my document look better. Any suggestions?

  Yes, try the new Themes feature of Word 2000. Open the **Format** menu, click **Themes**, and scroll through nearly zillions of designer themes. Apply them with a click of a button.

- How can I tell what style is applied to a paragraph?

  Word 2000 provides the **Style Area** to enable you to see the complete details of how styles are being used. Open the **Tools** menu and choose the **Options** command. Click the **View** tab and temporarily change the **Style Area Width** setting to 1 (or .5 to save space). You'll now see the style details. Get rid of it by deleting the width setting.

- How do I make changes to an existing style?

  To make changes to any style, change a paragraph with that style, and then select it. Make sure the style name is correctly displayed in the **Style** box on the Formatting toolbar, then press **Enter**. Click **OK** to confirm that you want to make these changes to the style.

Chapter 20

Customizing Word 2000

In This Chapter

- Add or remove buttons on your toolbars
- Add or remove commands on your menus
- Create a new toolbar
- Changing your right-click shortcut menu
- Adjust the view of your workspace

If you don't like something, change it! That's the rule in this chapter, demonstrating the new flexibility in Word 2000. Discover how to add or customize a button on your toolbar, add a command in your menu, or create your own unique toolbar. And if that's not enough for your creativity, try customizing your own shortcut menu that pops up when you right-click!

Customize Your Toolbars

Toolbars in Word 2000 were created by Microsoft to organize the most common commands so you can find and use them quickly. Because most people use a few buttons from both the Standard and the Formatting toolbars, Microsoft got the hint and simplified things. Your first view of a toolbar is actually the combination of the best of these two toolbars. If you don't like them, you are welcome to change them. For example, you can add and remove menus and buttons, create your own custom toolbars, hide or display toolbars, and move toolbars.

Put Anything on Those Toolbars!

In previous versions of Word, toolbars contained only buttons. Now toolbars can contain buttons, menus, hyperlinks, or any combination thereof.

Basic Toolbar Changes

Want bigger buttons? Don't like that combined Standard/Formatting toolbar? Don't want those menu commands to change places without your permission? Tired of waiting that couple of seconds to see your complete menu?

Answers to all of these can be found in one simple box. See for yourself. Click **Tools**, **Customize** and the **Options** tab. As shown in this figure, choose your desired options.

Figure 20.1: Take control of your toolbars and menus.

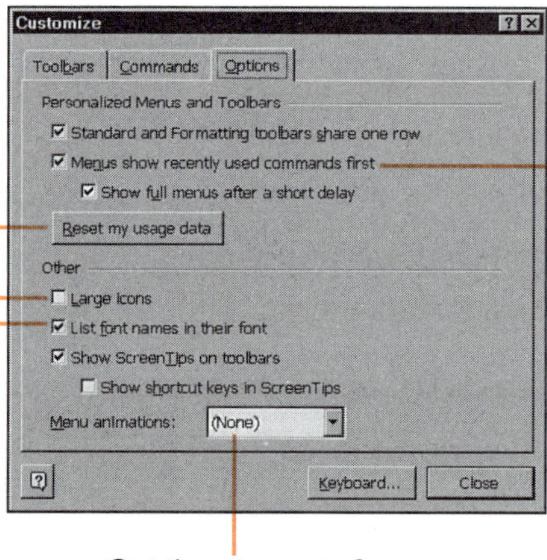

Noisy Toolbars?

You can turn off toolbar sounds if they disturb you. Open the **Tools** menu, click **Options**, and then click the **General** tab. Clear the **Provide Feedback With Sound** check box. This is a universal setting, however, which means this also affects all Microsoft Office 2000 programs.

Add a New Button to a Toolbar

You can add toolbar buttons for any commands and frequently used styles, AutoText entries, and fonts. The toolbar must first be visible on your screen, so if it's not, open the **View** menu, point to **Toolbars**, and then click the toolbar of your choice. Open the **Tools** menu and choose **Customize**. Did you notice that the Word 2000 toolbar just woke up and split into *two* toolbars? That's the full Standard and Formatting toolbars, awaiting your customization. Now click the **Commands** tab. In the **Categories** list, you see names for each group of buttons classified by function. The buttons for each category are displayed in the **Buttons** preview box. If you don't see the command you want under a particular category, find and click **All Commands** in the **Categories** box. You'll see *thousands* of them. When you find a button you really like, click and drag it right onto your toolbar. Really. If it doesn't land in the exact spot you want, just click and drag it to a new location. This is also how you can change the order of your buttons.

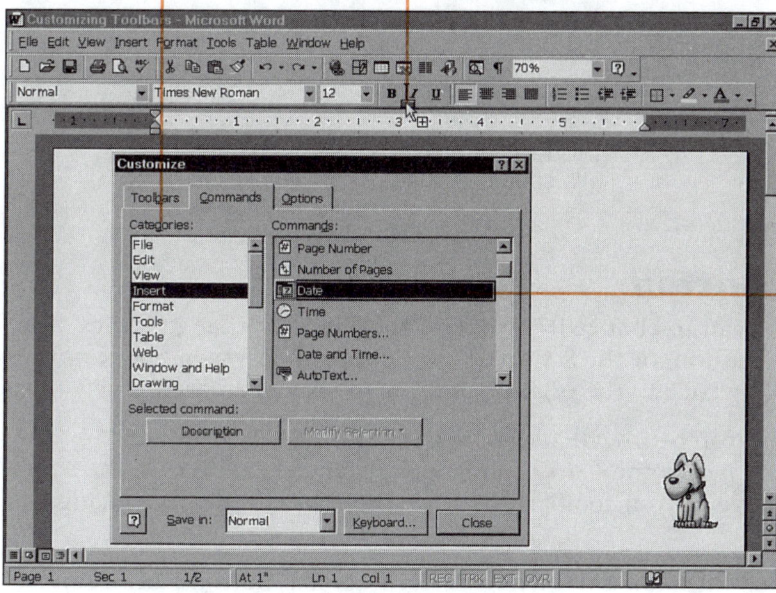

Figure 20.2: Add a useful button to your toolbar.

Don't like an existing button? Get rid of it now! As long as the **Customize** dialog box is open, just click and drag a button off the toolbar into some empty area and just let go. It vanishes. If you want to bring it back, just find it in the **Commands** box and drag it up again.

Figure 20.3: Complete customizing of any toolbar button.

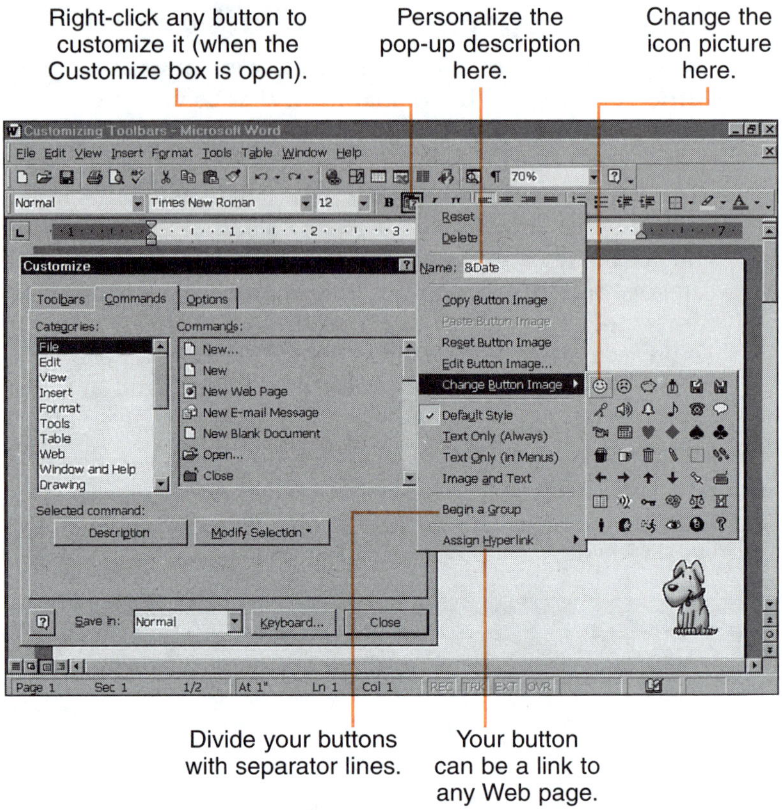

Edit Any Toolbar Button

Is your button boring? Want to change it? You have the power to change things, like the little picture on the button, or the ScreenTip words that appear when your mouse hovers over it, or resetting back to the original button. You can even draw a new one.

Make sure the button is visible on your screen, then open the **Tools** menu and choose **Customize**. Briefly ignore the **Customize** dialog box and right-click on the actual button you wish to change in your toolbar. You'll see the shortcut menu of changeable options.

The **Customize** dialog box must remain open to perform toolbar button editing, and sometimes you might need to move it out of your way to see the button you want to edit.

- To change the button icon to one of 42 new icons, click **Change Button Image** on the shortcut menu and choose one from the palette of images displayed.
- To change the button icon to something completely different, click the **Edit Button Image** and you'll open a graphics editor giving you almost complete freedom in drawing your own icon.

- You can divide your buttons into groups using separator lines. Click **Begin A Group** to add a line in front of this button.
- If you prefer words to pictures, choose **Text Only**. Sometimes a short word might be more helpful.
- To reset this button to the original settings, click **Reset**.

Once you see how easy this is, you might be tempted to change all of your toolbars. That's not recommended.

I suggest you create a new toolbar and keep all of your changes limited to that single toolbar. Then you can always return to the original toolbars if someone else needs to work at your computer.

Change the Order of Those Buttons, Too!

You can also change the order of buttons on toolbars (or commands on menus) by just clicking and dragging them to a different location. All you need is the **Customize** dialog box open at the time.

Create a New Toolbar

If you can think of a handful or more of important buttons you can't live without, then you're ready to build a whole new toolbar! You already know how to add the buttons to it; you just need to know how to create the toolbar itself.

If it's not already up on your screen, open the **Tools** menu, click **Customize**, then click the **Toolbars** tab to bring it to the front. Click the **New** button, and in the **Toolbar Name** box, type the name you want. In the **Make Toolbar Available To** box, click to choose the template or document you want to save the toolbar in, or leave it at Normal (the Normal Template), which makes it available all the time.

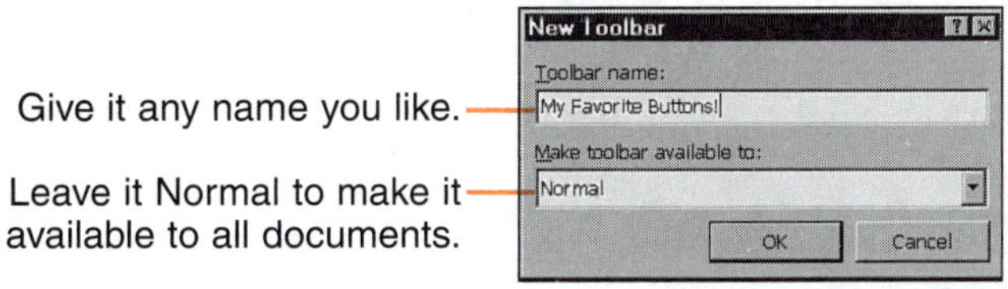

Figure 20.4: Name your new toolbar.

Figure 20.5: A new toolbar can contain your favorite buttons.

Voilà! Your new toolbar appears, even though it looks a little squished. You need to make it grow by adding buttons. Follow the same steps as before, clicking the **Commands** tab and dragging favorite commands to your new toolbar. When you have added all the buttons you want, click **Close**. Your buttons are saved.

Restoring Original Toolbar Buttons If You Change Your Mind

There's an easy way to put back the original toolbar buttons in Word 2000, just in case you change your mind. Open the **Tools** menu, click **Customize**, and then click the **Toolbars** tab. Select the toolbar you want to restore by clicking a toolbar name in the **Customize** dialog box. Click the **Reset** button. Finally, in the **Reset Changes** box, click the template or document that contains the changes you want to reset.

Customizing Your Menus

Yes, you can customize your menu bar the same way you customize any built-in toolbar, by adding and removing buttons and menus. You can change the wording, paste an icon next to it, or add lines to divide commands into groups. You can even insert hyperlinks.

Add a New Command to Your Menu

The menu bar is really nothing more than a list of commands. Some commands display a list of more commands. Many of these commands now have images next to them so you can quickly associate the command with its purpose.

Unlike your other toolbars, the menu bar cannot be hidden. It's always visible on your screen (with the one exception of the Full Screen View, when nothing but your document is in view). That takes care of the first step in customization. Now open the **Tools** menu, click **Customize**, and this time click **Commands**. Find the command you want to add, and then click and drag it up to the menu bar. When you drag on top of the existing menu bar commands such as File and Edit, you'll find that they open right up, enabling you to place the new command anywhere you want in the list.

Edit Your Menu Commands

First open the **Tools** menu and click **Customize** to open the **Customize** dialog box, which must be open whenever you edit menus or toolbars.

Getting to the desired menu command to edit it might be tricky the first time you try. Click to open a menu if you need to get to a command inside. Right-click the menu command you want to edit. You'll see the shortcut menu full of customization options. To add a menu command image, click **Edit Button Image** and choose from the palette. To change the name, click in the **Name** box and start typing. When you finish, click the **Close** button and your customization is saved.

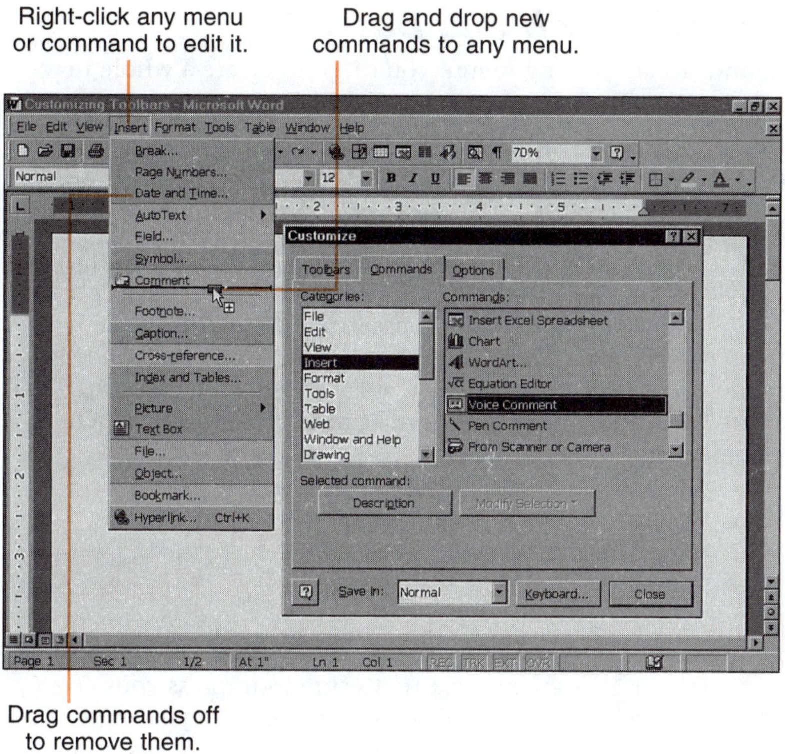

Figure 20.6: Customize any menu command.

What's That Ampersand All About?

An ampersand symbol (&) is usually wedged somewhere inside the name of your menu command. It's the secret keyboard shortcut, and you can create them yourself! You can add a single ampersand anywhere inside a menu command name, with no spaces. The letter immediately following the ampersand is the *shortcut key* letter, and is underlined when using your menu (the ampersand disappears). Now when you see this menu command, you can press the Alt key along with this key letter, and the command is executed. Some people think these shortcut keys are faster than using your mouse. One word of advice: Don't choose letters that have already been taken, such as Alt+F, which is a shortcut to open the **File** menu, or else you'll never be certain which command executes when you press the shortcut key.

Create a New Menu in Your Menu Bar

Instead of adding commands to an existing menu, you can also create a whole new menu. The steps are slightly different from those used to add a new toolbar.

Open the **Tools** menu, click **Customize**, and click the **Commands** tab to bring it to the front. Scroll to the bottom of the Categories and choose the **New Menu** command. In the Commands column, drag the **New Menu** command up to your menu bar and drop it where you prefer. If it doesn't land where you want, click and drag it to a different spot.

Your menu bar shines with its new entry! Of course, it doesn't do anything yet, because no commands are assigned to it. You know the routine: Find commands in the available categories and drag them up to this new menu. Afterward, you can edit them with a right-click and a selection from the shortcut menu that appears. When you have added all the commands you want, click **Close**.

But It's Covered Up!

If you can't see the **Commands** area because it's covered up by this shortcut menu, click **Text** again to close this column temporarily, and drag the Shortcut toolbar farther away from the Customize dialog box.

Impress Your Friends; Change Your Right-Click Shortcut Menu!

Here's a new trick that's sure to impress your geekiest of friends and perhaps make you more productive at the same time. By now you should be using the shortcut menus that pop up when you click the right mouse button. They often contain helpful commands like cut, copy and paste, and it's faster to click them here rather than sending your mouse up to the toolbars or menus. Well, why not customize these shortcut menus to contain your all-time favorite commands? The Customize dialog box makes it a snap.

Open the **Tools** menu, choose **Customize**, and click the **Toolbars** tab. Scroll to the bottom and click to select the **Shortcut Menu**. You'll see the Shortcut toolbar.

Keep this Shortcut toolbar up on your screen while you click the **Commands** tab on the **Customize** dialog box. Right now you're setting up the playing field.

Ready? Click to choose the **Text** column on the Shortcut toolbar, and then choose the shortcut menu you want to edit. For this example, click on **Text** near the bottom of this list, and you'll see a menu pop-up that displays the actual shortcut menu you see every day.

This menu stays open while you reach over to see the commands in the **Customize** dialog box. Browse through the categories to find the command you want, then drag and drop the command onto the desired shortcut menu (**Text** is a popular one). Any command can be dragged into any location. When you finish, click **Close** and your custom menu is saved.

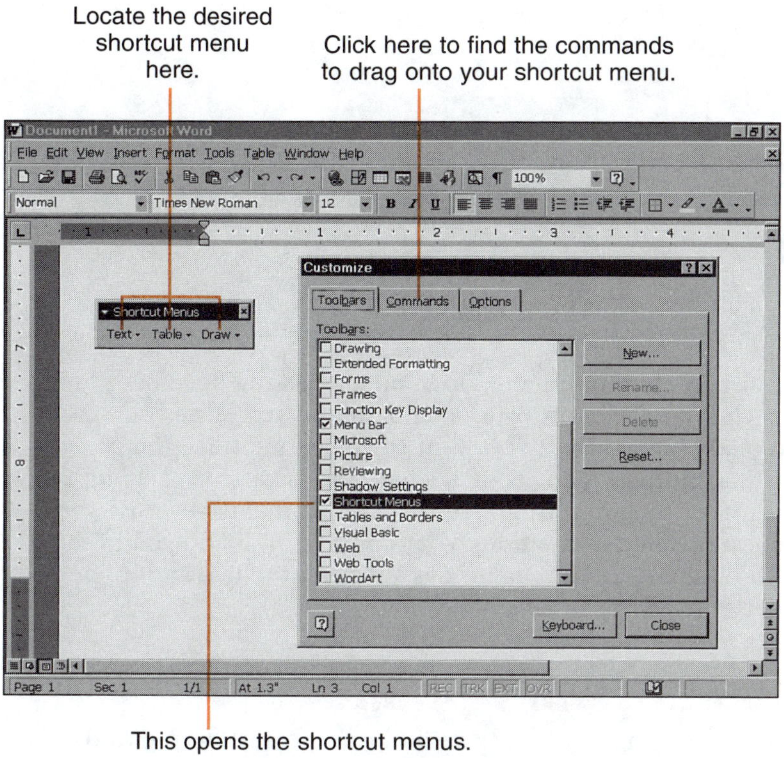

Figure 20.7: Choose the shortcut menu to customize.

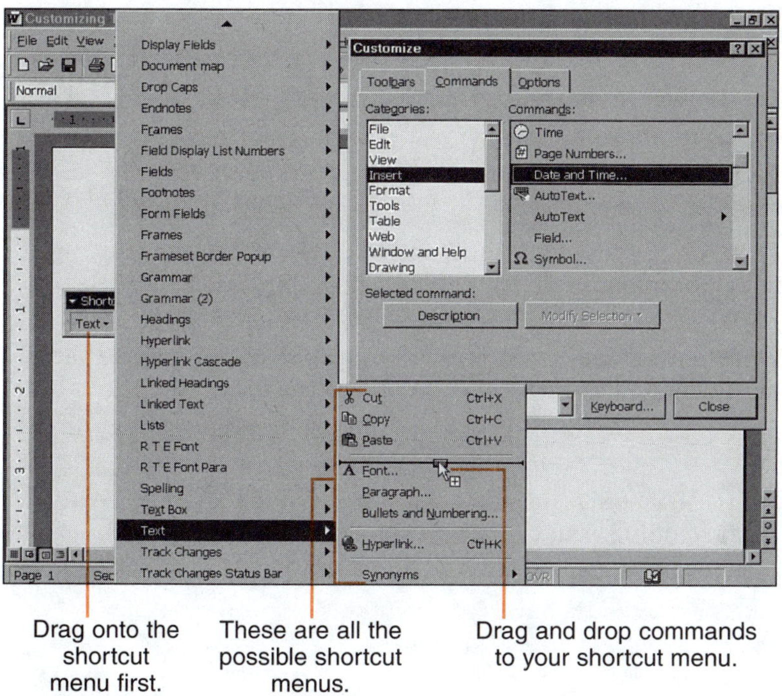

Figure 20.8: Drag the command onto your shortcut menu.

Figure 20.9: Your customized shortcut menu in action.

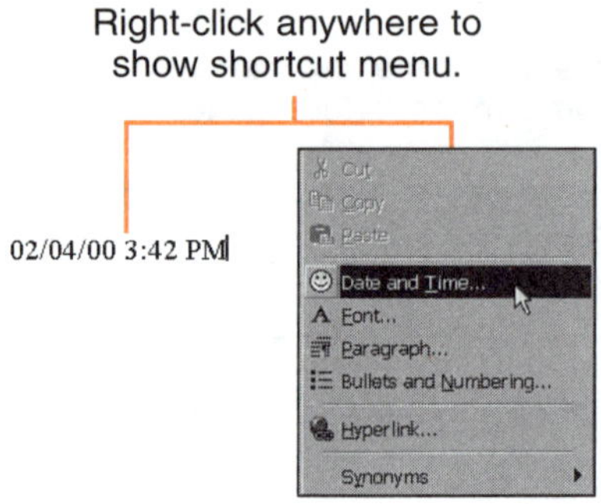

Now it's time to test your new shortcut menu! Open up an existing document or create a new one. Right-click anywhere in your document and you'll see your customized commands ready for action! If you want to go beyond this example, you need to remember that shortcut menus change based on what you're doing at the time. This is how they got their other name—the Context menu—because they change based on what you're doing at the time (your context). Why do you need to know this? Because each different context menu has a different name, and if you plan to change one, you'd better know its name!

Other Word 2000 Custom Options

The remainder of this chapter brings you other helpful ways to customize Word 2000 in an effort to make you more productive. Some change the way you see things; others change the way you do things.

Tips for Making Your Workspace Larger in Word 2000

If you find yourself constantly squinting at your screen with bloodshot eyes, why not give yourself a break? Here are some tips on how to make documents easier to see on your computer screen.

- **Run Word 2000 maximized.** Be sure you can see the Restore, not Maximize button, in the Title bar. If it's not maximized, click the **Maximize** button in the Title bar.
- **View only a single document at a time.** Make sure the document window is maximized inside Word, and don't waste space working in a split screen unless you are moving and copying information from one to the other.
- **Hide any toolbars you don't need.** Most people can get along fine without the Ruler or Status bar (or even the scrollbars).
- **Adjust Zoom control to maximize your comfort level.** You can choose Page Width to prevent horizontal scrolling. You can also type a number directly in the Zoom box for custom-viewing sizes.

- **Switch to Full Screen view.** Everyone should experience this at least once in his or her lifetime. Open the **View** menu and click **Full Screen**. You'll see nothing but your document (and a small **Close** button), even though the menus are still there! To prove it, slide your mouse pointer to the very top of the screen and the menu bar is exposed temporarily. To leave full-screen view, click the **Close** button (or press the **Esc** key).
- **Resize a floating toolbar.** To resize a floating toolbar, move the pointer over any edge until it changes to a double-headed arrow, and then drag the edge of the toolbar. Didn't know toolbars could float? Click and grab the left border of any docked toolbar, and you can drag it anywhere around your workspace.
- **Change the size of your toolbar buttons.** This might not make your workspace larger, but it might save your eyes so you can work longer. Open the **Tools** menu, click **Customize**, and click the **Options** tab. Select the **Large Icons** check box.

Changing Your View on Documents

Here's an important point before we start: Your document doesn't change just because you change your view of it. Why have more than one view? To help you and your computer perform at their best, depending on the task at hand. The only reason to change the view of your document is to help you see parts of it better, or work with it in a different manner. There is a suggested document view for each of the tasks you are trying to accomplish, whether it's editing (Normal view), reorganizing or working in very large documents (Outline view or Document Map view), creating a Web page (Web Layout view), manipulating graphics or pictures (Print Layout view), working with Headers and Footers, or preparing to print (Print Preview). You can even hide everything with Full Screen view.

Viewing What Does Not Print

To view special characters on your screen that do not print, make changes to your **View** options. Click **Tools**, **Options**, and the **View** tab. Select the check boxes for the characters you want under **Nonprinting Characters**.

If you want to customize the way Word 2000 displays your document, open the **Tools** menu, click **Options**, and browse the select options on the **View** tab. For example, you can display or hide items in your document (such as graphics, animated text, and field codes) or screen elements (such as scrollbars). The options that are available on the **View** tab depend on which view you're in.

Lots of Pictures? Want to Speed Up Scrolling?

Pictures take a fraction of a second longer to display than text. Lots of pictures may add up to several seconds of delay. If that's too long for you, you can speed things up, if you don't mind temporarily ignoring those pictures.

Click the **Tools** menu, choose **Options**, and click the **View** tab. Place a check in the **Picture Placeholders** box. Click **OK** to return to viewing your document. You now see an empty box for each picture, and it's faster.

Adapt to Multiple Languages

Need to create multilingual documents (mixed languages in the same document)? Then you must be tired of seeing all those red wavy lines as Word thinks you're misspelling the other language. Try the new *Language AutoDetect* feature, and Word automatically determines what language you are typing and applies the correct spelling and grammar checking.

This takes a few moments to set up initially. Click **Start**, point to **Programs**, **Office Tools**, and choose **Microsoft Office Language Settings**. Scroll until you find the language you need, and select it. Your choice is added and appears in the **Enabled Languages** box. Word needs to reboot your computer to add the new language. When your computer restarts, you can enable auto-detection in Word. Open the **Tools** menu, point to **Language**, and choose **Set Language**. Be sure to check **Detect Language Automatically**, and click **OK**. Word now acknowledges each language you've enabled.

Create a New Keyboard Shortcut

Shortcut keys are ways to quickly accomplish a task without using your mouse. For instance, to open your **Edit** menu you can press the **Alt+E** key combination. Touch typists love these shortcuts, because they can type much faster without stopping to touch the mouse.

You can assign a shortcut key to almost any command, macro, font, AutoText entry, style, or a commonly used symbol. Open the **Tools** menu, click **Customize**, then click the **Keyboard** button. Browse the **Categories** box until you find the desired command, and click to select it. In the **Press New Shortcut Key** box, type the shortcut key combination you want to assign. Any shortcut keys that are currently assigned appear in the **Current keys** box, to prevent you from changing existing shortcuts. Next, in the

Save Changes in box, click the current document name or template in which you want to save the shortcut key changes, or leave it at the Normal template to make it available everywhere. Finally, click the **Assign** button and then **Close**, and your new shortcut is ready and waiting for you.

For WordPerfect Lovers Only

If you are familiar with WordPerfect commands, you can customize your Word 2000 to react intelligently when you accidentally press those old key combinations. Word stops you at that instant and says, "Hey, that's not how we do things here. Try it this way…" If you're interested, click **Help**, **WordPerfect Help**, the **Options** button, and put a check in the following boxes:

- **Help for WordPerfect Users**. This prepares Word for the next time you need help. You'll see modified help screens slanted toward WordPerfect commands.
- **Navigation Keys for WordPerfect Users**. Once again, the WordPerfect command you know by heart won't actually work, but a help screen does pop up and explain the rules of the road for Word.

WordPerfect Commands Don't Work in Word

So what's the big deal about having these two check boxes if they won't make the WordPerfect commands actually work? Well, if you're an experienced typist with WordPerfect commands memorized, it's better to be forced to stop and read a help menu rather than to be allowed to continue typing, thinking your command was executed.

This **Help for WordPerfect Users** dialog box is full of all the standard commands you may remember from WordPerfect, and by selecting each command you get directions on using the Word equivalent. There's also a demo button for each command, enabling you to sit back and watch as the computer demonstrates the new command for you. Now, if only you could get it to write that report.

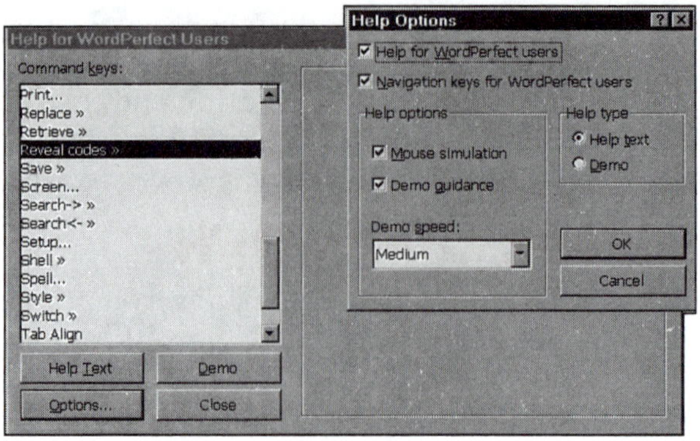

Figure 20.10: Your old WordPerfect commands can be recognized.

Where's Reveal Codes?

Sorry, Word 2000 still does not expose all formatting codes directly, as you can in WordPerfect, because Word 2000 stores many of these codes inside the paragraph symbol at the end of a paragraph. You can, however, choose to view many of the nonprinting characters in Word by checking the appropriate box in the **View** tab of the **Options** command on the **Tools** menu.

The Least You Need to Know

I now have 23 custom toolbars dancing on my screen with no room left to work, and I click randomly using my joystick (I now enjoy Word 2000 more than games). I hope you are more productive in customizing Word 2000 to suit your needs, especially if you gleaned some of the tips from this chapter.

- I forgot to read this chapter. How do I customize a toolbar?

  You can customize toolbars by opening the **Tools** menu and choosing **Customize**. Click the **Commands** tab to display what's available, then click and drag new buttons on or off any toolbar (or menu).

- Can I also customize a menu?

  Sure, it's just as easy using the same **Customize** dialog box. Click the **Commands** tab to display what's available, then click and drag new commands on or off any menu (or toolbar).

- How about that shortcut menu when I right-click? Can I customize it?

  Absolutely. Open the **Tools** menu, choose **Customize**, and click the **Shortcut Toolbar** found on the **Toolbars** tab. Drag and drop commands to any of the many shortcut menus available in Word 2000. To run a shortcut menu, just click the right mouse button at the desired location for the command.

- I hate using the mouse. Can I speed things up using the keyboard?

  Try creating your own keyboard shortcuts. Open the **Tools** menu, click **Customize**, then click the **Keyboard** button. Assign a new shortcut key combination to any of the commands in Word 2000.

- Can I get rid of everything on my screen and see nothing but my document?

  It's called **Full Screen** view, and you can find it quickly. Open the **View** menu and click **Full Screen**. Spend as much time as you like. When it's time to return, press the **Esc** key.

Chapter 21

Using Word 2000 with Excel, PowerPoint, and Access

In This Chapter

- Sharing information in Office 2000
- Hyperlinking to Office 2000 programs
- Displaying Excel data inside your document
- Sliding some PowerPoint into your document
- Beefing up your document with database information from Access

Okay, Word has some spreadsheet capabilities, but certainly no slideshow pieces or database power. Not by itself, anyway. That's why most people get Office 2000—it includes the whole shebang of sweet products! Oh, I meant suite of products. But you don't have to be an expert to figure out how to stick in a slide or nibble at a database; that's what this chapter is for!

Learning All the Ways to Share Information Between Programs

Not too long ago, sharing information from one program usually meant retyping that same information into the second program. It was bad news all around, because information changed with the times, and it was hard to keep all of the documents up-to-date.

Microsoft now provides lots of different tools to make it easy to share information between the Office 2000 programs. Each tool serves a slightly different purpose, so you should learn when to use what. You'll be glad to hear these tools work the same way in each of the different programs, so you have to learn a method only once.

Different Methods of Using the Same Data Twice

Let's say you're creating a budget report in Word 2000 and you need to reference a few facts and figures stored in either Excel, PowerPoint, or Access. Here are your choices for getting the information from one program to another:

- **Copy and Paste it**. Still the most common method, this duplicates the information in two locations. Pasting has come a long way now, and you can paste in different ways, from a simple copy of static information, or maybe a link that can be updated, or perhaps an embed that carries the tools with it.
- **Drag and Drop it**. This typically moves information, sometimes deleting it from the first location, and adding it to the second (dropping the selection onto the program icon in the Windows 95/98 or Windows NT/2000 Taskbar does the same thing). You can also use this method to create hyperlinks now (see below).
- **Link to it**. Use this method when you want the most up-to-date information included in one or more documents. One location is considered the source of the "real" information, while the other locations have a link to this source and the information stays updated automatically.
- **Embed it inside**. Besides the information, when you want to include all of the tools necessary to edit that information, you embed the information. It's like carrying around multiple programs inside your document.
- **Hyperlink to it**. Here's the Web way to leave the information where it is, and just jump directly to it when you feel the urge.

When to Copy into Your Document

The **Copy** command in Word is simple and should never give you any trouble. If you see something you like just the way it is, and you're happy that it always stays the same, use **Copy** to insert it into your document. It becomes a static addition to your document. You can think of it as a picture of the information you selected. You usually don't edit it anymore, except to get rid of it. No matter what information you choose, in any of the Office 2000 programs, you can always select it, click the **Copy** button, and then change to Word and click the **Paste** button to insert it into your document.

You can also move something into your Word document, and it acts as if it has been copied into your document. One way to move text, graphics, or other objects is to select them and click the **Cut** button. Move to Word, find the location you want, and click the **Paste** button.

Drag-and-drop editing is another way to move text, graphics, or other objects from one place to another, and the end result is as if you copied it there. You can drag and drop selected information from any of the Office 2000 programs into your Word document.

When to Link into Your Document

If you need to include information that is likely to change in the near future, you might be better off *linking* to that information, instead of copying it into your Word document. Linked information always remains up-to-date with the source of that information. The only requirement is that you always need to have access to the original source, in case it changes in the future. Linking is a good method to use when you want to share the same information between many documents and also when you want to share information among documents in an Office Binder.

You can link virtually any information from an Office program into your Word document. For instance, to make sure budget figures from an Excel worksheet are up-to-date in a quarterly report written with Word, you would copy and link the information. If the figures change, they can be automatically updated in your Word document.

To link existing information in any Office 2000 program, copy the information, and then switch to your current document in Word. Place the insertion point where you want the information placed. Open the **Edit** menu and click **Paste Special**, and then click to select the **Paste Link** option. Click **OK** and the object will be linked to your document.

Do you want to control when these links are updated? All you need to do in Word is open the **Edit** menu, click the **Links** command, and then click the name of the link you want. Choose the **Manual** button to set the link to update only when you specifically request an update; otherwise, the link is updated each time you open this document.

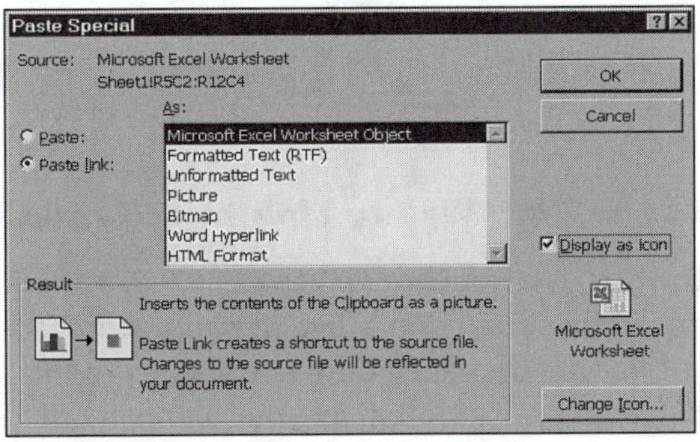

Figure 21.1: Linking data to an Excel worksheet inside your Word document.

When to Embed into Your Document

Sometimes you need to include information from another program, but you aren't sure if that program is available in the future. If this is your concern, then you should embed the information into your Word document. *Embedding* is the process of taking the selected information—and the program that created it—and merging it into your document. Once you've embedded an Excel worksheet for example, you are always able to edit the information. Just double-click it to see full-functioning Excel toolbars ready to help you, right inside your Word document!

Need to Keep File Size to a Minimum?

Link information instead of embedding it. Embedded objects increase file size because both data and application are stored in your document. A linked object, however, shows only the information; the rest is stored somewhere else as the source.

Remember, however, that there is no longer a link to the original source of your information, so if the source changes, the information in your Word document could be outdated.

To embed existing information in any Office 2000 program, copy the information, and then switch to your current document in Word. Open the **Edit** menu and click **Paste Special**, and then click the **Paste** button. To create and embed any new information, such as an audio clip, a graphic object, or an Equation Editor object, click where you want it to appear in your Word document. Open the **Insert** menu and click **Object**. On the **Create New** tab, choose the object you want. If you know the name and path of an existing object, click the **Create From File** tab, type the name of the file you want to embed (or click the **Browse** button to help you locate the file). The object is embedded in your document.

Here's the Web Way to Link to Information!

Try linking directly to your data source using the **Paste As Hyperlink** command found on the **Edit** menu. By clicking on a hyperlink in your document, you quickly jump to the source of information, including the application that created it. These destinations can include other computers on your company network, or locations on the Internet and the World Wide Web. Find out more about hyperlinks in Chapter 22, "Creating a Web Page in Word 2000."

When to Use Hyperlinks

Sometimes you need to link to current information, have it presented in the application that created it, and keep the document size as small as possible. Word 2000 uses a feature called a *hyperlink*, and you probably have experience using it already, in either the Windows Help menus or browsing a Web page.

Hyperlinks are nothing more than jump commands. Hyperlinks appear as blue-colored, underlined text in your Word document. Click a hyperlink and you immediately jump to the destination specified by the hyperlink. Hyperlinks are a great way to jump around common groups of documents quickly, and they work the same way in Microsoft Office programs as they do on the World Wide Web.

The advantage of a hyperlink is that your document doesn't have to carry around excess baggage (as in embedding) so your document file size remains small. In fact, as long as you know the application and data are always available, a hyperlink is probably the best way to link information to your Word document.

Sharing Information Between Your Office 2000 Programs

Each Office 2000 application includes convenient ways to copy, link, embed, or hyperlink information quickly from one program to the next. For example, in Microsoft Access, click the **Office Links** button to transfer database information to other Office applications. Here are specific examples that can help you share information between all of your Office 2000 programs.

Create Hyperlinks to Any Office 2000 Program

To create a hyperlink, start at a destination—for instance, the budget summary figures in an Excel worksheet. Click and drag to select the budget numbers that excite you, then click the **Copy** button. Change to your Word document and click where you want to insert the hyperlink. Open the **Edit** menu and choose the **Paste As Hyperlink** command. The hypertext that appears is either the name of the destination, a few words of identifying text or figures, or any name you choose.

You can also create a hyperlink if you drag and drop a bit of the destination text or object wherever you want a hyperlink to appear. It's a fast method to use when all destination documents are currently opened on your screen.

Get Excel Worksheet Information into Your Word Document

If you have some data existing in an Excel worksheet that you'd like to make part of your Word document, you can copy and paste selected cells directly into your document. Open the worksheet containing the data you wish to copy. Select the cells with your mouse, click the **Copy** button in Excel, click in your document where you want it to appear, and then click the **Paste** button in Word. A snapshot of the Excel data appears in your document.

If you feel daring, you can also drag and drop a selected portion of information from one program to the other. If the other program is open, but minimized, you can drop right on the task bar button for that document. The selected text is pasted right where you drop it, and the formatting is as crisp as it was in the original.

Excel 2000 Data Inside Your Word Document

Prefer a hyperlink in your Word document that jumps to that spot in your Excel worksheet? Try to drag and drop the top left cell of your choicest region of worksheet, and use the right mouse button to drag it onto your Word document. In the shortcut menu that appears, click **Insert Hyperlink**. You now have a working hyperlink in your Word document. Click it and you jump to that chosen spot in Excel. If Excel isn't open at the time, your hyperlink starts it automatically and finds the correct worksheet.

If you want to insert a new Excel worksheet into your Word document, just click the **Insert Microsoft Excel Worksheet** button on Word's Standard toolbar. A grid pops up that looks just like the one we used to create a table, and it works the same way. Click the size of worksheet you want to start with right on this grid (such as four rows, three columns, for example). Your document comes alive with what looks like a junior Excel worksheet sticking out at you. There's nothing junior about it, though, because all the Excel tools are now at your disposal while you work inside this object. Go ahead and fill it with data and use tools to sort, sum, or even graph this data. When you're finished, just click outside the worksheet (anywhere on your document) and you'll find the worksheet still there, but supporting tools hidden back in the woodwork. The worksheet is really part of your document. Double-click it and all the tools return.

You can also go the other way, and insert your Word document into your Excel worksheet. To do this, start Excel and open your worksheet. Now open the **Insert** menu and click **Object**. In the **Object** dialog box, find the object called **Microsoft Word Document**. Click the **Create From File** tab and click to check the **Link To File** box, in order to keep this document updated each time the original is changed in Word.

If the document is large, you might also want to click the **Display As Icon** box, which leaves an icon on the worksheet representing your document. Your reader simply double-clicks this icon to read the Word document.

Copying PowerPoint Information into Your Document

If you see information in a PowerPoint slide presentation that you want to include in a Word document, go get it! The easy technique is copy and paste, so start PowerPoint, open the presentation, and find the slide that holds your interest. Select the information on the slide using your mouse, and then click the **Copy** button. Now bring up the Word document and find the spot in which you'd like it to appear, then click the **Paste** button in Word. If you prefer to link this information, don't use the Paste button, but instead open the **Edit** menu and choose the **Paste Special** command. Now you have the opportunity for a **Paste Link**, which keeps this slide information in sync with the original presentation in PowerPoint. If someone updates that slide in the future, your document is updated automatically.

You might have noticed another helpful command while you were inside the **Edit** menu. It's the **Paste As Hyperlink** command, which is another way to present PowerPoint information in your Word document. Using the previous example, choose **Paste As Hyperlink** instead of Paste Special. Now, instead of seeing the actual slide data, you see a hyperlink that you can save in your Word document. All you do is click the hyperlink in your document and you jump to this exact slide in the PowerPoint presentation. After viewing the slide, you close PowerPoint, and you are returned to this exact spot in your Word document.

Incidentally, the opposite direction works just as well. If you prefer to have Word document information inside a PowerPoint presentation, copy and paste the selected text the same way, but start in Word and paste in PowerPoint. Or if you prefer hyperlinks, open the **Edit** menu in PowerPoint and choose **Paste As Hyperlink**. Either way, you can have Word text in your slide presentation.

If you prefer to create your own new PowerPoint slide from scratch while inside your Word document, open Word's **Insert** menu and click **Object**. Find **Microsoft PowerPoint Slide** on the **Create New** tab and then click **OK**. You'll have a new slide in your document, surrounded by the PowerPoint collection of editing tools at your disposal.

Slip a PowerPoint 2000 Slide into Your Document

You can also grab an entire slide or two (or a whole presentation) that appeals to you from a PowerPoint presentation and plant it firmly into a new Word document. To do this, start PowerPoint and open the presentation containing the desired slides. Click to select the particular slide you want to copy. Open the **File** menu in **PowerPoint**, point to **Send To** and choose **Microsoft Word**. In the **Write-Up** dialog box, you have your choice of page layout designs to be used with your slide. The default places the slide on the left, and presenter notes on the right. Next, choose either **Paste**, to copy this slide into your Word document, or **Paste Link**, which provides a link to this presentation file. If you expect the author of this slide to update it in PowerPoint and want the copy inside your Word document to be updated right along with it, choose **Paste Link**. Click **OK** and the slide is pasted as requested inside a new Word document.

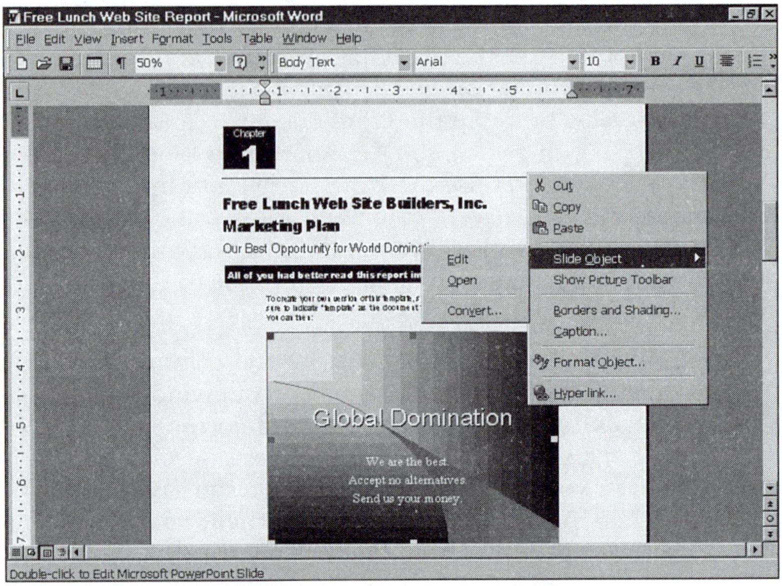

Figure 21.2: PowerPoint slides can be part of your Word document.

Link Your Document to an Access 2000 Database

Microsoft Access is a powerful relational database that can store almost anything you need. Once it's in there, you might decide that you want a copy of a portion of the database inside your Word document. For instance, you're creating a budget report and you want to include the latest budget summaries from the database. It can be done, and Access provides an easy tool to use just for this purpose. It's called the **Office Links** command, and it's available on the **Tools** menu in **Access**.

To give this a try, open Access and find the database table or report that contains the information you need. Select the region of data you want to include, open the **Tools** menu and click **Office Links**. In the **Office Links** dialog box, you must decide how you want the data to be copied into Word. The first option, **Merge It With MS Word**, is used to copy the selected data into your existing Word document. The second option, **Publish It With MS Word**, can be used to create a new Word document while inside Access. With either option, you have the data you need inside a Word document.

Copying and pasting data is also supported with Access, following the same steps as in Excel and PowerPoint. Select the data in Access, click **Copy**, change to Word and click **Paste**, **Paste Special**, or even **Paste As Hyperlink** from the **Edit** menu.

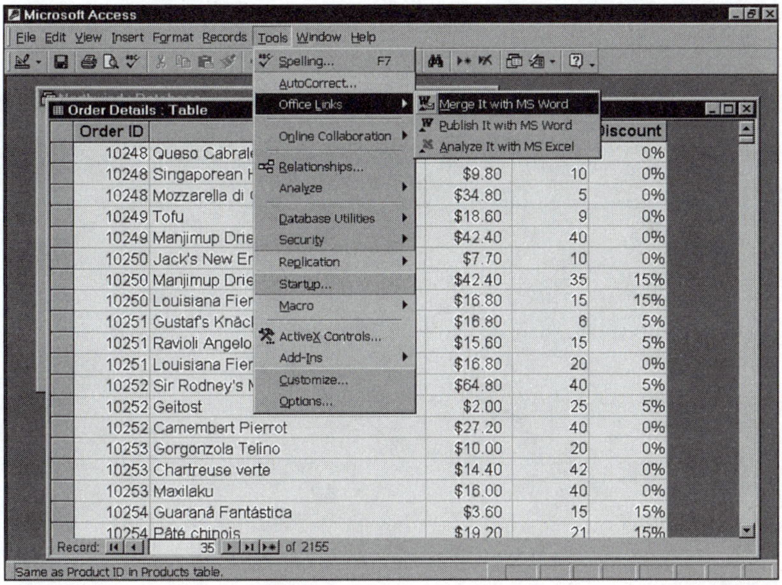

Figure 21.3: Even Access data can be presented in your Word document.

The Least You Need to Know

Word 2000 is an integrated component of Office 2000, which means you can benefit by using the absolute best tool for whatever your task may be. You can quickly move yourself, and your data, among these applications, in a variety of different ways.

- How do I create a hyperlink to a PowerPoint slide in my document?

  You can create quick hyperlinks to other Office 2000 programs. It's easiest if you get both programs running at the same time. Drag the selected object in the destination over to the place you want the hyperlink to appear. The hyperlink is created automatically.

- Can I hyperlink if the other program isn't maximized at the moment?

  Yes, just drag the selection onto the application's icon on the taskbar and continue holding down the mouse button until the application opens. Then drag the selection where you want it. The hyperlink will be created automatically.

- Can I get data from Excel, PowerPoint, and Access into my Word document?

  Yes, and you have several choices. The easiest method is to simply copy and paste the information, and Word will maintain the appropriate format for the data. Other options include hyperlinks, file linking, and file embedding.

Part 4

Creating a Web Page in Word 2000

So much can change in a few short years! Typing your first document with a computer was tough, but you got the hang of it. Now they're asking you to create Web pages, store stuff on the Internet, and your boss wants it done before noon! It's enough to make your head spin.

Word 2000 won't leave you spinning because it's full of features that help you cope with this new stuff. Why not use your original browser (your eyes) and allow these chapters to help ease your way into the modern world?

Chapter 22

Creating a Web Page in Word 2000

In This Chapter

- Using the Web Page Wizard or Web Templates
- Formatting your Web page
- Adding special effects to your Web page
- Creating hyperlinks

The world changes quickly, and Word 2000 has improved to help you change with it. The World Wide Web has become the standard method of sharing information, but until recently it's been difficult to create and support your own Web documents. Word 2000 finally meets that challenge by providing the proper tools to help you create Web pages.

Create a Web Page Fast

Do you need a certifiably beautiful, interesting, and most important—functioning—Web page but have only 15 minutes to spare? No problem, as long as you own Word 2000, because all the tools you need are provided. Pull up a chair and let's see how it's done.

The Web Page Wizard, at Your Service

Running the Web Page Wizard consists of answering several questions covering the function and visual style for a new Web page. It's fast and kind of fun. Open the **File** menu and click **New**. In the **New** dialog box, click the **Web Pages** tab, and then double-click **Web Page Wizard** to start.

Figure 22.1: Plenty of choices to create the pages you need.

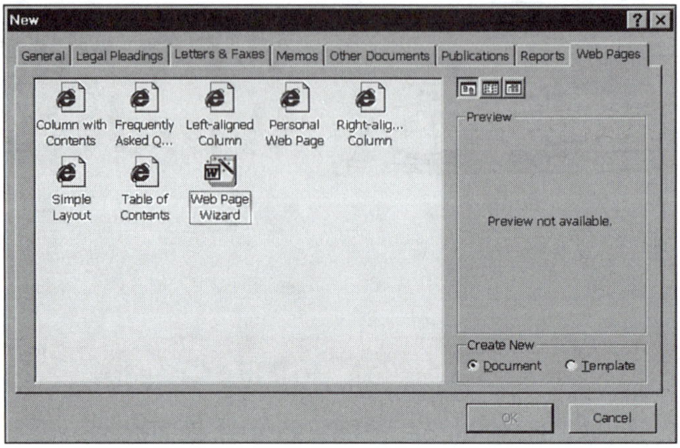

First, provide a **Title and Location** for your Web page. A suggested location is already provided in your Personal folder, but you can change it if necessary. Click the **Next** button and decide if you want vertical or horizontal pages on the **Navigation** page. Click **Next** and you've got the option to add more template pages now, especially useful once you are experienced and want to create lots of pages fast. Click **Next** again and you get the chance to rearrange the order of your new pages in the **Organization** box.

Finally, you can choose a visual theme for your page. These are color-coordinated combinations of text and graphics that follow a general theme, like an *Artsy* page, or perhaps a *Safari*one, or even a *Classic* theme if you want to look like everyone else. Besides choosing a theme, you can also decide on three options available for each theme, as shown in the figure. Click the **Finish** button and a striking new Web page appears on your Word 2000 screen.

So what's next? Just click on the **Insert Heading Here** and type the title for your Web page. Click the next line **Insert Subheading Here** and give credit to yourself, or perhaps a description, address, or warning label.

This is a good time to save this Web-page work of art. Click the **Save** button and provide a name and folder location. Notice that the file type is already set to Web page. Before going further in Web page customization, let's take a look at the other creation choice, the Web Page templates, and see what's different.

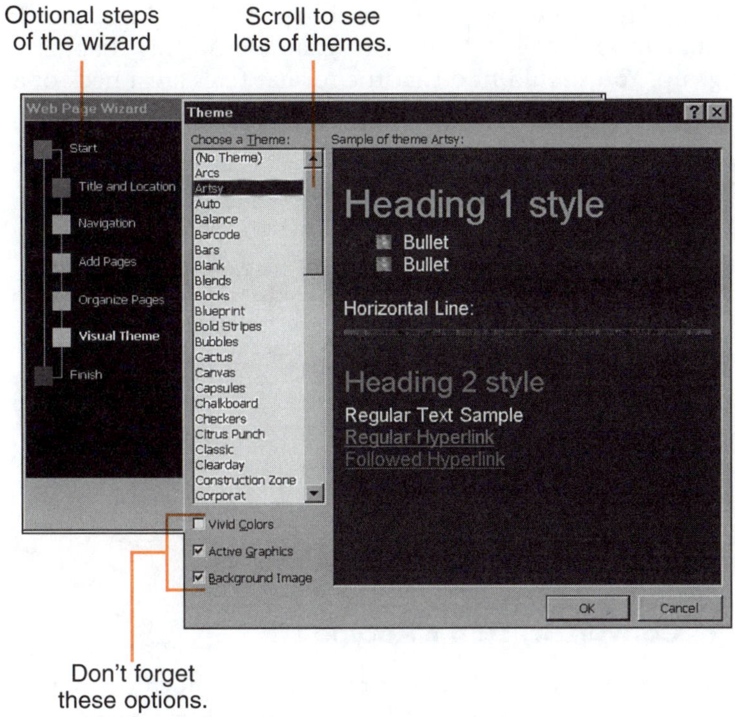

Figure 22.2: Visual Themes provide striking appearances for Web pages.

Build from Scratch Using Web Page Templates

Don't want to mess with the Wizard? Then try one of the many web templates included in Word 2000. Open the **File** menu, click **New**, and choose the **Web Pages** tab. You'll find a great assortment of the most common page types required by Web sites, including prealigned column pages, table of contents pages, and a great Personal Web Page that includes a complete Web site on a single page!

Also be aware that, on the **General** tab, you'll find the Web Page template, and it's the no-frills version of the Web Page Wizard. With no questions asked, it's just an ordinary Web page ready for you to customize and save. As you become more experienced, you'll want to try creating a page from scratch, and this template provides the canvas for your artistic expression.

Saving Any Word 2000 Document as a Web Page

Trivia question: Besides the Wizard and the various Templates, what's the third way to create a Web page fast in Word 2000? Answer: Just convert something you've already got! With the document opened, open the **File** menu and choose **Save As Web Page** and the document will be converted to a Web page. This is the real kicker in creating complete Web sites fast—you probably have most of the content already! Maybe you've already got a phone list document, job notices, employee profiles, and so on, in Word format. That's perfect, because they can be converted to Web pages fast.

It's not always simple and perfect, however, and you need to look at the conversion to see what formatting may have changed. Follow the examples in this chapter (and the next) to clean things up. You should find that the format fixes are a heck of a lot easier than re-keying all the information in your document.

Converting Several Documents at Once

Feeling lazy? Need to convert lots of existing Word documents into Web pages fast? Use the new **Batch Converter**. Place all the documents you want to convert into a single folder. Open the **File** menu, click **New**, and click the **Other Documents** tab. Double-click the **Batch Conversion Wizard** icon. You tell it where they are, where to put them when finished, and it knows what to do.

Convert It, Don't Retype It!

Creating massive amounts of Web pages shouldn't come as that much of a surprise to you, especially if you've seen government Web pages. They're very good, containing literally thousands of pages, and did you think that someone created each Web page from scratch? It's more than likely that they converted existing documents into Web pages.

Save Your Own Custom Web Page Template

Don't forget: Both the Web Page Wizard and the Web Page templates can be used to create your own custom templates. A custom template helps you keep all your pages looking consistent, besides saving you lots of time if you have many pages to create. You'll also reduce errors, because the common page parts are already tested and placed into the page.

To save a Web page as a template, open the **File** menu and click the **Save As Web Page** command. Choose **Document Template** in the **Save As Type** box, and provide a name you'll recognize in the future. Notice that the default storage folders for templates are displayed in the **Save As** dialog box; it's good practice to stay organized, so store this template in the Web Pages folder. The next time you start a new document by opening the **File** menu and clicking **New**, you see the new template listed in the **Web Pages** tab.

Glorify Your Web Page with Formatting Features

Now that you've got a great start to your Web page, it's time to customize it. Take advantage of many Word 2000 editing and formatting features, including automatic text correction, spelling and grammar checking, tables, and the list goes on and on. But not forever. If it happens that you can't seem to find a formatting option you desire, it usually means that a browser isn't capable of viewing it.

Basic Text Formatting on a Web Page

Almost all your favorite tools work on Web pages. Bold, italic, underline, strike-through, superscript, and subscript can be applied to text. You can align text with the **Align Left**, **Center**, or **Align Right** buttons. You can also change the font size of selected text, and your range is limited to supported Web page increments. Try the **Increase Indent** or **Decrease Indent** buttons on the Formatting toolbar to adjust indenting in standard Web increments.

Give That Web Page a Title

The Web page title is different from the heading text that appears at the top of a Web page. The title appears in the title bar of the Web browser when it's viewing your page, and it also appears in history lists and favorites lists, if someone stores a link to your Web page. So give your page a good title. Open the **File** menu and click **Properties**. Type the title you want in the **Title** box.

If you choose to ignore this step, your page still has a title. Word 2000 chooses a title based on the first few words or characters of your Web page.

Adding Bullets and Numbered Lists to a Web Page

Web pages are usually full of lists, and yours is easy to create. Just use the standard features of Word 2000 by clicking the **Numbering or Bullets** button on the Formatting toolbar. Or, if you don't want to bother clicking, just make sure the **AutoFormat** feature is turned on (found on the **Format** menu) to automatically create bulleted or numbered lists following your lead. You start the list, and AutoFormat continues it as you press the **Enter** key.

If the standard bullets are too boring for your page, change them. To add a new bullet for selected text, click **Bullets and Numbering** on the **Format** menu, and then select the bullet you want.

Pardon Me, but Where's the Numbered Outline?

Outline numbering works differently in Web pages, because they don't support automatic numbering. You can, however, simulate the look of an outline by indenting numbers in different levels and applying different numbering formats. Pick your top-level text and open the **Format** menu, click **Bullets and Numbering**, and then click the **Numbering** tab. Choose the number format that you want. Use the **Tab** key to indent the text that belongs to the next level in the list. Word 2000 can convert tabs in a numbered list to an indented level.

Break Things Up with Horizontal Lines

They're not as common as they used to be, but horizontal lines are still used quite often in Web pages to separate different sections of text. First, click where you want to insert the line in your Web page. Then be pleasantly surprised to see how fancy Word 2000 lines are by opening the **Insert** menu, choosing **Borders and Shading**, and clicking **Horizontal Line**. Scroll the selection and click to choose the line you want, then click **Insert Clip** as shown in the following figure:

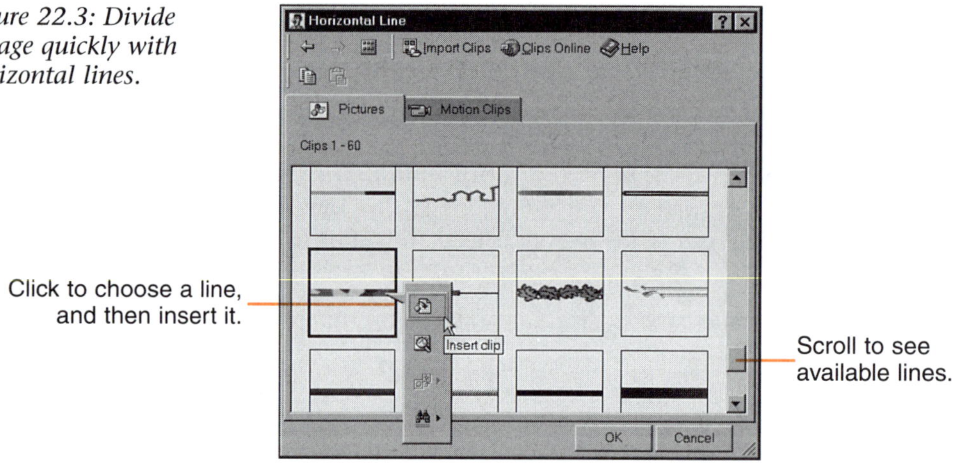

Figure 22.3: Divide a page quickly with horizontal lines.

Doing the Background Work on Your Web Page

What makes a Web page interesting, even if the words don't mean a thing to you? Background color and texture, of course! You can add or change the background color on any Web page by clicking it from a palette of colors. And adding texture is just as simple. Texture is the make-believe bumps and shading you can add to your flat background to make it appear three-dimensional.

Open the **Format** menu and point to **Background** (it's visible only while you're in **Web Layout** view). Review the palette of colors and click the color you want. It's always best to choose a background that contrasts with your text color (no yellow on white, or brown on gray, please). Although you can also click **More Colors** to see additional color choices, be forewarned that not all browsers can "see" these additional colors, and might substitute another color without asking your permission. To add a texture to your background, open the **Format** menu, point to **Background**, and click **Fill Effects**. Click to select the special effects you prefer for your background. You can choose only one texture per Web page.

Create Your Own Fancy Background

You can use any picture as a background for your Web page. Don't worry about the size; small pictures are *tiled*, or repeated, to fill the entire Web page.

Click the **Picture** tab and click the **Select Picture** button. Locate the folder where you've stored your picture, click to select your picture, and then click **OK**. Now use it in your Web page. Each time it's used, Word 2000 saves this new texture as a separate graphics file (with a name like STUCCO.JPG) in the same folder that you create and store your Web page.

You see these backgrounds and textures only while you're in **Web Layout** view. And don't forget, these backgrounds aren't designed for printed documents. They'll chew up printer memory faster than that newsletter from Chapter 18. Limit background colors and textures to your Web pages, or documents that you use online only.

If you change your mind and want to get rid of the background color, open the **Format** menu and point to **Background**. Click the **No Fill** command.

Coloring Your Words

All text on your Web page can be colored instantly using the **Font Color** button on the Formatting toolbar. Select the text, click the **Font Color** button, and choose a color from the palette. It's best to change the text color to contrast with the background color. Use lighter colors on darker backgrounds, and vice versa. Avoid using the color white for text, because white text won't print on many printers. Also avoid choosing a text color so light that it's hard to read without the background, because readers can adjust their browsers to ignore backgrounds.

Add Scrolling Text to Your Web Page

Ready for a little more action? How about a cute little marquee that flies across your Web page, like an invisible airplane pulling a banner across the sky? You even have control over the speed and scrolling behavior of your text.

First, click the line in your Web page where you want the scrolling text to appear. Open the Web Tools toolbar, and click the **Scrolling Text** button. Type the text that you want to scroll under **Type the Scrolling Text Here** box. On the **Size and Speed** tab, enter the height, width, and distance from text in pixels. Also, select the scrolling speed that you want.

Scrolling Text is one of those formatting options that might not appear to scroll in all Web browsers. The good news is that the text is still displayed (stationary), even if it doesn't scroll. Another tip—don't use more than one or two scrolling texts per page, or you slow it down needlessly, and the novelty wears off quickly for a visitor.

Inserting and Aligning Pictures in Your Web Page

Inserting a favorite graphic, clip art, or scanned picture can be as easy as clicking a button, as long as you know where it's stored. Open the **Insert** menu, point to **Picture**, and choose **From File**. Find your graphic with the **Browse** button and click **Insert** to plant it into your Web page.

Once the picture lands on the page, you can move it anywhere you like (you'll want to make sure you are using **Print Layout** view to do this). Get the hang of clicking the picture, and then pointing near the edge of it until you see the pointer change into the four-headed arrow. Click and drag it to a new spot. You can also stretch or scrunch it by clicking and dragging any of the picture handles. Be sure to save your Web page after you've added a picture. Need to align things? Make it easy on yourself and use the alignment buttons on the Picture toolbar that appears when you click on a picture. You can align images in Web pages to the left of text, to the right of text, or with no alignment so that they don't flow around the image.

Your Web Page Can Warble

Ever notice that some Web pages make sounds when you open them? That's called a *background sound*, and you can add one to your Web page. A background sound plays automatically as the reader views your Web page with a Web browser. The sound can be long or short, but short is preferred, to keep your Web page fast. You can also imitate a longer sound—if you play the shorter sound over and over. You can determine the number of times the sound repeats or have it play an unlimited number of times.

Where can you find sounds to use in your Web page? Try one of the many samples that are included in Word 2000. Click the **Insert Sound** button on the **Web Tools** toolbar and you'll open the **Background Sound** dialog box. Click **Browse** to see the samples or to look for your own sound files. If you want the sound to repeat, type the number of times in the **Loop** box, and then click **OK**. The sound is now part of your Web page and plays each time your page is accessed. You can also use sounds from other sources, including the Internet (www.midifarm.com is one example of a Web site offering sounds to download). Any sound file with the extension of WAV, MID, AU, AIF, RMI, SND, and MP2/MP3 (MPEG audio) formats can be inserted into your Web page. Your best bet is to use the MID or WAV files, because they provide the best sound quality while keeping the file size reasonably small. Once again, not all Web browsers support all sound formats, and the reader's computer must have sound support to hear them, so don't make the sound critical to understanding your Web page.

Hardware Requirements for Sound

Don't forget: In order to hear sound files in a Web page, your computer needs a sound card and speakers or headphones, as described in Chapter 12. If you want to record speech or other sounds, you'll also need a microphone that plugs into your sound card.

Your Web Page Can Do Video, Too

You can also add short video clips to your Web pages to make them more interesting. They can be fun and informative for your reader, but you should remember that they aren't supported by all Web browsers and they might take a long time to download. It's always good to provide text-based alternatives to videos you place in your Web page.

To insert a video clip, click the **Insert Movie** button on the **Web Tools** toolbar. In the **Movie Clip** box, click **Browse** to search for and select the video file you want. Now, do you see the **Alternate Image** box? That's where you can place a plain graphic in place of your video for browsers that can't do video. It's much better than a blank area. Likewise, you can include a comment in the **Alternate Text** box for viewers who have turned off graphics in their Web browser. In the **Start** box, click an option to specify how the video plays in a Web page. The easiest option isn't the smartest (unless your video is extremely short—less than a second or two). **Open** causes the video to play when the user opens your Web page. That means your reader must wait until the entire video is downloaded to completely open your Web page. **Mouse Over** is better, as it causes the video to play when the mouse pointer is placed over the video. Just as you can repeat a short sound many times to make it seem longer, you can also repeat short videos. In the **Loop** box, you can type the number of times you want the video to repeat.

Hear and See Them Now

You probably want to preview a sound or video after you've added to your Web page. Click the **Refresh Current Page** button on your Web toolbar and you'll experience the events programmed for your Web page opening.

Create Hyperlinks in Your Documents

Ready to learn one of the most important Web features of Word 2000? It's called a *hyperlink*, and you use them to jump back and forth quickly to different places. These destinations can be inside the same document or Web page, inside different documents stored in your computer or out on your network, in other Office 2000 program files, or even in remote locations out on the World Wide Web. Hyperlinks can even jump to recorded sounds and videos.

Hyperlink

A *hyperlink* is a jump to a location in the same file or another file represented by colored (usually blue) and underlined text, called *hypertext*. Hyperlinks can also be represented by a picture. You click a hyperlink to jump to a file, a location in a file, a Web page, a frame on a Web page, an email address, or anywhere out there on the Internet.

A hyperlink usually appears as an underlined word or phrase colored blue. But it can also be a picture that when clicked jumps to a different location. After using a hyperlink, its color changes to purple. This change helps you remember where you've been as you jump around the links.

There are basically three ways to insert hyperlinks. All have the same result, so choose the method that's easiest for your current situation.

- ➤ Just type the destination and use the automatic formatting features of Word 2000.
- ➤ Use the Hyperlink button when you want to browse for the destination address.
- ➤ Use a drag-and-drop operation to create hyperlinks within a document or between two opened documents.

Simply Type the Destination and Use AutoFormat Features

The quickest way to create a hyperlink is to simply type the destination and let the AutoFormat features of Word 2000 turn your typing into full-fledged hyperlinks automatically. For instance, to create a hyperlink that takes you to Microsoft's home page on the Web (even if you've never been there before), just type *www.microsoft.com* and those words automatically turn into a working hyperlink!

Need to link to another document stored on your computer or local network? Just type the full path and filename and watch it convert into a hyperlink automatically.

AutoFormat is also handy to include Internet email addresses in your document. For instance, let's say you run the Web page for the cafeteria menu, and you want to find out if the chili special has been the cause of recent employee turnover. Ask for feedback on the Web page and then type your email address. AutoFormat converts it to a hyperlink immediately. Your readers simply click on the address and an email is prepared automatically, with your correct address already included in the **To:** line. They just type a comment and send it.

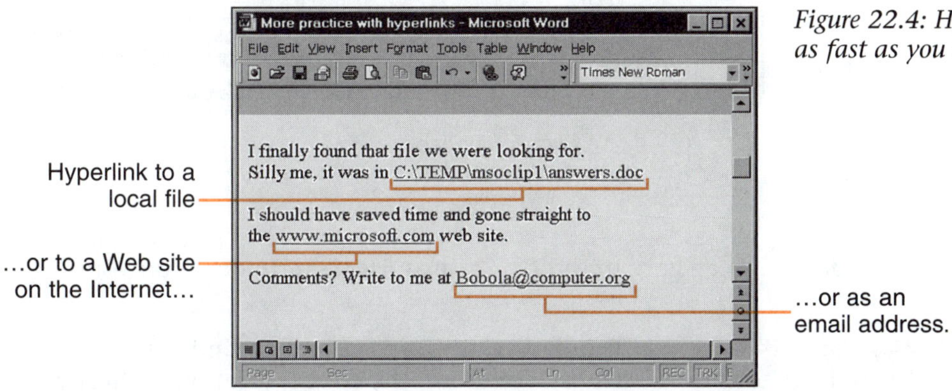

Figure 22.4: Hyperlinks—as fast as you can type.

To make all this magic happen, open the **Tools** menu and click **AutoCorrect**, to open the **AutoCorrect** dialog box. Click the **AutoFormat As You Type** tab. Under **Replace As You Type**, click to place a check in the **Internet And Network Paths With Hyperlinks** check box, and click **OK**.

Use the Insert Hyperlink Button

If you can't remember the exact destination for your planned hyperlink, or prefer to choose your own words for the hyperlink (called the *hypertext*), use this handy button.

Start by selecting the word or words to be used as the hypertext. Click the **Insert Hyperlink** button to open the **Hyperlink** dialog box, as shown in the following figure:

Figure 22.5: Choose a destination for your hyperlink.

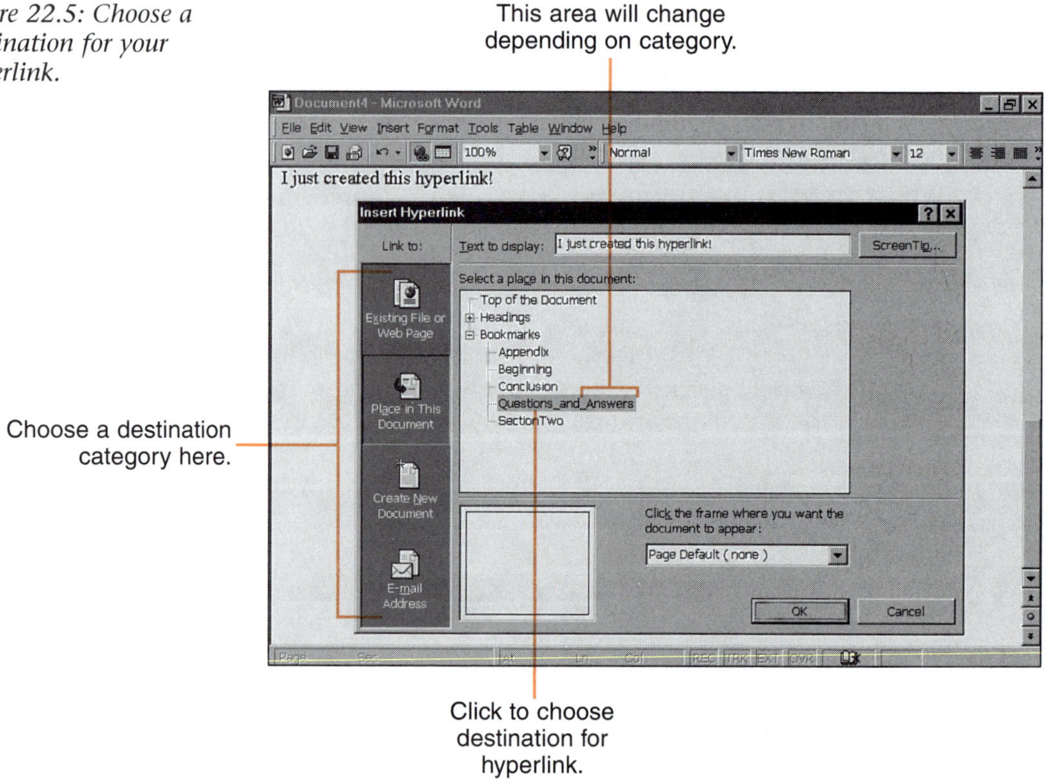

Choose the appropriate category in the **Link To** area. Here's a rundown on your options:

➤ **Existing File or Web Page**. Click **Browse** or **Web Page** and go find your destination. When you switch back to Word, the correct location is already filled in.

- **Place In This Document**. Use this to hyperlink to an exact location within the same document. You can select from the listing of either the style headings or any existing bookmarks.
- **Create New Document**. To hyperlink to something still in your head, but not yet on paper. The documents are named and created, and the hyperlinks are in place; finish the new documents at your convenience.
- **Email Address**. When you want to include a subject line in addition to the email address, use this option. When this hyperlink is clicked, an email already properly addressed, including a subject line, appears.

After choosing your **Link To**, complete the destination using either the available browsing buttons or by typing in the information. You can include optional text for **Screen Tip**; otherwise, your reader sees the destination when mouse rests on top of hyperlink. Click **OK** when you are finished and the working hyperlink is created in your document.

Bookmarks Make Hyperlinking a Snap

Bookmarks are invisible spots inside a document that you identify as something significant. It might be an important paragraph, chapter heading, index, chart, picture, or anything. Click to designate the location, then open the **Insert** menu and choose **Bookmark**. Provide any name for this location, as long as it does not contain any spaces. Click the **Add** button and this bookmark is saved.

Once you've got bookmarks in a document, it's a snap to hyperlink to them. In the **Insert Hyperlink** box, choose **Place In This Document**, and you'll see a listing of all available bookmarks.

Create a Hyperlink with a Drag and a Drop

Another way to create a hyperlink is to drag and drop a bit of the destination wherever you want the hyperlink to appear. It's a fast method to use when all destination documents are currently opened on your screen. It's also the easiest way to hyperlink between different Office 2000 products. For instance, you can drag a PowerPoint slide into your Word document, or a selected range from an Excel worksheet or even an Access database table right into Word document. Drop it at the location you want the hyperlink to appear. From now on, when you click this hyperlink, Word automatically recognizes the location of the information, opens the appropriate program, and displays the information.

The key to this is the drag. You need to drag with the right mouse button. When you drop it in your Word document, choose the command **Paste As Hyperlink** from the shortcut menu that appears. If it's not working for you, remember that both target and destination files must be saved first before a hyperlink can be created.

Hyperlink Between Frames

One of the coolest new features of Word 2000 is the ability to create frames in your Web pages, and you can create hyperlinks that jump between the frames (your Web page should already have frames created before you try this). Start by selecting the text or picture for creating the hyperlink, and click the **Create Hyperlink** button. In the **Link To** area, choose **Existing File or Web Page**, choose the destination file, and now look at the **Click the Frame Where You Want the Document to Appear** box near the bottom. It should resemble the frames of your document. Just click in the frame you want. Its unique name appears in the box and that frame becomes the target for your hyperlink.

Figure 22.6: Hyperlink to a frame in a Web page.

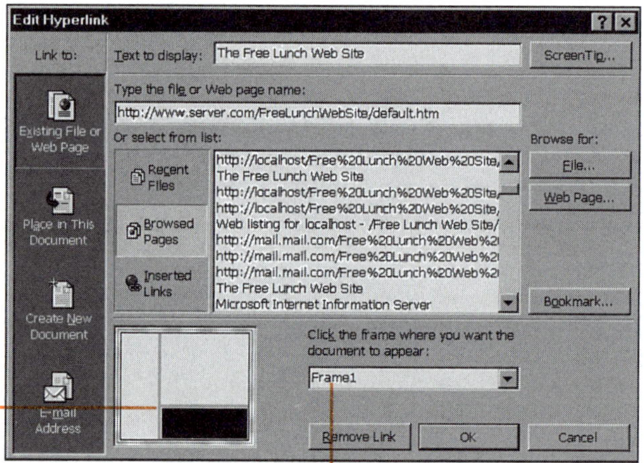

Changing Your Hypertext Words Once They're Created

Editing a hyperlink sounds easy, but there's a trick to it. You must first select the hypertext without launching it, and it's a skill that comes with patience. The trick is to click the hypertext with the *right* mouse button. In the shortcut menu that appears, point to **Hyperlink** and then choose the **Select Hyperlink** command. The hypertext is selected and you can change it by retyping or backspacing. Click outside the hyperlink when finished, and it is saved.

Removing Hyperlinks

To remove an outdated or obnoxious hyperlink, right-click on the hyperlink, point to **Hyperlink** on the shortcut menu, and choose the **Edit Hyperlink** command. In the **Edit Hyperlink** dialog box, click the **Remove Link button** and the hyperlink disappears. The hypertext returns to its previous formatting.

Buggy Hyperlinks?

If you're having problems with a hyperlink that once worked, consider these tips:

- The destination of the hyperlink may have been removed or renamed.
- The path to the destination may have moved to another location.
- If the destination is located on your intranet, check your network connections and make sure the server is available.
- The destination on the Internet may be too busy. Try to open the document later.

The Least You Need to Know

Creating a real Web page is easy in Word 2000, and browsing this chapter may have provided a few additional hints and tips.

- I know very little about the Internet but my boss needs a Web page. Can Word 2000 help me?

  Yes. Use either the **Web Page Wizard** or the **Web Template** to create perfect Web pages fast. Open the **File** menu, click **New**, and click the **Web Pages** tab to select a wizard or template. Follow the steps to create the Web page in simple steps until completion.

- What tools can I use to further format my Web page?

  Try any or all of the familiar buttons on the old Formatting toolbar. Also try adding a Theme, or changing the background colors. Then move up to the Web Tools toolbar and have some real fun. In fact, try using any of the tools available in **Web Layout** view, because if you can see the tool, chances are it can be used in your Web page.

- How can I include video and sound in my Web page?

    Two new buttons get the job done fast. You'll find the **Insert Movie** and **Insert Sound** buttons on the Web Tools toolbar. Add the location of your audio clip, video clip, or other file, and it appears on your Web page.

- How do I add a hyperlink to my Web page?

   Hyperlinks are used to provide additional or reference information in your documents or Web pages. When you click a hyperlink, you jump to its destination. To create a hyperlink, start by selecting some text, then click the **Insert Hyperlink** button, and provide the destination for the jump.

Chapter 23

Working with Web Frames and Other Tools

In This Chapter

- Working with Web page frames
- Creating tables for your Web page
- Consider these alternative format tools
- Previewing your Web page

Word 2000 is loaded with tools to help you build and maintain the latest designs in Web pages, including *frames* for dividing up your page and organizing your work. And you already know how to use many of the existing tools—the table creation and alignment tools, and the automatic proofing tools, for example—because the Web tools work the same way as their normal document counterparts. That frees up lots of time to learn the new tools that make snazzy Web pages a breeze to create.

Using Frames in Your Web Page

You probably see these while surfing the Web and secretly wish you could make them. Wishes do come true! Web pages can be divided into sections to help organize the content and keep certain areas on the browser screen at all times. When you divide a Web page into different areas, each area is called a *frame*. Most people stick a Web page in each frame. But, one of those pages is dedicated to holding everything together; it's called a *frames page*.

Open or create a Web page to practice constructing frames. They go in really fast, but don't worry—if something is not to your liking, click the **Undo** button (or press **Ctrl+Z**) and the frame is removed.

A New Toolbar for Creating Frames

Everything you need to create and edit Web page frames is found in the new Frames toolbar, or you can open the **Format** menu, point to **Frames**, and choose your weapon. The icons aren't much to look at, but the descriptions are near perfection, and only a few require an explanation:

- **Table of Contents.** Choose the frame to become your center of attention, and click this button.
- **To the Right or Left.** Frames magically appear on either side.
- **Above or Below.** Frames are created above or below the currently selected frame.
- **Delete This Frame.** Zaps the frame for good.
- **Frame Properties.** Brings up lots of controls regarding the borders, sizes, and initial page.

Click a few of these buttons to see how the frames chew up the screen real estate. You can stick a Web page in any frame. When it's time to save, remember you have an extra page managing all this, so provide a name for your new frames page when asked.

Figure 23.1: Click and create frames to organize your information.

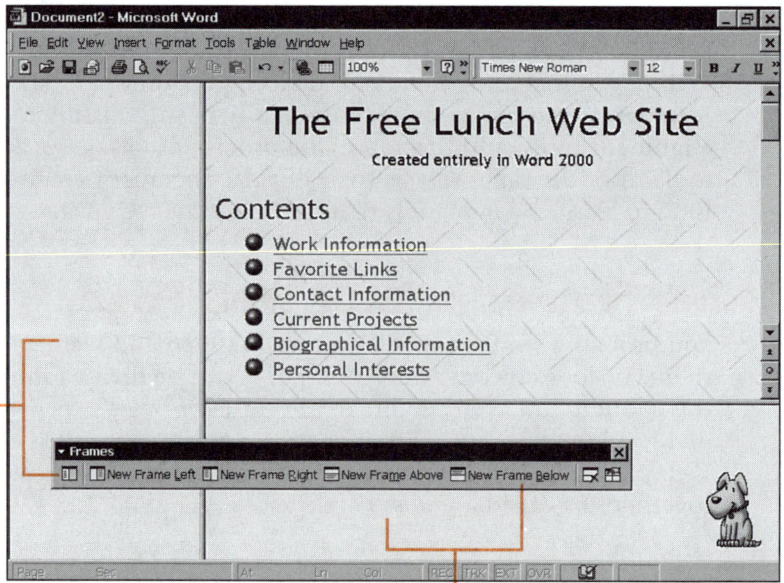

Add Header or Footer Frames First

Frames take about two seconds of planning, so think carefully. If you plan on having a frame across the top or bottom, you need to do it first. Got it? Open the **Format** menu, point to **Frames**, choose **New Frames Page**; on the **Frames** toolbar, click **New Frame Above**. Drag the borders to get the size and shape you need.

Likewise, you can click **New Frame Below** and have a constant footer bar at the bottom of your Web page.

Add More Frames As Needed

Now it gets real easy. After you've created your header and footer frames (if you needed them), you can add frames into the middle of your page. Click as close as possible to where you want the new frame. Open the **Format** menu, point to **Frames**, and choose the kind of frame you need.

Filling Your Frames With Stuff

After creating a frame, you may notice that it's empty. You can put something in it by just typing away. After all, it's just another Web page, and you know all about creating good Web pages.

If you want to fill it with an existing Web page or document, right-click in the frame and choose **Frame Properties**. This dialog box gives you complete control over this frame, including the content. Click the **Frame** tab, then click the **Browse** button to locate the document you want, as shown in the following figure:

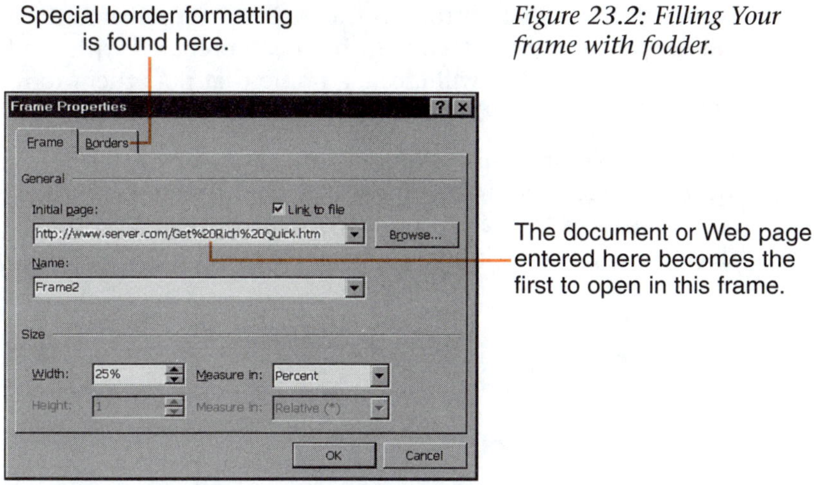

Figure 23.2: Filling Your frame with fodder.

Saving Frames

Once filled, frames should be saved, or else you lose them. Good thing it doesn't take much effort. Right-click in the frame you want to save and choose **Save Current Frame As**, then provide a name and folder in the familiar **Save As** dialog box.

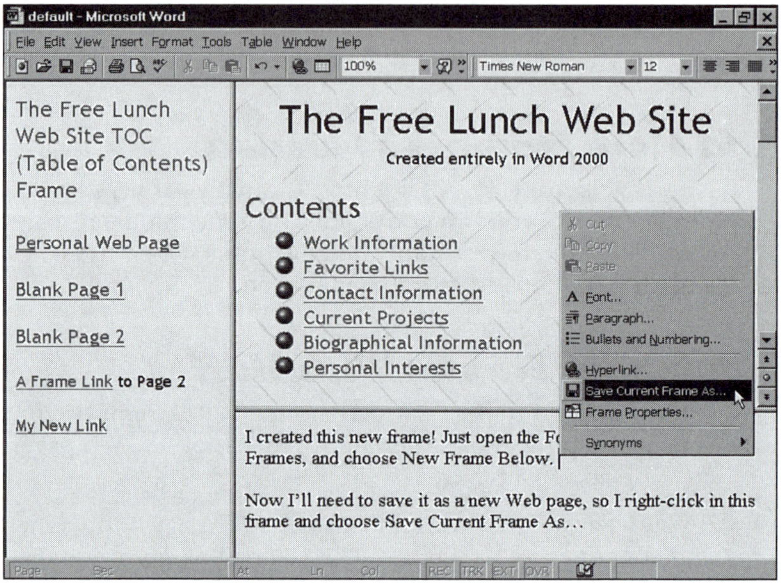

Figure 23.3: Saving a frame is easiest with a right-click.

When to Use the Table of Contents Frame

Notice the very first button on the Web Tools toolbar is the **Table of Contents in Frame** button. If your document has been prepared with field codes for a table of contents, this button will create a frame that puts them to use. You'll get a real table of contents frame with working hyperlinks that jump to each page of your web site.

No field codes in your document, you say? Are you sure? If you've used any of the wizards to create your document, the chances are good that you'll get a working table of contents. As long as you've consistently applied heading styles throughout your document, this button will probably drag out a decent table of contents.

Name That Frame!

All frames require a unique name, and Word provides very boring (but unique) names automatically. But you might want your own names, especially while building your hyperlinks. Click the frame you want to name. Open the **Format** menu, point to **Frames**, choose **Frame Properties**, click the **Frame** tab, and type the name in the **Name** box.

Editing Frames

Don't like the looks of your new frame? Go ahead and change it. Use the same process you've learned for manipulating windows.

- **Resize It.** You've got complete control over the height and width of any frame. Move your pointer over the border you want to change. When it becomes a double-headed arrow, drag in the direction you need.
- **Change the Content.** Click inside and edit to your heart's content. Right-click inside and choose **Frame Properties** if you want to swap out the entire page with another.
- **Delete It.** No longer friends with your frame? Dump it easily with a click to select it, then open the **Format** menu, point to **Frame**, and choose **Delete Frame**. And don't worry, whatever content was in the frame remains, plastered to the left side of the screen. This gives you the chance to save the content if you need it. If not, select it and delete it also.

Want Better Control With Frame Location?

To finely tune exactly how and where a frame aligns on your web page, open the **Format** menu, point to **Frame**, and choose what you need in the **Vertical** or **Horizontal** sections. Want the frame to move up and down with the paragraph it's anchored to? Check the **Move With Text** to lock the frame to a paragraph its anchored to. Or choose **Lock Anchor** to make sure it remains anchored to the same paragraph when the frame is moved.

Controlling Frame Appearance for Web Browsers

When you plan to allow people to view your creation with Web browsers, you also get to decide how much control they should have. Maybe you don't want them closing or resizing frames willy-nilly. Here's what you have complete control over:

- Allowing the resizing of a frame in a web browser
- Displaying border
- Displaying scrollbars

To control the appearance for any or all of these, open the **Format** menu, point to **Frames**, click **Frame Properties**, and click the **Borders** tab. Choose **Show Scrollbars In Browser**, **No Borders**, **Show All Frame Borders**, or **Frame Is Resizable in Browser**. Remember, these only apply to viewing the documents in a Web browser. You always have complete control while editing inside Word 2000.

Specifying Initial Web Page in a Frame

You receive complete control over the first web page that appears in each frame when your Web page opened in a Web browser. Click in the frame you want to set. Open the **Format** menu, point to **Frames Page**, choose **Frame Properties**, click the **Frame** tab, select **Initial Page** box, and locate the document.

Moving a Web Page that Contains Frames

Someday you may need to move your Web page to a different folder, or even a different Web server. Instead of searching for the folder and all the associated support files, pictures, and so on, do yourself a favor. Let Word 2000 move everything for you. Open the Web page, then use the **Save As Web Page** to specify a different folder or server. Word automatically moves all the supporting files and folders that relate to your Web page.

Set Your Table on a Web Page

If you lived through Chapter 13, you'll have no problem creating a table for your Web page. You use the very same Word 2000 table tools as you would in a normal document. Quick tables can appear with the click of a button, or you can decide to put your drawing talent to good use and sketch a completely custom table. Either way, you'll find tables to be indispensable additions to your Web pages.

Tables Inside of Tables

Word 2000 includes a new table feature that really helps when designing fancy web pages. It's called *nested* tables, and that means you can create a whole table inside another table. For example, you can pick a single cell of a table and actually create a new table inside that cell. Ours is not to tell you why, but to show you how.

Okay, we'll tell you why.

Nested tables help solve the one of the most common problems with web pages—splitting a page down the middle, from top to bottom, to help organize it. Create the first big table as simply two cells, a left and a right. Create a new table inside of the right cell (*nesting* it). Now you can put things on the left (like a picture or table of contents) and lots of organized details on the right and they stay in proper alignment.

Sure, you can accomplish the same goal using frames, but not all browsers can use frames, and all browsers perform faster using tables rather than frames.

Click inside an existing table cell and then click the **Table** button. Drag to the row and column number you need, and then watch as it scrunches into the space available.

Use Tables to Organize Your Web Page

If you're having trouble aligning your graphics and text on a Web page, try using a table as a layout tool. It works, and it's fast to create. Suppose you want your Web page to have a graphic on the left and a column of text on the right. Create a one-row, two-column table by clicking the **Insert Table** button. Insert the graphic in the left cell, and type the text in the cell on the right. What could be easier?

How Can You See the HTML and Other Stuff?

Someone may have told you that all Web pages are written in some special code with strange names like *HTML* (HyperText Markup Language), DHTML, SGML, and XML. They weren't lying. Even the simplest Web pages can consist of hundreds of lines of this coding. But, you never have to learn these languages because Word 2000 converts your work automatically. Someday though, you may want to see it for yourself.

See for yourself. To view the HTML source, open your Web page, then open the **View** menu and click the **HTML Source** command. You can also edit in this view, but only do so if you speak fluent HTML. When the excitement wears off, you can return to the regular view of your Web page by closing the Microsoft Development Environment.

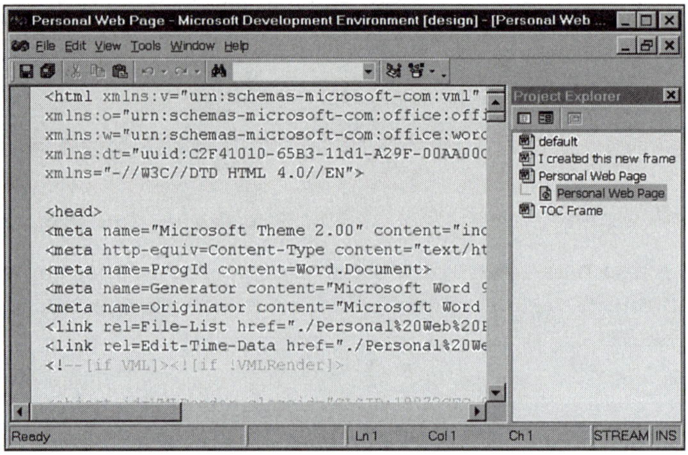

Figure 23.4: Yuck! The infamous Web language called HTML.

Do I Need to Understand HTML?

Heavens no! You don't even have to recognize the acronym. Word 2000 enables you to create Web pages in their final form, without understanding the language that's holding it all together. Web languages like HTML define the location and description of elements on a Web page. When you connect to a Web page, your Web browser creates the page you see by following the Web language instructions. Here, in this chapter, you can create complex pages in ignorant bliss, and Word 2000 takes care of converting things to the appropriate Web language.

Creative Substitutes for Unavailable Tools

You're familiar with the many tools that are available in Word 2000 while you create Web pages, including spelling and grammar checking, AutoCorrect, AutoText, tables, and so on. Some other features are customized to make Web work easier, like graphical bullets and lines. But some features just aren't there, like headers and footers for example. Web pages don't allow them. It's not a bug in Word 2000, it's just that the language of the Web doesn't support these formatting capabilities.

Here's a list of some currently forbidden formatting tools in Web pages:

- Line spacing
- Margins

- Character Spacing
- Embossed, Shadow, and Engraved Formats
- Kerning
- Text Flow Settings
- Spacing before and after paragraphs

So what do you do when you really need a particular formatting option? You compromise, get a little creative, and take a look at this cheat list.

- **Columns**. The standard newspaper columns aren't supported during Web creation, but you can use a table to create a two-column effect. Create a table in your Web page with two columns and only a single row. Start typing and continue to type in that row and your text grows into a column.
- **Paragraph Borders**. Borders around paragraphs aren't supported during Web creation, but you can place borders around graphical objects or tables. Try creating a large one-column, one-row table and type your paragraph inside. The table itself becomes the paragraph border.
- **Special Text Effects**. Some special effects like shadows, embossed text, and engraved text aren't supported in Web pages. You could always take a picture of the text and insert it as a graphic. It's not that difficult, it just has several steps. Get what you want on the screen, press **Shift+Print Screen**, now open the **Paint** program (found in your Accessories) and click **Paste**, and save it as your new graphic. For other effects, try substituting text effects that are supported on Web pages, such as strikethrough, bold, italic, colored text contrasting with background coloring, and scrolling text.
- **Headers and Footers**. Web pages don't have headers and footers. If you're converting a Word document to a Web page, the information is preserved, but it no longer is in a header or footer. You have to maintain it as normal text near the edges of your Web page. Common text near the top or bottom of your Web page, simulating headers or footers, can be included in your Web page templates to save you the time of entering it on each page.
- **Footnotes**. Footnotes aren't supported in Web pages, but you could substitute the formatting with horizontal lines and superscript numbering. A better solution is to convert all your footnotes to hyperlinks and use them as endnotes—click a number and you hyperlink to the reference elsewhere in the document. Click **Backward** to return to where you were.
- **Heading Styles**. The styles in Web pages are customized so they match the styles supported by HTML, the format for Web pages.
- **Cross-references**. Cross-references aren't supported in HTML, but you can manually create them using hyperlinks.

No Errors Here

The **Spelling and Grammar Checker** works on your Web page just like any ordinary document. It picks up errors in all parts of your Web page, including hyperlinks, scrolling text, and labels. And be sure to turn on the **AutoText** and **AutoCorrect** features to automatically correct common typographical errors while you type.

Design Toward a Common Browser

Want to ensure your design works for a specific version of a browser? Click to open the **Tools** menu, choose **Options**, and then the **General** tab. Click **Web Options**, and then the **General** tab. Select or clear the **Disable Features Not Supported By** and then choose your browser in the Browser box.

Web Page Preview and the Web Toolbar

When creating Web pages, Word 2000 can act a lot like a web browser. It can also work *exactly* like a web browser. With your Web page displayed, open the **File** menu and choose **Web Page Preview**. You'll see Word morph into a browser and show you exactly what the Web page looks like.

You also see buttons that operate just as they do on a browser. These buttons are also available on the Web toolbar, which you can view by opening the **View** menu, pointing to **Toolbars**, and choosing **Web**. Here's a quick review of the buttons:

Back. Click to jump to the previous page.

Forward. Click to jump to the next page.

Stop Current Jump. Cancel a jump that is taking too long.

Refresh Current Page. This updates the current page by reloading it.

Start Page. Press this and open the start page or home page. You can specify the start page using the Web toolbar.

Search The Web. This button opens a search page so you can search for words or phrases.

Favorites. You create this list of URLs—just click to go to the page. The Favorites folder contains shortcuts to files, folders, and hyperlinks you use often. Add your favorite shortcuts to the selected file, folder, or link here.

Go. This gives menu choices for setting Start and Search pages and more.

Show Only Web Toolbar. Press this to hide all toolbars except Web, allowing more room to see your Web page.

Address. You can type a URL here or click the pull-down arrow and see where you've been (or choose to go there again).

The New *Web Tools* Toolbar

Unless you are the ultimate geek perfectionist, you'll find all the professional Web page design tools you'll ever need on the new **Web Tools** toolbar. Here you'll find lots of new buttons, including picture placement and alignment tools, boxes, buttons, and check boxes, and even a script editor for custom programming. Custom help is available with all the features.

The Least You Need to Know

Frames are the new way of life. Word 2000 helps you enter this strange new world with a decent toolbar for creating and editing frames in your Web pages. A few other formatting tips were also tossed around in this chapter, to keep you on the cutting edge.

➤ What's a frame and why do I need one?

Frames help organize information on a Web page. When you divide a Web page into different areas, each area is called a *frame*. The Web page that holds several frames is called a *frames page*.

➤ Why can't I stick a header frame above my other frames?

Because you forgot to read this chapter. You should create header and footer frames *first*, before creating other frames in your Web page.

➤ Can Word 2000 help me create a table on my Web page?

Lots of them. Use the **Insert Table** button on the Standard toolbar. Use it the same way you create a table in a Word document. You can even create *nested* tables, which are tables created inside of existing tables.

➤ Why can't I place a picture and text side-by-side on my Web page?

You can; it just takes some creativity. Create a one-row, two-column table, and then type inside of one cell and paste a graphic in another.

➤ How can I see what my Web page really looks like?

Without travelling too far, you can open the **File** menu and click **Web Page Preview**. If you have more time on your hands, open your browser and point it at the document.

Chapter 24

Publishing Your Web Page on Your Web Server

In This Chapter

- Creating Web Folder shortcuts
- Working with Web Folders
- Taking Folders Offline for Editing
- Synchronizing Offline Folders with the Web Server
- Saving your pages to an Internet Service Provider

Most businesses now have the luxury of owning their own Web servers, and these are used internally on intranets, available to all employees. Many also have Web servers connected to the Internet. Well, now you can play with the rest of the world! This chapter shows how to actually publish your Web pages to a Web server, and you never have to leave Word 2000. Give it a try, and see if your pages can make it to the Top 10 Web Sites today!

Some Help From Your Network Administrator

You may need some help from your network administrator for activities in this chapter, because they require the use of the new *Microsoft Office Server Extensions* on your Internet server. These extensions are included free with Office 2000. Once they've been installed, you won't have to bother your administrator anymore—you'll be able to copy and manage your Web pages all by yourself.

Here's the procedure. You get the name of the Web server from your administrator, build your own shortcuts to it, and then save your Web pages to your shortcuts! That's actually intuitive, isn't it?

> **What Makes It a Web Server?**
>
> A "Web Server" is a computer that sends out Web pages in response to a request from a Web browser. With Office 2000, Microsoft adds the *Office Server Extensions* to make it easier to publish your work directly to your Web server.

Installing the Web Publishing Wizard

You need only do this once, just to get things set up. If you forget this step, you can still create Web folders but you won't be able to do the fancy stuff, such as synchronizing. Just click **Start**, **Programs**, **Accessories**, **Internet Tools**, and choose **Web Publishing Wizard**. Click **Next** to get started.

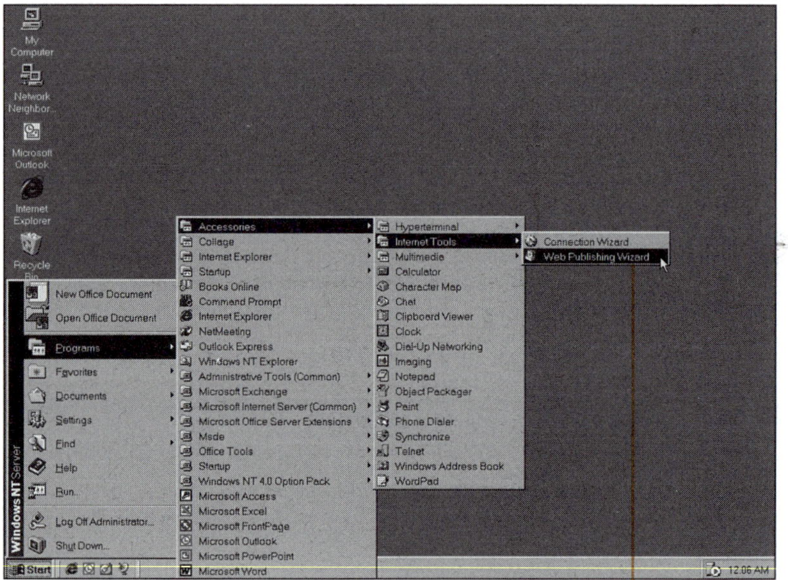

Figure 24.1: One-time installation of the Web Publishing Wizard.

The following figure shows that the most likely folder to publish has already been chosen. In most cases, this is the preferred location, but you can override it if needed. The **Browse** buttons help you locate other folders. Click **Next** to continue.

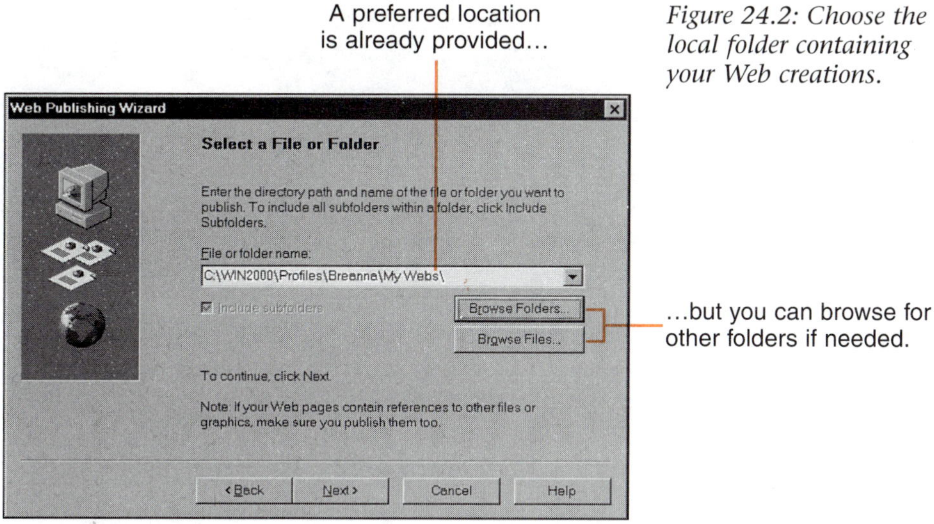

Figure 24.2: Choose the local folder containing your Web creations.

Now pick an easier name so you won't have to remember that long name in the preceding figure. We chose *Marketing Newsletter* for this example. It's not necessary, but if you're curious, you can click the **Advanced** button to choose between four different connection methods you plan to use. The default is **Automatic**, so you won't have to worry about it. When finished, click **Next**.

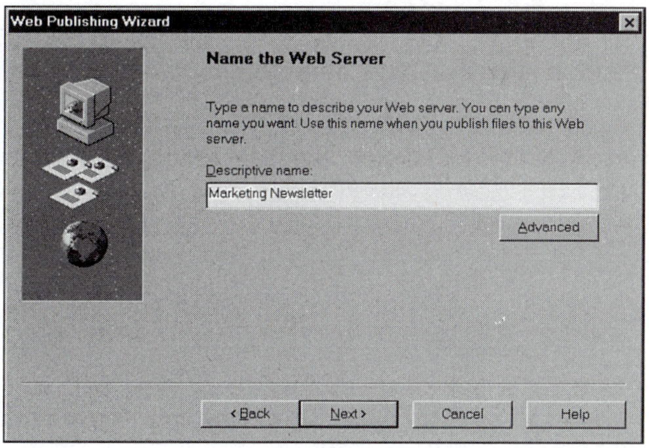

Figure 24.3: Provide a simple name for your shortcut to the Web server.

Now you need to identify your real Web server. This is the name of the Web server location where you are permitted to store pages. Your network administrator or Internet Service Provider (ISP) gives this to you, and you type it here. Click **Next** to continue. You may get another screen asking for the URL; type in the same information and click **Next** to continue.

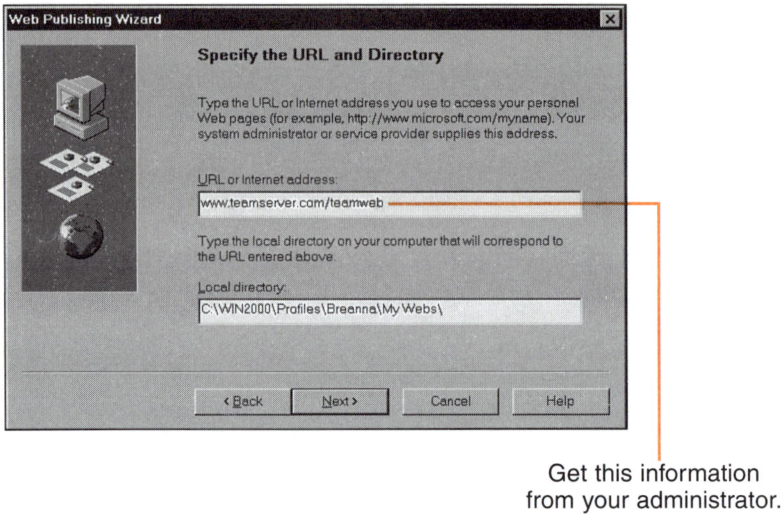

Figure 24.4: Point your shortcut to your real Web server.

Your computer now attempts to connect using the information you've used. If it fails, you get the chance to check for typos or loosened connections, or call to yell at your administrator for the correct location. But if it works, you get a smile on your face and the completion screen waiting for you to click **Finish**.

Working With Web Folders

A Web folder is simply a shortcut to a Web server. It enables you to forget the details of the server location, and remember just a simple icon you've created that points to a server.

When you create Web pages in Word, they are normally saved in your Personal folder on your local computer. When you are ready to publish your pages, you save them in a Web folder, and they are automatically moved to the proper spot on the Web server.

Saving to Web Servers

You need a *Web folder* to save your work to a real Web server. Creating Web folders is easiest using the **Add Web Folder Wizard**. You'll find this wizard icon inside **My Computer**, but it's even faster inside Word. Click the **Open** button and click the **Web Folders** button to see what you've got. If it's empty, you can add one now by clicking the **Create New Folder button**. As shown in the following figure, you are quickly asked to type the full name of the Web server location that has been provided by your administrator.

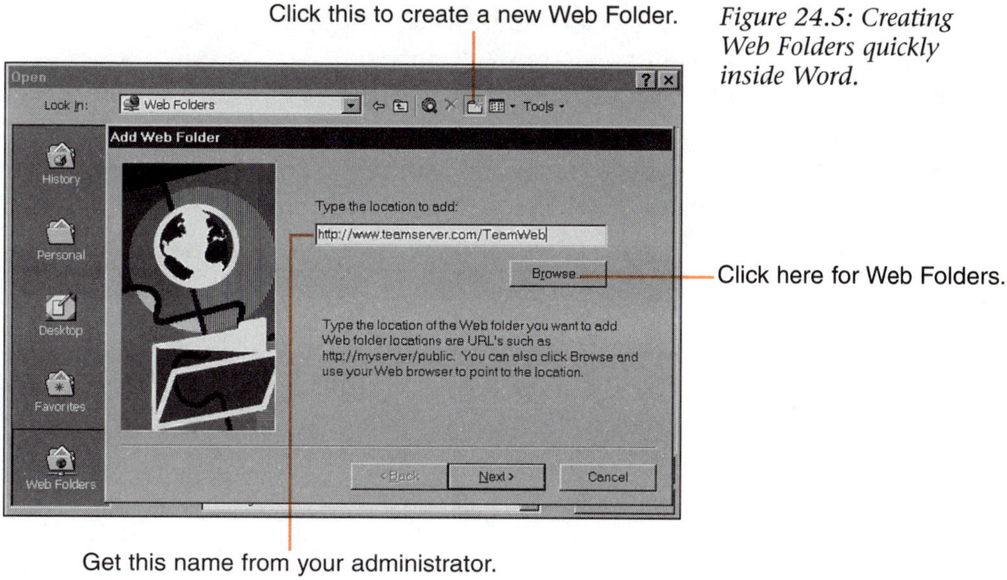

Figure 24.5: Creating Web Folders quickly inside Word.

Click **Next**, and type in a simple name for your new Web folder. You aren't renaming anything on the server—this just makes it easier for you to remember the location. Click **Finish** and it's built, ready for your content.

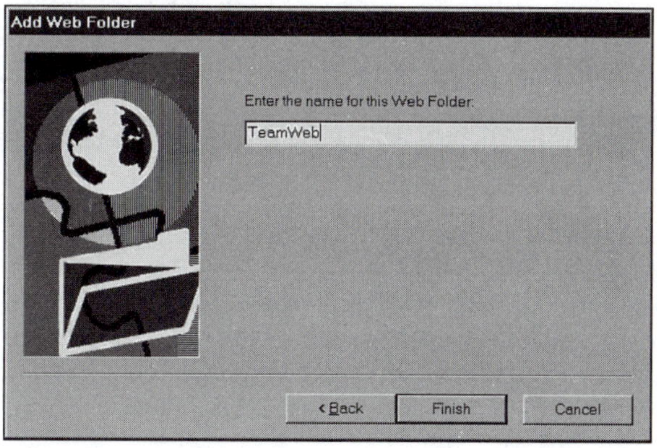

Figure 24.6: A simple name is all you need for your new Web folder.

Now it's time to store stuff in your Web Folder, such as Web pages! Create one or several Web pages as described in Chapter 22. When it's time to place them on your Web server (called *publishing* your Web pages), open the **File** menu and choose **Save As Web Page**. Click the **Web Folders**, choose your server folder, and click the **Save** button. Your Web pages are copied to the Web server. At that point, they become accessible to anyone with a Web browser who has access to your Web server.

Managing Stuff in Web Folders

Once you've created your Web folder and filled it with good things, you can manipulate the folder in familiar ways. You remember cut, copy and paste, drag-and-drop, Send-To and so on. And you've got three different ways to expose your Web Folders:

- **In Word 2000**. Right inside the **File Open** dialog box.
- **Inside your Web browser**. Use your familiar browser buttons.
- **In Windows Explorer**. As you would expect, and you can combine any of these three ways.

No matter how you get to them, the end result is the same, so try them all and stick with the one you like best.

The Fastest Way to Publish a Web Page

Would you believe one (or two) clicks from your mouse can start the ball rolling? Just expose a list of your Web page documents anywhere (as in **File Open** or Windows Explorer) and right-click the page you want to publish. Everything you need is on this menu. Point to **Send To** in the shortcut menu and choose **Web Publishing Wizard**. You can even send several at the same time. Hold **Ctrl** down while you select multiple pages, right click on them, and **Send To** the **Web Publishing Wizard** en masse.

The Wizard takes you through the basic steps: You choose the Web server from the list, it gathers all related files, and you click **OK**. The Wizard copies the Web page and all supporting files to the Web server and makes it available immediately. You can check now by using your Web browser.

Working on Your Web Pages "Offline"

Once your Web pages are running on the server, you don't want anyone to disturb them, including yourself. So if you need to update them, do it the professional way: Make a copy on your local computer, perfect your changes there, then stick them back on the server when you are absolutely sure they are ready. When you work with a Web page or folder locally, it is considered to be *offline*. Offline is the temporary state of storage while you work on them.

To take any Web Folder or page offline, locate it by clicking **Open** in Word and clicking **Web Folders** (you can also find them in **My Computer** or **Windows Explorer**). As shown in the figure, right-click the desired folder or file and choose **Make Available Offline**. The process begins immediately; you'll see a copy of the folder moved to your computer. Any editing you do now is done on this local copy.

Check mark means
folder is available offline.

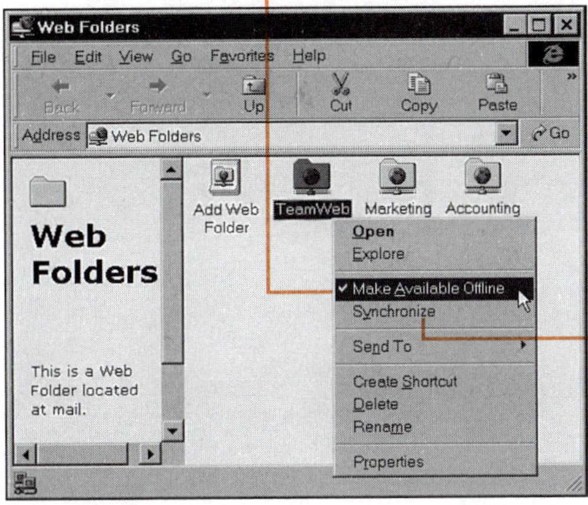

Figure 24.7: Update Web pages locally, and then synchronize with the server.

Click here for manual synchronization anytime.

When you've finished your changes, it's time to make your folder "online" again, so right-click the folder and choose **Make Available Offline** again, and the check mark is removed.

Replicating Web Folders to your Local Computer

If you plan to have your folder offline for longer periods of time (especially with Web pages that constantly change), you may want to *synchronize* your local folder with the server folder on a regular basis. Synchronize (or *sync*) means to compare two folders and if changes are discovered in one, apply them to the other.

Synchronizing Your Offline Pages

Word 2000 makes it easy if you are a casual synchronizer. You don't even need to think about the last 20 files you've changed—they are synchronized automatically. If you need more control over offline folders, you can synchronize them many ways:

- **Manual**. Performs a sync on demand whenever you want.
- **Logon/Logoff**. Only sync when logging in to or out of the network. The default sync process occurs when you log in to the network.
- **On Idle**. Wait until the computer isn't doing other work, and then start a sync.
- **Scheduled**. Performs a sync on a daily, weekly, or monthly basis.

To manually synchronize any offline folder or file, right-click it and choose **Synchronize**. You see the **Synchronize** dialog box and the sync occurs immediately. If you want to schedule automatic synchronization, click the **Settings** button in this dialog box. Click the tab describing the schedule category you desire, and select from the available options for that category.

Figure 24.8: Synchronize between your local work and the Web server.

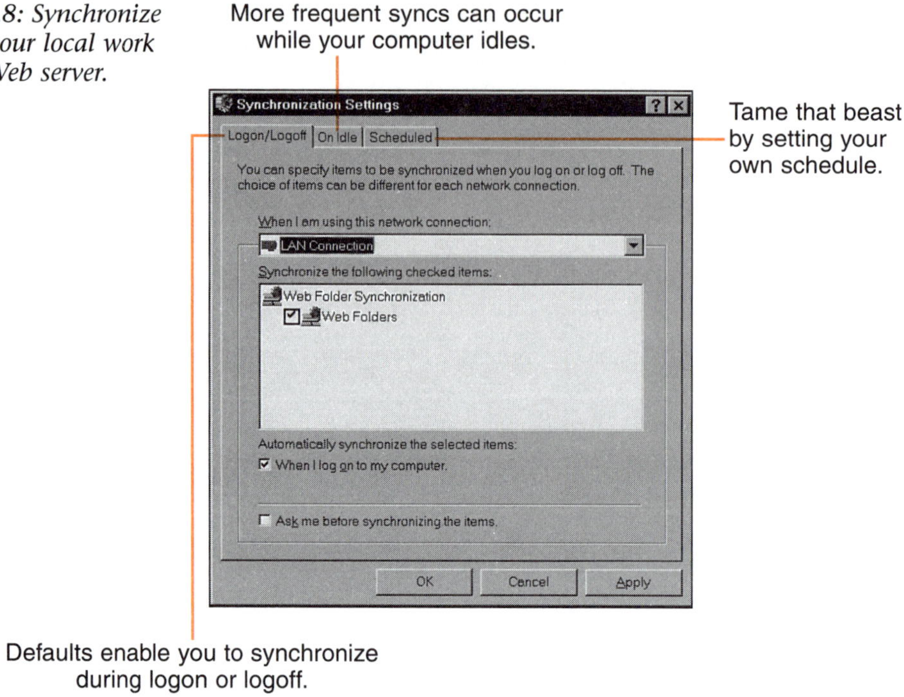

Synchronizing the Unexpected

Here's the general rule: During synchronization, the time and date stamp of each file is compared, and Word assumes the latest time stamp is your latest edit, and should replace the other. Most people operate this way, and no one complains.

But several people might be working on the same folder offline, and you may not want to blatantly overwrite someone else's changes (or maybe you do). In these cases, Word gives you a warning and enables you to control how differences are to be resolved. You can choose to:

- **Keep Both Versions**. In this case, don't change either one.
- **Replace the Version on the Web Server**. Your changes rule.
- **Replace the Version on Your Computer**. Ignore your changes and bring down the copy on the server.

Again, you'll see these options only if the synchronization process thinks something funny is going on, and needs your input. It's just a red flag to call your attention to the fact that someone else might also be making changes to these Web pages.

Sending Your Web Files to a Service Provider on the Web

To publish your Web pages on the Internet, you either need to locate an Internet Service Provider (ISP) that hosts (provides storage space for) Web pages or need to create your own Web server. The easiest way is to locate a service that hosts personal Web pages. It's a good idea to ask about limitations, such as the total amount of disk space allowed for your files. If you plan to use lots of pictures, forms, sounds, and video, you may want to ensure that your Web page service permits these features, because they involve additional storage and maintenance.

Once you've negotiated your own Web site, you'll need to deliver all the Web pages you've created. Be sure to keep the folder and subfolder hierarchy intact, and be sure to copy all the required files. You can save them to disk, or copy them electronically to your ISP using the instructions it provides.

Set the Language for Your Web Page

If you're planning for international exposure of your Web page, make sure you've got the language correct! Click **Start**, **Programs**, point to **Office Tools**, and choose **Microsoft Office Language Settings**. On the **Enabled Languages** tab, place a check in all the language boxes you need.

Tuning Your Web Page for High Performance

Even on a good day, the Internet isn't fast enough for us. The biggest bottleneck is usually your connection to the Internet, and that's what all of your Web pages files have to fit through. If you're mathematically inclined, your could add up the file sizes of all components on your Web page, and if it's a big number, Web browser viewing is slow. The best thing you can do to improve performance of your Web page is to keep the file size down. Here are some tips to show you how:

- **Keep Your Picture Sizes Small.** Sure, lots of good pictures make your Web pages more interesting, but people may not stay if it takes longer than a few seconds to load your page. Find or convert your picture files so they take up less room, such as simple line drawings, smaller-sized graphics, fewer colors, and so on. A good graphic photo editor comes with Word 2000 and can convert pictures to a format that uses less space (JPEGs are much smaller than BMP or PCX, but the picture looks pretty much the same).

- **Provide alternative text for graphics and tables.** Some users turn off the display of images in their browsers, and some Web browsers don't even support viewing tables. You should always include some alternate text for graphics, videos, and tables if they contain essential information, to guarantee that everyone sees something.
- **Re-use Little Bits of Things.** You can also repeat the same graphic or image whenever possible on your page. For example, when you use the same graphic for a bullet inside all your Web pages, the image is downloaded only once, even if it appears on several pages. This can save lots of little bits of time.
- **Trim the Video.** A video that's a few seconds long can take several minutes (or longer) to download on a slow computer, slow link, or slow Internet day. To decrease the file size of videos, you can consider black-and-white instead of color, reduce the height or width of the video, edit unneeded material, use fewer panels, and use file compression. And of course, instead of putting a video on your home page, choose a single frame and use it as a thumbnail hyperlink to the actual file. Your readers will thank you.

But It Doesn't Look the Same

Your Web page may not appear the same way to all people who view it, because some visitors may be viewing your pages with different Web browsers, possibly using different operating systems. While browsers support the same language, HTML, there are some differences among browsers. You should design a layout that is readable by the majority of visitors expected to visit your site.

The Mouse with the Wheel Helps You Browse the Web

If your mouse has a wheel between the buttons, it can do these clever tricks with the Microsoft Internet Explorer:

- **Hyperlink jumps**. You can jump to any hyperlink by pointing to it, and then "datazooming" forward. To datazoom, you press and hold down the **Shift** key while rotating the wheel button. To return to the previous topic, datazoom back by rotating in the opposite direction.
- **Scrolling**. You can scroll through a Web page by rotating the wheel button forward or back.
- **Panning**. You can continuously scroll through the current Web page by holding down the wheel button while moving the mouse.

The Least You Need to Know

After you've created your Web site, it's time to publish it for the world to see! This chapter helped you get ready for the big day with additional productivity tips.

- What's the fastest way to publish my Web page?

  Find it, right-click it, and choose **Send To** the **Web Publishing Wizard** on the shortcut menu. This wizard enables you to choose the Web server from a list, and then copies the page (or pages) and all supporting files to the server.

- Help! I can't find any Web Publishing Wizard!

  Relax. You need to install it first, and you need only do this once. Click **Start**, **Programs**, **Accessories**, point to **Internet Tools**, and choose **Web Publishing Wizard**. You'll need to know the name of your Web server, and your technical support staff should be able to provide it.

- How can I speed up my Web page?

  You can speed up Web pages by providing text alternatives to graphics, videos, and sound.

- Is there an easy way to see how my Web page looks with a browser?

  Yes, and you don't even have to leave Word 2000. **Web Layout** view provides a very close approximation, and it's the default view when you create Web pages.

- Can I really publish my Web pages to the Internet?

  Sure, especially if you work closely with an Internet Service Provider (ISP), that gives you instructions on how to submit your Web pages. The ISP provides an address, and you'll be able to send them directly from Word 2000.

Appendix A

Speak Like a Geek

By the End of This Appendix, You Will Be Able to...

- Control the computer by using the mouse
- Start and handle programs using Windows 95, Windows 98, or Windows NT
- Use buttons and menus to give commands
- Complain about your computer using the right words

This appendix is about *Windows*, the program that handles how you control all the other programs. A number of different versions of Windows are around, but you are probably using Windows 95, Windows 98, or Windows NT. These all work pretty much the same.

Maybe this is the first time you have used your computer, or maybe it's not. If you have used a computer before, you probably know most of the stuff in this appendix—but read it over anyway to become comfortable with the terminology used in this book.

A Mouse in the Hand

Attached to your computer is probably a white lump with two or three buttons on it. You use this device to control the computer. The Geeks in Charge of Naming Computer Things (GICONCT) decided that because you would be spending so much time with your hand on it, they should name it after something you would never put your hand on. It's called a *mouse*. You use the mouse by putting your hand on it and sliding it across a flat surface (usually a *mouse pad* made for just such usage).

Try sliding your mouse around. When you slide it, you should see something move on your computer screen. When you slide the mouse side to side, it also moves side to side. When you slide the mouse forward, it moves up the screen, and when you move the mouse back, it moves down the screen. This thing is called a *pointer*, and it's under your command. It will follow you to the edge of the Earth—or at least the edge of the screen.

Missing a Mouse?

If your computer doesn't have a mouse, it probably has a *trackball* (push your hand across the top of the ball, and the pointer is pushed in the same direction) or a *pad* (drag your finger across this flat rectangle, and the pointer is dragged similarly).

The Point of the Pointer

The pointer is used to point to different things on the screen. When you want to give the computer a command about a certain part of what's being displayed, you will use the pointer to tell the computer which part.

The pointer takes on different shapes at different times. Usually, it's an arrow, which makes a very clear pointer. When you are pointing to an area of text, the pointer might turn into something that looks like a thin, tall capital *I*. This is called an *I-bar*, and it's handy because you can put the thin vertical bar of the I between two letters, letting you point to a specific place in the text.

Sometimes the pointer turns into a picture of an hourglass. This means that the computer is busy doing something, and you will have to wait until it's done. If you get sick and tired of seeing the hourglass, it's either time to get a faster computer or time to go do something else, like whittling. (If you can whittle yourself a new computer, you can do both at once!)

Clicking's a Snap!

It's not enough to point to something to give a command. After all, the pointer is always pointing to something. You have to have a way of letting the computer know that it's time to act on what you are pointing at, and that's what the mouse buttons are for.

The mouse has at least two buttons. The left one is the one that you will use most of the time. When we talk about *clicking* something, we mean that you *point* to it with the pointer and then press the left mouse button. Don't hold it down, just push down and then let up on it quickly. To *double-click* something, you point at it and, instead of clicking once, you click twice.

Right-clicking is just like *clicking*, only you use the right mouse button rather than the left one. You won't do this nearly as often.

Lefties Are All Right!

If you have a mouse that's set up for left-handed use, you will use the right button for normal clicking, and the left button when we tell you to right-click.

If your mouse has three buttons, you probably won't be using the middle one, at least not in the beginning. That third button is there mostly for advanced users, who can set it up to do special things with certain programs.

Clicking a Button

On your screen is a rectangle with a little colorful Windows symbol in it and the word **Start**. It's probably in the lower-left corner of the screen. (If you don't see it, try pointing to the very bottom of the screen; a gray bar should appear with **Start** at the left end.) This is a *button*, a rectangular area on the screen that, when you click it, issues a command to the computer. At this point, the **Start** button is probably the only button on your screen, but soon you will have more buttons on your screen than there are on a dry cleaner's floor!

Notice how the button looks like it is pushed out from the gray bar that it is on. Try clicking the button, and you will see two things. One is that the button looks pushed in. This means the button is currently *active*, that it is having an effect. The other is that a list of items appear above the button. This list, called the *Start menu*, shows a number of commands that you can give to the computer. Pushing the Start button told the computer to show you the commands. Click the button again, and the list disappears and the button appears pushed out again.

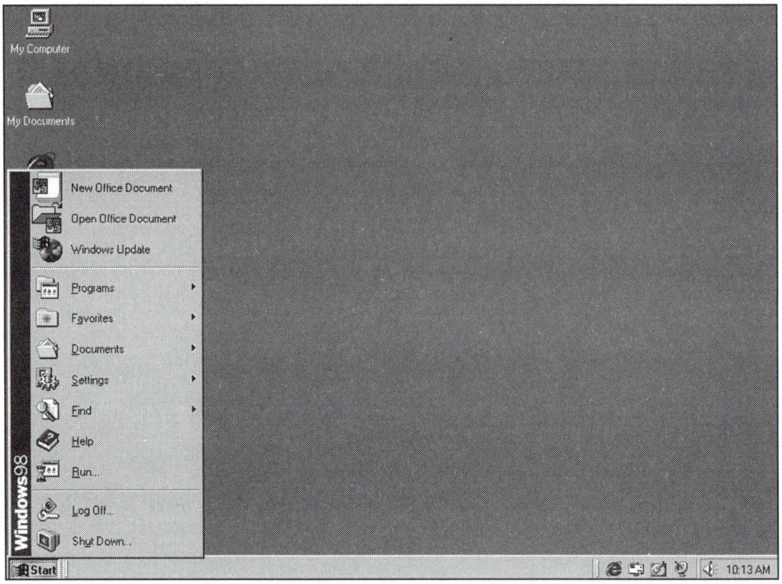

Figure A.1: Pressing the Start button made the Start menu pop up.

Try *right-clicking* the big open background area of the screen display (this is called the *desktop*). A short list of commands that you can choose pops up. This is called a *shortcut menu*. By right-clicking many things in Windows, you get a menu of commands that apply to what you clicked. Right-click the desktop, and you get a shortcut menu of commands that can change the desktop. Right-click a strawberry, and you get a strawberry shortcut menu, which isn't half as good as a strawberry shortcake menu!

Dragging Ain't No Drag!

Sometimes, you will have to move something from one part of the screen to another. This is called *dragging*, and it's quite easy. To take a swing at it, let's try dragging one of the *icons* around your desktop. (The icons are the little pictures with words underneath. Each one stands for a different program, file, or device on your computer.)

Find the icon with the picture of a computer on it (it probably says **My Computer** underneath it). Point to that icon. While pointing to it, push down the left mouse button and hold it down. With the button pressed down, slide the mouse around. A transparent copy of the image follows your pointer. It's the ghost of your computer!

Slide the pointer over to an area of the desktop where the ghost icon isn't overlapping any other icon. Let go of the mouse button, and one of two things will happen:

- The icon disappears from where you dragged it, and reappeared where you moved it to, or…
- The icons rearranged themselves in neat columns, with the icon appearing in a new spot.

If the second thing happened, it doesn't mean your dragging didn't work. Your copy of Windows is set up to keep the desktop tidy, and the moment it saw that something was out of the group, it neatened everything up. If your real desktop worked as well as your computer desktop, you would always be able to find a pencil when you needed one!

In either case, you can put things back to the way they were by dragging the icon you moved back to where you took it from. If the rearranging icons covered up the place where the icon was before, drag it just a bit higher on the screen than the icon that took its place, again making certain the ghost icon doesn't overlap any other icon.

When You Need a Menu

You have already seen how the Start menu and the shortcut menu can appear when you need them, hiding away like squirrelly, umm, squirrels the rest of the time. Menus provide access to tons of commands without taking up a lot of screen space when you don't need them.

Start Up the Start Menu, You Upstart!

Click the **Start** button again. Take a look at the Start menu. Each line has a picture and a word or phrase explaining what that command does. Some of the lines also have an arrowhead at the right edge, pointing toward the right. The arrowhead indicates that ancient native peoples used these menus, probably while running Windows 1273.

Actually, the arrowhead means that that command brings up another menu. Slide your pointer up the menu. Notice how, as the pointer passes over each command, it changes color. This color change is called *highlighting*. Just like the way that blue water in your toilet shows you that Tidy Bowl is there for you, the colored bar shows you that that command is there for you. Click the line marked **Programs**.

Programs had an arrowhead on it, so that means another menu will appear next to this one. It may be just one column, but it may be several. Find the line marked **Windows Explorer** (it should be near the end of the last column), and click it. This starts a program that lets you sort through the files on your disks.

Why Don't You Drop Down and See Me Sometime?

A big rectangle appears onscreen, filled with all sorts of stuff in it. This is the Windows Explorer *window*, the area of the screen where the Windows Explorer program displays controls and information.

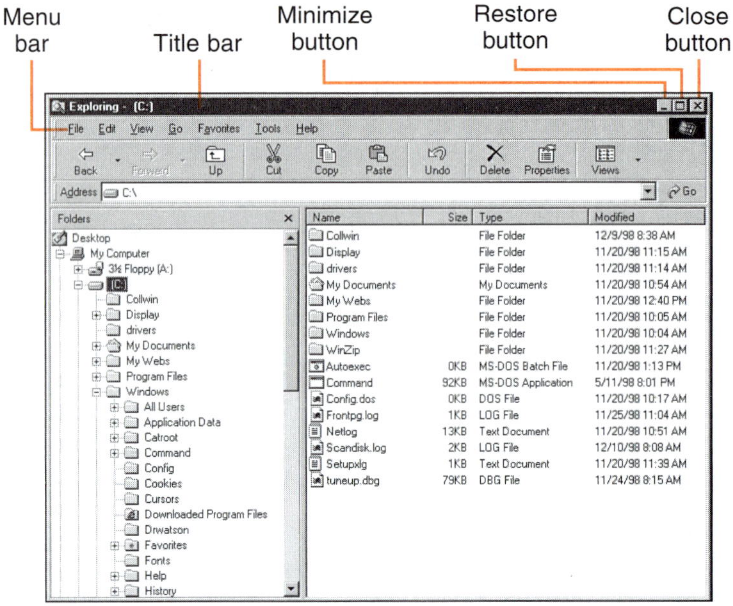

Figure A.2: Your Windows Explorer window may look different depending on your Windows version and settings.

At the top of a window are two bars. The first, called the *title bar*, has a name for the window. On the Windows Explorer window, it says **Exploring** followed by the name of your hard disk.

The second bar is called the *menu bar* (as opposed to, say, a *bar menu*, which would have a list of drinks and prices for those 10-year–old boiled eggs they keep in a jar). It has a series of words on it. Each word is the name of a menu. Try clicking the word **View**. A menu of commands appears below it—these are commands that have to do with the way that the program is displaying the list of what's on your disk. Try clicking the command **Refresh**. This tells the program to recheck what's on the hard disk and to display the information again; you should be able to see when the display is being redone.

Managing Menu Mishaps

If you accidentally bring down the wrong menu, don't worry. Just click the menu name again and that menu disappears!

Some programs try to keep their menus simple using a system called *personalized menus*. This means the program guesses which commands you're likely to use and shows only those commands when you click the menu. At the bottom of the menu will be a down-arrow. Click the down-arrow, and the rest of the commands become visible.

Keyboard Kwikies!

Sometimes you don't want to keep moving your hand back to the mouse and then back to the keyboard, you just want to keep typing. Reaching your foot for the mouse is too much exercise after a while! Luckily, there are ways to give menu commands without clicking the menu.

If you click the **Edit** menu, you will see some commands with things like **Ctrl+V** or **Ctrl+A** on the ends of them. This tells you the shortcut for that command. For example, the **Ctrl+V** on the end of the Paste command means that you can do a Paste command at any time by holding down the key marked **Ctrl** and pressing the key marked **V**. Other keys you might see referred to include the **Shift** key and the **Alt** key. If a menu item is followed by **Shift+Alt+X**, for example, that means that you can issue that command by holding down the Shift key and the Alt key, simultaneously, and pressing the X key. Of course, if you are new at typing, you might need both hands and your nose to do this.

On the menu bar, one letter of each word is underlined (for example, the V in View is underlined.) This means that you can bring the menu up by holding down the **Alt** key and pressing the underlined letter's key (such as **Alt+V**). On the menu that appears, one letter in each command is underlined; just press the key for that letter (such as the R in Refresh) to issue that command. So, in full, to get the refresh command, press **Alt+V**, and then let go of the Alt key and press the **R** key. It may sound like a lot of work—but if you think that's a lot of work, you should talk to your grandpa, who will tell you that real work is carrying 16 tons of rocks a mile up hill every day, just to earn your lunch (a rock sandwich). (Of course, your grandfather actually sold shirts for a living, but that's no reason why you should have it easy!)

Gray Means No Way

Most of the menu commands are in easy-to-read lettering, probably black. If you see one that's almost the same color as the background (probably gray), it means that you can't use this command now. (These are commands that only work under certain conditions.)

Windows Don't Have to be a Pane!

If you're using several programs simultaneously, you can end up with a screen full of windows, overlapping and even completely hiding each other. This can make your desktop as messy as that "stuff" drawer in your kitchen, where you *know* there's an almost-working 9-volt battery, if only you could find it! Luckily, there are tools that let you move around windows, change their size, and even hide them for a while (very handy if you are playing Space Bunny Attack and hear your boss coming).

Wipe Away Your Window

At the right end of a window's title bar are three buttons. The first, which has a straight line in it, is the *Minimize* button. Click this, and the window disappears! Don't worry, it's not gone for good, so you can still help the Space Bunnies save the galaxy. If you look at the *taskbar* (the bar with the Start button on it), you will see a button with the title of each window you are currently using. Click the button that has the title of the window you just minimized, and the window reappears, good as new, with each Space Bunny still intact.

Seize the Size!

The middle button will have one of two pictures of it. If it has two overlapping rectangles, this window is currently in *Full-Screen mode*, so that it automatically takes up all the screen space available. When a window is in Full-Screen mode, you can't move it or change its size. It is seemingly invincible, but for one fatal flaw, its Achilles' Heel (or, for those of us with more modern heroes, its Kryptonite): If you click this button (called the *restore* button), it goes from Full-Screen mode to *Resizable* mode, and then you can do what you want with it! You have torn down all of its defenses!

If the middle button has just a single box on it, the window is already in Resizable mode. Clicking this button (called the *maximize* button) will put the window into Full-Screen mode. This is good if you want to see as much as possible in the window. (More Space Bunnies!)

Become a Mover and a Shaker... and a Resizer!

For you to move a window, it has to be in Resizable mode. Point to the window's title bar and then drag it. Depending on how your computer is set up, you may be dragging the whole window or just an outline of it. Drag it up, drag it down, drag it, drag it all around! When you let go of the mouse button, the window will now be where you dragged it to!

If you want to change the size of a window, point at the lower-right corner of the window. The pointer will turn into a slanted arrow with arrowheads in both directions (like a "two-way" street sign would look, if there were any need for such things!). Try to drag the corner, and you will find that you are moving the corner of an outline of the window. Move it so that the outline is the size that you want the window to be, and then release the mouse button. The window will now appear in the rectangle. With a little practice, you will get so quick at dragging that you will be ready for the drag races!

Wiping Out the Window

The button on the far right of the title bar, the one with an **X** in it, is the *Close* button. After you finish using a window, click this and the window disappears. This also tells the computer that you are done using the program that opened the window; so if you are running a program where you create a file (like a word processor), be sure you have saved the file before clicking this.

Let's Rap About Dialogue!

Sometimes, a program wants to ask you for information. To do that, it uses a *dialog box*, a type of window. Most dialog boxes don't have a menu bar and can't be resized, but they can be moved around. More importantly, you give the computer the information it wants with one. Or, if you don't want to buckle in to the computer's demands, you can just ignore the dialog box. Of course, then the computer won't do what you want it to, but sometimes it's important to show who is boss!

A dialog box is a basically a form. Just like paper forms can have blanks to fill in, boxes to check off, items to circle, and so on, computer forms have a lot of different ways of getting information. After all, filling out a form on a computer should be just as much fun as filling out a paper one!

To see some of these in action, click the **Start** button and select the **Find** command. When the second menu (sometimes called a *submenu*) appears, pick the **Files or Folders...** command. (The ... at the end of a command name lets you know that if you select that command, you will get a dialog box. You can't complain that you weren't warned!)

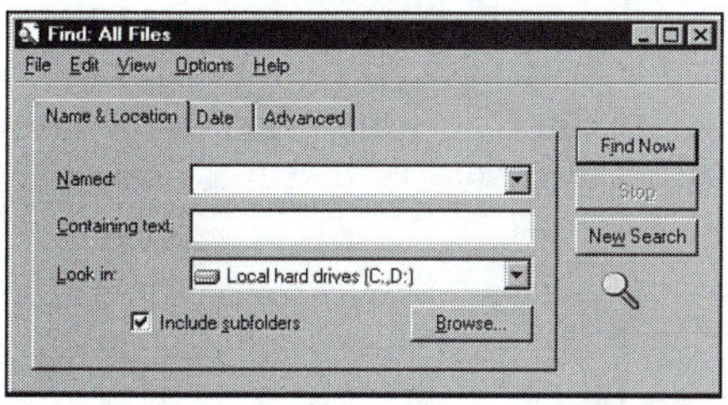

Figure A.3: A dialog box.

Tab: It Isn't Just for Dieters Any More!

On the Find File dialog box, you can see a file folder shape with a form on it. At the top of it, in the tab where the name of the folder would go, are the words **Name & Location**. Next to it are two other tabs, just as if you got a set of good file folders with the staggered tabs. Click one of those other tabs, and another form appears. Clicking the three tabs, you can easily choose which form you want to work on!

A Text Field Is the Type for Type

Check the **Advanced** tab and the **Name & Location** tab. On one of them (depending on which version of Windows you are running), you will find a white area marked **Containing Text**. This is a *text field*, one that you can type into. To put some words into that field, click in the field, and then type. You can use the cursor keys and the Backspace key to correct any typos you make. Or, you can leave your mistakes in, and just confuse the computer!

Drop Down and Give Me Twenty!

On the **Advanced** tab is a field labeled **Of type**, which has a button at the end with a down arrow. This is a *drop-down list*, good for choosing one item from a list of items. Click the button (the *drop-down button*, which is a better name for it than *Mildred*), and a list of items will appear under it. Click any item, and the list goes away, and that item appears in the field.

What the Scroll Is That?

At the right side of the *drop-down list*, you will see a vertical bar with a box inside it. This is a *scrollbar*, which sounds like a wizard's tavern. Actually, it's Windows's way of telling you that it has more to show you than it can fit in the area it has to work in. The bar area represents the whole list. If the box is at the top of the bar, it means you are seeing the start of the list; if it's at the bottom of the bar, you are looking at the bottom of the list.

To see more of the list, just drag the box down the bar. The lower you drag it, the farther down the list you will see. (If you see a sideways scrollbar at the bottom of a display, it means that what the computer is trying to show you is wider than the space it has. A sideways scrollbar works just like a regular one, if you are lying down!)

Check Out the Check Box!

Click the **Name & Location** tab. At the bottom of the form you will see a little box marked **Include subfolders**. This is a *check box*. It either has a check mark in it, which means *yes*, or it's empty, which means *no*. To change a check box from checked to unchecked (or vice versa, or even the other way 'round), just click it!

Option Button, Option Button, Who's Got the Option Button?

Click the tab marked either **Date Modified** or just **Date**. At the left of the form, you will see two columns of circles. These circles are called *option buttons*. These "buttons" are used to select one thing from a small list of choices; you use them to select one from a list of choices, and when you select one by clicking on it, a dot appears in the circle. You can only have one button selected in each column at a time; when you click one, the dot disappears from the previous selection.

Try clicking the lowest option button. When you click it, the field next to that option turns white; but if you then select the button above that one, that field turns gray. That's because that field is only used if you use that option; when it turns gray, the computer is telling you that you don't have to fill it in. Think of the fields like fields of snow—a white field is good to be in, but stay away from the gray ones!

The Least You Need to Know

- Sliding the mouse across your desk moves a pointer on the screen.
- *Clicking* means to point the pointer at something and press once on the left mouse button.
- *Double-clicking* means to point at something and press the left button twice, quickly. *Right-clicking* means to point at something and press the right button once.
- A *menu* enables you to select from a list of commands, by clicking the menu name to bring up the list and then clicking the command you want.
- A *dialog box* is a form that the computer displays, asking you for information.

Glossary

The word processing world has its own language. If you want to be accepted, you need to learn some of the lingo. This glossary helps you get started.

Accelerator keys Keys that activate a command without opening the menu. Usually a function key or a key combination (such as Alt+F10) is displayed next to the menu command. To use an accelerator key, hold down the first key while you press the second key.

Add-Ins Document templates that automate the creation process. You can use existing templates as add-ins, design your own add-ins, or purchase add-ins created by other companies for use in Word 2000.

ASCII file A file containing characters that can be used by any program on any computer. Sometimes called a text file or an ASCII text file. (ASCII is pronounced "ASK-EEE.")

Border A line placed on any (or all) four sides of a block of text, a graphic, a chart, or a table.

Bulleted list A list similar to a numbered list made up of a series of paragraphs with hanging indents, in which the bullet (usually a symbol such as a dot or check mark) is placed to the left of all the other lines in the paragraph. A bulleted list is often used to display a list of items or to summarize important points.

Cell The box formed by the intersection of a row and a column in a Word table. The same term is used when describing the intersection of a row and a column in a spreadsheet. A cell may contain text, a numeric value, or a formula.

Clip art A collection of prepackaged artwork whose individual pieces can be placed in a document.

Clipboard A temporary storage area that holds text and graphics. The Cut and Copy commands put text or graphics on the Clipboard. The Paste command copies Clipboard data to a document. The new Office Clipboard holds up to 12 items.

Columns Vertical sections of tables. See also *newspaper-style columns.*

Cropping The process of cutting away part of an imported graphic.

Cursor The vertical line that appears to the right of characters as you type. A cursor acts like the tip of your pencil; anything you type appears at the cursor. See also *insertion point.*

Data source A special document file containing information (such as names and addresses) that is later merged with another document to produce form letters or mailing labels.

Desktop publishing Advanced word-processing that combines text and graphics used to create newsletters, brochures, flyers, résumés, business cards, and so on.

Dialog box A special window or box that appears when the program requires additional information prior to executing a command.

Document Any work you create using an application program and save in a file on disk.

Document map A view in Word 2000 that displays a column of document headings on the left, enabling you to quickly browse the structure of a document.

Document window A window which frames the controls and information for the document file you are working on. You may have multiple document windows open at one time.

Drag Pressing and holding the mouse button when moving the mouse pointer from a starting to an ending position.

Drop cap An option used to off-set the first letter in a paragraph. The letter is enlarged and set into the text of the paragraph at its upper-left corner.

Embedded object An object that maintains a connection to the application that created it so if changes are needed you can access that application by double-clicking the object.

End mark Mark designating the end of the document. As you enter text, this mark moves down.

Field Part of a file record containing a single piece of information (for example, a telephone number, ZIP code, or a person's name). A field is also a code inserted into a document which is updated when the document is opened, such as the Date field.

File The computer term for your document. Anything can be placed in a file: a memo, budget report, graphics or images. Each document you create in Word 2000 is stored in its own file.

Folder A place to store documents. Folders can exist on disks or hard drives, and folders can be stored inside other folders. Before Windows 95, folders were known as subdirectories.

Font Any set of characters that share the same typeface (style or design). Fonts convey the mood and style of a document. Technically, font describes the combination of the typeface and point size of a character (as in Times Roman 12-point), but in common use, it describes a character's style or typeface.

Footer Text that can be reprinted at the bottom of every page within a document. Footers appear in the lower margins of a document.

Footnote A place to store extended detailed information referenced in the main body of a document. Footnotes usually appear above the lower margin and reference the location by using matching superscript numbers.

Formatting Changing the look of a character (by making it bold, underlined, and slightly larger, for example), a paragraph (by centering it on a page, indenting it, or numbering it), or a page (changing margins, page numbers, or paper orientation).

FTP Short for File Transfer Protocol, a set of rules governing the transfer of files between computers. You can send Web pages created in Word to your Internet Service Provider using FTP.

Function keys The 12 F keys on the top (or sometimes side) of the keyboard. F keys are numbered F1, F2, F3, and so on. These keys are sometimes used to enter various commands in the Word 2000 program.

Grammar Checker A special program within Word 2000 that reviews your grammar and offers suggestions on improving it. This feature is now combined with the Spelling Checker and can be set to automatically check grammar as you type your document. See also *Spelling and Grammar Checker.*

Graphic A picture which can be imported into Word in order to illustrate a particular point.

Gutter An unused region of space that runs down the inside edges of facing pages of a document; it's the part of each page that is used when the pages of a book or a magazine are bound together.

Handles Small black squares that surround a graphic or text box after it is selected. Handles can be dragged to change the size or shape of a graphic.

Hanging indent A special kind of indent in which the first line of a paragraph hangs closer to the left margin than the rest of the lines in the paragraph. It is typically used for bulleted or numbered lists.

Hard drive A nonremovable disk drive that stores many megabytes or gigabytes of information.

Header Text that can be reprinted at the top of every page within a document.

Home page The first Web page providing the entrance to a Web site.

HTML Short for HyperText Markup Language, the programming language used for creating Web pages.

HTTP Short for HyperText Transfer Protocol, a set of rules that govern the exchange of information between a Web host and a client (a Web browser on your computer). The address for every Web server starts with http.

Hyperlink A jump to a location in the same document or another file represented by colored and underlined text or by a graphic. You click a hyperlink to jump to a file, a location in a file, an HTML page on the World Wide Web, or an HTML page on an intranet.

Icon A small graphic image that represents another object, such as a program or a tool.

Indent The amount of distance from the page margins to the edges of your paragraph (or the first line of a paragraph).

Insert mode The default typing mode for most word processors and text editors. Insert mode means that when you position your cursor and start to type, what you type is inserted at that point, and existing text is pushed to the right.

Intelligent field Text within a Word document that is updated automatically as changes are made. Some intelligent fields, such as the date and time fields, are updated when the document is opened or printed.

Intranet A small version of the Internet, usually private and designed for the business needs of a single company, using the popular tools of the Internet (like Web browsers and search engines) for employee access to company information. Intranets are typically not directly connected to the Internet in order to maintain higher performance, controlled access to information, and security of information.

Kilobyte A unit for measuring the amount of data. A kilobyte (KB) is equivalent to 1,024 bytes.

Landscape orientation Your document is oriented so that it is wider than it is long, as in 11-by-8 1/2 inches. The opposite of landscape orientation is portrait.

Leader Dots or dashes that fill the spaces between tab positions in a list.

Linked object An imported object (such as a graphic) that maintains a connection to the program that created it, so that if changes are made to that object, those changes can be updated (either automatically or through a command) into your document. A linked object is stored separately from your Word document.

Links Also known as hyperlinks, these are icons, pictures, or highlighted text that connect one source of information to another, including locations of information in other documents, other programs, graphic, sound or video files, and Internet sites.

Macro A recorded set of instructions for a frequently used task which can be activated by pressing a specified key combination. Macros resemble small programs.

Margin An area on the left, right, top, and bottom sides of a page that is usually left blank. Text flows between the margins of a page.

Megabyte A standard unit used to measure the storage capacity of a disk and the amount of computer memory. A megabyte is 1,048,576 bytes (1,000 kilobytes). This is roughly equivalent to 500 pages of double-spaced text. Megabyte is commonly abbreviated as M, MB, or Mbyte.

Menu A list of commands or instructions displayed on the screen. Menus organize commands and make a program easier to use.

Menu bar A bar located at the top of the program window. This displays a list of the names of menus containing the commands you use to edit documents.

Merging The process of combining information stored in a data source (such as names and addresses) with a main document (such as a form letter) in order to produce a series of form letters or mailing labels.

Mirror margins An option you can use when creating magazine-like reports. When open, the pages of your report would face each other.

Mouse A device that moves an arrow (or other pointing symbols) around the screen. When you move the mouse, the pointer on the screen moves in the same direction. Used instead of the keyboard to select and move items (such as text and graphics), execute commands, and perform other tasks. A mouse gets its name because it connects to your computer through a long "tail," or cord.

Mouse pointer An arrow or other symbol that moves when the mouse is moved. When the mouse pointer is over text, it changes to a large I-shaped symbol. When the mouse pointer is over an element on the screen, it usually takes the shape of an arrow.

Mouse wheel The wheel located between the buttons on the Microsoft IntelliMouse. You can spin this wheel with your finger to scroll, zoom, and pan Word 2000 documents easily.

Multimedia The general term used to describe information observed using more than one of the five senses, particularly sound and motion. Documents containing multimedia might include animated graphics, sound effects, and motion picture video.

Newspaper-style columns Similar to the column style found in newspapers. Text in these columns flows between invisible boundaries down one part of the page. At the end of the page, the text continues at the top of the first column on the next page. Columns can be "interrupted" by graphics (pictures or charts) that illustrate the story being told.

Numbered list Similar to a bulleted list. A numbered list is a series of paragraphs with hanging indents, where the number is placed to the left of all other lines in the paragraph. A numbered list is often used to list the steps of a procedure in the proper order.

Overtype mode The opposite of Insert mode that is used in word processors and text editors. Overtype mode means that when you position your cursor and start to type, what you type replaces existing characters at that point.

Page break A dotted line which marks the end of a page. A page break can be forced within a document by pressing Ctrl+Enter.

Pane What Word 2000 calls the special boxes that you use when adding headers, footers, and comments. In Normal view, a pane appears in the bottom half of the document window. (Since it's part of a window rather than being a separate box—like a dialog box—it's called a pane.)

Paragraph Any grouping of words that should be treated as a unit. This includes normal paragraphs as well as single-line paragraphs (such as chapter titles, section headings, and captions for charts or other figures). When you press the Enter key in Word 2000, you are marking the end of a paragraph.

Point size The type size of a particular character. There are 72 points in an inch. Font families usually have only certain point sizes available; if you need larger or smaller letters than your font offers, switch to a different font.

Portrait orientation Your document is oriented so that it is longer than it is wide, as in 8 1/2-by-11 inches. This is the normal orientation of most documents. The opposite of portrait orientation is landscape.

Pull-down menu A type of menu containing selections for a Main menu command. Pull-down menus are activated by clicking them, and the menu appears similar to the way a window shade can be pulled down from the top of a window frame.

Readability index A measure of the educational level a reader would need to understand easily the text in a given document. It is determined by counting the average number of words per sentence and the average number of characters per word. A good average is about 17 words per sentence. The capability to assess the readability of your document is a feature built into Word 2000.

Record In a data file, a record is a collection of related information contained in one or more fields, such as an individual's name, address, and phone number.

Ruler The thin bar in Word 2000 that makes it easy to set tabs, stops, indentations, and margins.

Scaling The process of resizing a graphic so it does not lose its proportions.

Scrollbars Bars located along the bottom and right sides of the document window. Use scrollbars to display other areas of the document. To scroll around a document, you can either click the arrow boxes on either end of the scrollbar, click one side of the scroll box, or drag the scroll box within the scrollbar.

Section A part of a document that has different settings from the main document (for such things as margins, paper size, headers, footers, columns, and page numbering). A section can be any length: several pages, several paragraphs, or even a single line (such as a heading).

Selection bar This invisible area runs along the left side of the document window. It provides a quick way for you to select a section of the text you want to edit.

Selection letters A single letter of a menu command, such as the x in Exit, which activates the command when the menu is open and you press the key for that letter.

Shading The box of gray that is placed behind text or behind a cell in a table in order to emphasize it.

Shared document A document set up to allow a group of users to access and modify it.

Shortcut menu A small pop-up menu that appears when you point at an object and click the right mouse button. Shortcut menus contain commands that are specific to the object you're pointing at. For example, if you point to a block of text and click the right mouse button, you'll see a shortcut menu for copying, moving, and formatting text. Shortcut menus are also referred to as context-sensitive menus because they sometimes change based on what you are doing.

Shrink to Fit If only a small amount of text appears on the last page of a short document, you may be able to reduce the number of pages with this feature. In order to shrink the document, Word decreases the font size of each font used in the document.

Spelling and Grammar Checker A special program within Word 2000 that assists you in correcting spelling and grammar errors within a document. In Word 2000, misspelled words are underlined with a red wavy line; grammar errors are underlined with a green wavy line.

Split bar Located on the right side of a document window; when you double-click this bar, the window splits vertically into two smaller windows called panes.

Standard toolbar One of the most often used toolbars because it contains the most commonly used commands (such as opening, saving, and printing a document) in button form.

Status bar Located at the bottom of the program window, the status bar displays miscellaneous information about your document, such as the page and section number, the current line and column number location of the insertion point, and the new spell checker status icon.

Style A collection of specifications for formatting text. A style may include information for the font, size, margins, and spacing to a section of text. When you apply a style to a block of text, you format it automatically (according to the style's specifications).

Style Area An area that can be made to appear at the far-left side of the Word 2000 screen, and that displays the name for the style of every paragraph in a document.

Tab A keystroke that moves the cursor to a specified point. Tabs are used to indent paragraphs or align columns of text.

Table Used to organize large amounts of data in rows and columns. Tables consist of rows (horizontal) and columns (vertical). The intersection of a row and column is called a cell.

Template Defines the Word environment, such as margin settings, page orientation, and so on. The template also controls which menu commands are available and which buttons are located on the various toolbars.

Text area The main part of the document window. This is where the text you type appears.

Text box A drawing object that takes advantage of the Word 2000 Art features, such as 3D effects, fills, backgrounds, text rotation, sizing, and cropping. Used as an invisible container to position text or graphics at a specific location in a document, or to make text flow around other text and drawing objects.

Text file A type of file that contains no special formatting (such as bold), but simply letters, numbers, and such. See also *ASCII file*.

Toolbar A bar across the screen that presents the most common Word commands in an easy-to-access form. For example, clicking one of the buttons on the Standard toolbar saves your document.

URL Short for Uniform Resource Locator, an address for an Internet site. An example of a URL is `http://www.whitehouse.gov`. The "http" stands for HyperText Transfer Protocol, which means this is a Web document. The "www" stands for World Wide Web, and the remainder of the URL identifies the name of the company or organization.

View mode A way of looking at a document. Word 2000 comes with several view modes: Normal, Web Layout, Outline, Print Layout, Print Preview, Document Map, and Master Document.

Web browser Any of several programs you can use to navigate the World Wide Web. The Web browser controls the look of the Web documents and provides additional tools for jumping from one Web document to another. Examples of Web browsers include the Microsoft Internet Explorer and the Netscape Navigator.

Web Layout view A new view in Word 2000 that displays the formatting of a Web page.

Web page A document on a server that is viewed with a Web browser.

Web server A computer on the Internet dedicated to storing and serving up Web documents for clients requesting them from computers with Web browsers.

Web site A location consisting of one or more Web servers that provides storage of Web documents.

Word processor A program enabling you to enter, edit, format, and print text. A word processor can be used to type letters, reports, and envelopes, and to complete other tasks you would normally use a typewriter for.

Word wrapping Causes text to remain within the margins of a document. As the text you're typing touches the right margin, it's automatically placed at the beginning of the next line. When you insert text into the middle of a paragraph, the remaining text moves down. If you delete text, the remaining text in the paragraph moves up.

World Wide Web A collection of interconnected documents stored on Web servers all over the world. These documents can contain text, pictures, video clips, sounds, and links to other documents. You navigate through the Web by clicking hyperlinks or typing URLs inside your Web browser.

Wrapping A feature of Word 2000 allowing text to flow smoothly around a graphic with different levels available to control the distance between the text and graphic.

Index

A

B

E

F

L

M

N

O

P

Q-R

S

T

U

V

W

X-Y-Z

Other Related Titles

The Complete Idiot's Guide to Microsoft FrontPage 2000
Elisabeth Parker
ISBN: 0-7897-1806-5
$16.99 US

The Complete Idiot's Guide to Microsoft Outlook 2000
Bob Temple
ISBN: 0-7897-1981-9
$16.99 US

The Complete Idiot's Guide to Windows 98
Paul McFedries
ISBN: 0-7897-1493-0
$14.99 US

Easy Windows 98
Shelly O'Hara
ISBN: 0-7897-1484-1
$19.99 US

The Complete Idiot's Guide to Microsoft Access 2000
Joe Habraken
ISBN: 0-7897-1900-2
$16.99 US

The Complete Idiot's Guide to Microsoft PowerPoint 2000
Nat Gertler
ISBN: 0-7897-1866-9
$16.99 US

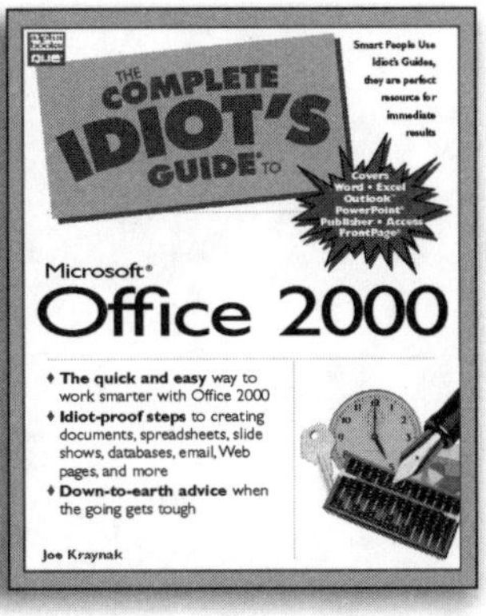

The Complete Idiot's Guide to Microsoft Office 2000
Joe Kraynak
ISBN: 0-7897-1848-0
$16.99 US

The Complete Idiot's Guide to Microsoft Excel 2000
Sherry Kinkoph
ISBN: 0-7897-1868-5
$16.99 US

que®
www.quecorp.com

All prices are subject to change.